"Khalil Marrar brings us a closely reasoned, powerfully documented, and gracefully written analysis of the OTHER lobby and efforts to shape US policy in the Middle East. A valuable antidote to the simplicities that continue to distort this long running tragedy."

J. David Singer, University of Michigan

"This is an important and much-needed book. Marrar uses the politics of a two-state solution for Israel and Palestine as a window through which to see the activities and prospects of the pro-Arab lobby in the United States. Part of the creativity of this work is that Dr. Marrar not only studies how pro-Arab lobby groups in the U.S. have tried to influence public opinion and foreign policy, he also shows how the arrow points in the other direction—the way that the Arab lobby is influenced and constrained by events in America and abroad. This thorough and provocative examination helps fill a tragic gap in our knowledge of ethnic interest group politics, and serves as a must-read for students of American foreign policy and ethnic interest group politics."

Patrick J. Haney, Professor of Political Science, Miami University

The Arab Lobby and US Foreign Policy

The US foreign policy stance on Israel–Palestine has shifted considerably in recent years, from a position of "Israel only" to one which embraces both Israel and Palestine in a call for peace. This volume assesses why the US stance has evolved in the way that it has, concluding that while international factors cannot be overlooked, developments within the United States itself are also crucial.

After years of vacillating on Palestinian national aspirations, the majority of Americans, the author notes, have come to favor the establishment of an independent Palestinian state on the West Bank and the Gaza strip. Considering what accounts for changes in US policy on Israel–Palestine, this volume:

- delivers a thorough assessment of the role of international and domestic factors in shaping US policy in this area;
- considers how US policy has evolved from the Camp David negotiations of the 1970s up to the occupation of Iraq in the mid-2000s;
- explores the significance of American public opinion and the pro-Israel and pro-Arab lobbies in the evolution of US policy.

The Arab Lobby and US Foreign Policy will be of interest to students and scholars of foreign policy and political science, current affairs, and American studies.

Khalil M. Marrar is Professor at DePaul University, USA. He has served in editorial positions at the *Arab Studies Quarterly* and the Association of Arab-American University Graduates.

Routledge Research in American Politics

The Arab Lobby and US Foreign Policy

The two-state solution

Khalil Marrar

Routledge
Taylor & Francis Group

LONDON AND NEW YORK

First published 2009
by Routledge
2 Park Square, Milton Park, Abingdon, Oxon, OX14 4RN

Simultaneously published in the USA and Canada
by Routledge
270 Madison Ave, New York NY 10016

Routledge is an imprint of the Taylor & Francis Group, an informa business

Transferred to Digital Printing 2010

Typeset in Times New Roman by
Taylor & Francis Books

British Library Cataloguing in Publication Data
A catalogue record for this book is available from the British Library

Library of Congress Cataloging in Publication Data
The Arab lobby and US foreign policy : the two-state solution / Khalil
Marrar.
   p. cm. Includes bibliographical references.
   1. United States–Foreign relations–Middle East. 2. Middle East–
Foreign relations–United States. 3. Lobbying–United States. 4. Pressure
groups–United States. 5. Arab-Israeli conflict–1973-1993. 6. Arab-Israeli
conflict–1993- 7. Palestinian Arabs–Politics and government–1973-1993. 8.
Palestinian Arabs–Politics and government–1993- 9. Israel–Politics and
government–1973-1993. 10. Israel–Politics and government–1993- I. Title.
II. Title: Arab lobby and U.S. foreign policy. III. Title: Arab lobby and
United States foreign policy.
   DS63.2.U5M385 2008
   327.73056–dc22
   2008021678

ISBN10: 0-415-77681-3 (hbk)
ISBN10: 0-415-58662-3 (pbk)
ISBN10: 0-203-88739-5 (ebk)

ISBN13: 978-0-415-77681-3 (hbk)
ISBN13: 978-0-415-58662-7 (pbk)
ISBN13: 978-0-203-88739-4 (ebk)

To my Mother, Aysheh Marrar.
Everything I am, I owe to her.

Contents

Appendices

Preface

When I started thinking about American foreign policy, the domestic pressures acting on it, and its adoption of the two-state solution to the Israeli–Palestinian conflict, I never knew that writing about these subjects would involve traveling all over the United States to conduct research and present findings. I was spellbound by what I had learned and wanted to share it with anyone that would listen. Of particular concern was American support for a Palestinian state as a matter of national interest. I was taken aback when I discovered that the popular and scholarly literature had little to say about the "pro-Arab lobby," which has for decades sought a solution to the Arab–Israeli conflict, particularly as it involved the Palestinians. I wrote this book to examine the role and potential of the pro-Arab lobby in US foreign policymaking by considering its relationships to public opinion and its pro-Israel rival. I also wanted to look at how its advocates viewed their positions in the foreign policy milieu. This is an especially important task as the new American president deploys US power in order to resolve crises all over the world, particularly in the Middle East.

Producing a work like this is an incredibly laborious process but there were precious people along the journey that made life worthwhile. And although I could never convey the depth of my gratitude to all of them nor fully appreciate the support they gave me, I shall settle for enumerating the ways in which they stood by me. Their presence, help, and love propped me up during the most difficult moments. Their celebration turned modest accomplishments into my greatest milestones. To them I turned for advice and solace. At every step of the way, they were there, generously offering the spirit that sustained me.

I wish to thank my family, my father Mousa, brothers Hussain, Hassan, and Mohamad, sisters Shatha and Fatenah, sister in law Samar, nieces Acille and Lisa, and nephews Gavyn, Abdallah, Ali, and Kamil. Not only did they get me through the mundane, their tender love allowed me to strive for and attain what would otherwise have been beyond reach. And while my dear mother, Aysheh, the center of our family, lived to see me lovingly through the exhausting stages of writing this manuscript, she died suddenly before having a chance to enjoy its completion. In addition to praying for her soul so that one day I may see her in heaven, everyday I thank God for being blessed with her wisdom, her grace, and the family she cherished. To her I dedicate this book.

Next, I offer my gratitude to Sherri Stone Replogle, who wholeheartedly gave me encouragement, fondness, and camaraderie of the soul. I also wish to thank Vince Mahler for his learned sustenance throughout the years. Ghada Talhami will forever have a place in my heart for her affectionate and nurturing mentorship. The direction offered by Gunes Murat Tezcur and Alexander Grigorescu helped turn my initially sophomoric musings into what I hope is mature scholarship. Jamal Nassar read some early drafts and offered seminal insight. I am forever indebted to him and to Manfred Steger for passing on the torch of wisdom to me and the rest of their intellectual posterity. Both Nassar and Steger made me understand that the philosophic life is worth living.

I owe many thanks to the people and institutions that afforded me their resources. Hussein Ibish extended to me an invaluable opportunity to learn first-hand about Arab American leadership in Washington. I am also grateful for the interviewees of pro-Arab organizations, including Khalil Jahshan, Rafi Dajani, Christine Gleichert, Mary Rose Oakar, Nabil Mohamad, Helen Samhan, Rebecca Abou-Chedid, Marvin Wingfield, James Zogby, and Peter Timco for graciously giving me their thoughts. Christina Zola's tenacious efforts secured essential interviews. Jason Riefler helped improve my argument and appendices. The evaluation and skepticism of Norm Finkelstein inspired me to think more clearly.

Kyle Christensen, Matthew Crosston, Michael Cairo, Richard Wandling, Elizabeth Bloodgood, Patrick Callahan, Ali Abunimah, J. David Singer, Virginie Grzelczyk, Richard Sobel, Sterling Johnson, and Patrick Haney delivered excellent feedback during the final push to complete this project. Mike Budde and Wilma Kwit helped me obtain a variety of resources and support. Hussein Zaghal, Safa Hamed, Ron Miller, Sarah Diel-Hunt, John Majer, Issam Nassar, Azam Nizamuddin, Shakeela Hassan, Gretchen Grad, Haneen Ahmad, Amal Eqeiq, Larry Bennett, James Block, Scott Hibbard, Valerie Johnson, Azza Salama Layton, Catherine May, Christina Rivers, Rose Spalding, Wayne Steger, Harry Wray, Dick Farkas, Shiera Malik, Molly Andolina, Zachary Cook, Anna Law, David Barnum, Ola Adeoye, Clement Adibe, Kathryn Ibata-Arens, Hyung-min Joo, Michael Mezey, Phillip Stalley, Claudio Katz, Suzan Mezey, Tracy Pintchman, Patrick Boyle, Thomas Engeman, Peter Sanchez, Heather Fowler-Salamini, Greg Guzman, Stacey Robertson, John Williams, Brad Brown, Jef Powell, David Lulkin, Kevin Suess, George Jolly, Gina Meeks, and Nora Rabarczyk offered friendship and assistance. I offer special thanks to David Jesuit and Central Michigan University for inviting me to address their students and faculty; they offered terrific input. Heidi Bagtazo, Amelia McLaurin, Lucy Dunne, Andy Soutter, and Paola Celli of Routledge deserve unique recognition for faithfully assisting in the preparation of the book and getting it out to the world.

I also want to thank DePaul University, Loyola University, Bradley University, Illinois State University, Elmhurst College, Heartland Community College, Richard J. Daley College, and Lake Forest College for their generous economic, library, and academic support. The US Congress, Centennial Center for Visiting Scholars, Hala Foundation, American-Arab Anti-Discrimination Committee, Arab American Institute, and American Task Force on Palestine kindly facilitated my stays and research in Washington. Financial support from the Artinian Award and the Olin Fellowship helped me avoid having to choose between living and learning. Conferences of the American Political Science Association, the International Studies Association, the Midwest Political Science Association, the Southern Political Science Association, and the Illinois Political Science Association provided my work much needed exposure and critical feedback. I wish to express my warmest gratitude to my past and present students, who eagerly helped me frame and expound my ideas. To all mentioned above, and countless unnamed others, I humbly devote the strengths of this work, while the weaknesses eternally belong only to me.

Abbreviations

AAAN	Arab American Action Network
AAI	Arab American Institute
AAUG	Association of Arab-American University Graduates
ACLU	American Civil Liberties Union
ADC	American-Arab Anti-Discrimination Committee
ADL	Anti-Defamation League
AFSC	American Friends Service Committee
AIPAC	American Israel Public Affairs Committee
AJC	American Jewish Committee
AMC	American Muslim Council
APN	Americans for Peace Now
ARAMCO	Arabian American Oil Company
ATFP	American Taskforce on Palestine
CAIR	Council on American-Islamic Relations
CCA	Christian Coalition of America
CMEP	Churches for Middle East Peace
DFLP	Democratic Front for the Liberation of Palestine
DOP	Declaration of Principles
EI	Electronic Intifada
EU	European Union
FPA	Foreign Policy Analysis
GWOT	Global War on Terrorism
IDF	Israel Defense Forces
IFCJ	International Fellowship of Christians and Jews
MPAC	Muslim Public Affairs Council
NAAA	National Association of Arab Americans
NAACP	National Association for the Advancement of Colored People
NCC	National Council of Churches
NER	Near East Report
OAS	Organization of Arab Students
PA	Palestinian Authority
PAC	Political Action Committee
PLO	Palestine Liberation Organization

SPIP	Strategic Peace Initiative Package
UN	United Nations
UNSC	United Nations Security Council
US	United States
USCCB	National Conference of Catholic Bishops
WINEP	Washington Institute for Near East Policy
ZOA	Zionist Organization of America

1 US foreign policy and the two-state solution

Introduction

When it comes to US policy toward the Israeli–Palestinian conflict, is there such a thing as a meaningful pro-Arab lobby capable of countering pro-Israel pressure? Or is it the case, as some have asserted, that in comparison to the pro-Israel lobby, "pro-Arab interest groups are weak to non-existent?"[1] The very fact that the American public and its policymakers have come to prefer the two-state solution suggests that such remarks may be overly dismissive of factors that, aside from the pro-Israel lobby, play a role in US policy concerning Israel and the Palestinians. And, given the increasingly common position that "the overall thrust of U.S. policy in the region is due almost entirely to U.S. domestic politics,"[2] this book makes the case that reactions to domestic *and* international developments by public opinion, policymakers, and the pro-Arab lobby, in addition to the pro-Israel lobby, are important to understanding the American posture toward the Israeli–Palestinian conflict, particularly as it pertains to unprecedented calls for a Palestinian state from the highest levels of the US government.

First, a brief background on the US foreign policy shift in question is in order. After the 1967 war between Israel and its Arab neighbors, American policymakers heightened their support of the Jewish state as a Cold War ally. Israel strengthened its hold over the West Bank and Gaza while the United States denied the Palestinians' right to self-determination on those captured territories. It was widely believed that the exercise of that right posed a threat to the Jewish state's existence.[3] As the relationship between the US and Israel deepened into a "strategic alliance" under the Ronald Reagan administration and a Congress dominated by the pro-Israel lobby, American policy rejected Palestinian nationalism while acquiescing to Israel's dominion over the occupied land.[4] Decades later, the United States remained committed to its Jewish ally but for reasons that will be the focus of the chapters to follow, accepted Palestinian autonomy and ultimately sought a two-state solution to the Israeli–Palestinian conflict. According to President George W. Bush, the two-state vision and the roadmap for peace designed to implement it, command nearly universal support as the best means of achieving a permanent peace and an end to the Israeli occupation that began in 1967. United Nations Security Council resolutions have repeatedly spoken of the desirability of establishing two independent states, Israel and Palestine, living side by side within secure and recognized borders.[5]

The resolutions referred to by President Bush include 1397 (2002) and 1515 (2003). All concerned international actors, including Israel, the Palestinian Authority (PA), the European Union (EU), the Russian Federation, and the Arab League,[6] have endorsed the two-state solution as articulated by the Bush administration's "roadmap," which outlined steps for a "permanent two-state solution."[7]

Unofficially, the concept of granting the Palestinians independence over the West Bank and Gaza in order to secure peace went back to the Jimmy Carter presidency.[8] After the Camp David Accords, signed on September 17, 1978, President Carter envisioned – but never made explicit – a Palestinian homeland on the territories that Israeli Prime Minister Menachem Begin referred to as "Judea and Samaria."[9] *Official* American support for the "limited autonomy" precursor to the two-state solution, however, only emerged in the post-Cold War era under the sponsorship of President Bill Clinton. While in principle, the US supported the peace proposals of United Nations Security Council (UNSC) resolutions 242 (1967) and 338 (1973), which called for Israeli withdrawal from the territories occupied in June 1967, with the partial exception of the Carter administration, American leaders since Lyndon B. Johnson did not recognize the Palestinians as a people deserving of their own homeland.[10] However, beginning with the Intifada (1987) and through the fall of the Berlin Wall (1989), the end of the first Gulf War (1991), and the subsequent collapse of Soviet communism (1991), American designs shifted toward a political solution to the Israeli–Palestinian conflict, which in the post 9/11 period was enshrined by the international consensus on the roadmap.[11] As will be demonstrated later, even though it is necessary to rely on international factors in order to explain the two-state plan, the monumental systemic changes of the past three decades by themselves do not account for the shift in US strategy. Instead, there were interactions between international events and domestic factors that may have corresponded to changes in American policy toward the Israeli–Palestinian conflict.

Why two states?

Therefore, this work focuses on the factors that related to US policy moving from unyielding support for its strategic ally by ignoring Palestinian national aspirations during the last decade of the Cold War to backing the two-state solution during the 2000s. Specifically, the question under examination is as follows: why has the US shifted from an "Israel only"[12] position toward the Israeli–Palestinian conflict to supporting an "Israel *and* Palestine" formula for peace? Currently, the two-state solution persists despite forceful arguments that its time has passed and that the only viable peace option is of a binational state solution.[13] And while one state for both Jews and Arabs may be the ideal solution for some, the reality is that American policy and the international community preferred two states. In order to assess how this reality emerged on the US diplomatic front, three domestic factors will be examined for their roles in American foreign policy and its preference for the two-state solution. These include: (1) public opinion and its interaction with policymakers' perceptions regarding the Israeli–Palestinian conflict, (2) the pro-Israel lobby, and most importantly for the purposes of the present work, (3) the pro-Arab lobby's relationship to these domestic factors.[14] All three will be traced out during the following periods: the late 1970s Camp David era and during the 1980s when Israel became a strategic ally of the US under Ronald Reagan; the George H. W. Bush presidency and the end of the Cold War; during the Clinton years of the Oslo peace process (1993–2001); and through the wars on terrorism and in Iraq (after 2001). Two identifiable international orders existed during those periods: Cold War bipolarity between the US and the Soviet Union during the late 1970s–1980s and post-Cold War American military, political, and economic hegemony in the 1990s and 2000s.[15]

Aside from it being the issue of the day, this study will conclude by partaking in the two states versus one state debate.[16] It will do this for a number of reasons related to "facts on the ground" in the Israeli–Palestinian conflict and because of the political situation in the US. First, before its occupation of the West Bank and Gaza, Israel was already a multinational state in which Arabs were granted citizenship.[17] At the time of this writing, over 20 percent of its population is non-Jewish.[18] Second, after 1967, Israel populated the newly occupied territories with Jewish settlers. Presently, their number is estimated at anywhere from 300,000 to over 450,000.[19] According to Rashid Khalidi, the entrenchment of the settlements makes "the creation of a viable, sovereign Palestinian state alongside Israel impossible."[20] Third, if the entity principally called for by the roadmap did come into existence, the American–Israeli understanding that settlements will stay in the West Bank and that Palestinian territories including Gaza may remain under Israeli military control would create Bantustan conditions for the Arab inhabitants and thus ensure the perpetuation of violence.[21]

Despite all of that, Israel and its lobbying interlocutors in the US wish to maintain Jewish majority and have opted to keep the population of the occupied territories out of the state's political system.[22] The US supports this position and has dedicated its diplomatic energies to resolving the conflict through the two-state arrangement, something that would allay Zionist fears of losing Jewish domination. Although that solution faces many obstacles, American policy and the international consensus that rallies around its peace proposals insist on it.[23] Hence, this study will examine how the two-state solution became embedded in US policy after the end of the Cold War when it was not even an option before. To do that, it looks at the following issues surrounding the domestic factors under analysis. First, even though public opinion has tended to support Israel, a Palestinian state has enjoyed increasing popular backing.[24] This fact raises the following question: what was the role of public opinion in the eventual adoption of the two-state solution as a part of American policy? Second, while the pro-Israel lobby never recognized the national rights of the Palestinians, its interest in maintaining a democracy exclusively for Jews in the Middle East has meant that it had to countenance the possibility of an Arab political establishment on the West Bank and Gaza. This was particularly the case after the first Intifada when the Palestinians, through pro-Arab forces operating in the US, showed the futility and brutality of Israeli occupation. Consequently, this study will look at the impacts these developments had on the two lobbies' approaches toward foreign policy. Third, since recognition of the Palestinians' legitimate rights was something that may not be credited to international events alone and because that is something that groups like the American Israel Public Affairs Committee (AIPAC) actively opposed, we must look at the growing strength and potential of the pro-Arab lobby and variances in the pro-Israel lobby. How did activism by both sides interact with policy regarding the two-state solution, and what are the future prospects of those interactions? While public opinion and pro-Israel pressure groups have been thoroughly discussed in the literature, the often-dismissed pro-Arab lobby remains worthy of a great deal of foreign policy analysis (FPA).[25] But before delving into these issues, the perspectives underlying the present analysis will be examined.

Understanding foreign policy decision-making

Ethnic lobbying and FPA

Much of the foreign policy research tends to center on the relationship between domestic organizations and the people they seek to influence on the one hand, and the ideological commitments of the actors involved in policymaking on the other.[26] Against this backdrop, FPA has looked at the forces shaping national interests and the actions they promote. Most analysts echo a similar grand conclusion: the traditional realist paradigm, which has maintained that rational states will act in their self-interest, does not neatly capture the decision-making reality.[27] Nevertheless, to say that realism no longer dominates the study of foreign policy would be a mistake. Still, numerous scholars have made it their business to analyze foreign policy through competing approaches.[28] For example, while Ole Holsti recognized the value of realist explanations, he argued that "ideas" are crucial to policymaking.[29] Likewise, even when affirming the realist logic in foreign policy decisions, scholars have to account for intrastate components, moving away from the "billiard ball" model.[30] Others look at the role of complex phenomena such as globalization, terrorism, and international governance in order to explain behavior.[31]

Seeking to offer alternative explanations, a growing number of scholars have focused on sub-state factors that shape motives behind policy conduct.[32] There has been particular interest in domestic agents that try to push their agendas against the grain of what would otherwise be in the national interest. Flying in the face of realist doctrine, this was precisely the argument of Melvin Small, who dedicated an entire history to the influence of domestic politics on the scheme of foreign policymaking.[33] In his *Democracy and Diplomacy*, Small chronologically outlined the role of domestic groups in shaping international outcomes, the power struggle between the various branches and departments of government, and the impacts of diverging economic interests. This approach yielded many important contributions to FPA, most notably for the purposes of the current analysis, that ethnic groups, from Irish to Native Americans, have exhibited similar patterns of political behavior but experienced different outcomes from their attempts to lobby their government on a wide range of domestic and international affairs.

Like other communities, Arab Americans have tried their hand at influencing US policy, albeit with limited success.[34] Their leadership has maintained that its lack of power directly relates to the strength of groups making up the pro-Israel lobby.[35] Such a line of reasoning, however, according to Georges Corm, "effectively exonerate[s] the US government from moral responsibility toward the Arab world's just claims and demands."[36] Consequently, pro-Arab pressure groups have sought attention from policymakers to the region's problems, particularly as they stem from the failure to resolve the Israeli–Palestinian conflict. Their efforts have centered on pushing American policy toward a solution, which would give Palestinians an opportunity to normalize their relations with Israel, the Arab countries, and the rest of the world. It is widely recognized that because of its support for Israel, the US is complicit in the Jewish state's intransigence surrounding that issue. This has led foremost figures within the policymaking elite to conclude that the US must engage in "renewed and sustained commitment ... to a two-state solution."[37] Such a course of action, however, has to face the fact that vacillation on Palestinian statehood as outlined in the roadmap is closely related to the pro-Israel lobby's immense endowment. Writing on American foreign policy post 9/11, Vaughn Shannon observed, "how the US Congress came to be so pro-Israel may have a lot to do with interest groups," particularly AIPAC.[38] Aside from being intimately familiar with how to win policymakers and public opinion to Israel's side, that organization is particularly good at knowing who to target in Congress, something that Marie Hojnacki and David C. Kimball have concluded is essential to lobbying efforts in Washington.[39] Accordingly, the pro-Israel lobby has enjoyed immeasurable weight in the Beltway establishment. This phenomenon, as Abraham Ben-Zvi reminded us, dates back to the 1960s, particularly after Israel's crushing defeat of its foes in 1967. By adapting to growing competition from Palestinian state supporters, not to mention the changing international terrain after the end of the Cold War, pro-Israel groups continue to shape policy in the present.[40]

Yet for so long, with some notable exceptions that will be looked at later, the influences of ethnic blocs such as those of Jewish and Arab Americans were largely overlooked. This led Patrick J. Haney and Walt Vanderbrush to observe, "the study of U.S. foreign policy, and foreign policy analysis more generally, has paid relatively little attention to the roles and powers of ethnic interest groups and the full range of their activities."[41] In the present, however, scholarship on the pro-Israel lobby and the interests of its constituency have engendered intellectual earthquakes and turned the heads of scholars and pundits throughout the world.[42] And while the pro-Arab lobby has received marginal consideration when compared to its pro-Israel challenger, many questions arise from the focus on ethnic lobbies. A noteworthy question concerns the extent to which those lobbies, coupled with the public opinion they seek to influence, interact with policy. And, if these factors do have an impact, the logical issue would be exploring how they have done so in the past and how they may continue to do so in the future. Since there has been an affirmation of the significant pressure that ethnic lobbying groups try to exert on foreign policy, many have detailed the "who and how" of the Washington lobbying game and the strategic dimensions of interest articulation.[43]

Harkening back to an earlier time, this approach to FPA emphasizes domestic variables to complement international or systemic explanations.[44] Increased attention towards globalization during the 1990s and 2000s brought inquiries centered on "informational" lobbying.[45] Such approaches consistently involved microanalysis of organizational subsections. Most attempted to glean how lobbyists tailor information in order to achieve particular policy ends.[46] The proliferation of this type of scholarship went hand in hand with attempts to identify a set of factors that act on the foreign policy of the world's only superpower in the aftermath of the Cold War. Concerning the Middle East, since that is where a disproportionate amount of American power rested after the fall of the Berlin Wall, some tried to gauge various influences on efforts at bringing peace to the Israeli–Palestinian conflict.[47] Right up to the present, foreign policy research continues to center on specific interests. Preference has been given to individuals and organizations at the domestic level over nebulous phenomena such as the changing nature of the international order to explain policy behavior.[48]

Although domestic factors dominated the study of foreign policy, we must not overlook the fact that all analyses assumed the power vacuum created by the departure of the Soviet Union from the global scene. Thus, even though the literature today focuses on specific actors and factors at the domestic level, we must acknowledge international conditions when looking at the larger context. Regardless of which study we focus on, we see that domestic actors have to interact with and ultimately adapt to changes at the state and structural levels. Without such adaptation, the actors under examination would have ceased to exist long ago. Indeed, the mark of any inquiry's worth is its ability to make sense of past events much in the same way that a scholar cannot meaningfully approach the current political reality without accounting for a variety of historical agents through a toolbox of approaches.

The robustness of the field of FPA provides the appraisal of factors shaping policymaking with a number of possibilities to consider. Studies interested in the intersection between the foreign and domestic arenas have looked at a number of forces and their interactions with the US position on the Israeli–Palestinian conflict.[49] According to Kathleen Christison, during the administration of George W. Bush, there were several developments that were responsible for the US bias toward Israel, including the preoccupation by both countries with fighting terrorism, the personal rapport between President Bush and the Jewish state's leaders, the pro-Israel/evangelical Christian lobbies,[50] and dominance of neoconservative ideology in American government. Christison's analysis showed the multiplicity of factors one can examine when analyzing foreign policy decisions, particularly US support for the Jewish state.

While it may be argued that shared culture is one of the most important reasons behind the American–Israeli alliance, that *alone* does little to explain policy behavior. Rather it needs to be scrutinized in conjunction with other factors. For instance, as will be shown throughout the pages to follow, while the US may show a preference for Israel because of cultural commonality, this by itself does not account for the success of the Zionist agenda in American foreign policy. However, when coupled with a strong Israel lobby that recreates and plays up the perceived cultural, social, economic, and political bonds between the two nations – while distancing the Arab world in those same characteristics – then *and only then* do we have a more viable explanation of favorable policy toward the Jewish state.[51] The same may be applied to past weaknesses and future potential of the pro-Arab lobby. For reasons that will be looked at later, Americans do not see themselves as having as strong a connection with the Arab nations relative to Israel. Therefore, the already "less vocal and less effective" Arab lobby, according to William Quandt, was even more at a disadvantage, particularly during the Cold War.[52] As that rivalry began to unravel, the pro-Arab lobby's achievements and strengths would begin to depend upon its ability to elucidate the plight of the Palestinians under Israeli occupation and on efforts to convince Americans to identify with their struggle.[53]

The discussion so far shows the intersection between various global dynamics and the factors of this study, public opinion and policymaker perceptions interacting with the two lobbies. When trying to discuss that interaction, one would be hard pressed to find any work on foreign policy that does not fit into the *general* scholarship outlined above. Accordingly, the *specific* literature on American policy in the Israeli–Palestinian conflict is informed by the grand theory of FPA. As a part of that literature, this study tries to navigate between the individual, state, and structural levels of approach to foreign policy by examining the American course of action on resolving the Israeli–Palestinian conflict during the "friendship" across time between two "first world," Western democracies, the USA and Israel.[54] When policymakers supported the political formulae that would ultimately lead to the roadmap, there was a milieu of issues that made the agenda for a Palestinian state possible. As will be argued elsewhere, political influence on and perceptions of American interests during distinct international contexts engendered the articulation of the two-state solution and the difficulties involved in realizing it.

While this manuscript primarily attempts to examine the significance of domestic factors on foreign policy conduct, the international environment in which that takes place as well as the characteristics of the states under examination are also important. However, this study ultimately sides with Fareed Zakaria's contention that "the parsimony of systemic theory is useful for some purposes ... [however, d]omestic politics explanations can be more useful in explaining events, trends, and policies that are too specific to be addressed by a grand theory of international politics."[55] This position is especially useful when looking at the relationship between the US and Israel, since we cannot explain American policy, particularly its specific preference for the two-state solution, by international events alone.[56] To do that would miss crucial piece of the puzzle. We now turn to domestic and international explanations of US policy toward the Middle East and their links to the present investigation.

US foreign policy in the conflict

American Middle East involvement is an agonizing paradox. On the one hand, the US has sought to maximize its ostensible self-interest in the pre-dominantly Arab/Muslim region. On the other, that interest is constrained and oftentimes harmed by its commitment to Israel, a perceived settler colony.[57] Many attribute that commitment directly to the powerful influence that the Israel lobby exercises in Washington, DC.[58] Before the imple-mentation of glasnost and perestroika, two Soviet political reforms that, among other developments, were responsible for the end of the Cold War, conservative Illinois Congressman Paul Findley observed, "it is no over-statement to say that [the pro-Israel lobby] has effectively gained control of virtually all of Capitol Hill's action on Middle East policy."[59] Its strength in shaping US policy disturbs the necessity for evenhandedness in dealing with the problem of the Israeli–Palestinian conflict. Findley even went so far as to say that Israel "lobby groups function as an informal extension of the Israeli government."[60] He found this state of affairs unacceptable for two reasons.

First, the Israel lobby does not protect American interests but rather those of the Jewish state. Second, US and Israeli interests rarely correspond to one another and in fact often clash. Yet, the Zionist lobby consistently pushed its agenda through with much celebration by members of Congress. Because there was little resistance to its power at the time he wrote his work, Findley like others, tried to appeal to a sense of doing what is in the national interest of the United States. In particular, this meant trying to resolve the Israeli–Palestinian conflict with a fair-minded approach that allows both sides to discuss peace in a way that does not endanger the survival of the other or American security.

There was pessimism about the likelihood of that happening, however. Because of the sheer strength of its lobby, Findley discovered that the desires of Israel too often drowned out the American interest. At the heart of support for the Jewish state was (as it remains today) the *perception* that its lobbying machine would destroy anyone that would dare challenge it. Since aiding Israel is the single issue of concern for that lobby, it has been relatively easy to point out dissenters and to bring them disrepute wherever they happened to be in government. Moreover, pro-Israel groups do not just operate in the Beltway. They have the ability to blackmail in academics and the media as well.[61] Their clout lies not in their capacity to offer rewards for those that support Israel, but rather in stirring up fear of punishment in those that may withhold their consent. To counter that, Findley urged those who would "dare speak out" to institute a "broad educational program" to show how pro-Israel policies have harmed the United States.[62] However, such a program was and still is very difficult to organize because of the fear of reprisal and the ability of many vocal Zionist outfits to dull oppositional messages. The pro-Israel dogmatism that Findley observed may be compared to the McCarthyism of the 1950s when government officials were not only too afraid to speak out against abuses because of worrying about themselves being next in line for penalty, but they also mistrusted those around them.[63] In the "special relationship" between the US and Israel, it has become taboo or prohibitively costly to even think about the stakes in the Middle East outside of the Jewish state's interest. This was not something limited to the strategic alliance of the mid-1980s, when Findley wrote his work.[64] Pro-Israel partisans continue to lobby for a restoration of that state of affairs, as will be demonstrated later.

Picking up where Findley left off, Cheryl Rubenberg proposed two domestic factors for the "extraordinary and contradictory union" between the US and Israel. The first involved

> a perception, based on the erroneous assumptions and a total misunderstanding of the complexities of the Arab world but that nevertheless acquired the legitimacy of absolute truth in dominant sectors of the American foreign policymaking elite, that saw Israel serving as an extension of American power in the Middle East and a strategic asset to U.S. interests.[65]

Rubenberg added that the second factor is "the power of the pro-Israeli lobby in American domestic politics."[66] Both factors have been documented in the literature on US policy in the Israeli–Palestinian conflict.[67] Rubenberg outlined their evolution from Israel's founding in 1948 until its 1982 invasion of Lebanon. During the 1980s when Findley and Rubenberg completed their works, the two-state solution was neither on the agenda of policymakers or the lobbies that sought to influence them. This study will add to the literature exemplified by Findley and Rubenberg by bringing their analyses up to date through an assessment of how lobbying, joined with public opinion, related to the preference of American policy for resolving the conflict after the end of the Cold War and through the war on terrorism.

Even though works like Rubenberg's and Findley's were too early to account for the advent of the peace process after the collapse of the Soviet Union, they did provide a great deal of insight. On public opinion/perception, Rubenberg argued that because of Israel's spectacular performance against its Arab foes, "the June 1967 war marked a turning point in the U.S.-Israeli relationship" since it forced Americans to appreciate Israel's might.[68] Military prowess by itself, however, does not create alliances. It took leadership to unite the two states, something that Rubenberg attributed to Secretary of State Henry Kissinger, who "was particularly wedded to the notion of Israel as an extension of American power and was highly instrumental in institutionalizing the thesis both in ideology and practice."[69] In this case, the vision of a principal statesman in the administrative branch coincided with the Israel lobby's congressional agenda resulting in the close relationship between the two sides that flowered into the "Memorandum of Understanding," which engendered the strategic alliance of the 1980s.

Furthermore, Rubenberg highlighted several factors that made the pro-Israel lobby particularly potent in the outcome of American foreign policy that, as will be shown, applied both before and after the end of the Cold War. According to her, in addition to their "impressive" access to the media, plentiful financing, sharp public relations skills, and "unified support of the Jewish communities of the United States,"

> the unique success of the pro-Israel lobby on the American political landscape was also related to other factors: 1. the *congruence* of the lobby's objectives with elite perceptions; 2. the ability of the lobby to tie Israel into the Cold War anti-Communist consensus ...; 3. the evolving role of Congress on Middle East issues and the ability of the lobby to influence Congress; 4. the strength of pro-Israeli sentiment in public opinion ...; 5. the growth of 'Christian Zionism' as part of the increasing Christian fundamentalist movement in the United States; and 6. the success of Jewish groups and individuals in the social process known as interfacing, which led to coalition building with non-Jewish groups.[70]

With adjustments by the pro-Israel lobby to changes in public opinion toward resolving the Israeli–Palestinian conflict and concomitant challenges by the pro-Arab lobby, the above factors, with the exception of the second, still apply in the present. Even before September 11, the Israel lobby tried to replace communism with Islamist ideology.[71] In the post-9/11 world, that lobby touted the Jewish state as a leader along with the US in the global war on terrorism.[72]

The continuing debate on lobbying

A lobbyist, according to Thomas Dye, is a "person working to influence government policies and actions."[73] By this definition, lobbying may take place either directly or indirectly.[74] Lobbying for Israel involves both forms and does so effectively. However, on behalf of the Palestinians, it takes place mostly through indirect means – by influencing opinion and disseminating information when called upon by government officials and media outlets.[75] In this regard alone, the Israel lobby has much more weight than its Arab counterpart does. This is why, compared to the latter, the former receives the lion's share of attention in the investigation of ethnic lobbies acting on US foreign policy.[76] Since the 1980s, when Rubenberg and Findley dedicated their scholarship to exposing the pro-Israel lobby, the pro-Arab lobby has increased its potential to become more competitive after the Intifada and the onset of the peace process.

While the ominous force of the Israel lobby on American foreign policy was documented during the last decade of the Cold War, John Mearsheimer and Stephen Walt reinvigorated the discussion during the war on terrorism. According to them,

> other special interest groups have managed to skew U.S. foreign policy in directions they favored, but no lobby has managed to divert U.S. foreign policy as far from what the American national interest would otherwise suggest, while simultaneously convincing Americans that U.S. and Israeli interests are essentially identical.[77]

From this introductory statement, Mearsheimer and Walt went through great lengths to show why the powerful influence of the Israel lobby harmed American interests, as evidenced by US involvement in wars resulting in exorbitant losses of blood and money. Although the Israel lobby has convinced American policymakers that it is in the US interest to be Israel's benefactor, Mearsheimer and Walt concluded that the Jewish state has been nothing but a "strategic liability."[78] The US obligation to Israel places it at odds with opinion throughout the world, not just in Arab/Muslim countries.[79] Hence, as the 2006 war in Lebanon demonstrated, just as Africans, Asians, Europeans, and Latin Americans were outraged by the Israeli invasion of a sovereign country, the United States moved to protect its ally against any censure or sanction by the international community regardless of how flagrant its actions may have been perceived.[80] Likewise, American policymakers have refused to apply pressure on Israel to make good on the roadmap, despite support of a Palestinian state.

Mearsheimer and Walt explored several possible reasons as to why the US would commit itself to such unpopular actions in order to support Israel – was it: to back the "underdog," to aid a democratic regime, to compensate Jews for past injustices and genocide, or even to enjoin "good" versus "evil?" The answer to every one of these questions is a complex "no."[81] Instead, according to Mearsheimer and Walt, the Israel lobby meticulously constructed the reasons behind US support of the Jewish state. Pro-Israel advocates have conducted campaigns of intimidation and misinformation in order to strengthen the "strategic alliance" between the US and Israel and to make it seem as if the two countries' friendship has existed from time immemorial. Presently, the Israel lobby posits that the American–Israeli alliance finds itself united against a common enemy: Islamic terrorism. Contrary to this position, Mearsheimer and Walt argued, "the United States has a terrorism problem in good part because it is so closely allied with Israel, not the other way around."[82]

Like Findley and Rubenberg, after outlining the Israel lobby's characteristics, its campaigns to manipulate the media, silence dissent, and to police academia, Mearsheimer and Walt moved to show its effects on US foreign policy.[83] They found that in addition to forcing acquiescence in support of the Jewish state, the Israel lobby has succeeded in convincing the US to enter into operations against its national interest. These include "demonizing the Palestinians," the invasion of Iraq, shunning prudent engagement with rogue states such as Iran, Syria, and Libya, and attempting the geopolitical transformation of North Africa, the Middle East, and Central Asia.[84] Such conclusions have set off a firestorm of debate. While some, spearheaded by Alan Dershowitz and Eliot Cohen, dismissed the Mearsheimer-Walt position as anti-Semitic, many others took it more seriously but emphatically argued against it. A summary of those arguments is as follows: (1) American interests in the Middle East would be the same even without a pro-Israel lobby; or (2) that lobby is powerful because it espouses beliefs already held by most policymakers.[85] Responding to their critics, Mearsheimer and Walt have presented further evidence in their book, and have maintained that pro-Israel actions will continue to undermine the US role in the Middle East by destabilizing the region while bringing global indignation about American policies.[86] Iraq for example, is a much more dangerous place for Americans and coalition countries than it was under Saddam Hussein.[87] While his elimination from power and execution may have furthered the interests of Israel, an arch-rival of the Arab nationalism championed by Ba'athism, it did little to secure an already precarious American position there.[88] This was traceable to Zionist and neoconservative efforts in Washington.

Mearsheimer and Walt as well as many others have studied the powerful effects of the pro-Israel lobby on American policymaking but few have grappled with the pro-Arab lobby.[89] It is well known that the reason for this is the relative weakness of the latter vis-à-vis the former.[90] However, when American policy pursued peace, notably by adopting the two-state solution to the Israeli–Palestinian conflict, the pro-Arab lobby underwent dramatic changes. In the present, since the pro-Israel lobby is interested in maintaining Jewish supremacy in Israel, the two-state solution may be something on which both lobbies may agree. Apart from this possibility for agreement, each side has tried to push policy toward furthering its own goals in the Israeli–Palestinian conflict. The Israel lobby is interested in supporting the Jewish state's actions, from occupation over the Palestinians and building the security wall to negotiating on its own terms.[91] Meanwhile, many in the pro-Arab lobby support "the recognition of Palestinian rights to a *viable* state founded upon the June 4, 1967 occupied territories through multilateral agreement."[92] It is noteworthy that the two-state solution has such wide appeal that it would provide common ground to otherwise diametrically opposed sides. In this context, Tony Smith wrote, "the result in domestic American politics was for the first time a collaboration between mainstream Arab and Jewish Americans for a goal they all shared."[93] Nevertheless, the pro-Israel lobby is primarily interested in ensuring the alliance between the Jewish state and the US against the Palestinians and for articulating Israel's interests, even when they do not include the pursuit of peace as outlined by numerous international decrees and the roadmap. Conversely, the pro-Arab lobby, "bringing together competing interests from over twenty-two nations," because of relative weaknesses in the same attributes that make the pro-Israel lobby such a force to be reckoned with, has not been as effective in influencing US policy on the Israeli–Palestinian conflict.[94] On that Janice Terry wrote,

> if they hope to compete on anything approaching even terms [with the Israel lobby], pro-Arab groups would be wise to adopt long term, unified and vigorous agendas. To mount successful lobby campaigns, Arab American organizations need to expand and develop the trend toward unified efforts. [The Arab-American Anti-Discrimination Committee] and other Arab American and Muslim organizations have had some success in countering stereotypes, particularly at the grassroots level, but even in this realm much remains to be done. Undoubtedly, the attacks of 11 September, the subsequent war in Afghanistan, the occupation of Iraq, Israeli attacks in the Occupied Territories and the concomitant increase of suicide bombings, have all exacerbated the problems faced by Arab American domestic pressure groups.[95]

While the promise of Arab lobby effectiveness continues to grow as Americans tackle issues in the Middle East, the problems of the war on terrorism have intensified Israeli attacks not just on the Palestinians and others in the region but also on the foundation of a viable two-state solution through land expropriation with support by groups like AIPAC.[96] In this climate, pro-Arab advocates have yet another challenge against that resilient foe. The post-9/11 terrain has seen a reaffirmation of the alliance between Israel and the United States against terrorism. This means that the presumably compatible interests of the two states provide the pro-Israel lobby with more sway compared to the pro-Arab lobby.

In the present, however, the pro-Arab lobby may become influential for several reasons. First, the pro-Arab lobby's support for the two-state solution may ironically benefit from efforts by the pro-Israel lobby to keep the Jewish majority status quo in Israel. Thus, if Israel was to maintain itself as a political entity in which Jews continue their demographic superiority, then the creation of a Palestinian state consistent with the US roadmap is the only long-term option on the policymaking scene in which the pro-Israel lobby operates. Second, the increasing population of Arab and Muslim Americans due to migration and birthrate may have a corresponding intensification of lobbying efforts.[97] Third, particularly after 9/11, Arab and Muslim Americans are more visible and vocal.[98] Even if this does not make a difference in direct lobbying, it may have an effect on public opinion, which already favors the two-state solution. The increasing potential for Arab Americans and their allies to "become more influential in their government's decision making on the Middle East signals a counterweight to the pro-Israel lobby that may produce more even-handed policy outcomes."[99] Regarding the Israeli–Palestinian conflict, the pro-Arab lobby has always pressed for:

> 1. opposition to Israel's occupation of the West Bank [and] Gaza ...; 2. the need to cut U.S. aid to Israel to prevent the "establishment of illegal settlements and annexation of occupied territories, including Jerusalem"; 3. the need to enforce American arms control laws "with reference to Israel's misuse of United States supplied military equipment ...;" and 4. the need for a Palestinian state.[100]

While not on the American agenda during the 1980s, these goals have become necessary conditions for the practicability of US peace proposals in the 1990s and 2000s, *regardless* of whether or how they are pursued.

On those and other issues, the pro-Israel lobby has enjoyed a significant place in policy decisions.[101] AIPAC is the most powerful pro-Israel lobby and represents a good deal of support for the Jewish state in the US.[102] This exemplar of the Israel lobby seeks unconditional friendship between the two sides. It does this through, among other tactics, contributions to members of Congress, which according to Rubenberg, "are carefully targeted to individuals whose committee assignments will involve them in legislation concerning Israel."[103] For the most part, AIPAC's fortune has corresponded to the general success of the Jewish state. Before and during the 1980s strategic alliance, AIPAC worked tirelessly to bring about and maintain that relationship. It has been "committed to promoting, preserving and protecting strong and consistently close relations between the United States and Israel."[104] This commitment existed both during and after the Cold War. However, while the United States pursued a peace framework during the 1990s and 2000s that would ultimately result in the two-state solution, AIPAC resisted that formula, something that may explain why it did not come to fruition after the 2005 roadmap deadline. Prior to the end of the Cold War, AIPAC maintained, "an independent Palestinian state in Judea, Samaria and Gaza is unacceptable."[105] After the fall of the Soviet Union, AIPAC moved from outright rejection of the two-state solution to acquiescence, although it has tried to frustrate its accomplishment. Possible reasons for that shift will be inspected with emphasis on the failure to produce a Palestinian state, despite support for it in the United States and throughout the world. To analyze the American preference for two states, public opinion and its relationship to policy will be considered.

Public opinion and policymakers

Studying public opinion and its impacts on decision-making continues to be a productive enterprise. Thus, Richard Sobel observed,

> a fundamental premise in our democracy is that government policy reflects the will of the people. In an ideal sense, what the government does should derive from citizen opinion. In actuality, what the government does derives only imperfectly from citizen preferences. Yet the public's beliefs and attitudes do guide and constrain public policy, in foreign as well as domestic affairs.[106]

The task of the student of public opinion then is to figure out how it guides and constrains foreign policy. In the American context, the historical debate seems to focus on isolationism versus interventionism.[107] Since the US has consistently intervened in the Israeli–Palestinian conflict, whether through its longstanding support of Israel or by issuing the roadmap, what is needed is an examination of the variables involved in shaping public opinion and its influence on policymakers' actions toward foreign involvement.

American decision-making is guided by variety of factors, particularly popular sentiment. However, there is uncertainty about the extent to which citizen preferences influence foreign policy. As a case in point, while a majority of Americans favors the two-state formula, US policymakers have lacked the will to apply enough pressure on Israel to bring it into being.[108] Perhaps this is due to entrenched support for the Jewish state in the American psyche. Therefore, this study will examine how backing for Israel stems from the Judeo-Christian consciousness of the majority of Americans, something that belongs to the cultural studies sub-field of FPA.[109] Such an examination however, would be incomplete without understanding how pro-Israel forces are responsible for playing up attitudes of affinity between Americans and Israelis. These attitudes permeate the highest levels of decision-making where foreign policy is conceived and implemented.[110]

Looking at the US position toward Israel, we see that wide-ranging support by the American public of the Jewish state offers few constraints, particularly in its treatment of the Palestinians. Although little is known about the conflict between them, Americans' general mood tends toward favoring one side over the other. How does such a disposition influence foreign policy? Public opinion scholars have developed numerous theories to explain the interplay between their focus and the outcome of American policy. Most posit a complex relationship.[111] Hence, decisions on the American position in the Israeli–Palestinian conflict stem from interactions between the foreign policy elite and a variety of players. That elite is influenced by strong lobbying voices in Washington wishing to see favorable policy outcomes. Once such policies are articulated, public opinion moves *further* toward either support or disinterest. This is one possible path in the relationship between popular sentiment and foreign policymaking that will be examined in more depth. Another is where opinion guides decision making, such as the public favor of Israel creating a positive policy atmosphere for its supporters. When it comes to that, the challenge is to pinpoint with some certainty the form in which the public interacts with policymaking. This may only be done with a thorough examination of polling data and comparing it to policy positions.

Before doing that, what can be done with confidence now is to look at the nature of public opinion as it spills over into the halls of government. In 1981, Mohammed K. Shadid argued

> it is quite clear that domestic support of Israel goes well beyond the boundaries of Israeli and American-Israel lobbying groups. There is a strong sentiment in American moderate and liberal circles (and often among conservatives as well) that Israel is a nation "in the image" of the US: "democratic, progressive," and western in outlook. Certain American fundamentalist groups even regard Israel as the fulfillment of biblical prophecy. In addition, many American supporters perceive Israel as an essential, strategic ally in an unstable region, the "bulwark against communism and radical nationalism" in the Middle East.[112]

During the decade after the end of the Cold War, Israel lost an important attribute, that of "bulwark against communism." However, with much work by pro-Israel advocates, it continued to enjoy everything else ascribed to it by Shadid and presently is understood to be a staunch ally against terrorism, something with which scholars like Mearsheimer and Walt took issue. The belief of Israel as a likeminded "friend" and of the Palestinians simply as its "enemy," persists today despite changes in the international landscape.[113]

There was a brief period after 9/11 when Americans began to question that mindset and whether the Israeli–Palestinian conflict had a role to play in the terrorist attacks.[114] This line of questioning evaporated as other events like the invasion of Iraq and terrorism against European cities took center-stage.[115]

Before 9/11, many concerns threatened positive opinion toward Israel. A long standing argument, persisting both before and after the Cold War, has been that the cost "Israel is likely to pay in the long run if it persists in its policy of holding onto the West Bank and the Gaza Strip will be the deterioration of support in the United States."[116] While this may have been true before the beginning of the 1993 peace process, its culmination in the roadmap that called for two states may have reinvigorated backing for Israel in the US. With the perception that it will "give" the Palestinians a state as demonstrated by its willingness to negotiate, not to mention its "withdrawal" from Gaza, attentive American minds may believe that the Jewish state is willing to quit occupying another people, therefore relieving it of blame. At the point that the two-state solution seems to be suffering failure, whether because of terrorism or the election of Hamas, the positive view of Israel would allow culpability to be placed squarely on the Palestinians. After all, the Jewish state gave up so much and the Palestinians failed to provide anything in return. This understanding contributes to further public support of Israel in the present, particularly after the failed Camp David talks in 2000. It will continue to inform ways of thinking about the conflict and its resolution well after the round of negotiations started at Annapolis in 2007.

In addition to the positive view of Israel, many have pointed out that public opinion toward the Palestinians involved a lack of knowledge about Arabs, their history, and political environment. Hence,

> the United States ... has a long tradition of sympathy for peoples striving to attain sovereign nationhood generally, and for persecuted peoples in particular which was likely to bring forth a friendly attitude toward the aspirations of Jewish nationalism. And while it is true that Jewish nationalism conflicted with Palestinian Arab nationalism, American opinion, quite apart from the influence of powerful Jewish propaganda, was apt to give priority to the Jewish claim to national restoration in Palestine, because of its connection with the Bible, over the Arab case about which it knows very little even today.[117]

Although made in 1963, this observation still has a great deal of truth in the present. However, after the 1967 war, Israel proved capable of defending itself. This monumental development did not square with the archetypal notion of Jews as a persecuted community. And since the Palestinians remained the only party in the Arab–Israeli conflict that did not have a state, it was likely that Americans would, under the proper guidance by voices for peace, be sympathetic to their aspiration for statehood, as is demonstrated by majority support of the two-state solution. Where this will be tested however, is in whether a Palestinian state was prevented from coming to fruition primarily because of the Zionist lobby or because of the persistent lack in understanding the Arabs, particularly the Palestinians. At this point, it must be noted that both of these issues may undergo change because of the potential of Arab American groups and other supporters of Palestinian statehood in confronting the pro-Israel lobby and the related possibility that the public will become more educated about the Middle East from an equitable perspective.

If not informed by this perspective, evenhandedness in American policy on the Israeli–Palestinian conflict rests at least on the ability to frame the debate in terms that are more neutral. As it stands, the contemporary mood toward the Palestinians involves the following.

> Despite the fact that Palestinians are now recognized to have a national existence and national aspirations, U.S. policymakers are still, in their focus on Israel's interests and perspective, able to a great extent to block out the Palestinian viewpoint. Israel's security still takes precedence in U.S. calculations of what constitute fair and reasonable peace terms, and Israel's readiness to negotiate still determines U.S. readiness to mediate. The question of Palestinian security has rarely entered U.S. calculations, and Palestinian readiness to negotiate has rarely pushed the United States to press forward with a mediation effort.[118]

Blocking out the Palestinian viewpoint takes place on the levels of elite perception and public opinion and is the first hurdle that has to be overcome in order pressure Israel toward the realization of the two-state solution. The primary task when looking at this issue, however, is asking why despite the difficulties involved in getting public and policymaker opinion to correspond with the appropriate position for peace, did the two-state solution become the prevalent method to address the national concerns of the Israelis as well as the Palestinians.

This is an especially poignant question since "public opinion is increasingly recognized as a central factor in the decisions about U.S. foreign relations."[119] When it comes to Middle East policy, it plays a role that is both inhibited and channeled by numerous political forces, particularly lobbies, policymaker perception, and various other agents of socialization such as the media.[120] And while American attitudes toward the Middle East in general, and the Israeli–Palestinian conflict in particular, suffer from a lack of knowledge about the peoples involved, the default position shows that "the people of the US broadly subscribe to the belief that they have a genuine national interest in the survival of Israel as an independent state."[121] Hence, American public opinion varies little on the *principles* behind US support for the Jewish state. The prevalent conviction in the political right is that much of what Israel does may be justified in the name of Western civilization,

Jewish independence, biblical prophecy, or a combination of these reasons. On the left, many believe that the Jewish state serves to protect its citizens against anti-Semitic crimes such as those committed by the Nazis during the 1930s and 1940s, and therefore ought to be supported. On both sides of the political spectrum, most have been convinced that Israel's policies serve the US.[122] Still, Americans remarkably favor a Palestinian state. This shows that while public opinion and foreign policy may be committed to a one-sided principle, there are nuances worthy of investigation when it comes to proposals for peace in the Israeli–Palestinian conflict.

Examining public opinion on the Israeli–Palestinian conflict during the late 1970s–1980s, after the end of the Cold War, and during the war on terrorism, this study expects to find changes in what was believed to be a solution to the conflict related to how international events were conveyed and perceived.[123] While very high levels of support for the two-state solution emerged a year after the historic "handshake" between Arafat and Rabin, this study will grapple with how the 1993 Declaration of Principles (DOP) related to public opinion.[124] Also, it will examine what effects the two lobbies had on efforts to resolve the Israeli–Palestinian conflict after the end of the Cold War and during the war on terrorism. Whereas only a minority of Americans supported the two-state solution in the initial stages of the Arab–Israeli peace process – which dated back to the late 1970s but disappeared during the Reagan years – a majority backed an important part of President Bush's strategy in the war on terrorism, the *explicit* call for the two-state solution in the roadmap.[125] As will be shown later, this type of support for a Palestinian state places the Arab lobby and supporters of peace in a better position in their aim of pushing American power toward ending the conflict.

Historical synopsis[126]

As mentioned earlier, during the Reagan years, Israel gained a special place in America's approach to the rest of the world. Not only was the Jewish state perceived as a shield against Soviet influence in the Middle East, it was also seen as a defender of the free world and the American interests that served it. According to Karen Puschel, four factors "lead to a dramatic improvement in US-Israel relations" during the early 1980s.

> First, three key personalities would either be replaced or would undergo a significant change in views, and the National Security Council would play a more important role in US-Israel relations. Secondly, the failure of US policies in the region would lead to a reassessment of ways to achieve US interests in the Middle East. Third, the Soviet Union would reemerge as a much more potent factor in US strategy in the Middle East. Finally, domestic pressures would build for an improvement in US-Israel relations.[127]

These developments defined the scope of policy toward the Israeli–Palestinian conflict through the rest of the 1980s and have implications in the present. While important for US–Israel cooperation, they also contributed to the American policy of ignoring Palestinian national aspirations, something that was capitalized upon by an effective Israel lobby.

Although the Cold War ended in 1991, the Bush administration continued its predecessor's rejection of any viable solution to the Israeli–Palestinian conflict. Two factors began changing how the United States perceived that conflict. First, the Intifada made the Israelis and their American ally realize the increasing difficulty of occupation.[128] In the United States, the pro-Arab lobby would take advantage of the Palestinian uprising to mount a sneak attack on the hegemony of pro-Israel forces on government policy and public opinion. Second, Arab American pressure groups vehemently campaigned to drive home the point that the Gulf War was exhibit A in the case that unsavory characters in the region such as Saddam Hussein could use the Palestinian problem to stir the masses to their side, thereby undermining the stability of Middle East regimes that fought in the coalition to expel Iraq from Kuwait.[129] Despite these efforts, the US did not take any significant measures to change its policy during the remainder of Bush's term in office. "In fact," Rubenberg argued, "the Bush administration maintained the historical consistency of US policy toward the Palestinians including the rejection of the Palestinian right to self-determination, to an independent state, and to leaders of their own choosing."[130] Still, in response to the Intifada and the first Iraq War, one of the Bush administration's key accomplishments was that it facilitated peace talks at Madrid (1991) between Israel and various Arab parties.[131] This study will examine how the Intifada, the first Gulf War, and the end of the Cold War were seized upon by domestic pressure groups in the US. It will also look at the role of those developments in the peace process.

Talks at Oslo and the DOP took place between Israel, the Palestinians, and the US under the Clinton administration.[132] They heralded unprecedented negotiations, which moved forward at a higher rate of progress than Madrid. While it appeared that Clinton's presidency represented a shift in policy toward the Israeli–Palestinian conflict, most agree, "when Bill Clinton took over the presidency from George Bush in January 1993, his Middle East agenda was largely fixed, at least in strategic terms."[133] However, it was under Clinton's watch that Israelis and Palestinians *formally* and *jointly* accepted the land for peace formula, which would underlie the two-state solution. This study examines the interplay between the factors under consideration and that watershed agreement. Particularly, it will look at the role of those factors in the failure of American policy to realize Clinton's vision of peace.

After a last ditch effort to restart talks at Camp David, Clinton's tenure ended and George W. Bush came to power. While the Bush administration "has been severely criticized for not taking a sufficiently active role in trying to solve the Israeli–Palestinian conflict," the sheer amount of issues confronted by the White House, from the terrorist attacks on 9/11 to the invasion of Iraq and the subsequent insurgency took away from the Israeli–Palestinian conflict receiving the required attention.[134] Nevertheless, in the beginning of his term, Bush treated the situation with a "hands off" approach. This nearly became a mantra in the early months of his presidency.[135] However, "hands off" meant that the US would support Israel as it had in the past while leaving the Palestinians to fend for themselves in an increasingly bloody conflict after the beginning of the al-Aqsa Intifada in 2000. In any case, this approach ended during the aftermath of the brutal events of 9/11.[136] Pursuing its enemies from Osama bin Laden to Saddam Hussein, the US had to act in order to secure acquiescence to its global war on terrorism (GWOT, in the neoconservative parlance). The result was the "roadmap."[137]

Methods of inquiry

Overview

An interesting set of questions emerges from the examination above and the one which will occupy the rest of this book. First, how did international developments both before and after the end of the Cold War through the beginning of the war on terrorism influence public opinion, policymaker perception, and lobbying efforts concerning the eventual adoption of the two-state solution as the cornerstone of American policy toward the Israeli–Palestinian conflict? Second, what was the interaction between the two lobbies and public opinion? Third, how did policymaker perception and lobbying relate to global events involving the United States, Israel, and the Palestinians? These questions will be analyzed in the course of the following: the Camp David Accords era of the late 1970s, the forging of the strategic relationship between the United States and Israel in the 1980s, US reactions to the Intifada, its intentions behind the first Iraq War, its role in the Israeli–Palestinian negotiations after the end of the Cold War, and its approach to the conflict during the war on terrorism and in the second Iraq War.

Opinion/perception

In order to study public opinion and policymaker perceptions as they affect and are influenced by American foreign policy, polling data will be analyzed. Such a query tells us a great deal about public opinion and its weight in policymaking. Polls from Gallup will be inspected for changes concerning the Israeli–Palestinian conflict.[138] In particular, the following will be looked at: (1) How did Americans perceive Israel and the Palestinians during the late 1970s and through the 1980s? (2) How did they view the conflict between the two sides during that timeframe? (3) Was there a change in that view during the Intifada, the subsequent recognition of the Palestine Liberation Organization (PLO), and the commencement of negotiations? (4) How did Americans' views change after the end of the Cold War? (5) Specifically, how did their opinion change regarding the two-state solution after the first Gulf War; during the pax Americana of the 1990s; during the war on terrorism; and in the second Gulf War to oust Saddam Hussein from power? The variations in public opinion will be examined in how they related to foreign policy elites' perceptions (and vice-versa), and what role they played in the pursuit of the two-state solution to the Israeli–Palestinian conflict.

Despite overwhelming support for Israel, the emergence of the two-state solution signals sympathy with the Palestinians, who since the late nineteenth century have struggled for an autonomous political order of their own.[139] The issue is this: if the relationship between Israel and the United States is so solidified, how could anyone thinking about US policy during the 1980s have forecasted the possibility of the two-state solution? If indeed public opinion is important in the determination of foreign policy, then what happened to cause a sway in the direction of something favoring the Palestinians when nearly all of the cards were stacked so heavily in favor of Israel?[140] Could it be the realization that Israel cannot remain a state for Jews without a Palestinian state, or was it something altogether different? If the two-state solution is perceived as serving the interests of either one side or the other, then how did that view come about? These questions will be framed through an in-depth analysis of public opinion and policymakers' perception during the periods under examination.

Pro-Arab lobby

The pro-Arab lobby has two dimensions, foreign and domestic. Foreign lobbying often takes place on behalf of nation-states with their own economic or political agendas, including petroleum exports and weapons sales. Some countries like Saudi Arabia directly attempt to influence American policy on the Israeli–Palestinian conflict through their contacts with government officials in the administrative and legislative branches.[141] While these lobbying efforts are important, they are difficult to examine in any consistent manner because of their often secretive and informal nature.[142] Consequently, this study will primarily focus on the domestic Arab lobby and its pro-Palestinian state allies, which include peace activists of all backgrounds and Jewish American organizations interested in a secure Israel through land for peace.

Two groups have for the most part undertaken *direct* domestic Arab lobbying efforts in the United States: the now defunct National Association of Arab Americans (NAAA),[143] established in 1972 by Richard Shadyac, and the Arab American Institute (AAI), founded in 1985. While the latter aimed for the "political empowerment" of Arab Americans, the former sought to counter AIPAC.[144] There are additional groups, such as the American Taskforce on Palestine (ATFP), the American-Arab Anti-Discrimination Committee (ADC), and others that indirectly, and somewhat directly, oppose the Zionist political message. To get a sense of their lobbying efforts, they will be looked at during the timeframes under analysis. The investigation of these groups seeks to address the following: (1) When does support for the two-state solution come about? (2) What is the nature and scope of that support? (3) Is there a relationship between that support and the shift toward the two-state solution? (4) What bearing do they have on public opinion and policymakers? This inquiry involved interviews conducted with members of the pro-Arab lobby in the seat of American policymaking, Washington, DC.[145] Through firsthand accounts, the purpose of these interviews was to understand attempts to influence foreign policy. Of particular importance were variances in support for the two-state solution as well as methods to articulate its necessity for US interests.

Interview questions were broken down into the following categories: "organization information," "foreign policy," "resolution," "public opinion/policymakers," "vis-à-vis other lobbies," and "miscellaneous." The first category, "organization information," was meant to gather information on the organization's characteristics through the professional perspective of the interviewee. These included the organization's objectives, how it pursued them, and its position on the Israeli–Palestinian conflict in the era after the Cold War and if applicable, before the end of the Soviet–US rivalry.[146] The "foreign policy" category sought to understand the organizational view on American national interests in the Israeli–Palestinian conflict. Important here were issues surrounding the "special relationship" between the US and Israel and which side that relationship better serves. The foreign policy questions aimed to understand how specific international events have shaped methods of influencing American policy toward the Middle East in general and in the Israeli–Palestinian conflict in particular. While no questions were asked about the war on terrorism, it was assumed participants would address it, as they unanimously did.

The third category, "resolution," attempted to find out what each group considered the best way to resolve the Israeli–Palestinian conflict. While it was understood that all would point to the two-state solution, the status quo of American policy, they were asked about the one-state solution. Since there are seemingly insurmountable problems with both solutions, participants were asked to explain why they chose one particular solution over any other way to resolve the conflict.[147] The fourth category, "public opinion/policy makers" included a series of questions meant to find out how the organization interacts with public opinion and policymakers' perspectives. While direct pro-Arab lobbying on Capitol Hill is very limited, it was anticipated that participants would outline their indirect efforts at shaping national policy. Interviewees were questioned about how their organizations handle public opinion, and whether they have access to officials in charge of national decisions. As had been pointed out earlier, because of the restricted leverage of the pro-Arab lobby on policy when compared to the Zionist lobby, it was expected that participants would address how that comparative weakness limited their access to policymakers in Congress and the White House. Participants were also asked to explain how they could overcome challenges to influencing foreign policy, particularly from pro-Israel competitors. Given the nature of political discourse, all of the pro-Arab weaknesses are strengths of the pro-Israel lobby. To delve into this issue further, in the section on "other lobbies," pro-Arab lobbyists were asked to evaluate the two sides. Finally, the "miscellaneous" category was meant to draw out conclusions about the future of the pro-Arab lobby, given its past and present during the distinct periods in the history of American policy toward the Israeli–Palestinian conflict.

Pro-Israel lobby

Unlike the pro-Arab lobby, advocates for Israel refused efforts to meet and formally interview. This presented challenges to symmetrically inspecting both lobbies. To try to overcome those, the pro-Israel lobby's endeavors to influence American foreign policy will be analyzed by looking at mission statements and press releases from AIPAC, which according to Rubenberg, "is registered as a domestic, not a foreign, lobby, having been exempted from the Foreign Agents Registration Acts."[148] There is also a variety of literature that will be examined around Jewish political action committees (PACs), which sheds light on their policy preferences, their contributions to members of government, public information activities, and direct lobbying efforts in the halls of Congress. While this data has not been readily available, the best attempts were put forward at researching it. Since AIPAC is the most powerful pro-Israel group, it will be treated as the main representative of the pro-Israel lobby in the United States, which at this time includes over fifty-one organizations.[149] And even though the "pro-Israel" lobby is not homogeneous – for instance, there are many groups that favor a settlement with the Palestinians even as Israel has shunned it – the truth remains that AIPAC has dominated the discourse on what it means to favor the Jewish state: following its government's position without regard for the consequences.

Another dimension that will be considered about the pro-Israel lobby is how persons that share its Zionist ideological persuasion have gone on to serve in high government positions that directly manipulated policy. During the Reagan, first Bush, Clinton, and second Bush administrations, key advisors have either come from the ranks of the pro-Israel camp or have resolute sympathy for the Jewish state.[150] Of particular interest is the significance of those individuals on American behavior toward Israel. As is the case with other factors examined here, the primary focus for the investigation of the pro-Israel lobby will be on how its actions interacted with policy in the direction of (or away from) the two-state solution to the Israeli–Palestinian conflict. This will be done by looking at: (1) What form does action on the two-state solution take? (2) Does the Israel lobby represent American interests in the Israeli–Palestinian conflict or does it follow the Israel government line? (3) What effects has it tried to have on public opinion and policymakers? In order to address these questions, Israel lobby websites and the literature surrounding its political efforts in the US will be valuable. Since that lobby has been studied extensively and because of the fact that its key representatives rebuffed attempts to meet, the chapter discussing them may present a lesser contribution than what may be gained by the one on the often-neglected pro-Arab lobby. Even so, after the roadmap, we sorely need a better understanding of the pro-Israel lobby's posture toward the two-state solution through a historical assessment of its evolving techniques to influence American foreign policy decisions.

Conclusion

Support for a state of Jewish majority, even from within Israel, benefits the longstanding aspirations for Palestinian statehood. If indeed Israel is the democracy esteemed by American public opinion, backed by policymakers, and championed by the pro-Israel lobby, then it cannot maintain itself as a Jewish state while occupying or treating as second-class citizens an ever-growing population that is non-Jewish. All concerned parties understand that situation as untenable. However, American ambivalence has been a chief source of maintaining it, even though the US has strongly called for the two-state solution, something that was echoed across partisan lines.[151] Having gone unheeded, these calls present a key dilemma in American foreign policy thought: how can the US both steadfastly back Israel in its status quo ante while at the same time affirming the Palestinians as a national community deserving of a state? This dilemma forces the consideration of another scenario for peace, the one-state solution, which will be done in the concluding chapter of this book.

The post-9/11 era is riddled with pitfalls for US policy toward the Israeli–Palestinian conflict, which according to James Zogby, have reduced international activism "to simply alleviating the suffering of the mess made during the war on terrorism."[152] However, the pro-Arab lobby currently has an opportune moment, one in which the Palestinian "problem," a sore point of American global relations, could be resolved with separate states. This is especially significant since Palestinian statehood, a key plank of pro-Arab lobbyists, their backers, and peace camp allies, has support most notably from an American government that is considerably influenced by the Israel lobby. Indeed, in the post-Arafat-Sharon-Bush era, the roadmap – which has its conceptual roots in the periods of the Camp David Accords and the immediate aftermath of the Cold War – is everywhere an accepted model for peace. It is hoped that the questions surrounding the political evolution behind the two-state consensus raised by the chapters to follow can offer a unique understanding of where American foreign policy has been, and where it might be headed next considering: positive sentiment for Israel with a central footnote of majority public and official American support for the existence of a Palestinian state; the immense strength of the pro-Israel lobby; and the prospects for the pro-Arab lobby to capture the spotlight of leverage because it wants the same thing sought by nearly everyone else, an Israel secure as a Jewish state. Now that the main issues and the literature surrounding them have been outlined, the inquiry will move to public opinion and policymaker perceptions.

2 Public opinion and foreign policy perception

Introduction

What is the role in American foreign policy of the intersection between lobbying, public opinion, and elite perceptions? In 1977, Robert H. Trice wrote,

> the domestic political environment surrounding the governmental foreign policy-making system in the United States includes a variety of elements that have the potential to affect policy outputs. The domestic sources of foreign policy are widely recognized, and include interest groups, mass public opinion, and the printed and electronic media. These nongovernmental elements are assumed by many to have a significant impact on the course of the government's foreign policy activities. ... As a result, the nature and degree of the direct effects, and even more so the secondary effects, of domestic factors on governmental policy remain lively topics of debate.[1]

Although stated decades ago, much of this observation still holds true in the present, particularly as US policy has taken a central place in world affairs after the end of the Cold War. There has been an outpouring of work from a variety of perspectives on the issues taken up by Trice, which has demonstrated the effects of public opinion, interest groups, and other factors on foreign policy.[2] And because such scholarship has contributed a great deal to our understanding of the interaction between domestic phenomena and foreign policymaking, their methodology will be useful to the current task of investigating how public opinion relates to the US-led international consensus on the two-state solution.

Specifically, this chapter has three aims.[3] First, it will look at how Americans perceived the Israeli–Palestinian conflict during the late 1970s after the signing of the Camp David Accords between Egypt and Israel through the 1980s "strategic alliance" between the Jewish state and the US. Looking at that period, we may inspect public opinion nuances and their relationship to policy on Palestinian claims to national self-determination. There is quite a bit of interaction between public opinion, policymakers' perception, and policy outputs during these concluding years of the Cold War. As the Israel–US relationship deepened under Reagan's administration and a Congress dominated by the American Israel Public Affairs Committee (AIPAC) during that timeframe, the Palestinian question was sidelined as Washington not only refused to constrain Tel Aviv's policies toward the Arab nations, it also gave the Jewish state military, economic, and political support for its actions.[4]

Second, this chapter will analyze public opinion during the end of the 1980s and the beginning of the 1990s, roughly the entire period of George H. W. Bush's presidency and Clinton's first year in office. Four significant international events span that timeframe. The Intifada was brought into the American consciousness, an occurrence welcomed by pro-Arab pressure groups and their allies (1987–93); the invasion of Kuwait by Iraq and the consequent Gulf War which engendered the perception that something needed to be done about the Palestinians, whose leadership was on the wrong side of the war as evidenced by a well publicized cordial meeting between Palestine Liberation Organization (PLO) leader Yasser Arafat and Iraqi President Saddam Hussein shortly after the invasion (1990–91);[5] the Soviet Union and the Cold War came to an end heralding a "New World Order" in which the United States no longer feared communist annihilation (1991–92),[6] a development that gave the pro-Arab and pro-Israel lobbies a new policy landscape in which to operate; Arabs and Israelis began negotiations at Madrid (1991); and the signing of Oslo's Declaration of Principles (DOP) by Israel and the Palestinians on the White House Lawn with much media fanfare (1993).[7] During the peace process, Arab American activists received "equal access time to government officials and the media" with their rivals in the pro-Israel lobby.[8] This chapter looks at how these events related to a shift in public opinion more amenable to the existence of the Palestinians as a national community on the world stage. Third, the analysis will turn to looking at public opinion dynamics after the events of September 11, 2001. In particular, it will focus on variance in public opinion during the culmination of Oslo in the roadmap (2002), which outlined a two-state solution to the Israeli–Palestinian conflict, through the beginning of the second Gulf War, which ousted Saddam Hussein from power in Iraq (2003).

The periods outlined above are significant not just for their international developments, but also because they overlapped with major changes in domestic public opinion and simultaneous revisions in strategy to influence "hearts and minds" by pro-Arab and pro-Israel advocates in the United States. Worthy of examination here is why American public opinion and policy went from granting the Palestinians no diplomatic recognition during most of the 1980s to insisting on their right to have a state that would exist side-by-side with Israel after 2002. Hence, the central question of this chapter is what were the impacts of changes in public opinion on the roles of pro-Israel and pro-Arab organizations and their efforts on American foreign policy, which has called for a two-state solution to the Israeli–Palestinian conflict? This inquiry seeks to contribute to the debate over public opinion's relationship to interest groups and their interactions with policymaking.[9] It will test the well established hypothesis that public opinion shapes political output.[10] Mainly, the treatment below will look at whether foreign policy behavior and the elite perceptions surrounding it influence public opinion or whether the relationship is the other way around. Regardless of the outcome, it will demonstrate that special interest groups on both sides of the Arab–Israeli conflict have a substantial stake in influencing public opinion for the following reasons. First, if foreign policy and elite perceptions shape public opinion, then direct lobbying is the better bet for any group seeking influence, since only policymakers matter. Second, if there is a two-way effect between public opinion and foreign policy, then the manipulation of popular sentiment as well as direct pressure on politicians by interest groups are optimal to controlling policy. Third, if public opinion shapes foreign policy, then influencing how citizens view world affairs will determine policy outcomes. All strategies are assumed to adapt to major international events. While the second strategy obviously offers the best possible path for pressure groups, it is also true that in a world of limited resources, the pro-Arab lobby and its pro-Israel rival must prioritize and focus their efforts in order to minimize their costs and maximize desired policy outputs. Hence, what follows is an examination of the role of public opinion in the ultimate preference for the two-state solution.

The Cold War

Advancing the "strategic relationship"

Despite some notable efforts to humanize them, the late 1970s and early 1980s were a bad time for how Palestinians were viewed, with "little regard for Israel's occupation over them."[11] As pro-Arab advocates and scholars like Mohammed K. Shadid were calling on the US to "bring an end" to an "internationally threatening conflict" by searching "for a just and equitable resolution of the Palestinian situation," the American public and its policymakers barely recognized the Palestinians as a people worthy of attention.[12] Some have argued that this was informed by a general lack of recognition for non-Western people and a long established narrative about the "Orient" built upon a series of misunderstandings.[13] According to Douglas Little, "U.S. policymakers from Harry Truman to George W. Bush tended to dismiss Arab aspirations for self-determination as politically primitive, economically suspect, and ideologically absurd."[14] On the flipside, there has always existed a wide-ranging belief that Israel and its "Zionist pioneers were ineluctably transforming the dream of a Jewish state into Middle Eastern reality through blood, sweat, and tears." With attitudes like this, it is of little wonder that during the 1980s the US nurtured a profound alliance with Israel.[15]

Reflecting that, year after year, Americans tended to view the Jewish state with favor. When asked about the warmth of the Israel–US relationship in 1986, the majority of Americans responded with high marks.[16] While that has been a continuing theme in opinion polls of the 1980s, responses about the Palestinians, when they were considered at all, have been misinformed, sometimes hostile, but always preferring that they be kept at a distance from American support. Many attribute this fact to the framing of Israel as a partner of the West in the Cold War,[17] a task that in no small measure preoccupied its lobbying camp in the US. The Jewish state, with its conventional and nuclear military might, was believed to be a natural ally while the much weaker Palestinians and other Arab nations were seen as unacceptably neutral or worse, sympathetic to the Soviet Union.[18] Pro-Israel lobbyists unearthed many examples to support this view, such as Gamal Abdel Nasser's founding of the non-aligned movement and his flirtation with the Eastern Bloc during the 1950s and 1960s. Decades later, public opinion polls expressed enormous concern for Israel and its region.

In the 1980s, there was great worry about the Middle East, especially its position in the Russo-American rivalry. During 1985, 58 percent of Americans believed that the problems between Israel and the Arab states would have a "great chance" of becoming a source of "a major U.S.-Soviet confrontation or war."[19] Another 25.5 percent thought that the hostile relationship between Israel and the rest of the Middle East had a "moderate chance" of bringing the superpowers into confrontation. This meant that close to 84 percent of Americans saw the region as a major Cold War issue. In this type of atmosphere, Israel seemed to be a crucial ally available to the United States if Soviet influence crept into the region, as it often did. For that reason, American leaders maintained strong ties with the Jewish state. Consistently, policymakers thought that they must keep a steady stream of aid flowing to Israel. The proportion of them responding in that manner during the 1980s usually topped 75 percent.[20] Consequently, US backing for Israel only deepened over the years.

Strong elite support often mirrored popular opinion that affirmed the extraordinary relationship between the two states. During 1986, policymakers were asked about where their sympathies lay in the Middle East, whether with Israel or with the Arab states. Over 60 percent of them responded that they sympathized "more with Israel." This meant that American assistance, public opinion, and elite perceptions converged throughout the era of the strategic alliance. More support for Israel in thought meant a corresponding amount in practice. The American approach to the Israeli–Palestinian conflict seemed not only one-sided, since that would assume another side existed, but to support Israel as the *only* bona fide actor in its regional neighborhood. Money and weapons poured into the Jewish state as it built up settlements and furthered its hold on the occupied territories. When Israeli actions resulted in counteractions by the Palestinians, those responsible were branded terrorists and had to reckon not just with Israel's military, but also with further contempt by American citizens and policymakers alike.

American Middle East strategy granted Israeli security supreme priority during the latter half of the 1980s. When policymakers were asked in 1986 whether they would respond with military force to protect the Jewish state against an Arab attack, nearly 57 percent said they would do so.[21] This poll was striking considering the backdrop of American ambivalence about foreign intervention, particularly during the age of the "Vietnam Syndrome."[22] Hesitation about international involvement was shown in a poll during the same timeframe, in which the majority of Americans opposed using troops in order to rescue Israel.[23] Still, during the 1980s, at least among policymakers, it virtually became an extension of the territorial United States. For many, an assault against it would have been analogous to an attack on the US mainland. While this represented tension between public opinion and what policymakers believed, the fact is Americans generally held Israel in very high esteem. Well aware of that fact, decision-makers were more pro-Israel than their constituents.

Certain were the stakes Americans attributed to their alliance with Israel. In a question about "vital interests," a majority (nearly 76 percent) believed their country had "political, economic, and security" reasons to be allied with the Jewish state. When answering this question, most defaulted to the common understanding of Israel as a friend. American support meant that Israel continued its policies of undermining Palestinian national aspirations with impunity, often in direct violation of international law and the explicit wishes of the United Nations. Eventually, the Palestinians no longer acquiesced to living under occupation. By the end of 1987, they revolted en masse, a movement that came to be known as the Intifada, which aside from attempting to "shake off" Israel, helped the domestic pro-Arab side seek change in the way Americans viewed the conflict. According to Khalil Jahshan, the Intifada provided that effort "with resounding evidence that the deplorable situation in the Middle East could no longer be tolerated by anyone in the United States."[24]

The Intifada years

By 1988, the Palestinian uprising was in full swing. Americans received news about Israeli aggression toward a population struggling against military occupation by, for the most part, the use of nonviolent techniques.[25] As stories from the West Bank and Gaza made their way into the print and electronic media, pro-Arab advocates reached out to fellow Americans to convey Palestinian suffering under Israel's control. Subsequently, empathy for the Jewish state began to show weakness. At issue was how a country with "purity of arms"[26] could be so ruthless to women and children who too often were on the frontlines of the uprising. While most Americans viewed it favorably despite its attempts to put down the Intifada, many saw Israel's actions "dealing with the Palestinian riots" as "too harsh."[27] Some began to question the policies that the Jewish state had engaged in since the 1967 war and the consolidation of its authority over Arab territories. And although American support for Israel did not abate, there were increased calls for peace with its neighbors, which a simple majority of Americans (about 51 percent) believed was possible and therefore ought to be pursued by US policy during a survey taken in 1988, the Intifada's first full year.[28]

Regarding how peace might be accomplished, in the same survey, Americans were asked, "do you favor or oppose the establishment of an independent Palestinian nation within the territories occupied by Israel in the 1967 war?" In answer to this, 30.30 percent supported an "independent nation," 26.51 percent opposed it, and 43.19 percent chose "don't know." This showed that attitudes during the late 1980s were at best edging toward support for Palestinian statehood and at worst ambivalent about it. Nearly two years after the beginning of the Intifada, Alvin Richman put opinion polls in perspective.

> The American public (1) is closely divided about whether the Israeli reaction to the disturbances has been "too harsh," (2) remains con-siderably more pro-Israel than pro-Arab or pro-Palestinian in its sym-pathies, (3) is inclined to approve a Palestinian homeland that does not threaten Israel's security, and (4) supports an active U.S. diplomatic role in the Middle East.[29]

It was widely understood that the Intifada showed the Jewish state and the world that the Palestinians refused to accept their subjugation.[30] Two points were rarely emphasized, however. First, concern about the conflict as por-trayed in the daily news cycle confirmed the pro-Arab message that Israel's reaction to the Intifada was unendurable. Second, it showed the American public and its policymakers that Israeli and Palestinian misery might be alleviated by a political formula based on United Nations Security Council (UNSC) resolutions 242 and 338.[31] This was the only way out of the occu-pation's harsh conditions for the Palestinians and a conduit for Israel to save face under mounting international pressure against its measures to quell the uprising.

While 1988 was a watershed year because of developments in the Israeli–Palestinian conflict, change in US policy toward it had limits set by domestic sentiment. Richman mapped the public opinion terrain of the late 1980s by looking at three priorities: "(1) assuring Israel's security, (2) satisfying Palestinian national aspirations, [and] (3) satisfying Israeli territorial claims based on possessions during earlier times."[32] Americans have always accep-ted the first goal when considering Middle East policy and continue to do so at the time of this writing. The mutually dependent second and third goals have been more elusive in both public opinion and as they relate to policy-making. Since the two-state solution was not yet considered a US aim, other issues took precedence. In fact, more pressing was the need to maintain the Israeli–Egyptian peace a decade after the Camp David Accords (1978). Following that settlement between the two former enemies and Ronald Reagan assuming office, American policy throughout the 1980s strategic alliance primarily concerned itself with Israel's security. This came at the expense of the Palestinians, even as it was understood that the interests of peace and stability depended upon political agreement between Israel and the people it occupied.

Whereas ignoring Palestinian aspirations corresponded to the deepening Israel–US alliance and the concurrent growth in the Israel lobby's power to sway policymakers, there was sizeable minority support for the two-state solution among Americans, which dated back to the late 1970s. One instance of this was a poll taken in 1979, which asked a question similar to the one conducted a decade later: "do you think a separate, independent Palestinian nation should be established or do you think the Palestinians should continue to live as they do now in Israel and the neighboring Arab nations?" To this question, 36.92 percent said "establish separate nation," 25.03 percent stated "continue as they do now," 2.97 percent answered "other," 25.28 percent held "no opinion," and 9.80 percent gave no answer.[33] Two things are noteworthy about this poll when compared to the one conducted in 1988.[34] First, the percentage of those believing in the necessity of the two-state solution was actually higher in 1979 than in 1988. This was remarkable since American public opinion waffled on support for the two-state solution a year prior to the 1979 poll.[35] Second, it demonstrated that the intensification of the "Memorandum of Understanding" between the US and Israel under AIPAC's direction in Congress and the Reagan administration's increasingly rejectionist path on the Israeli–Palestinian conflict, coincided with a downturn in support for an independent Palestinian state in the 1988 poll.[36]

This was not always the case during the 1980s. In a 1982 poll, the first full year of Reagan's term in office and of the strategic alliance between Israel and the US, over 41 percent of Americans supported "a separate, independent Palestinian nation" versus 21 percent who believed that they should "continue as they do now."[37] Taken a month after Israel's invasion of Lebanon on June 6, 1982, this poll may have been a reflection of growing knowledge that the status quo in the Middle East did not serve the interests of peace, a point that pro-Arab pressure groups worked to instill while arguing for a political solution to the conflict.[38] What all of this showed was that – as in the above example of military intervention to rescue Israel[39] – public opinion only gradually matched up with foreign policy outcomes. Hence, even though the Reagan administration and Congress rejected Palestinian autonomy, their successors considered the idea as demonstrated by peace efforts from Madrid to Annapolis. International events had a relationship to change in Americans' opinion. In the wake of the Lebanon invasion and later the Intifada, the necessity for peace between the Arabs and Israel became more pressing.

Nevertheless, with stepped-up focus on the Cold War during the Reagan years, particularly as the pro-Israel lobby had convinced policymakers that the Jewish state was the best defense against communism in the Middle East as expressed by the 1981 Memorandum of Understanding, what many in the public affirmed was optimal to resolve the Israeli–Palestinian conflict took a backseat to what were perceived as more compelling matters.[40] Under Reagan's watch, the Soviet rivalry preoccupied foreign policy elites.[41] Meanwhile, the strategic relationship forged between the US and Israel meant that public opinion polling, which showed some level of support for Palestinian statehood, was viewed by the establishment in Congress and the White House as a prima facie threat to the Jewish state's existence. This overlapped with privileging Israel and a disregard for Palestinian anguish in the occupied territories. One could see then why the Intifada broke out in 1987, a response to Israeli policies that were unconcerned by any significant constraints from the American benefactor.

The Gulf crisis

Two occupations

The world was rapidly changing during and after 1989. The fall of the Berlin Wall signaled the beginning of the end for the Soviet Union, the Warsaw Pact, and the Eastern Bloc. While the Germans chipped away at that symbol of their division, American sympathy toward Israel as a strategic ally in the Cold War began to lose its luster. In the Middle East, Israel and the Palestinians were going through their second year of struggle during the Intifada. The Reagan era ended with the election of George H. W. Bush. Although the world was undergoing an epic transformation, Bush wished to stay the course of his predecessor's policies.[42] Despite being controlled by the Democrats, Congress concurred with the newly elected Republican president's position on the Israeli–Palestinian conflict. The forces of global change and the evolving domestic situation, however, forced continuities and discontinuities in policy. Continuities existed as the US treated Israel through the lens of the strategic relationship. Discontinuities were rampant since the tectonic plates of the international arena were quivering with the collapse of the rivalry between the United States and the Soviet Union. The conclusion of the Cold War meant that the US no longer had to pick its battles based on what the USSR might do next, directly or through proxy.[43] This presented many problems for American foreign policy, since there was no longer a fixed point of reference on which to base decisions.[44] It also meant that the pro-Israel lobby would soon lose its icon of the Jewish state as an ally against the Soviet Union and communism. The conflict between Israel and the Palestinians was not spared from the transformation of the global power balance. Each side understood the implications for its own future.

But before the official end of the Cold War on December 25, 1991, Iraq's invasion of Kuwait in the summer of 1990 shocked the world community. Under orders from Saddam Hussein, Iraqi forces faced little resistance as they sped toward Kuwait City and occupied the rest of the country. The challenge Iraq did face came from American and global opinion as the invasion was swiftly condemned.[45] During November 1990, while Operation Desert Shield was still in progress, Americans were polled on sending troops to the region. Particularly interesting was a question on the use of force if Iraq attacked Israel. A majority of participants (67.18 percent) supported protecting the Jewish state while a minority (24.56 percent) opposed it.[46] From this poll, we see that in addition to ensuring US interests in the Persian Gulf, an important matter for Americans regarding military deployment against Iraq was the protection of Israel. In the realm of public opinion, however, war was not inevitable. A remarkably high percentage of participants (67.57 percent) favored combining discussion of "the Palestinian problem in Israel" with talks about "the Iraq/Kuwait" situation. This meant that public opinion made the link between the Gulf crisis and the Israeli–Palestinian conflict, something that most pro-Arab advocates agreed was necessary to American evenhandedness in the Middle East.[47]

Additionally, during the Gulf crisis, in the often-asked question of which side they sympathized with – a question that often ends up with Israel getting a disproportionate amount of sympathy from the public and policymakers – a larger percentage of *foreign policy elites* said the Palestinians (35.28 percent) as opposed to Israel (32.89).[48] This was a significant outcome since policymakers usually supported Israel without regard to the Palestinians. It also contrasted to public opinion polling during the same period, in which 33.80 percent of Americans sympathized with Israel while only 13.68 percent chose the Palestinians.[49] These polls demonstrated the following about the period leading up to the Gulf War: (1) there was a disconnect between public opinion, which favored Israel, and policymakers that showed some preference toward the Palestinians; and (2) the Gulf crisis may have contributed to a mindset shift regarding the Israeli–Palestinian conflict, but not one that would necessarily remain constant or alter policy outcomes. Nevertheless, the poll showing more elite sympathy toward the Palestinians, when coupled with public opinion favoring combining the two occupations in US decision-making, provided an example of considerable change in traditional perceptions of Israel and therefore an opportunity to discuss alternative approaches to the status quo.

Iraq's invasion of Kuwait and Saddam Hussein's appeal to the Palestinians, regardless of its intent, forced policymakers and their constituents to demand a remedy to the serious situation in the Middle East.[50] Most Americans right up to President Bush began to realize that actors like the Iraqi dictator might use the Palestinian issue as a cover for rogue actions. Indeed, while the invasion of Kuwait and the unlawful appropriation of its oilfields overwhelmingly served Iraqi interests, Iraq's leader claimed that he was taking such action on behalf of the Palestinians.[51] Hence, when his armed forces moved into Kuwait, many Palestinians welcomed them as liberators from a regime that treated them with contempt under second-class status.[52] Likewise, the Palestinian leadership, exiled in Tunisia at the time (the result of Israel's invasion of Lebanon), viewed the Iraqi dictator as someone that stood up to injustices against their compatriots in the occupied territories and throughout the Middle East. This was the case even though most Palestinians realized first-hand that the invasion and occupation of another country was criminal.

The Gulf crisis showed US policymakers that military action by itself to protect Kuwait was not enough. The region had to be put in order. This would not happen unless American policy pursued a solution to the Israeli–Palestinian conflict, something that many were keenly aware of in the wake of the Gulf crisis. In a poll of the US foreign policy elite during October of 1990, a few months before Operation Desert Storm to dislodge Iraq from Kuwait, the following question produced noteworthy results.

> Which of the following approaches do you think the U.S. should take with regard to the issue of the Israeli-occupied territories and the possibility of a Palestinian homeland – The U.S. should not pressure Israel at all and should let Israel pursue whatever policy it thinks best; The U.S. should exert diplomatic pressure on Israel to negotiate a settlement but not reduce economic and military assistance; The U.S. should reduce economic and military assistance if Israel does not negotiate a settlement; or The U.S. should cut off all economic and military aid if Israel does not negotiate a settlement? [Answers] The U.S. should not pressure Israel at all and should let Israel pursue whatever policy it thinks best (5.57%), The U.S. should exert diplomatic pressure on Israel to negotiate a settlement but not reduce economic and military assistance (36.07%), The U.S. should reduce economic and military assistance if Israel does not negotiate a settlement (49.60%), The U.S. should cut off all economic and military aid if Israel does not negotiate a settlement (7.43%), DON'T KNOW/REFUSED (1.33%).[53]

The position of policymakers confirmed what had been suspected all along: peace in the Middle East depends to a significant part on US evenhandedness. One possible way to accomplish that would have been to place conditions on aid to Israel. The Bush administration eventually tried to do just that.[54] In January of 1992, Bush's secretary of state James Baker indicated that allotted loan guarantees to the Jewish state would be frozen until it halted the expansion of its settlements in the occupied territories.

Most in Congress disagreed with the administration's move.[55] This was because action against Israel had very negative political consequences for its supporters, particularly in the legislative branch.[56] The public, after all, sympathized with Israel while its lobby was hard at work tarnishing the reputation of those that stood against it. Still, policymakers understood that there was also an appreciation for resolving the Israeli–Palestinian conflict among voters. Therefore, a few of them went along with denying Israel some support in order to slow settlement-building activity. Moreover, there was a confluence of public opinion and Washington policy on the eve of the Iraq War, particularly between what the American people thought was the proper solution to the conflict and policymakers' concerns about peace. In October of 1990, the public was polled about "the establishment of an Independent Palestinian nation within the territories occupied by Israel in the 1967 war." While 30.36 percent opposed this proposition, 36.24 percent favored it, with 33.4 percent not knowing or refusing to answer.[57] Hence, just as policymakers worried about the threat to peace posed by Israeli settlements, public opinion tended toward support, albeit marginally, for the two-state solution.

In the larger picture, the convergence of public opinion and that of officials during the Gulf crisis provided us with a functioning circuit of foreign policymaking that operated in the following manner. A higher percentage of the public supported the establishment of a Palestinian state on the territories occupied during the 1967 war, was generally less sympathetic to Israel than before, and believed that aid to it ought to be curtailed;[58] policymakers sympathetic with the Palestinians called on the Jewish state to halt settlement activity so as to not jeopardize the chances for resolution through the land for peace framework *or* face cuts in support; the US then proceeded to follow through with that warning and delayed aid; as a result, Israel pledged for the time being to stop the growth of settlements; American policy resumed support. In short, this sequence of developments reflected citizen and elite preference through decisions necessary for the desired outcome. In the case of the Israeli–Palestinian conflict and the larger situation throughout the Middle East, that outcome is peace. The foreign policy circuit of American–Israeli–Palestinian affairs, however, rarely functions properly.

A considerable reason for that has to do with the generally cynical attitude toward peace. During the Gulf crisis, for example, when Americans were asked about its prospects in the Middle East within the next five years, 41.61 percent of them answered that peace was possible and 48.67 percent said that it was not.[59] Now, while violence in the region was ominous, we must consider that a lot happened after this poll outcome within the timeframe asked about, including peace conferences at Madrid and Oslo and the DOP, which outlined steps for Israel and the Palestinians to settle their differences under US mediation. Perhaps pessimism about the likelihood for peace had to do with the turbulent nature of world affairs at the time. After all, as that poll was conducted, Iraq occupied Kuwait, the Palestinians were in full rebellion against an increasingly violent Israeli crackdown, and the Middle East in general looked bloody. The question therefore becomes, what were the interactions between public opinion, elite perceptions, and foreign policy outcomes in the months preceding and during Operation Desert Storm?

Beginning with public opinion prior to the war, most Americans ulti-mately refused to link Iraq's invasion of Kuwait and Israel's occupation of Palestinian lands. While this seemed contrary to the poll taken just months before,[60] it may be explained by the fact that war was imminent. Americans were more likely to tie the two occupations together when diplomacy was ongoing than they were as force became the only option. Hence, on the eve of the showdown between coalition and Iraqi forces, when asked whether the US should work out a diplomatic solution to the Gulf crisis by tying Iraq's invasion to Israel's occupation of the West Bank and Gaza, most Americans (69.44 percent) rebuffed the idea and believed that withdrawal from Kuwait should happen without conditions.[61] This view mirrored President Bush's call on Iraq to quit Kuwait unconditionally or face military consequences. Withdrawal, of course, did not happen. As a result, the United States started an air assault and later a ground campaign to accomplish what Bush ordered. The war threatened to bring Israel into confrontation with Iraq because of the latter attacking the former with Soviet-made Scud missiles.[62] Under US pressure, however, Israel sat out the Gulf War. Meanwhile, the majority of Americans polled showed sympathy for the Jewish state.[63] This was due, in no small part, to it showing restraint, a fact thoroughly seized upon by Zionist organizations in the US. Regardless of how it was domestically spun, Israel's staying out of the war helped the United States because it prevented escalation, something that would have undermined the coalition of Arab states fighting side-by-side with American forces in order to expel Iraq from Kuwait.

Israel, however, was not in the clear as far as American thinking was concerned. In the midst of the Gulf War, when asked whether the US should push Israel "to compromise to achieve peace with the Palestinians," 44.65 percent believed that it should while 37.23 percent said it should not. Still, pressure on Israel or the lack thereof by the United States was linked to narrowly defined and immediate interests in the Gulf War. Hence, a majority of Americans believed that if Israel did not retaliate against Iraq, it should not be required to negotiate a settlement to the Palestinian issue.[64] Rather, the disbursement of money was more of a priority for public opinion. Thus, when asked about what steps the US should take after "thinking about Israel and the attacks it has suffered from Iraq," 45.52 percent supported increasing financial aid to the Jewish state for staying out of the war while 48.32 percent opposed it.[65] During a time of major crisis, Americans cast aside the Israeli–Palestinian conflict, as demonstrated by their preference for the US *not* pressuring Israel to make peace if it had shown restraint. Yet public opinion was against increasing aid to the Jewish state even if it stayed out of the Gulf War. During those extra-ordinary times, defeating the Iraqi enemy was the main concern for policy-makers and the public, taking precedence over the conflict between Arabs and Jews.

The task ahead

After the Gulf War ended, the focus came back to finding a solution to the Palestinian problem. US pressure on Israel no longer merely sought to keep it out of the war. Instead, it focused on enticing the Jewish state to negotiate. The poll below showed the public mood behind this quite well.

> Which of the following approaches do you think the U.S. should take with regard to the issue of the Israeli-occupied territories and the possibility of a Palestinian homeland – The U.S. should not pressure Israel at all and should let Israel pursue whatever policy it thinks best, the U.S. should exert diplomatic pressure on Israel to negotiate a settlement but not reduce economic and military assistance, the U.S. should reduce economic and military assistance if Israel does not negotiate a settlement, or the U.S. should cut off all economic and military aid if Israel does not negotiate a settlement? [Answers] The U.S. should not pressure Israel at all and should let Israel pursue whatever policy it thinks best (25.64%), The U.S. should exert diplomatic pressure on Israel to negotiate a settlement but not reduce economic and military assistance (35.23%), The U.S. should reduce economic and military assistance if Israel does not negotiate a settlement (18.14%), The U.S. should cut off all economic and military aid if Israel does not negotiate a settlement (14.28%), DON'T KNOW/REFUSED (6.71%).[66]

While this demonstrated a good level of support for Israel, it also showed that Americans wanted to resolve the conflict by pressuring the US ally. Most of those polled placed some level of importance on "a peaceful solution to the Israeli–Palestinian problem in the Middle East."[67] After defeating aggression in the Gulf War, Americans had conveyed feelings of efficacy in resolving world problems.[68] There was both a sense of pride in the accomplishment of routing the Iraqi forces and "liberating Kuwait," and contempt for the people these actions were intended to help. Douglas Little put this sentiment best in his comparison between the contemporary American–Middle East relationship and the one that existed dating back to the time of Mark Twain. According to him, "Twain was among the first to interpret the U.S. relationship with the Middle East as the byproduct of two contradictory ingredients: an irresistible impulse to remake the world in America's image and a profound ambivalence about the peoples to be remade."[69] This mentality showed pessimism about the ability of Middle Easterners to be helped out. Yes, Americans felt superior because of their stunning performance in the Gulf War. However, the burdens ahead seemed daunting because the people themselves were helpless, as was demonstrated by constant fighting between Arabs and Jews during the Intifada and by Iraq's takeover of its predominantly Arab/Muslim neighbor.[70]

Hence, during their celebrations of military victory, Americans were still glum about prospects for peace. When asked about its likelihood between Israel and the Palestinians after Iraq's expulsion from Kuwait, more people said that peace was less likely.[71] This showed that against the grain of self-congratulatory ecstasy after the war, the public understood that the key to peace might have to do not simply with getting Iraq out of Kuwait but also with Israel ending its occupation of Arab lands. This point was incessantly put forward by pro-Arab pressure groups and had significant political cover.[72] Thus, in a poll taken a few months after Iraq's defeat, the majority of Americans indicated that Israeli withdrawal from conquered territory would "very likely [or] somewhat likely ... bring lasting peace to the Mideast."[73] This outcome was remarkable since the public returned to making the link between Iraq's occupation of Kuwait and the Israeli occupation of Arab lands even though it refused to express that opinion in the dire times of war. American policymakers eventually heeded public opinion and, along with Soviet leaders, called for an end to the Arab–Israeli conflict with more urgency after the end of the Gulf War. Since by occupying the West Bank, Gaza, the Golan Heights, and Southern Lebanon, Israel violated the same international conventions that Iraq did by its invasion of Kuwait, the question that pro-Arab forces argued must be asked was why there was such a glaring double standard. The data suggest that this question was intuitively begged and ultimately, the American public may have linked the two illegal occupations, Israeli and Iraqi, together as culprits of Middle East instability. In the aftermath of the Gulf War, pro-Arab pressure groups labored to capitalize on that realization.[74] However, despite having public and elite sympathy, this position on the Gulf crisis could not be sustained in the face of resilient support for Israel. Thus, the public backed the immediate and unconditional expulsion of Iraq from Kuwait while the Jewish state continued to occupy and unlawfully settle Arab lands.

Still, the majority of Americans favored withdrawal from territories occupied in 1967 in return for Arab recognition of Israel's right to exist.[75] Unfortunately for Arab American lobbying efforts, by the same token, more Americans held the Arabs responsible for the Israeli occupation. According to a survey taken in September 1991, when asked, "do you think Israel or the Arab countries is more to blame for the lack of progress in settling their differences?" 22.50 percent answered Israel, 36.79 percent blamed the Arab countries, while 22.57 percent faulted both equally.[76] Where the blame was placed depended a great deal on Americans' generally favorable view toward Israel and their concurrent lack of sympathy for the Arab states. It also corresponded to official support of Israel, even in its occupation of the Palestinians at a time when the US was demanding and received UNSC resolutions to condemn the invasion of Kuwait by Iraq and went to war under their auspices with the help of a broad coalition of states. Did public and policymaker dispositions allow for such a contradiction in American foreign policy?

The answer depended on which polls one consulted. For instance, while Americans generally favored the Jewish state, they also, at least during the late 1970s and throughout the 1980s, showed an inchoate preference for a Palestinian state. Politicians only caught on to the preference for a solution and attempted to begin its implementation during the 1990s under President Clinton's leadership, something that "brought much hope."[77] Through it all, the public and policymakers tended toward favoring Israel. Nevertheless, when asked, "in general, do you think Israel has too much influence on U.S. policy, not enough influence, or about the right amount," 46.89 percent of the public said that Israel had "too much" influence while 35.92 percent thought that it was "the right amount."[78] In general, Americans do not like to see foreign meddling in their affairs but many saw the Jewish state as doing exactly that. Therefore, their preference for Israel has always been wary, but paradoxically generous. How could that be? Possible answers to this question will be discussed later. For now, the analysis will be limited to looking at the role of public opinion and policy on the conflict under the Clinton administration during the 1990s.

After the Cold War

The Clinton peace

President Bill Clinton's tenure in office signaled a new era of US policy toward the Israeli–Palestinian conflict.[79] During his first week in office, Americans were asked a question, the answer to which broke with the trend of US refusal to condemn Israeli actions: "do you favor United Nations sanctions against Israel to bring back 400 Palestinians deported to the no-man's-land in Lebanon, or should the United States block any such sanctions?" In answer, 41.21 percent of Americans favored UN sanctions against Israel for deporting civilians from their homes and 37.49 percent said that their country should block them.[80] A poll like this may have given reason for optimism regarding evenhandedness in the Middle East. After all, the Cold War enemy was defeated and the US no longer had to keep its interests fixated on fighting against the communist threat, which for so long the Israel lobby toiled to conflate with the Jewish state's enemies.[81] Nevertheless, the fact that more Americans supported sanctions may have signaled that the US could have been on a path to mediate conflict in a more equitable manner.

After the end of the Iraq War and the collapse of communism, that was precisely what the pro-Arab lobby sought. It was widely believed that public opinion was essential to evenhandedness.[82] Pro-Arab advocates tried to ensure a political atmosphere in which the US would no longer deny the Palestinian claim to sovereignty over the territories occupied by Israel. And although the peace process may have been condemned as just an American–Israeli smokescreen to avoid dealing with the reality on the ground, granting the Palestinians legitimacy in US foreign policy thought was a decent start when compared to their rejection in earlier decades, particularly under the presidency of Ronald Reagan and the anti-Soviet strategic relationship.[83] Satisfying Palestinian national aspirations no longer had to be contained to the sphere of public opinion; it now began taking root in American policy, a process that would become the precursor of the Bush roadmap.

During the early 1990s, public opinion reached a milestone regarding the two-state solution as a *majority* favored it on the eve of the 1993 White House handshake between Palestinian leader Yasser Arafat and Israeli Prime minister Yitzhak Rabin. Asked, "in general, do you favor or oppose the idea of an independent Palestinian state within the territories occupied by Israel since the 1967 war," 52.50 percent of Americans favored it and 25.45 percent opposed it.[84] This showed the pulse of public opinion reflected a tangible formula for peace by a majority. Accordingly, there was a relationship between what poll respondents thought should be the end of US policy and elite perception of the feasibility of attempting to fulfill Palestinian national objectives. Such congruence of thought between citizens and their leadership offered a clear impetus for US efforts to arbitrate peace between Israelis and Palestinians. Meanwhile, most Americans had some amount of confidence that the Jewish state would meet its obligations to peace.[85] In regards to the PLO, the level of confidence was drastically lower but still positive. Overall, the building blocks for a resolution of the Israeli–Palestinian conflict were in place. Public opinion supported the two-state solution and had some faith that all sides would cooperate; Israelis and Palestinians showed a willingness to negotiate, and President Clinton, the chief American policymaker, tried to be the trustworthy broker both sides sorely needed. Even before the signing of the DOP, there was a convergence of most factors influencing foreign policy, including American public opinion and willingness by the Israelis and Palestinians to make peace. AIPAC's acquiescence and the pro-Arab lobby's encouragement paralleled these developments. During the heady days of the early 1990s, there was much reason for optimism.[86]

That, however, was not cause enough for generosity. Even though Americans preferred peace through a Palestinian state, public sentiment was against paying for it.[87] When asked whether the US along with other countries should provide economic aid to the Palestinians, a resounding 65.41 percent opposed the idea and only 29.88 percent favored it.[88] In this regard, Americans had an interventionist appetite when it came to addressing world problems but took an isolationist stand when it came to bankrolling efforts to do so. This was no surprise and is analogous to American public opinion being voraciously in favor of education and other forms of welfare but opposed to the taxation that would pay for them.[89] At any rate, most supported the peace process. An overwhelming majority favored the "land for peace" formula outlined in UNSC resolutions 242 and 338 that were buried during the Reagan era only to be uncovered after the Intifada and the end of the Cold War. Hence, 79.85 percent of Americans favored the following statement in a poll taken during the early 1990s: "Israel and the P.L.O. have reached a new agreement in the Middle East. It would give the Palestinians control over some land in the occupied territories. In return, the P.L.O. has agreed to end terrorism and recognize Israel's right to exist."[90] The US-led mediation that allowed for such agreement also ranked high with Americans. Nearly 77 percent placed some level of importance on developing a peaceful solution to the Israeli–Palestinian conflict.[91] As in the present, there was in the past a general will to see peace in the Middle East, which in the post-Cold War period translated into policymakers perceiving and acting upon the necessity for a solution to conflict through diplomacy.

While they had some level of confidence in and priority for peace through the two-state solution, Americans showed caution about whether Oslo would lead to a durable arrangement. In a 1994 survey that asked "how likely is it that the recent agreement between Israel and the P.L.O. will lead to lasting peace – very likely, somewhat likely, not too likely, or not at all likely," only 3.30 percent said "very likely," 33.60 percent answered "somewhat likely," while almost 61 percent answered "not too likely [or] not at all likely."[92] Here, a sense of mistrust pervaded public opinion. The hopefulness that swept through the world after the end of the Cold War did not carry over to perceptions of the Middle East. Meanwhile, concern for Israel was still firm. A majority of Americans (63.74 percent) believed the US had a vital "political, economic, or security" interest in the Jewish state.[93] Accordingly, many wished to either increase or maintain political and economic aid to Israel as well as defending it in case of invasion by Arab states, a remote possibility given the fact that Israel had negotiated peace treaties with key members of the Arab League and was the only Middle East power armed with nuclear weapons.[94] It is quite curious that public opinion favored shedding treasure and blood for Israel considering that during 1995, more Americans were interested in the storied O. J. Simpson murder trial than in the Israelis and Palestinians accomplishing further peace agreements.[95] Congress reflected that mindset and policymakers were weary of foreign involvement as being too risky since it would result in little return from their constituents but may entail potentially high expenditures.[96]

Despite their relative lack of attention, many Americans maintained their sympathies with Israel and their pessimism about the two sides ever settling their differences, as demonstrated by polls in 1997. In the perennial question of where their sympathies lie "in the Middle East situation," 37.93 percent chose Israel while only 8.33 percent answered "Palestinian Arabs."[97] A combination of generalized disinterest and sympathy toward the Jewish state characterized public opinion. Policymakers may in such conditions reward Israel at the expense of the Palestinians with relatively little cost. Thus, even though the Cold War had ended and the geostrategic need for keeping Israel happy diminished with it, American policymakers for the most part still stood with the Jewish state to uphold the tendency of their electorate, if for no other reason. Pro-Israel lobbyists busied themselves with maintaining that state of affairs while trying to replace the vacuum left by communism with terrorism as the new enemy in the 1990s.

Under US brokering, the peace process reflected not just the power imbalance of the conflict, but also the inclination of public opinion. Peace was not something that most Americans thought was possible. When asked "do you think there will or will not come a time when Israel and the Arab nations will be able to settle their differences and live in peace," 56.54 percent said no, even as their commander-in-chief was working toward that end.[98] This was not surprising considering that hostilities between Arabs and Jews flared up throughout the 1990s, particularly toward the end of the decade. However, it begs the question of how policymakers should act in a system that forces them to pay attention to a constituency laden with skepticism. To a policymaker concerned with public opinion polling, this is the way things appeared: on the one hand, citizens were fond of Israel and believed that it should have American support with few lapses during unusual times; on the other hand, they did not know much about the predicaments of the Arabs in general or of the Palestinians in particular but when asked about either, they knew enough to feel that Arabs were not able to make peace and therefore ought not be trusted; but really, there was no peace to be had anyway because both sides will never settle their differences. Well, how do policymakers in a democracy act under such conditions? In the same way that they have acted throughout the Israeli–Palestinian conflict: supporting Israel and for the most part ignoring its adversary.[99]

Throughout the rest of the 1990s, Americans tracked global events in a very disconnected manner. Four years after the Israelis and Palestinians signed the DOP, over 70 percent of Americans stated that they followed the situation "not too closely" or "not at all."[100] Similarly, Congress lacked attention to developments abroad.[101] This was the case despite "the intensifying economic rivalry of Europe and Japan, and the emergence of intermestic issues like global warming."[102] Concerning the Middle East, US policy was increasingly left up to the president and his advisors, especially when it came to complex matters such as peace. AIPAC succeeded in adapting to the problems presented by the Intifada and the end of the Cold War insofar as it oversaw the constant flow of support to Israel as part of the peace dividend. This period saw expansion of settlements under prime ministers Benjamin Netanyahu and Ehud Barak.[103] Still, the supply of US dollars and political backing to Israel continued. That would present many obstacles to the pursuit of peace.[104]

At the same time, asked if the US should take sides in the Israeli–Palestinian conflict, 73.85 percent of the public was content with the answer that it should not.[105] When placed in context of opinion trends, this answer was peculiar. On the one hand, Americans believed that the US should defend Israel against Arab attack, an unlikely event anyway considering the sheer power imbalance between the two sides. On the other, they believed that their country should not take a side. In addition, more Americans sympathized with the Israelis than with the Arabs or Palestinians.[106] Nonetheless, in 1998 many Americans believed that the US had not placed enough pressure on Israel.[107] According to polling data, public opinion held that the Jewish state should be compelled to allow for the possibility of Palestinian statehood. In 1999, 51.63 percent favored the establishment of a Palestinian state compared to 28 percent that opposed it.[108] In the same poll, even more agreed with the two-state solution when Palestinian territory was defined as "the West Bank and the Gaza strip."[109] And although the public supported Israel throughout the late 1990s, more Americans believed that military aid to the Jewish state ought to be decreased, reflecting the public's discontent with the frustration of US designs for a solution to the conflict.[110] While President Clinton was often disappointed with the outbursts of violence that plagued the region, he had a mandate to pursue peace, as most Americans believed that US foreign policy should at some level concern itself with ending the Israeli–Palestinian conflict.[111]

By the beginning of the new millennium, the peace process had reached its pinnacle or nadir, depending on one's perspective. Public opinion still sympathized with Israel more than with the Palestinians, thought the US should take no sides – even as it actively aided Israel, believed in peace as a chief foreign policy goal, and still did not know much about the conflict.[112] During 2000, there was a significant decrease in support for the two-state solution. Whereas in years past, Americans favored it by majority levels, in July support for the two-state solution shrank to 33.56 percent in favor and 31.02 percent opposing it. This was the lowest level of support since 1977 when that type of polling began. Still, at least the July 2000 poll had a larger fraction favoring the two-state solution than not, while most wished the US to remain a neutral arbiter, reflecting Clinton's self-proclaimed "honest broker" position and his repeated attempts to bring Israelis and Palestinians together to hammer out the details of final negotiations.[113]

By September 28, 2000, with Sharon's march on the Dome of the Rock along with over 1,000 Israeli security officers, the peace process was in crisis. In response to that Jerusalem incident, the Palestinians engaged in some of the most considerable acts of resistance since the end of the first Intifada in 1993. Participants and observers of this uprising dubbed it the "second Intifada." According to a key pro-Arab lobbyist, "everything that went right with the first Intifada went wrong with the second one. We [pro-Arab pressure groups] had less room to maneuver in order to influence fellow citizens."[114] Thus, American public opinion turned from support to ambivalence about the peace process and showed anxiety about a workable settlement under US direction. According to a poll taken in October, less than two weeks after the outbreak of the second Intifada, over 80 percent of Americans registered to vote in the 2000 election were either "very concerned" or "somewhat concerned" about violence in the uprising resulting in war between the two sides.[115] The situation was indeed spiraling out of control. Scenes from the occupied territories of Israeli soldiers clashing with

Palestinians harkened back to the first Intifada. Palestinian police forces turned their guns in vain against the better equipped and well trained Israeli army. In the quarrel between civilians throwing rocks and small arms police going up against one of the most powerful militaries in the world, the results were cataclysmic. Even counting Israeli casualties from suicide bombings, the outcome was about ten dead Palestinians for every Israeli killed.[116] Most of the fatalities on both sides were civilian. As waves of violence continued to escalate, a majority of Americans believed that the region would never be peaceful.[117]

Clinton's failure, Bush's victory

By December of 2000, Americans were enmeshed in the outcome (or lack thereof) of the presidential election. Supreme Court case Bush v. Gore consumed national attention and kept the mounting Israeli–Palestinian conflict out of the spotlight. Lame duck President Clinton failed in his last ditch efforts to bring the peace process to conclusion as the two sides reached no agreement. It was said that Barak gave all he could only to be rebuffed by Arafat.[118] After the collapse of numerous summits, both sides were dead-locked in battle. The winner of the American election was decided to be George W. Bush, the man who would try to succeed where his predecessor failed. However, before we get to Bush's work toward peace, we must look at a powerful bloc of the public that had strong convictions about Israel's role in American foreign policy: the religious right. Because of this group's millenarian disposition toward the Jewish state, they did not believe in nor wanted US policy to seek a just resolution to the Arab–Israeli conflict.[119] Their vote propelled the new American president into office.[120] Forming alliances across his uneasy but determined political base, religious conservatives' views are important to the examination of policies on Israel during Bush's tenure in office. The president defined himself as a member of their ranks.[121] His perceptions of foreign affairs were very much shaped by that persuasion.

Israel has always occupied a special place in the hearts and minds of evangelical Christians.[122] Their beliefs may be broken down into three parts: (1) Israel is the fulfillment of ancient biblical prophecy; (2) Palestinian claims to the land are illegitimate; and (3) Jewish settlements are a natural extension of Eretz Israel, a land given to the Chosen People by God.[123] From these three tenets flows the following advocacy.

> All of the land west of the Jordan River is part of Eretz Israel, the historic land of Israel. However, many Israelis choose not to exercise their claims to the entire area if such restraint will advance the cause of a just and lasting peace. These Israelis would share the land with the Palestinian Arabs so long as Israel's legitimate security requirements are met and Israel retains its Jewish character.[124]

While most Americans may not agree with that particular statement,[125] its effects would become strongly pronounced in the ventures of President Bush and his advisors. During their time in office, Israel sought to control the West Bank, and its population of Palestinians while remaining Jewish itself. As had been seen by years of conflict, this was never going to happen and remains a painful paradox since Bush had agreed with Sharon that removing the settlements would be impractical.[126]

That agreement fit into a long string of ambiguities by the Bush administration. After all, the two-state solution, a part of American of public opinion – but not of explicit US policy until after 2002 – since the late 1970s, did not come to President Bush immediately. Instead, when he first got into office, one of his first statements was that he was going to take a "hands off" approach to the Israeli–Palestinian conflict, fully understanding its effects of violence as usual where more Palestinians died than Israelis.[127] With the withdrawal of the US resolve on making peace, Israel was more able to treat the Palestinians anyway it saw fit. Bush's supporters in the religious right could not be happier about that since it meant reversing the path on which the liberal President Clinton had placed the Jewish state. Accordingly, in his first few months in office, Bush, true to his base, was not interested in pressuring Israel to make concessions that it did not deem conducive to its interests.[128] In many ways, during those few months of the president's "honeymoon," Israel's interests virtually became America's interests. In essence, the US supported the Jewish state militarily and economically, while conveniently taking a political hands off approach when it mattered to the security of the region.

The global war on terrorism

9/11

September 11th ferociously altered the hands off approach. The United States was attacked by al Qa'eda, which claimed the Palestinian problem as one of its main grievances against the West.[129] Even though it was never publicly articulated, the White House through its actions understood that the war on terrorism involved defusing – or at least giving the perception of doing so – the Israeli–Palestinian conflict, regardless of the al Qa'eda leadership's motives for clinging to the issue.[130] On March 12, 2002, at the request of President Bush, the Security Council issued Resolution 1397. Through it, the international community as represented by the United Nations demanded the solution that President Clinton could never *explicitly* call for during his stewardship of the peace process, "affirming a vision of a region where two States, Israel and Palestine, live side by side within secure and recognized borders."[131] This pronouncement solidified what public opinion and pro-Arab pressure groups had hoped for since the beginning of the peace process, namely a call for the two-state solution to the Israeli–Palestinian conflict based upon UNSC resolutions 242 and 338.[132] Months later, the Bush administration would unveil its roadmap outlining steps for implementing Palestinian statehood.[133]

Aside from the profound impacts that it had on US Middle East policy, the events of 9/11 affected public opinion as well. While the sites of the World Trade Center, the Pentagon, and the plane crash in Pennsylvania smoldered, Americans were asked about military and economic aid to Israel. A minority said that military aid should be increased but an overwhelming majority responded that economic aid to the Jewish state should either be *decreased or cut off*.[134] Meanwhile, Americans did not change their historical opinions about Israel. On sympathies, whether the US should choose a side, and general support for the Jewish state, they responded within historically ordinary levels.[135] There was, however, renewed hopelessness perhaps reflecting the prevailing mood of catastrophe in the country after 9/11. Asked whether Arabs and Israelis will be "able to settle their differences and live in peace," 58.58 percent of Americans said no.[136] Still, most believed that peace ought to be the chief foreign policy goal.[137]

Needless to say, the events of September 11 dramatically increased attention to the region. In April of 2002, most followed "the situation in the Middle East" either "very closely," 34.06 percent, or "somewhat closely," 45.32 percent.[138] This was an expected outcome since the terrorist attacks were linked to political strife in the Arab/Muslim states, which produced all of the 9/11 hijackers. Regardless of why Americans were taking notice, policymakers understood that they had to act in the public spotlight. It seemed that the more attention Americans paid to the Middle East, the more cynical they became about prospects for peace. A total of 60.96 percent believed that Arabs and Israelis would not be able to compromise on a solution to the conflict.[139] Be that as it may, most Americans did have a sense of what needed to be done in order to improve the situation between Israelis and Palestinians. A near unanimous majority (91.75 percent) agreed with President Bush's demand that the Palestinian Authority "stop encouraging suicide bombing against the Israelis." Equally as important, when asked if they approved or disapproved of President Bush's request "that Israel withdraw from the Palestinian territories it has occupied in the West Bank," Americans approved by 71.10 percent.[140] While supportive of moves by both sides to increase the ikelihood of peace, most saw violence by the Palestinians as "terrorism" but viewed the same by Israel as "legitimate acts of war against their opponents," and accordingly understood the latter as "justified" and the former as "unjustified." This may be attributed to fact that the US pursued its enemies after 9/11 in a manner similar to that of Israel's war on the Palestinians. Pro-Israel advocates worked tirelessly to make that link. Nonetheless, a majority of Americans believed that fighting should halt on both sides.[141]

Regime change

Although violence did not stop, three months after UNSC resolution 1397 called for the two-state solution, Americans favored a Palestinian state by a substantial majority (74.38 percent).[142] However, after this poll, US policy efforts toward the Middle East were dedicated to removing Saddam Hussein from power. Bush administration officials believed that after the fall of the Taliban and the establishment of a pro-US government in Afghanistan, such action was the next step in the global war on terrorism.[143] Yet public opinion polling showed that Americans did not agree with that move. Well before the second Iraq War, more of them thought that the higher priority for US policy should be "working to establish peace in the Middle East between the Palestinians and Israelis" (52.10 percent) than "working to overthrow Saddam Hussein in Iraq" (42.45 percent).[144] And while some would later contend that the US went to war against Iraq in order to further Israel's interests, the public has generally been opposed to that.[145] In particular, Americans thought that regime change was a "bad reason" for involvement in Iraq even as a majority of them understood that it would help the Jewish state.[146] Although the public tended to esteem Israel, it did not for the most part wish the US to do its bidding. Astonishingly, even as the US was busy pursuing terrorists in Afghanistan, public opinion favored war against Iraq if it would have helped Israelis and Palestinians achieve peace. When asked whether "paving the way for a peace agreement between the Israelis and Palestinians" was "a goal worth going to war over," a majority of Americans (56.68 percent) said that it was and a minority (39.47 percent) said that it was not.[147]

In this instance, polls taken around the outbreak of the US invasion of Iraq presented a significant discrepancy between public opinion and foreign policy. To summarize, Americans took interest in war against Iraq if such action prevented terrorist attacks and helped the Israelis and Palestinians accomplish peace. However, the Bush administration constructed a terrorist threat in Iraq where none had existed (that country had no responsibility whatsoever for the 9/11 attacks)[148] and ostensibly called for the two-state solution to placate its constituents, not to mention the international community including the Arab states, so that it could pursue its invasion. Such action showed an acute example of the general will not being followed in the policy conduct of the US, even though the Bush administration was politically savvy enough to give the impression that it was bowing to public opinion pressure. At a time when the Israeli army had Chairman Arafat and his cabinet imprisoned in their offices, was increasingly squeezing the iron grip of its occupation, and was destroying all remaining vestiges of the Palestinian Authority, the US government turned a blind eye and sought war in Iraq contrary to public sentiment. If such action indeed only furthered the Israeli position in the Middle East, then American policy did not at all follow the expression of public opinion in favor of peace through the two-state solution. Rather, policymakers beginning with President Bush did the exact opposite. Hence, Iraq was invaded, its regime removed, and the Israelis and Palestinians were further apart on peace than ever before.[149] From this point onward, the US would become entwined in Iraq, as American power would be committed to nation building instead of peacemaking.

However, there is a strong counterargument to the account presented above. Perhaps Bush and his advisors as well as their Israeli counterparts could not imagine a Palestinian state with the perceived threat to the Jewish state posed by Iraq under Saddam Hussein.[150] In this case, the plan for regime change might have had the tripartite effect of (1) safeguarding the US against the construed threat of Iraqi weapons of mass destruction;[151] (2) advancing Israel's security to a threshold that would have allowed for the harmless existence of a bordering Palestinian state; and (3) ensuring the emergence of democracy in the Middle East starting with the government in Baghdad, a move thought to strengthen liberal tendencies throughout the region, particularly in a newly created Palestine. If this line of reasoning is carried to its conclusion – and there is no reason to believe that these were not genuine rationales at the time of the US invasion[152] – we may see that President Bush wanted to bring about a Palestinian state that was both democratic and did not imperil American or Israeli interests. In this context, the White House may only be faulted for pursuing the wishes of the American people through different means. Simply put, if we took the contentions for invading Iraq at face value, we may see that it was a required step in order to bring about a Palestinian state, thus honoring what the public wanted. However, US shortcomings in Iraq have rendered moot the administration's arguments concerning regime change, regardless of whether they had any legitimacy at the outset of war in 2003.

In the wake of action against Iraq, a slight majority of Americans were more optimistic about prospects for peace between Israelis and Palestinians. When asked the recurrent question of whether they thought "Israel and the Arab nations will be able to settle their differences and live in peace," 50.98 percent of Americans said yes.[153] This response coincided with the "mission accomplished" sentiment that swept the political landscape in the aftermath of the collapse of the Ba'athist regime and the capitulation of Saddam Hussein's army.[154] Even though Bush strayed from public opinion through his Iraq campaign, a large majority (well over 84 percent) of Americans still placed some foreign policy premium on the "development of a peaceful solution to the Israeli–Palestinian situation."[155] In response, after the fall of Baghdad, President Bush briefly turned his attention to the Israeli–Palestinian conflict, but accomplished very little as other issues preoccupied his mind and American policy throughout the world. These included a mounting insurgency – and later an embryonic civil war – in Iraq, the unrelenting resurrection of the Taliban in Afghanistan, and an increase in terrorist "chatter" about attacks on the US and its allies, among others. Throughout, American policy would have some interesting interactions with public opinion on the Israeli–Palestinian conflict, as was demonstrated by two noteworthy polls taken during the middle of 2003.

Those polls showed public opinion moving in two distinct directions: (1) attributing some level of religious significance to the Arab–Israeli conflict, and (2) having less concern about President Bush dedicating his energies toward Middle East peace.[156] Turning to the first direction, Americans were asked the question below.

> Which of the following comes closest to your view about the land in Israel and other countries in the region of the world known as the Middle East – It is a holy land that has personal religious significance for you because you believe events that the Bible predicted will eventually occur there, It is a holy land that has personal religious significance for you for other reasons, or It is a land that is historically significant but does not have any personal religious significance for you? [Answer] It is a holy land that has personal religious significance for you because you believe events that the Bible predicted will eventually occur there (29.80%), It is a holy land that has personal religious significance for you for other reasons (19.82%), It is a land that is historically significant but does not have any personal religious significance for you (46.88%), DON'T KNOW (3.00%), REFUSED (0.50%).[157]

This poll showed that when it came to the Middle East, almost half of the population might have reflected Bush's religious convictions. His increasing tilt toward a faith-based approach to policy corresponded with Americans placing value on the religious significance of the conflict.[158] Still, it did not have any such value for many people. Bush, however, has always been keenly aware of the importance of the Christian bloc to his political success in domestic as well as in foreign affairs. When viewed in that light, the above poll has a good deal of consequence and may indicate that public opinion set the field in which policymakers from the president on downward had to operate.

As for the second direction, something that might be related to the increasingly religious view of the conflict, Americans became less concerned about US foreign policy pursuing peace. When asked whether President Bush should make "achieving a peace agreement between Israel and the Palestinians" his top priority, only 17.48 percent said that he should do so.[159] Compared to previous polling in which the public demanded that US policy seek Middle East peace, this poll showed that Americans became preoccupied by other events that were the byproduct of the Bush administration's war making on two simultaneous fronts, in Iraq and Afghanistan. Both polls outlined above demonstrated that public opinion corresponded to foreign policy conduct in ways worthy of further investigation.[160]

Months after the Iraq War, the "mission accomplished" sentiment evaporated and the public grew increasingly pessimistic. A substantial majority no longer believed that Israel and the Arab nations would ever make peace. One poll showed that 59.70 percent of Americans thought it was not possible.[161] Many placed some fault on Israel for the stalemate. In an October 2003 poll, over 68 percent blamed Israel "a great deal [or] a moderate amount."[162] Meanwhile, in the midst of American soldiers dying in the escalating insurgency, not to mention thousands of Iraqi casualties,[163] new fears about national security emerged. Over 91 percent of Americans considered "the conflict between Israel and the Palestinians [as a] critical" or "an important" threat.[164] And although they were not too convinced that the conflict would be resolved, many had some level of confidence in their policymakers. For example, prior to his reelection in November 2004, 45.17 percent of Americans approved President Bush's handling of the Israeli–Palestinian conflict compared to 40.94 percent that disapproved.[165] Furthermore, a higher percentage embraced his management of the situation when compared to his rival, presidential candidate John Kerry.[166] This might have been related to the fact that Bush was perceived as more friendly to Israel than his principal competitor, something that the public appreciated.[167] As always, Americans had more sympathy and favorable views toward the Jewish state than they had for all Arab nations.[168]

Conclusion

American public opinion showed a preference for the two-state solution both before and after 9/11. Arab and Jewish Americans favored it at higher percentages than the rest of their compatriots because they have traditionally felt more impacted by the outcomes of war and peace in the region.[169] Most expressed support for the Bush roadmap, which worked in conjunction with UNSC resolutions calling for the establishment of a Palestinian state on the West Bank of the Jordan River and Gaza. US policymaker perceptions reflected public opinion in this important respect. And with *unanimous* international endorsement, not to mention the wishes of the Israelis and Palestinians themselves, the roadmap has enjoyed more support than most foreign policy issues out there. All involved actors believe that the two-state solution would bring peace to the hundred years' war that has plagued US interests in the Middle East and throughout the world.[170]

The data above showed that the two-state framework is the only solution prevalent in the American political discourse. More importantly, from its humble beginnings in the late 1970s to majority support after Oslo through September 11, public sentiment toward the two-state solution appeared to have had some impact on policymakers approaching the Israeli–Palestinian conflict with the roadmap. The preceding analysis showed that public opinion did indeed set the parameters for elite perceptions and policy options toward that stubborn problem. This is why: (1) no statesperson may talk about the need for peace without invoking the two-state solution, (2) US policymakers have adopted what seemed to be the path of least resistance amongst the American people and throughout the entire world, and (3) it is unlikely any other solution will emerge as a serious choice in elite policy circles anytime soon. Nevertheless, in American policy toward the conflict, decision-makers have not *meaningfully* chosen to bring about a Palestinian state, even as the public continually expressed support for it as the only solution that would have brought peace. This was demonstrated by the fact that the US roadmap has not reached fruition by 2005, the year in which the two-state solution was supposed to come into existence. Meanwhile, public opinion and policymakers continued to have sympathy and support for Israel. That may have had a significant role in preventing the US from effectively pressuring the Jewish state toward the establishment of a Palestinian one. Currently, it appears as if the peace process only takes place on an Israeli timetable, with the Palestinians having little control over its progress or outcome.[171]

The preponderance of evidence examined in this chapter has shown that in most cases, public opinion has overlapped with foreign policy actions before, during, and after the peace processes undertaken in the post-Cold War era. The following conclusions may be made from examining those periods. First, before the deployment of US troops, the public understood Iraq's 1990 invasion of Kuwait in relation to Israel's occupation of Palestinian land. However, in the heated period of Desert Shield when war was in the air, Americans refused to consider the Israeli–Palestinian conflict as a condition for negotiations with Saddam Hussein. Instead, popular opinion went hand-in-hand with policymakers' rejection of such a proposition, demanding the unconditional withdrawal of Iraqi troops from Kuwait. In that instance, the first President Bush had political protection for his approach to Iraq. Over a decade before the Gulf crisis, President Carter took advantage of public opinion in support of peace between the Arabs and Israel by successfully brokering the Camp David peace process. In essence, Carter showed the world that the land for peace formula worked as demonstrated by the agreements signed by Anwar al-Sadat and Menachem Begin, which stopped hostilities between Egypt and Israel. The Camp David Accords also flew in the face of the popular but anti-Semitic perception that the Arabs were implacably bloodthirsty and that the survivors of the Holocaust could never make peace with anyone that was not Jewish. As a result, support for the two-state solution emerged in the American imagination as a way to end the impasse between Israel and the Palestinians with a model based on the Camp David Accords, consistent with the wishes of the international community as expressed by the United Nations. During the 1980s, that imagination waned under the rejectionist Reagan policies and a reinvigorated neoconservative establishment of Cold War warriors.[172] It was also then that the pro-Israel lobby appealed to the strategic alliance, which was credited to the success of its political past of influencing the American public and the perceptions of its leaders.

Second, the end of the Gulf crisis and the Cold War involved a return to the peace optimism of the 1970s, corresponding with Bush's and later Clinton's desires to implement UN resolutions demanding land for peace.[173] Such action forced the issue of the two-state solution back into the court of public opinion. As was seen during the Reagan era, however, the public would not have weighed in on any solution that was not in the realm of possible action as policymakers shunned Palestinian national aspirations. After Oslo, Clinton's inability to bring peace during his time in office resulted in the second Intifada and the consequences in the United States looked at above. Later, the George W. Bush presidency's hands off approach in the midst of violent upheaval in the occupied territories not only made matters worse, it also signified a disconnect between public opinion, which favored the two-state solution, and policymaking that was, for all intents and purposes, nonexistent prior to the terrorist attacks on the American mainland. The attacks of 9/11 forever changed the course of US foreign policy.[174] The effects of that change were mixed. As has been seen, consistent with popular sentiment, US policymakers called for the two-state solution while invoking UN resolutions that have yet to be enforced. Israeli vacillation between unilateral withdrawal to the other side of the security wall on the one hand, and reinvading the occupied territories to attack the Palestinians on the other, when combined with seemingly immovable Jewish settlements, only created new and long lasting problems for the two-state solution.[175] Under such conditions, public preference for the two-state solution will not be realized, absent a *determined* effort by American policymakers, who as the next chapter will demonstrate, have to answer to the pro-Israel lobby.

3   The effects of the pro-Israel lobby

Introduction

Unified on the issue of securing political, economic, and military aid to the Jewish state, well financed and armed with talented advocates who have deep convictions about their cause, the Israel lobby is the envy of most other pressure groups.[1] With first-hand experience of that powerful lobby, former Republican Congressman Paul Findley stated, "our political system is seriously handicapped by the absence of unfettered discussion of what is best for the United States Middle East policy. The Israeli side is the only one that is seriously considered."[2] With such pre-eminence in the policymaking game, the Israel lobby has had a hand or at least a say in nearly every American decision on the Middle East for over half a century. It has constantly sought to improve its mission of: (1) pressuring policymakers to make decisions that favor Israel; (2) emphasizing its centrality for American interests particularly vis-à-vis Arab parties but also against communism during the Cold War and terrorism after its end; and (3) working with activists and thinkers that have dealings in government, academics, the media, and private businesses involved in Middle East affairs.[3]

During the Cold War years of the late 1970s throughout the 1980s, the pro-Israel lobby managed to convince policymakers and the public of the Jewish state's special relationship with the United States, particularly as it developed into a strategic alliance against the Soviet Union. Its strength intensified during that time, since it had an American administration under Ronald Reagan and his advisors on the Middle East who shared its values and mission.[4] Even well before Reagan's election, at the behest of the Israel lobby, the Jewish state enjoyed explicit support from large blocs of government officials. In 1975, to note but one example among a seemingly infinite number of others, seventy senators sent President Gerald Ford a letter "expressing their views in support of Israel" and outlining the extent of the Israeli–US relationship thus:

> a substantial majority of the Senate wrote you urging a reiteration of our nation's longstanding commitment to Israel's security "by a policy of

continued military supplies and diplomatic and economic support." Since 1967, it has been American policy that the Arab-Israel conflict should be settled on the basis of secure and recognized boundaries that are defensible, and direct negotiations between the nations involved. We believe that this approach continues to offer the best hope for a just and lasting peace.[5]

Considering its aim for peace, strikingly missing from the letter was the fact that Israel had occupied and settled Arab lands since 1967 against the expressed wishes of the international community as outlined in United Nations Security Council (UNSC) resolutions 242 and 338.[6] In particular, the Senate's letter to President Ford failed to mention the Palestinians, the people most affected by occupation. Since they did not possess a state, the letter further diminished their existence as it only referred to "nations [read as states] involved."

By the 1980s, the US became more entrenched in its special relationship with Israel as its supporters in Washington gained a deeper appreciation by *both* Congress and the White House.[7] Although the administrative branch is less susceptible to lobbying than the legislature, presidents have often understood the necessity of the pro-Israel lobby in the passing of their agendas in Congress. Advocates on behalf of the Jewish state have consistently gained access to powerful policymakers with provisions of "education" through policy talking points. They have helped elect presidential candidates that would offer Israel more support relative to others. In general, Israel's pressure groups knew how to play the political game as they tried to advance its friendship with one of the world's greatest superpowers.

Although many failed to see it then, the Cold War was on its last legs during the 1980s. In those years, supporters of the Jewish state maintained that it was the supreme weapon in the Middle East against communism. Having been convinced of that position, Congress in conjunction with President Reagan's administration declared the *strategic* value of Israel to US interests.[8] In the words of Thomas A. Dine, executive director of the American Israel Public Affairs Committee (AIPAC), the 1980s were not just a time of "transformation in the relationship" between the US and Israel, it was also a time of "revolution" in their alliance.[9] This was solidified by most of the domestic factors acting on foreign policy. As has been examined elsewhere, public opinion was in favor of Israel, the US had forged the strategic alliance with it in 1981, and accordingly policymakers from the White House to Capitol Hill applauded the value of that relationship.[10] In front of a room packed with AIPAC activists, supporters, and well-wishers during 1986, Dine triumphantly summarized the Israel lobby's involvement with policymaking in the following way.

Congress functions both as a forum through which public opinion is brought to bear upon the whole federal government and as a medium for gathering and disseminating information for the enlightenment of the people. Capitol Hill is the repository of our democratic principles. It is in Congress that laws are made and national policy codified. No one appreciates these facts more than those of us in this room tonight – AIPAC's members and staff. The barometer by which one measures Israel's standing among the people of America is what takes place on Capitol Hill. Here U.S. support for Israel is built, maintained, and advanced. Congress is the bedrock of the U.S.-Israel relationship.[11]

This understanding has always animated the approach that AIPAC took in bringing American power to bear on the Israeli–Palestinian conflict.[12] Under President Reagan's leadership, the executive branch picked up where the legislature left off, making the American–Israeli relationship one of the most prolific alliances between two states in modern history.

In order to trace out that relationship and the bearing of the pro-Israel lobby on American policymaking as it pertained to the Israeli–Palestinian conflict from the decline of the Cold War to its end and beyond, this chapter will engage in the following objectives. First, it will try to identify the pro-Israel lobby's nebulous position on the two-state solution.[13] The lobby's attitudes on land for peace and Israeli withdrawal from occupied territories will be analyzed as indicators of that. Although military withdrawal by itself would not create *sufficient* conditions for a viable Palestinian state, that action is *necessary* for its existence. Second, this chapter will assess whether AIPAC pursued joint American–Israeli interests in the conflict or if it merely reflected the wishes of status quo elements in the Jewish state.[14] The importance of this issue is accentuated by the fact that AIPAC's defenders view it as an organization that primarily looks out for American interests. Moreover, AIPAC is registered as a domestic lobbying group and not as an organization acting on behalf of a foreign government.[15] Third, this chapter will look at the nexus between Israel lobbying personnel and policymakers. Specifically, it will highlight the sometimes-blurred line between pro-Israel advocates and US government officials. Fourth, this chapter will examine the influence of Israel lobbying groups on both public opinion and elite perceptions. Through this, it will map out variances in the pro-Israel lobby's techniques during key international developments to push US policy in directions favored by its constituents. Fifth, this chapter will explore the adjustments that the pro-Israel lobby had to make in order react to domestic changes, particularly the preference for the two-state solution and the concurrent growth in strength and potential of the pro-Arab lobby. To accomplish the previous two aims, AIPAC's public statements will be considered.

Sixth, the chapter will conclude by analyzing whether the strength of the pro-Israel lobby lies in the fact that most American policymakers and public opinion concur with it on support for the Jewish state or if it creates that agreement. This discussion will also involve assessing implications of the ostensibly shared culture between Israel and the US.[16] The analysis that follows will be limited to the general timeframe of this study: the late 1970s and 1980s through 1990–91 at the height of the American–Israeli relationship during the Cold-War; the changing international environment surrounding the end of the bipolar system and during the "New World Order" after the first Gulf War and Madrid (1991); the Oslo peace process and the advancement of Palestinian autonomy during the Clinton era; and the events of the "war on terrorism," particularly after the passage of UNSC resolutions 1397 and 1515, and the inauguration of the George W. Bush roadmap (2002–3).

Lobbying for Israeli–US alliance in the Reagan-Bush eras

From special to revolutionary

History has taught that whereas Congress has often provided *continuity* in policy on the Israeli–Palestinian conflict, the White House was responsible for *changes*.[17] Hence, every new president takes a few months to assess how to best practice American power. Many choose to continue the legacy of their predecessors while others try to take foreign policy in new directions. When it came to Reagan and his successor, particularly during the first two years of Bush's administration, both acted toward Israel in ways more similar than they were different. After the first Iraq War and the end of the Cold War, however, President Bush, as will be seen later, took American policy in a different path. Meanwhile, the representatives and senators that came to power during the tenures of both presidents pretty much continued the policies of previous Congresses. That led Steven Siegel to conclude, "in trying to understand why the United States acts in a particular way at any point, the approach of key policy formulators in Washington must be investigated."[18] To do that during the Reagan-Bush eras, we must look at the strategic alliance between the US and Israel and its interactions with the pro-Israel lobby during the 1980s and early 1990s.

What was the nature of that alliance? To address this, we turn to the "Memorandum of Understanding between the Government of the United States and the Government of Israel on Strategic Cooperation," which was declared on November 30, 1981, over ten months after President Reagan was sworn into office. Its preamble clearly set the tone of the relationship between the two sides.

> This memorandum of understanding reaffirms the common bonds of friendship between the United States and Israel and builds on the mutual security relationship that exists between the two nations. The parties recognize the need to enhance strategic cooperation to deter all threats from the Soviet Union to the region. Noting the longstanding and fruitful cooperation for mutual security that has developed between the two countries, the parties have decided to establish a framework for

continued consultation and cooperation to enhance their national security by deterring such threats to the whole region.[19]

By itself, this message of intent made the job of pro-Israel lobbyists in the US much easier. Israel and the United States would join their interests in the Middle East to ensure that the region was free from Soviet aggression. Under this type of relationship, AIPAC, the leading pro-Israel lobbying organization, would use its status as a domestic pressure group to assist in the development of policy toward a state favorably embedded in American sentiment, and after the memorandum, a country that became strategically integral to US interests in the Middle East.[20] Indeed, during the 1980s, the confluence of public opinion and policymaker perceptions overwhelmingly allowed for support of most actions taken by Israel in the name of the strategic relationship. This was shown almost immediately when Israel invaded Lebanon in 1982.[21]

The Jewish state's free hand in Lebanon allowed the Israel Defense Forces (IDF) to pursue the elimination of its archrival, the Palestine Liberation Organization (PLO), at the time headed by Yasser Arafat.[22] With no intervention from any country that could match Israel's strength, Lebanon was laid in ruins.[23] Palestinian civilians were massacred under the invasion, with the most despicable acts of brutality taking place in Sabra and Shatila at the hands of Lebanese Phalange militias.[24] The carnage outraged the world.[25] The invasion of Lebanon and its consequences demonstrated a disconnection between calamitous events in the Middle East during the 1980s and American inability or unwillingness to react to them. Why? Many attributed this to the strength of the pro-Israel lobby, particularly its pressure on policymakers, the media, and public opinion.[26]

Several other characteristics of that lobby made it an especially formidable group. According to Richard H. Curtiss, they included the following.

Pro-Israel PACs [Political Action Committees] ... have deliberately sought non-descriptive titles to mask their purpose from the American public. ... Neither [AIPAC] nor any of the PACs that follow its guidance have ever registered as foreign agents ... yet their principal concern is to lobby Congress to maintain or increase ... military and economic assistance to any elected government of a foreign state, Israel. During the two-year 1988 election cycle, Israel received well over $6 billion in direct U.S. taxpayer grants, a return ... of more than $1,105 in taxpayer grants for every $1 spent on lobbying Congress for such aid. Another special feature of AIPAC and the pro-Israel PACs is that, prior to the administration of President Bill Clinton, virtually all of their activities have been in opposition to administration and ... private sector initiatives. ... AIPAC and its affiliated PACs are virtually the only PACs in Washington whose campaigns are designed to transfer American jobs to overseas competitors, and whose successes expose to danger overseas

American military and diplomatic personnel ... businessmen and tourists. *This danger results not from U.S. measures in defense of U.S. interests against unfriendly states, but from U.S. measures in defense of Israeli refusal to negotiate land for peace with its Arab neighbors.*[27]

This lengthy excerption of the pro-Israel lobby's functions demonstrated the magnitude of its influence on policymaking both during and after the Cold War. Equally as important, it expressed the ambivalence that AIPAC and its affiliates have had about the land for peace arrangement, even after Israel accepted peace settlements with Egypt in 1978 and could have engaged in similar negotiations with the Palestinians. It is to this issue that we now turn.

Rejecting "land for peace"

Throughout the 1980s, pro-Israel groups ensured that the Jewish state would negotiate on its own timetable by eliminating pressure to do so while maximizing American aid. This delayed the land for peace formula. While the blame for that may fall on AIPAC and its supporters, there has always been disagreement on the extent to which lobbies influence foreign policy outcomes.[28] In 1977, William Quandt wrote:

interest groups typically suffer from a number of disadvantages in trying to influence foreign policy. First there may be internal divisions that weaken their effectiveness. Second, they are unlikely to have the resources, in money and information that would allow them to present their case effectively. Third, lobbyists have a strong tendency to seek out those who already agree with them rather than trying to make converts. Fourth, lobbyists are vulnerable to counterpressures, especially from the powerful federal bureaucracy.[29]

Although these are fine points about the limitations of interest group influence, Quandt agreed, "not all of these drawbacks affect pro-Israeli groups." In fact, since his work in the late 1970s, the pro-Israel lobby has only gained in strength, unity, and numbers, and has succeeded in its attempts to foil the land for peace scheme, the *cornerstone* of the two-state solution.[30] By the 1980s strategic relationship, AIPAC continued to insist that a "Palestinian state in Judea, Samaria and Gaza" is "unacceptable" for Israel's interests and by extension, those of the US.[31] Pro-Israel groups sought to influence policy away from that solution or any other by educating the public and pressuring elected officials in Congress and the White House on the dangers posed by land for peace. In this regard, supporters of the Jewish state have always possessed a refined ability to coordinate the rejection of any concession. As always, the Israel lobby not only brought public salience to the issues on the table of policymaking toward the Middle East, it was also capable of influencing how individual members of Congress vote. It did that through what Quandt referred to as the "anticipated reaction" principle, whereby policymakers seldom vote on the merits of particular legislation, but rather on how powerful interests would react to their vote.[32] As a result, rarely did Congress consider American interests through the land for peace framework.

Charged with coordinating pro-Israel groups on Capitol Hill and elsewhere, AIPAC created for its cause a nationwide support network. "This network may be broadly divided into four categories which are only formally independent of AIPAC," wrote Mohammed K. Shadid. They include:

> (1) Congressmen, Jewish or non-Jewish who have a personal commitment to the Jewish cause; (2) Congressional staff members; (3) other Israel lobbyists, organizations, the Israeli embassy, and influential or strategically placed Jewish individuals in the Administration; and (4) Jewish constituents in the Congressmen's home states.[33]

This strategy functioned effectively during the 1980s by forcing policymaking to take into account grassroots support, which was channeled by pro-Israel organizations in cities throughout the country.[34] Shadid's work detailed typical examples of actions taken by Israel's network, which included the following.

1 Conferring on a regular basis with members of the Israeli government on issues of concern to them in the US.
2 Getting pro-Israeli ideas across to influential newspaper columnists.
3 Advising candidates for office on Middle East issues.
4 Interviewing with "people in Congress ... sometimes by people in Israel, more often by leaders of the American Jewish community."[35]

Such an approach allowed for deeper influence by connecting Israeli interests to politically central factors that act on American foreign engagement. Consequently, the *national* network described by Shadid during the 1980s would become an ever more effective outfit for AIPAC's activities on Capitol Hill to express the Israeli government position in the 1990s negotiations with the Palestinians, particularly on issues of land for peace, security, and autonomy. In the peace process, the characteristics of proposals favorable to Israel at the elite level appeared to permeate from the grassroots of American society.

Adding further strength to the Israel network, American Jews come out to vote in larger numbers than other groups, and while they have traditionally tended to the left, groups like AIPAC have appealed to the Democratic and Republican parties, both of which consistently dispatch representatives to pro-Israel organizations' annual meetings.[36] Engaging both sides of the partisan isle, AIPAC has unfailingly been quick to remind policymakers and US citizens that despite their ideological differences, they must unite in their support for Israel, which is the best ally of American values and strategy. Those that strayed from that type of thinking were swiftly punished, something that also occurred across party lines. Congressman Findley maintained "House and Senate members do its bidding, because most of them consider AIPAC to be the direct Capitol Hill representative of a political force that can make or break their chances at election time."[37] *Perception* is what mattered when officials assessed policies on Israel or attempted to formulate new ones. Accordingly, throughout the early to mid-1980s, the Palestinian question was kept out of any reasonable debate in Washington. In those years, as Golda Meir once remarked, it appeared as if there was "no Palestinian people."[38] Their presence in American foreign policy was muted, if not to serve the Israeli interest, then to preserve the position of politicians terrified to speak out against the pro-Israel line taken by a near unanimous majority in government. During the heydays of the 1980s, fear was the hallmark of techniques employed by AIPAC, which was understood to "function as an informal extension of the Israeli government."[39]

Findley mischievously noted how pressure from pro-Israel groups created some amusing situations. Quoting Don Bergus, former US ambassador to Sudan, he wrote "at the State Department we used to predict that if Israel's prime minister should announce that the world is flat, within 24 hours Congress would pass a resolution congratulating him on the discovery."[40] To be sure, Israeli prime ministers never made such proclamations. The types of perilous statements they did put forward in the 1980s were far more implicit and frequently backed by American policymakers. Israel shunned international law outright, as demonstrated by its disregard for any peace proposals coming out of the international community or the US leadership.[41] Hence, shortly after taking office, President Reagan outlined an agreement built on the land for peace provisos but was flatly denied by Israel and its lobby.[42] Even though they snubbed his proposal, Reagan would seek AIPAC's help in keeping American Marines in Lebanon during 1983.[43] The 1980s were replete with such examples of Israeli rejection of Palestinian rights, US acquiescence, and policymaker cooperation with pro-Israel groups.

While toeing the Israeli government's line and monopolizing Washington's Middle East policy with its own agenda, AIPAC has worked to silence dissenting voices, particularly from sides favoring evenhandedness. Findley demonstrated this with a vivid example.

AIPAC is as successful at keeping lawmakers from visiting Arab countries as it is in presenting only Israel's views. When the National Association of Arab Americans, working through the World Affairs Council of Amman, invited all congressmen and their spouses to an expense-paid tour of Jordan with a side trip to the West Bank in 1983, a notice in AIPAC's Near East Report quickly chilled prospects for participation. It questioned how Amman, without Israeli cooperation could get the tourists across the Jordan River for events scheduled in the West Bank. It also quoted Don Sundquist, a Republican Congressman from Tennessee, as expressing "fear" that if any of his colleagues accepted the trip they would be "used" by anti-Israeli propagandists. Only three Congressmen made the trip. A 1984 tour was cancelled for lack of acceptances.[44]

This illustration is emblematic of efforts to dissuade policymakers from taking any stance that may detract from backing for Israel. Withholding support to the Arabs while lavishing it on the Jewish state became the order of the day.[45] Accordingly, advocating land for peace at a time when Israel rejected it so vigorously would have been akin to political suicide. This is something that Findley realized, hence the reason for his work. Throughout his text, he chronicled numerous instances when "American interests demanded peace and stability in the region," which would have been realized by Israeli withdrawal "from occupied Arab territories in return for Arab acceptance of Israeli sovereignty and territorial integrity."[46] That of course did not happen, due in large part to the power exercised by the pro-Israel lobby in Congress and on the administration.

In sum, the peace so essential to American interests in the Middle East never took place as AIPAC and other groups frustrated its pursuit. Findley lamented such circumstances.

> Those who criticize Israeli policy in any sustained way invite painful and relentless retaliation, and even loss of their livelihood, by pressure by one or more parts of Israel's lobby. Presidents fear it. Congress does its bidding. Prestigious universities shun academic programs and grants which it opposes. Giants of the media and military leaders buckle under its pressure. Instead of having their arguments and opinions judged on merit, critics of Israel suddenly find their motivations, their integrity, and basic moral values called into question. No matter how moderate their criticism, they may be characterized as pawns of the oil lobby, apologists for Arab terrorists, or even anti-Semitic.[47]

Facing these hazards, supporters of land for peace, when Israel's lobbying arms have done everything in their power to stifle it, quietly retreated from their standpoints. Consequently, American interests took a backseat to Israeli pressures from within the decision-making arena and throughout the US body politic. Seth P. Tillman summarized this relationship well when he wrote that support for the Jewish state gave it "the means to withstand all verbal pressures and reproaches and to continue to impose solutions contrary to the desires and interests of the United States."[48] This made Israeli politicians and advocates on their behalf in the US feel invincible. The latter participated in the pluralist policymaking competition very well, and the rewards to the former were incessant supplies of American sustenance.

However, this was never prudent, something that Rubenberg wrestled with during the mid-1980s.

> After thirty-five years of this protracted and destructive conflict, rationality demands that Americans deal with the realities of the Middle East and attempt to comprehend the weltanschauung and sensibilities of the Arabs who did not eagerly welcome the usurpation of their land, the dispossession and displacement of their people, and the creation of an exclusive Jewish state in their midst.[49]

Transitioning from Reagan to Bush

As the Reagan years were coming to an end, AIPAC and other pro-Israel groups forcefully opposed the land for peace requisite of the two-state solution. This was their position all along, particularly in reaction to the possibility that Camp David's success in assuring peace between Israel and Egypt may have fostered American policymakers to seek the same of the Jewish state with the Palestinians or others in the region. That did not happen thanks to the convergence of the following: (1) the strategic relationship between Israel and the US against Soviet communism, (2) intense lobbying efforts by AIPAC and company that faced little competition, (3) pro-Israel elite sentiments in the US, (4) American public opinion favoring the Jewish state, and (5) the relative passivity of Palestinians living under occupation. And while Israel maintained peace with the Egyptians because it was in its interest to do so, the same did not hold for dealings with the Palestinians. Pro-Israel organizations tried to make sure that politicians did not have any second thoughts about Israel's occupation. The Jewish state preferred control over what it perceived as docile Palestinians who sat on Judea and Samaria but feared Egypt's military campaigns to take back the Sinai in 1973.[50] This was the case until the Intifada of December 1987. It was during that time that Israel and its promoters in the US realized that controlling the Palestinians no longer seemed feasible or possible. Still, with the kind of support that the Jewish state enjoyed from the Washington establishment, new policies to repress the Palestinians could be tried. If they failed, there were other options to control them as Israel was armed with support from its American ally, not to mention its immense and unparalleled military arsenal.

For the most part, Israel could not overcome the Palestinian uprising as day by day, the occupied territories proved ungovernable. While the violence mounted, AIPAC continued to press in favor of occupation. However, the Jewish state, its supporters on Capitol Hill, and the new American administration headed by President George Bush realized that the situation in the Middle East was coming to a head as a gradually more vocal pro-Arab lobby sought to bring the misery of occupation to light by exploiting the events of the Intifada in the media and pushing the Palestinian uprising into policymakers' perceptions.[51] Strategies had to be developed and deployed in order to address the increasing difficulties Israel faced. Hence,

> Secretary of State James Baker's May 1989 address to ... (AIPAC) ... called on the Arabs to demonstrate their readiness for peace and on the Israelis to "abandon their dream of a Greater Israel." Such statements answered the demand for some larger vision of the American diplomatic destination, but the immediate task was ... defined as one of helping the parties just get started on the right road. And those "parties" (to pin down an eternally elusive diplomatic circumlocution) now emphatically included the Palestinians as primary players – thanks in no small measure to the uprising they had managed to sustain. In practice, this meant that Washington would drop both the international conference and the tight "interlock" between interim and final status arrangements and concentrate instead on getting to direct political talks between Israelis and Palestinians. This, it was hoped, would transform the Intifada into a political dynamic, substituting statements for stones and bargaining for bullets. And since Israel had the upper hand, it was from Israel that the United States sought agreement on a way to launch this transformation.[52]

It became overwhelmingly clear that the American interest in Middle East peace coincided with Israel's desire to rid itself of the Intifada. Accordingly, AIPAC and its partners silently went along with the framework of a future peace process that would involve the Palestinians.[53] This allowed the Bush administration to feel free in trying to facilitate dialogue between Israel and its neighbors.

When Iraq invaded Kuwait, efforts by the Bush administration to broker peace were sidelined and yet their necessity was brought into focus. The outcome of that war had significant impacts on the Israel–US relationship. Months after the Gulf War's conclusion, on September 12, 1991, the White House found itself at odds with Capitol Hill over loan guarantees to the Jewish state.[54] President Bush threatened to veto legislation intended to provide it with an economic boost, consequently undoing AIPAC's efforts in Congress.[55] Israel forces in Washington would not forget that and the president, like others before him, would eventually suffer the consequences. However, Bush succeeded in some of his efforts to stymie support for Israel unless it worked for peace, something widely seen as serving the interests of the US in the Middle East and capitalizing on its successes in the Persian Gulf and the Cold War.[56] While his efforts would lead to a "chill" in American–Israeli relations, negotiations took place at Madrid, Spain during the end of October 1991.[57] Madrid allowed for a framework that attempted to encourage the start of negotiations between Israel, Syria, Lebanon, Jordan, and the Palestinians.[58] Its preliminary agreements, however, were not binding. Also, the conference never addressed the aspirations of the

Palestinians, thanks in no small part to the fact that the Bush negotiating team was staffed by personnel that refused to apply any significant pressure on Israel to compromise.[59]

Nonetheless, heightened negotiations between the Arab states and Israel would not have happened had it not been for the manner in which domestic pressure groups interpreted and conveyed to policymakers and their constituents the fall of the Berlin Wall, the Intifada, and the Gulf War. These historical events not only "reshaped the basic political order of the Middle East," they had profound impacts on methods to influence US foreign policy.[60] AIPAC and other Israel lobbying firms had to accept global changes. However, through them they strictly followed the Israeli government's guidance.[61] Accordingly, the Palestinians were rejected as a national community deserving of a state while their leadership was embraced insofar as it would bring order to the troubled occupied territories. The PLO would ultimately become the unofficial police of the Jewish state, erasing years of rejection by numerous Israeli governments that branded all Palestinian political actors as terrorists.[62] In Washington, pro-Israel measures were not only limited to Congress, they also permeated the Bush White House and the American delegation to Madrid, headed by Martin Indyk, former deputy director of research at AIPAC. Hence, we see that despite tensions between President Bush and the Jewish state, its lobby at least through its former members, still managed to exercise direct power over the peace process and the status of the Palestinians. However, the ensuing vision for Palestinian autonomy brought the unintended consequence of a rise in visibility of the pro-Arab lobby during the Bill Clinton presidency.

After the Cold War: Clinton's ascendance

Times of optimism?

Months after Clinton took office, the Palestinians signed the Declaration of Principles (DOP) in September 1993. This was a time for renewed hope that Israelis and Palestinians would settle their differences. After all, the Cold War had ended, the US played a bigger role in the Middle East after expelling Iraq from Kuwait, and was now mediating peace. The agreement between Israeli Prime Minister Yitzhak Rabin and PLO chairman Yasser Arafat signified mutual acceptance. Looking at rough estimates, the Palestinians were to accept Israel as the legitimate sovereign over 78 percent of historic Palestine while the Jewish state would allow them to have a political entity on the remaining 22 per cent.[63] Internationally, now that Cold War divisions were fading, there was some hope about the new arrangement brokered by President Clinton. The DOP and the ensuing peace process were believed to signal the end of the century-old conflict.

Optimism over the DOP, however, flourished in a context of sustained American support for the Jewish state, which changed little since the Cold

War period of the 1980s as the pro-Israel lobby began to find new ways to paint the Palestinians in a negative light. Meanwhile, Clinton appointed former pro-Israel lobby personnel to key positions in crafting peace. Old-time AIPAC player and Madrid negotiator Martin Indyk was assigned to the Middle East policy desk at the National Security Council. Samuel Lewis, former ambassador to Israel, was selected for the State Department's policy planning team. Dennis Ross, from the Washington Institute for Near East Policy (WINEP), a pro-Israel think tank closely aligned with AIPAC, was appointed coordinator of the peace talks. Under these three men, the peace process would be fixed to Palestinian "limited autonomy," with Israeli sovereignty over the majority of the occupied territories.[64] Given Israeli military control over Palestinian population centers under that arrangement, peace had to overcome many challenges. Eventually, the entire peace process would be perceived by many as a fraud at best, and at worst, a catastrophe. As early as 1995 Joe Stork lamented

> from Madrid to Oslo was a defeat for the Palestinians; from Oslo to Washington it was a rout; from Washington to Cairo (May 1994) it was a catastrophe, the second for the Palestinian people. The success of American (and Israeli) policies was total.[65]

Without a doubt, the mid-1990s were a period of wild success for AIPAC and the pro-Israel lobbying it coordinated in the peace process. The Palestinians were being policed by their own "autonomous" government in order to diminish the problems their occupation presented to the Jewish state while former pro-Israel lobbyists, given US government credentials and high-level security clearances, dominated policies on the Middle East. Meanwhile, even though the international community believed that a *fair* and final negotiated settlement was imminent, when the 1996 presidential election came around, "friends of Israel agreed that never in history had they had a greater friend in the White House than Bill Clinton."[66] Of course, Clinton also appealed to a wide variety of Americans that were interested in voting on issues other than US policy toward Israel. As a result, he won decisively. After Clinton's victory, the pro-Israel lobby would mount further campaigns to ensure that the Jewish state would give up little save for the rhetoric of recognition and further autonomy toward the Palestinians. It also began to reckon with the fact that American Jews were undergoing political transformation, and on the issue of Israel, were finding increased support from the right-wing Christian bloc in the US.[67] During these times of change, the *New Yorker* remarked:

> Jews earn like Episcopalians and vote like Puerto Ricans. For decades, this was traditional and iron law of New York politics (and, lest the joke police be suiting up, it was a remark known best of all among Jews). But

for some time now it has been clear that Jews have been getting more conservative – or, at least, more inconsistent – in their voting patterns. And though there are no polls to prove it, it is possible that Benjamin Netanyahu could have won among the Jews in the metropolitan area by about the same slim margin as he did in Israel.[68]

Jewish Americans were never the only supporters of AIPAC. After Clinton's reelection, the pro-Israel political right in the US was gaining momentum, a development that would benefit supporters of the Jewish state.[69] Christian evangelism was on the rise, as well as nationalist and secular conservatism (under the banner of "neoconservatism"). In the 1990s, these developments were still too early to determine much in elite politics.[70] However, they did force AIPAC to begin countenancing its future in American politics by appealing to Americans of all ideological varieties.[71]

Having moved in that direction, AIPAC could wield power in the left, center, and right of the US political spectrum, something that would serve it well regardless of who was in office or which party had more seats in government. Moreover, there was an ever more entrenched relationship of support for Israel in the United States under the Clinton administration. This was due in no small part to the pro-Israel lobby acting on a wide range of agents of socialization including the media, educational institutions, and houses of worship, all of which shaped public opinion.[72] As has been previously demonstrated, even though the public favored a Palestinian state, it also showed remarkable levels of sympathy for Israel, something that gave AIPAC the perception of wide support for its programs. In 1997, this would lead Charles Lipson to surmise, "in effect ... [AIPAC] worke[d] to translate broad but inchoate popular support into effective backing for specific policies, such as U.S. aid or the sale of advanced military technology" to Israel.[73] AIPAC also used preference for Israel in its work to vigorously prevent the same exchanges from taking place between the US and Arab parties.[74] However, it lacked popular support in its actions to stifle the emerging preference for the two-state solution. Throughout the 1990s, Americans, regardless of their political affiliation, supported peace in the Middle East through a Palestinian state.[75] However, they also sympathized with Israel by significant margins. The pro-Israel lobby managed to solidify that support at the grassroots and to harness it at the highest levels of decision-making. The outcomes favored Israel when it came to drafting policies on the Middle East and served to defer the meaningful realization of land for peace.

In addition to channeling public sentiment for Israel toward outcomes that went against the popular will for the two-state solution, the pro-Israel lobby was a great source of disseminating partial knowledge on the Middle East to the highest levels of government officials. One AIPAC aide noted:

it is common for members of Congress and their staffs to turn to AIPAC first when they need information, before calling the Library of Congress, the Congressional Research Service, committee staff or administration experts. We are often called upon to draft speeches, work on legislation, advise on tactics, perform research, collect co-sponsors and marshal votes.[76]

Obtaining information in that way may place Congress's guardianship role over citizens' welfare in jeopardy. Even if AIPAC was not acting on behalf of a foreign government, the particulars with which decision-makers act must originate from sources with no stakes in the outcome of foreign policy. Failure to adhere to that standard may have contributed to the lack of evenhandedness when approaching issues such as land for peace. Rather than being apprised of that situation, Americans and their leaders were informed of Israeli benevolence in negotiations and the Palestinians' nefarious ineptitude when it came to peacemaking. Controlling information thus was yet another testament to the strength of the pro-Israel lobby on Capitol Hill. When its experts were not busy serving the interests of the Jewish state indirectly, they were involved in determining policies by controlling the details animating them.

Pro-Israel tanks

In addition to its work with government, the pro-Israel lobby has been very effective at propagating knowledge to specialized and mass audiences through its think tanks.[77] Organizations like WINEP have always engaged in producing op-ed pieces and articles that influence policymakers and the public. In one example relevant to the two-state solution, when Hillary Rodham Clinton commented on the peace process resulting in a "Palestinian state" as an important part of long-term US interests, she was blasted by Robert Satloff, executive director of WINEP, who argued that since American policy under her husband's watch toward "final status" was intentionally ambiguous, the First Lady's remarks were unacceptable.[78] This example was only the tip of the iceberg during the late 1990s as the production of partisan thought by think tanks like WINEP dotted the political landscape.[79] There was an uneasy relationship between power and objectivity. Groups like WINEP do intellectually what AIPAC and other pro-Israel organizations perform in the halls of government. Whereas one side concerns itself with ideas, the other works fervently in the activist realm to turn theory into practice. To be sure, the ability to frame issues in a manner that suits a particular political agenda is nothing new. Pro-Israel think tanks produced an excess of facts and figures that made it easier to impede the two-state solution as a danger to the Jewish state, something that had been the constant position of Israelis like Benjamin Netanyahu and others of his political ilk both before and after Oslo.[80]

Furthermore, the creation of knowledge by pro-Israel lobbyists and think tanks often employed emotional and psychological tools. For instance, anytime someone spoke of the need for evenhandedness during the 1990s, that person was attacked as anti-Semitic.[81] If not directly from pro-Israel lobbyists, this charge came from think tanks supportive of their mission. Both Jews and non-Jews have been subjected to this repellent label. According to Nasseer Aruri and Muhammad A. Shuraydi,

> silence on the issue of Jews and Judaism is more than demanded; it is enforced with psychological and material penalties. The charges of Jewish self-hatred, the new anti-Semitism, and the encouragement of another holocaust are complicated by the highly organized and well-financed Jewish political apparatus and institutional structure. Examples abound, and one only need mention AIPAC ... and the ADL (Anti-Defamation League) to strike fear in the hearts of many who want to question contemporary Jewish understandings in relation to America and Israel.[82]

The strength of the Israel lobbying network became apparent at once to anyone in academic institutions or in government who questioned American vacillation on resolving the conflict.[83] As Findley and numerous others found out decades earlier, there was no room for dissent when it came to support of the Jewish state. Too often, American support for Israel was the conclusion that the facts followed. That remained true during and after the period of Oslo optimism, even though pro-Israel pressure groups had to adapt to the domestic and international realities outlined above.

AIPAC, Bush, and the wars on terrorism and Iraq

The rebirth of a giant

If everything that has come so far demonstrates the resilience and authority of the pro-Israel lobby, the fallout from the terrorist attacks of 9/11 would make it even more potent. Months before he came to power, George W. Bush was a candidate committed to Israel.[84] He ran as a devout Christian who "believed" in the Jewish state and did not think that it was in the US interest to "nation-build." Stated during his foreign policy debate with Vice President Al Gore, this Bush doctrine seemed to fit the interests of Israel quite well.[85] It promised the Jewish state friendship on religious and political grounds and offered the Palestinians no aid in breaking free from occupation. Such a position was exactly what the pro-Israel lobby sought in an American president, particularly after the start of the 2000 Intifada in which the Palestinians rebelled yet again. Whereas the largely unarmed 1987 Intifada showed the world that the Palestinians would no longer tolerate occupation, the violent second Intifada demonstrated that they could not govern themselves.[86] At least this was the narrative that the hard-line Israeli government wanted to convey to its American ally through its domestic proxy. Candidate Bush's platform suited that vision well. It would declare dead an ailing peace process by summarily rejecting intervention in the Israeli–Palestinian conflict except when it came to supporting the Jewish state as a matter of course. Needless to say, after his electoral victory, the new president began to dull the US pursuit of peace.

In fact, the "peace process" became problematic for the Bush administration, according to Aruri.

> [Secretary of State Colin] Powell, in an obligatory speech before AIPAC in March 2001, affirmed the unwavering strategic alliance between Israel and the United States ... and the determination of the United States to help Israel maintain a qualitative military edge over all the Arab states. What is new in those speeches, however, was the de-emphasis of the "peace process" and the Palestine question. ... This was clearly a move not only to distinguish the new administration from the legacy of President Clinton, but also a means to signal a change in the priorities of the Bush administration. Perhaps more significant in the reprioritization of American policy toward the Palestine question are statements by both Bush and Powell ... changing the description of America's role from "catalyst for peace" (under the Bush Sr.-Baker team) to "honest broker" (under Clinton) to "facilitator for peace negotiations" who will "assist but not insist," according to Powell. That is, the United States will facilitate peace negotiations once the initiative has been taken by the two relevant parties. The initiative will not emanate from Washington, and furthermore, for such negotiations to restart, "violence" and "terrorism" must be reduced or come to an end.[87]

The Palestinians alone were charged with ending "violence" and "terrorism." As far as American policy was concerned, the Israeli government, being a legitimate state authority, was immune from such demands since it was acting in self-defense against acts by extralegal foes, or in the post-9/11 lexicon, "unlawful enemy combatants."[88] The position taken by the Bush administration after 9/11 was only the beginning of a long series of events that helped pro-Israel pressure groups make the case to the president and members of Congress that the Palestinians ought to be included as targets in the struggle against terrorism.[89] Government officials were fed a regular diet of information that made the connection between the Palestinians and other rogue entities.[90] In most cases, when it came to policymakers and the public, the Israel lobby needed to make no case at all as the desire to "take the fight to the terrorists" was already the order of the day after the attacks on the US. However, without 9/11, during the first half of 2001, pro-Israel advocates had to cozy up to the new president who, despite being predisposed toward the Jewish state, was still formulating his policies and reevaluating his predecessor's positions on the Middle East and elsewhere.

Indeed, the first few months that President Bush was in office were a time of courtship between him and the pro-Israel lobby. Once he adopted the "hands off" approach to the Israeli–Palestinian conflict, Bush ensured that the Jewish state could try to squash the Intifada undisturbed. Still, as the Israeli government proved unable to stop the uprising, Bush's CIA director George Tenet tried to bring agreement with the Palestinians through the following program.

> (1) Immediately resume security cooperation, including eventual joint patrols, to replace the adversarial posture on the ground; (2) take immediate measure to enforce adherence to Israel's unilateral ceasefire, including Palestinian arrests of those committing acts of terrorism; (3) provide information on terrorist threats to each other and the US, and take operations to prevent attacks; (4) prevent persons from using areas "under their respective control to carry out acts of violence; (5) forge "an agreed-upon schedule to implement the complete redeployment of IDF to positions held before September 28, 2000;" and (6) develop a timeline for the "lifting of internal closures" and "reopening of internal roads," bridges, airports, and border crossings.[91]

This brought little relief as the violence escalated. It did make an effort at reining it in from the Palestinian side but gave no assurance of any permanent Israeli withdrawal. From the Tenet Plan, it appeared that the Bush "hands off" approach was only a facade.[92] The US was still active in Middle East affairs, only now the central principle behind the peace process, ending the occupation, became muffled. The burden for cessation of hostilities was placed squarely on the Palestinian side.

As tragic as the events of September 11, 2001 were, they gave AIPAC and other pro-Israel lobbying organizations a renewed sense of purpose. As the rubble smoldered, American and Israeli interests became resolutely similar: combating terrorism.[93] In 1981, AIPAC's chairman stated, "[u]nless you can always translate [your proposals] in terms of what's in America's interest, you're lost."[94] Twenty years later, the job of "translating" for the pro-Israel lobby became much easier. After expressing its condolences for the thousands of dead Americans, AIPAC fervently worked on giving al Qa'eda a Palestinian face. Under its direction, a key subject in foreign policy circles became the extent to which the US would support Israel's fight against terrorism. There were, after all, many similarities between the Palestinians and al-Qa'eda. While the latter was "a stateless terrorist organization [that] attacked the United States,"[95] the former also lacked a state and illegitimately attacked the Jewish state. As far as AIPAC was concerned, the task became clear: make linkages between the Palestinian Authority (PA) and the "global terror network." Such action would justify Israeli efforts at destabilizing the inchoate Palestinian government, including massive bombing campaigns against its offices in Ramallah and nearly killing Arafat in the rubble of his burned out and all but demolished compound, which ultimately became his prison until the last few months of his life.[96]

Although AIPAC gained an enhanced position from the connections made between Palestinian resistance and global terrorism, its strong hand may have been undermined since the pendulum of foreign policymaking moved from Congress to President Bush almost overnight. "Following September 11," noted Thomas Ambrosio, "the Bush administration assumed decisive control over U.S. foreign policy, with some describing a return to an 'imperial presidency.'"[97] Such a shift certainly impacted pro-Israel groups like AIPAC, which have traditionally operated at the congressional branch of government. However, President Bush understood that he still needed AIPAC in Congress to help pass legislation for fighting the war on terrorism.

Throughout the US and the world, there emerged a clear consensus on eliminating the terrorist threat wherever it existed. If other states were able to help, they may join the "coalition of the willing" in order to combat the global menace. In this regard, by destroying the PA's infrastructure, the Jewish state did what pro-Israel groups passed off as America's bidding without even being asked. Its compensation remained support by policy-makers and a newfound respect for being a committed ally in the war on terrorism, which now incorporated a Palestinian enemy. For the pro-Israel lobby, such a perception got it out of the dilemma faced by all other foreign entities: "less tolerance for endorsement of foreign policies that appear to support interests overseas" during times of crisis in the United States.[98] Simply put, Americans faced with the noxious threat of terrorist catastrophe on their homeland internalized and supported Israel's struggle even though it took place thousands of miles away.

Through the conduit of the pro-Israel lobby, the Jewish state closely identified its interests with those of the United States.[99] While this was the case before 9/11, after that dreadful day, Israel simply got away with much more in its efforts against the Palestinians. There was little room for criticism in a world that became deeply polarized, as was made clear by President Bush's crucial statement shortly after September 11: "either you are with us, or you are with the terrorists."[100] Such a determination meant that since the Palestinians were viewed as the "bad guys" and the Israelis as the "good guys," something that was demonstrated by numerous polls of US public opinion,[101] the alliance with Israel became even stronger and the already dominant position of influence that the pro-Israel lobby had enjoyed became more pronounced.[102] As Americans internalized Israel's struggle, AIPAC stepped up campaigns to turn that sympathy into policy.

Meanwhile, the US and the Sharon government became more wedded in their approaches to the Palestinians after the terrorist attacks on American soil. White House officials and members of Congress cared even less about an occupation that involved "collective punishment, closure and isolation, economic strangulation, starvation, massive bombardment of residential areas with American supplied F-16s and helicopter gunships, assassinations, and deliberative maiming of demonstrators."[103] If Palestinians resisted, they were placed in the same camp as Islamic fundamentalists that were the object of American targeting.[104] To make peace with such monstrous enemies of civilization was akin to treason, a view the pro-Israel lobby was quick to seize upon and nurture.[105] Even more dangerous, because of their intensified attacks against Israeli civilians during the Intifada, militants hijacked the spotlight from the internationally sanctioned Palestinian government. In a world overly focused on terrorism in the months following 9/11, they became the de facto voice of the Palestinian people as distinctions between lawful and unlawful resistance blurred. The more Palestinian extremists committed acts of terrorism, the more Israel felt justified in undermining the PA. Ironically, this only strengthened the terrorists since the moderate PLO government was the sole authority charged with ensuring Israel's security.

While some came out against Israel's occupation of Palestinian lands after 9/11, the policies undertaken by the Bush administration both before and immediately after the terrorist attacks reaffirmed it.[106] This went against the grain of American interest, which demanded a constructive role in resolving the Israeli–Palestinian conflict through land for peace. It seemed like that, however, was a moot point since there was no peace to be had in the wake of the terrorist attacks and as the Jewish state furthered its occupation and appropriation of Palestinian territory.[107] Moreover, Israel's swift destruction of most Palestinian government apparatuses only meant that the pro-Israel lobby in the US would have further reason to bemoan the fact that there was no partner with which to negotiate.[108] During the Clinton era, Arafat's "inability" or "lack of courage" to make peace were often blamed by Israel and its supporters for the stalemate. After 9/11, the obliteration of the Palestinian leadership crippled all efforts to make peace. Left to their devices, the Israeli government backed the Palestinian leadership into a corner. During those dark days, it seemed as if all options for peace had faded. The proverbial table on which both sides would have sat to negotiate was being charred by the reign of the war on terror. Still, there was hope in the midst of chaos.

On November 19, 2001, as violent confrontations between Israelis and Palestinians continued, Secretary of State Colin Powell forever changed the tune of American policy toward the Israeli–Palestinian conflict by declaring before a Louisville, Kentucky audience "we have a vision of a region where two states – Israel and Palestine – live side by side within secure and recognized borders."[109] Moving away from the "hands off" approach, this was a monumental announcement. In the context of the historical tendency of American foreign policy, it was revolutionary. For the first time ever, a high administration official spoke *publicly* and *explicitly* of "two states" as the ideal solution. Such action flew in the face of cynics on the US role in the conflict. Powell, however, did not stop at the future prospect for the two-state solution. Against the wishes of Israel and its supporters, he vehemently condemned the occupation by saying that "the overwhelming majority of the Palestinians in the West Bank and Gaza have grown up with checkpoints and raids and indignities ... too often, they have seen their schools shuttered and their parents humiliated." In addition, the secretary of state observed, "the Israeli settlement activity has severely undermined Palestinian trust and hope. It preempts and prejudges the outcome of negotiations and, in doing so, cripples chances for real peace and security."[110] Before Powell, a serving American statesman would have never publicly articulated such a position. During the war on terrorism, however, the two-state solution became necessary.

Months after Powell delivered his speech, President Bush outlined his vision of a two-state solution to the conflict while calling for a new Palestinian leadership.

> For too long, the citizens of the Middle East have lived in the midst of death and fear. The hatred of a few holds the hopes of many hostage. The forces of extremism and terror are attempting to kill progress and peace by killing the innocent. And this casts a dark shadow over an entire region. For the sake of all humanity, things must change in the Middle East. It is untenable for Israeli citizens to live in terror. It is untenable for Palestinians to live in squalor and occupation. And the current situation offers no prospect that life will improve. Israeli citizens will continue to be victimized by terrorists, and so Israel will continue to defend herself. In the situation the Palestinian people will grow more and more miserable. My vision is two states, living side by side in peace and security. There is simply no way to achieve that peace until all parties fight terror. Yet, at this critical moment, if all parties will break with the past and set out on a new path, we can overcome the darkness with the light of hope. Peace requires a new and different Palestinian leadership, so that a Palestinian state can be born.[111]

As he made this announcement, President Bush was surrounded with National Security Advisor Condoleezza Rice, Secretary of State Colin Powell, and Secretary of Defense Donald Rumsfeld. This was meant to signify both that the key players of his cabinet were on board with his plans and that the US would commit its energies from each of the state entities represented by the personnel on the Rose Garden. The speech was intended for all concerned parties: the American public, pressure groups, lawmakers, the Israelis and Palestinians, and the entire world. Peace in the Middle East had been charted a new path that took into account the realities of the international situation in the period after September 11, 2001. President Bush's vision of two states to resolve the Israeli–Palestinian conflict as outlined above became known simply as the "roadmap."

Many have questioned the intentions of the Bush roadmap, particularly as the air was heavy with the possibility of war against America's next target after Afghanistan in the war on terrorism, Iraq.[112] Was the call for the two-state solution designed to co-opt the Arab states into aiding or at least acquiescing in the efforts to oust Saddam Hussein from power, a fundamental goal of the Bush administration that was only heightened after 9/11? Or, did the US propose the two-state vision because it realized that the Palestinian predicament was partly to blame for the 9/11 attacks? The answer might involve both. In any case, it is not possible to delve into such discussion with any certainty since the intentions surrounding the Iraq War – aside from weapons of mass destruction, the oppressiveness of Saddam Hussein, etcetera – remain fundamentally concealed at the time of this inquiry.[113] What is known, however, is that (1) the Iraq War did help Israel by eliminating a major regional threat to its hegemony, a regime that ostensibly supported Palestinian terrorism; and (2) the roadmap endeavored to assuage an issue that has dogged American–Arab relations, the Israeli–Palestinian conflict in which the Jewish state occupied an Arab people and turned many of their ranks into refugees living in wretchedness.[114]

As war became imminent, AIPAC briskly argued, "both in Iraq and in the Palestinian areas, prospects for peace and stability depend on new, truly reformed leaderships."[115] Here again, we have pro-Israel advocates exploiting the foreign policy concerns of the times. It was as if they and American policymakers were engaged in a complementary power play. As the US sought to expel Saddam Hussein from power, AIPAC wanted Arafat dislodged from the negotiating position conferred on him by Oslo. Such a move may have greatly harmed efforts to resolve the Israeli–Palestinian conflict, if for no other reason, then simply because it took away from the pursuit of peace. Hence, the only moderate Palestinian party and its chairman were being asked to leave the scene of the peace process. This would spell trouble for Israel since it would lose a valuable Palestinian negotiating partner and would therefore prolong the misery of conflict between the two sides. Still, AIPAC did not care about these long-term implications and scrupulously worked to accomplish in American policy what Israel wanted.[116]

Days after the outbreak of the Iraq War, the Bush administration took its vision for the two-state solution to the pro-Israel lobby. Secretary of State Colin Powell was dispatched by invitation to AIPAC on March 31, 2003 to give a speech at its annual convention, which characteristically brought all major pro-Israel groups under one roof. Powell advanced the two-state vision in the following way.

> President Bush outlined a bold vision for peace based on two states existing peacefully, side-by-side – a secure, Jewish, democratic State of Israel, and a viable, peaceful, democratic, independent State of Palestine. ... And one fact is unmistakable. The president's vision requires an end to the use of violence and terror as a political tool. ... The president's vision puts clear obligations on the Palestinians. The Palestinian state must be based on transformed leaderships and

institutions that end terror. The Palestinian government must be trans-parent and accountable to the people. Above all, the Palestinian state must be a real partner for peace with Israel. Israel has clear obligations, too. It must take steps to ease the suffering of Palestinians and diminish the daily humiliation of life under occupation. Israel must also help put economic hope in Palestinian hearts by helping revive the devastated economies of the West Bank and Gaza. Settlement activity is simply inconsistent with President Bush's two-state vision. As the president has said, "as progress is made toward peace, settlement activity in the Occupied Territories must end."[117]

In addition to delineating the obligations of Israelis and Palestinians under US leadership, this statement highlighted the administration's insistence on peacemaking. While the immediate behind-the-scenes reaction from AIPAC is not known since it exists in private memoranda, the positions taken by the pro-Israel lobby in its public statements were well documented, as conveyed by its influential biweekly Capitol Hill publication, the *Near East Report* (NER).

Eluding the two-state solution

Members of Congress and AIPAC representatives were trying to blunt the effects of the roadmap after Powell's speech. As President Bush formally presented the Israelis and Palestinians with details of his plan, the NER featured a letter meant to hinder action on the two-state solution.

Leaders of the House and Senate are circulating a letter to President Bush saying any "roadmap" for Israeli–Palestinian talks should be based on the guiding principles he outlined in a speech last June 24. These principles include "the establishment of a new Palestinian leadership that is transparent, accountable, free from the taint of terrorism"; pro-gress based on "benchmarks of real performance"; and negotiations only between "the parties themselves" and the United States "in order for progress to be lasting."[118]

After passing through Congress, that letter was sent to President Bush. It was intended to place a disproportionate weight of peace on the Palestinians and made no mention of Israel's occupation in violation of the Oslo agree-ment and international law or the violence that the IDF committed against the Palestinians. In short, the letter sought to ensure that the administration could not move on Middle East peace evenhandedly. AIPAC and its allies in Congress recounted everything that the Palestinians were doing wrong, but failed to mention how the administration itself perceived the Israeli occupa-tion as a foundational obstacle to peace in the region. And since Congress controlled the purse, which would finance President Bush's grandiose vision for peace, the administration had to observe the letter's demands in order to preserve political capital with legislators and the pro-Israel lobby that sought to sway them.

Nevertheless, in accordance with calls for new leadership, the Palestinians appointed a new figure to head the PA. Mahmoud Abbas (Abu Mazin) became prime minister and Arafat took a backseat after years of isolation by Israel and the United States. This move, however, did not result in the US taking steps to compel Israel to ease its occupation of the Palestinian population in the West Bank and Gaza. Weeks after Abu Mazin's appointment, AIPAC commentators began to condemn the new Palestinian government, arguing that it was "moving in the opposite direction" on dismantling terrorist organizations.[119] Ignored was the fact that years of Israeli military strikes against the PA's security system meant that no new government would have been able to halt violence from renegade factions. Furthermore, there was no recognition of the relationship between occupation and terrorism.[120] As far as AIPAC was concerned, the Jewish state could flaunt international conventions until the Palestinians performed the nearly impossible task of quelling *all* resistance to an ongoing occupation without the means to do so. The American policymaking elite pretty much adopted the same position. Early calls for Israel to end its occupation were perceived at best as rhetoric to make it seem as if the US was engaged in constructive action on the Israeli–Palestinian conflict, and at worst, as a veneer for more sinister intentions in the region. US policy seemed to take the blame off the Jewish state while the entire world viewed its occupation as the catalyst for violence. Through all of this, AIPAC was proud to mention that the American administration was calling on Prime Minister Abu Mazin to take "concrete steps" to stop the violence with no commensurate outline for Israel to end its occupation.[121]

Along with the Bush administration's deeds to squeeze the Palestinian leadership, AIPAC was lobbying Congress to pass new laws regarding the conditions under which a Palestinian state would be recognized. In May 2003, the NER reported,

> the House International Relations Committee approved legislation declaring that a "Palestinian state should not be recognized by the United States" until the Palestinians elect new leaders, dismantle the terrorist infrastructure and reform their society as President Bush called for in his June 24, 2002, speech on the Middle East. The provision was included in the fiscal year 2004–5 Foreign Relations Authorization bill, which also authorizes U.S. aid to Israel.[122]

So, in addition to its support of Israel, Congress was now working to make opposition to a Palestinian state the law of the land. AIPAC's demands on a besieged population set up unattainable standards. Hence, the two-state solution, as envisioned by the Bush administration, was in danger of becoming a pipedream. The Palestinians were asked to end terrorism even though the phrase itself had no widely agreed upon definition or effective strategies to stop it. Furthermore, social reform is not something that could be engineered and implemented overnight by a virtually deceased Palestinian government without a state.[123] Even the United States with its great military might, abundant economic capital, and stable socio-political establishment could neither stop international terrorism nor transform its social fabric at home in any immediate sense. All of this meant that the realization of a solution to the conflict was rendered precarious, less than a year after Bush announced his roadmap.

Antipathy towards the roadmap, however, was never explicit in any way. All along, Congress claimed that it shared Bush's vision, but that Palestinian statehood would not happen unless the administration stuck to its own words on concrete actions to curtail terrorism.[124] Congress, however, had no regard for the flipside of the equation, mainly that Bush called on Israel to scale back its occupation. Such disregard for the Jewish state holding up its end of the bargain meant that violence only escalated, since the US was gridlocked on bringing to bear its diplomatic muscle on attempting, in good faith, to resolve the Israeli–Palestinian conflict. Under AIPAC's guidance, Congress willfully ignored the conditions on the ground in the occupied territories even as hard-line Prime Minister Ariel Sharon was cognizant of the difficulties Palestinians faced under occupation. This was something that AIPAC itself recognized when it reported that Sharon had "vowed to restore normal Palestinian life and improve the humanitarian situation," and that he understood "the importance of territorial contiguity in the West Bank for a viable Palestinian state."[125] Despite that, AIPAC continued lobbying to tighten the noose around prospects for a Palestinian state.

At this point, there seemed to be an apparent disconnection between what Israel was doing and what AIPAC sought in its efforts. While Sharon's rhetoric seemed to support Bush's roadmap, the Israel lobby was doing everything that it could to oppose it by focusing only on the Palestinian side of the equation for peace. Upon closer inspection, however, AIPAC was asking for the same thing as Sharon. Both stipulated that in order to have *any* state, Palestinians would have to stop terrorism, renounce any leadership with ties to terror, transform their society, and renew their acceptance of the Jewish state without conditions. As demonstrated above, meeting these goals was not possible, particularly under the Israeli occupation that most Palestinians felt compelled to resist. Still, AIPAC and its congressional friends continued to sing the same tune: the roadmap's realization may "only happen if terrorism is not allowed to defeat it as it has every agreement and cease-fire since the signing of the Oslo Accords."[126] Such cynicism showed that the pro-Israel lobby did not accept any foundations for a Palestinian state, even as it claimed to support Bush's roadmap in its public utterances.[127]

Making matters more complicated, Israel began constructing a new "security fence" that would later be ruled a violation of international law and a threat to the realization of the two-state solution and peace in the Middle East.[128] Since they financed its building with their tax dollars, Americans share culpability for that violation and in preventing the likelihood of a stated US foreign policy objective, the creation of a viable Palestinian state. What has AIPAC's position been on the building of the wall? The NER is filled with apologies for it. Statements such as "the fence is a necessary measure to prevent terrorist attacks," and "Israel is working to minimize the fence's impact on the Palestinians," line its pages.[129] In reality, the wall has proven itself a disaster for both sides. Virginia Tilley wrote, "the Wall will not secure Israel from the trouble ahead, for the Palestinian nation is unlikely to wither peacefully" adding "their misery and anger in their impoverished national ghetto would still foster unrest that would plague Israeli politics, security, and society."[130] Such conditions would neither be in American or Israeli interests. Yet, the pro-Israel lobby has continued to applaud the wall, which may have already brought about the conditions decried by many.[131]

In addition to its attempts to frustrate Palestinian statehood, AIPAC is actively engaged in calling for sanctions against other Middle East parties, particularly Iran, Syria, and Saudi Arabia.[132] While looking at each of these cases demands a great deal of attention – more than could be done here – what is important to stress in the context of this chapter is that AIPAC has often raised issues that detract from the pressing needs of the peace process between Israel and the Palestinians. That type of diversion from the task at hand for American foreign policy has been particularly acute since Bush announced his roadmap. This was the case with the second Iraq War, which essentially has been a black hole for the focus of America's Middle East policy.[133] Looking at that war, we see that in a single stroke, it forced the US to shift its focus away from the Israeli–Palestinian conflict toward toppling Saddam Hussein, the dictator which Israel believed was one of its greatest threats in the region.[134] Currently the US is bogged down in Iraq.[135] According to some, President Hussein's removal by the US and ultimate execution may be considered one of the pro-Israel lobby's greatest achievements.[136] This, and the seemingly unattainable threshold for Palestinian statehood combined with factional fighting in the occupied territories, has created great obstacles for the two-state solution.

While attempting to derail the creation of a Palestinian state, AIPAC has rejected any other framework for peace. As an ever-increasing number of thinkers have raised the possibility of one state for Israelis and Palestinians, AIPAC has feverishly argued that such a thing would be disastrous.[137] According to the NER, the one-state solution would "be an appalling idea" that has foreign origins in the Arab world and Europe; in addition to eliminating Israel, its realization would "endanger the lives of Jews everywhere."[138] However, with Israel continuing to usurp land by building its wall and bulldozing Palestinian homes and livelihood, the probability of a viable alternative has been gravely diminished. The remaining options are either an

Israel that rules over Bantustans of personae non gratae in the occupied territories or a unified democracy for all of its citizens, one state for both Palestinians and Israelis, which is the cause of much derision by AIPAC and is nowhere to be found in policymaker sentiment. So, the only feasible solution in existence is that of two states. However, in the midst of other issues facing American policy, Israel's delay tactics, and its lobby's efforts at blocking any progress toward the two-state solution, the bloodshed will continue as possibilities for peace become dimmer. Meanwhile, despite its stated commitment to the roadmap, as demonstrated by talks at Annapolis and elsewhere, the Jewish state has vowed to maintain the security wall, and has previously "disengaged" from Gaza on a superficial basis as that territory continues to fall apart.[139] Through all of this, its actions have drawn accolades as American leaders have referred to Israeli behavior as "historic and courageous."[140]

US support for Israel, however, did not stop at praise. In a well publicized 2004 meeting between Israeli and US officials, the two-state solution was dealt a severe setback. AIPAC summarized the agreement that took place between the two sides in the following way.

> Through extraordinary cooperation, the two allies forged an agreement that encompasses difficult and complex issues, including support for a secure and defensible Jewish state and a separate Palestinian state; strong U.S. backing for Sharon's planned disengagement from Gaza and parts of the West Bank and for Israel's right to defend itself against terrorism; an American recognition of Israel's need to permanently hold on to some West Bank settlements; and a U.S. rejection of the notion that millions of Palestinian refugees from the 1948 Arab-Israeli war and their descendants could return to what is now Israel instead of their own independent state. While embracing such historic measures, President Bush also reaffirmed the United States' commitment to strengthening Israel's security and right to defend itself, including its ability to take actions against terrorist organizations.[141]

This arrangement meant that the Jewish state would not allow for a viable peace because (1) of its permanent settlements, which break international law and undermine the contiguity of any future Palestinian entity; and (2) it would violate its neighbor's territory (or for that matter, the sovereignty of any other state in the region) any time it deemed such action necessary to fight terrorism.[142] Hence, the bilateral agreement between the US and Israel for disengagement offered neither genuine withdrawal nor peace. Furthermore, a Palestinian state cannot exist without its future leaders being a party to agreements made to decide their people's future. Israel's advocates often treat that concept with contempt.[143] The pro-Israel position – that "the Palestinian Authority would first have to end terrorism and demonstrate a firm 'commitment to peaceful co-existence with the State of Israel'" in order to resume serious negotiations about any two-state arrangement – puts such contempt into practice.[144]

Conclusion

While this chapter has discussed the strength and changes of the pro-Israel lobby's strategy over the years, particularly in seeking to frustrate the land for peace framework of the two-state solution, we must remember that the Israel lobby is not the only agent acting on American policy toward the Middle East. Instead, there are numerous other factors, such as policymakers' favoritism of Israel over the Arabs (something that, as the previous chapter showed, is reflective of public opinion), and more importantly, as Noam Chomsky and Joseph Massad put it, "general US opposition to independent nationalism" or scorn for "national liberation in the Third World."[145] Although those particular issues require further inquiry that falls outside the scope of this analysis, it would suffice to say that the US administration under President Bush, consistent with the wishes of the American people, has declared its intention to broker the founding of a Palestinian state. However, given the power of the pro-Israel lobby and its hegemony in the discourse on American interests, US policy has been unable to bring the two-state solution to fruition. On the one hand, President Bush talked about "a successful Palestinian democracy" being "Israel's top goal," and called on the Jewish state to "freeze settlement activity, help Palestinians build a thriving economy and [to] ensure that a new Palestinian state is truly viable, with contiguous territory on the West Bank."[146] On the other hand, the concessions given to Israel, as called for by its lobby, placed a roadblock in the way of that type of a Palestinian state.

Is such action in the American national interest or does it merely serve Israel's desire to stave off Palestinian statehood? Put another way, would US policymakers act in accordance with American interests and public opinion on the two-state solution had there been no groups like AIPAC, or did the pro-Israel lobby force them to act in ways that prevent the existence of a Palestinian state and to pass such action off as part of the national interest? Such questions have no simple answers; however, what may be concluded with certainty is that AIPAC and the rest of the pro-Israel lobby are much more effective and powerful *because* policymakers and public opinion agree with their basic premise that the US ought to support Israel for a multiplicity of reasons, be it to maintain stability by frustrating Third World or independent forms of nationalism, to fight inimical ideologies, or to root out terrorism.[147] Such a consensus, however, did not necessarily lead to the *specific* policies that the US implemented during the periods under examination. In fact, as this chapter has demonstrated, the pro-Israel lobby helped focus American behavior. It did so by adapting to variances in public opinion toward the two-state solution, by challenging pro-Arab voices, and by renewing its sense of mission and that of the state it represented in a changing international landscape.

In conclusion, most analysts of US policy on the Israeli–Palestinian conflict agree that the pro-Israel lobby is effective because of "the *congruence* of the lobby's objectives with elite perceptions."[148] No one would be able to counterbalance the pro-Israel lobby's strength unless there was first and foremost, a stated American interest in doing something that does not simply accept the interests of the Jewish state alone. The two-state solution is precisely that. Land for peace, the cornerstone for that solution, has been accepted not just internationally and by domestic factors such as public opinion and foreign policy elites, it is a premise to which even the pro-Israel lobby has nodded. A press release by the Conference of Presidents of Major Jewish Organizations, the umbrella group of pro-Israel organizations,[149] "supported, and continues to support, the decision of the Government and Knesset of Israel to disengage from Gaza and parts of the West Bank."[150] The devil of this statement, however, is in the details: Israel will keep major settlements in the West Bank. This alone shows that a Palestinian state has become nearly impossible under current conditions. However, the unanimous agreement on land for peace, despite whether or how it may be pursued, means that there are foreign policy possibilities that may bring peace after all. Those, however, do not come from AIPAC and its friends, but rather from a potentially powerful pro-Arab, pro-peace lobby, now that the two-state solution is an integral part of the US agenda on the Israeli–Palestinian conflict. This subject will occupy the next chapter.

4 The effects and potential of the pro-Arab lobby

Introduction

Given its weakness when compared to its pro-Israel counterpart, the pro-Arab lobby has had a spotty history in the United States.[1] Its very existence is often contested even from within its own ranks. For example, when phoning Arab American organizations to set up interviews with their representatives for this work, it was dismaying to hear the person on the other end state "there is no Arab lobby in Washington, DC."[2] Perhaps the definition of "lobby" that was being utilized in this instance narrowly considered the term as an organization that directly influences government officials by telling them how to vote on particular legislation or face consequences in either votes or campaign contributions. By that definition, Arab groups have only a handful of agents on Capitol Hill with limited resources, not enough to constitute a "lobby" in the same sense as the American Israel Public Affairs Committee (AIPAC). Lobbying, however, involves much more than prompting Congress members on how to vote. It is an integral part of "domestic support for or opposition to foreign policy" and is one of the most effective forms of political action, which "expresses itself in various forms, ranging from letter-writing and editorializing to demonstrations and bomb-throwing."[3] Moreover, lobbying is an essential component of the "domestic structures," which "function as important inputs into the making of foreign policy, and define the broad internal limits within which decision-makers feel compelled to operate."[4] It may be direct or indirect, may aim at the executive or the legislature, or may focus on shaping public opinion. Foreign governments or citizens' groups may lobby to secure favorable policies. The sources of funding for lobbying may come from domestic sources or from abroad. In short, lobbying is about providing inputs to affect policy outputs. A lobbyist is a "person working to influence government policies and actions."[5] If that person takes action to change any of the myriad factors acting on foreign policy, he or she is engaged in some form of lobbying. The organization that employs such a person would be considered a "lobby," which under US law, influences "the passing or defeat of legislation."[6]

If we were to take the strictest forms of the above descriptions, we see that a pro-Arab lobby has always existed with domestic and foreign actors.[7] Its lobbying not only included attempts to whisper in the ears of policymakers, but contemporarily also involves putting pressure on them in less direct ways such as giving money during election seasons, telephone, email, and/or petition campaigns, influencing public opinion through newsletters, television or radio appearances, and so on.[8] While pro-Arab organizations have dedicated themselves to differing mission statements, their operatives engage in similar tasks. Their personnel spend time on Capitol Hill attending committee hearings and afterwards rubbing elbows with lawmakers. When they are not in Congress, they make use of telephone and facsimile communications to reach out to key members. These advocates focus on figuring out the "who's who" of the Washington policy establishment and target policymakers with their positions on issues of interest to the Arab American community and others that share its concerns. They seek to provide information to people in power with the hope of swaying their attitudes on legislation concerning their constituency. To do that, they have to gauge the political pulse of elected officials and their appointees in order to develop proper tactics for gaining influence. Often, the work of a lobbyist involves reaching out to and persuading congressional staffers that have increasingly become the eyes, ears, and sometimes even the ethical compass of politicians too busy to be involved in the minutia of drafting policies or assessing their outcomes.[9]

Although direct lobbying is essential to effectively shaping policy, pro-Arab leaders dedicate the majority of their time and resources to indirect means of pressure in order to represent the interests of the 1.2 million Americans of Arab ancestry.[10] Their staffs compose press releases, track policy dynamics, recruit donors, allies, and organizational members, while at the same time trying to act as the liaison between the Arab American community, its government, and the general public. One of the most important functions of pro-Arab representatives is to speak at civic forums in the hope of manipulating sentiment in favor of their preferences. This takes place not only through regular appearances at various media and institutional outlets throughout the country, but also by responding to phone calls and other electronic communiqués from parties interested in the standpoint of the Arab American community.[11] Pro-Arab personnel also engage in debates with opposing factions, particularly those representing pro-Israel interests, and provide data not readily accessible in the mainstream.[12]

The activities described above are simple examples of the complex principal occupations of foreign and domestic pro-Arab lobbying organizations. And while foreign lobbies run the gamut of interests from industry to charity on behalf of countries throughout the Middle East and North Africa, the *domestic* pro-Arab lobby will be the focus of this chapter since it is more overtly and methodically involved in trying to influence American policy on solutions to the Israeli–Palestinian conflict.[13] There are other good reasons for the analysis below. First, the understudied domestic pro-Arab lobby needs further inquiry, particularly after the two-state consensus. Aside from unifying Arab and Muslim Americans, the widely accepted two-state framework has brought US-based organizations that articulate their preference for a solution to the Israeli–Palestinian conflict more attention from government officials and the public.

Second, whereas AIPAC has been meticulously studied, there has been relatively little investigation of its opposition, based on ethno-national concerns for the Palestinians.[14] It is true that many interests in Washington have tried to offset the hegemony that AIPAC has had on US policy toward the Middle East. Those include religion-based organizations like Churches for Middle East Peace (CMEP), Muslim Public Affairs Council (MPAC), the National Council of Churches (NCC), and the Council on American-Islamic Relations (CAIR),[15] and industry groups such as the now defunct Arabian American Oil Company (ARAMCO).[16] While these organizations have done a tremendous amount of advocacy, none of them is as committed to the Arab American regard for the Palestinian question in the same way that AIPAC and its allies claim to be dedicated to Jewish American interest in Israel. The assessment that will occupy the rest of this chapter is needed considering that when asked about their foreign policy concerns, Arab and Jewish Americans overwhelmingly cite the Israeli–Palestinian conflict as the issue with which they most identify.[17] Accordingly, studying pressure groups acting on behalf of both people to address that conflict when they deal with American policy is of supreme necessity.

Third, US law restricts *direct* lobbying by foreign governments on policies towards themselves or their allies and besides, Americans generally do not feel comfortable with alien pressures on their policymakers. That is not to say that foreigners do not try to influence US policy. One only has to look at behind-the-scene meetings between various heads of state and American policymakers for examples of that. Since critical issues raised during such meetings often remain secret, there is no way to study them systematically except through memoirs written long after policy decisions have been made.[18] In comparison, there are plenty of ways to research the domestic elements of the pro-Arab lobby, including its public forums, electronic or otherwise, published paper material,[19] its financial contributions, and by conducting interviews.[20]

Using these resources, this chapter sets out on the following goals to examine the pro-Arab lobby. First, it will look at the genesis and nature of its support for the two-state solution. This is a critical issue since Arab American pressure has not always sought that solution to the Israeli–Palestinian conflict, particularly as conveyed by President George W. Bush's roadmap, where Israel would retain 78 percent of historic Palestine while the Palestinians would have their state on the remaining 22 percent. Accordingly, this chapter will look at the evolution of pro-Arab lobbying efforts regarding American policy toward resolving the Palestinian question in that manner. Second, it will consider the extent to which US policy shifted toward the two-state solution as a result of the pressure applied by pro-Arab voices, which will be analyzed in their public opinion and policymaker-oriented forms. While it is not possible to establish causality between that pressure by itself and its impacts on new policies, we may be able to investigate how lobbying helped to facilitate and solidify existing policy dispositions. Third, and most importantly, this chapter will look at the *potential* of the pro-Arab lobby in Beltway politics, now that American foreign policy corresponds to one of its chief aims, the two-state solution as outlined by US-sponsored United Nations Security Council (UNSC) resolutions and by the Bush roadmap, which called for "two states, Israel and Palestine, [to] live side by side in peace and security."[21] The chief issue here is how domestic and international factors interacted with the functions and capabilities of the pro-Arab lobby.

The aims of this chapter will correspond to their relevant timeframes from the decline of the Cold War to the wars on terrorism and in Iraq, the international phenomena examined by this book. Specifically, the pro-Arab lobby will be looked at through the following historical lens: throughout the development of the "strategic alliance" between Israel and the US after the 1981 "Memorandum of Understanding between the Government of the United States and the Government of Israel On Strategic Cooperation;"[22] during the Intifada (1987–93) and the first Gulf crisis (1990–91); around the end of the Cold War, particularly during the Madrid and Oslo peace negotiations (1991, 1993) and in the era of President Bill Clinton; and finally, during the war on terrorism and the toppling of Saddam Hussein's Ba'athist regime (2001–3 and beyond). Interviews with and observations by pro-Arab lobbying officials will guide the inquiry below.[23] They involved representatives of the following organizations: American-Arab Anti-Discrimination Committee (ADC), American Task Force on Palestine (ATFP), Arab American Institute (AAI), Hala Foundation, and the National Association of Arab Americans/Association of Arab American University Graduates (NAAA/AAUG).[24] In regards to American foreign policy, the collective purpose of these groups, particularly of the individuals representing them, has been to gain recognition for the following.

> Palestinians are a part of an international peace process represented by their leaders. They want to negotiate a just and lasting peace to the entire Middle East conflict. Palestinians want, more than anything else, to have what up until now they have been denied – the recognition that they are a people with the right to their own flag, passport, and elected government. They want peace and security and a permanent place in Palestine.[25]

For reasons that have been looked at elsewhere and will be further analyzed later, such recognition was categorically denied during the 1980s under Israel's strategic alliance with the US. That continued until the Cold War neared its end, when the US began to accept some principles of Palestinian aspirations as expressed by the Intifada and mediated by the domestic pro-Arab pressure groups.

Cold War lobbying

Losing the game

Former president of the NAAA Joseph Baroody once remarked,

> we can't represent the Arabs the way the Jewish lobby can represent Israel. The Israeli government has one policy to state, whereas we couldn't represent the "the Arabs" if we wanted to. They're as different as the Libyans and Saudis are different, or as divided as the Christian and Moslem Lebanese.[26]

This statement gave the dilemma of the pro-Arab lobby in a nutshell. Its divisions are exacerbated by the fact that it is up against some of the most successful interest groups in history, collectively known as the pro-Israel lobby.[27] While, as previously shown, the latter is highly structured, organized, financed, and united, the former suffers from weaknesses in the same qualities.[28] To get a sense of this poignant disparity, one only has to take a cursory glance at the difference in contributions made by the two sides. From 1990 until 2002, pro-Israel political action committees (PACs) gave a total of $48,985,897 to political candidates compared to only $296,830 contributed by all Arab and Muslim pressure groups *combined*.[29] Considering this staggering difference, there is no competition between the two sides in terms of who could give more money. Hence, when the two lobbies contend to influence policy in one way or another, the pro-Israel lobby has an undefeated record if we assume that economic clout engenders political power.

However, two features give the pro-Arab lobby some competitive strength. The first has always existed, while the second was born in the 1990s after the end of the Cold War and matured with the declaration of the roadmap during the war on terrorism. Turning to the first, although divided by nationality and religion, almost all Arab and Muslim Americans have some sympathy for the plight of the Palestinians. This led prominent Israeli professor Yossi Shain to point out, "indeed, given the diversity of the community – in terms of quasi-national homelands, religions, and ideological persuasions – the Palestinian cause could be said to have provided the very foundation for pan-Arab ethnic identity in America."[30] Still, not all Arab American leaders *actively* advocate on behalf of the Palestinians, although most of them inevitably declare their views in favor of a "just solution to the Middle East conflict."[31] Hence, to restate Baroody's position,[32] while the pro-Arab lobby cannot represent "the Arabs" as a united political group, it has been able to express something that they have had in common, concern for the Palestinians. Second, the pro-Arab lobby has developed much more potential than it possessed in the past, since its position that the Israeli–Palestinian conflict should be resolved through the two-state solution corresponds to official perceptions at the highest levels.

This was not always the case. Despite constant calls from pro-Arab groups for a shift in US policy toward an understanding of the Palestinian position, *elite* American support for the two-state solution was nonexistent for most of the Cold War period.[33] This was exacerbated by strife within the Arab American community. Well before the Reagan administration and the advancement of Israel's strategic relationship with the United States in the 1980s, something that gave the pro-Israel lobby more strength, "pro-Arab activity in the US has suffered from lack of direction."[34] Such a condition was the result of divergent opinions along ethno-national, ideological, and religious lines. The problems did not stop there. Several groups founded during the late 1960s and early to mid-1970s would cease to function only a couple of decades later. Groups like the NAAA or the Organization of Arab Students (OAS), for example, have become relics of the past. This was especially troubling in the case of the NAAA, instituted "to counter the effects of AIPAC on US politics, particularly at the congressional level."[35] And even though at its height in the 1970s that organization touted over 200,000 members committed to "persuade Congress to revise its overall commitment to Israel," its leadership conceded that it has "not been effective in changing Congressional sentiment on Middle East policy."[36]

There were other reasons for the lack of effectiveness and eventual demise of one of the most powerful Arab lobbying groups in Washington. First, during the height of the Cold War, public opinion viewed Arab Americans unfavorably particularly as many Arab states were perceived as enemies of the US special ally in the Middle East, Israel.[37] Second, and related to the first, the NAAA had to compete against established and well financed pro-Israel groups that worked in a hospitable atmosphere where policymakers agreed with their basic position that Israel ought to be America's priority. Furthermore, according to Beverley Milton-Edwards and Peter Hinchcliffe, political figures, particularly in the White House, understood that "given the powerful influence of the Zionist (pro-Israel) lobby in US domestic politics, it would be a bold or rash administration that took any action that might arouse its ire. Especially at election time!"[38] Third, during a time of persistent crises in the Middle East, the Arab American community and its leadership did not have a specific *and* accepted solution to bring to bear on the Israeli–Palestinian conflict. Instead, Arab American organizations were primarily starting out from the rudimentary place of reducing negative sentiments toward Arabs in the Middle East and in the US.[39] Only secondarily did they dedicate their energies to particular formulae such as land for peace in order to resolve the Arab–Israeli conflict in a fair manner consistent with US interests. All of these reasons for the failures of the pro-Arab lobby stem from a basic theorem of foreign policy analysis (FPA): when there is no basic perception or recognition of a lobby's goals on the policymaker level, there is little or no effective action to be taken.[40]

Reinventing the Palestinian question

During the 1980s, when Israel practically became a strategic part of US territory, at least in public opinion and elite perceptions, policymakers grew increasingly unsympathetic to the Palestinian question.[41] As far as they were concerned, there were no Palestinian *people* to deal with aside from the handful of terrorists that menace Israeli and American interests throughout the world. Even though it was a lobbying aim of Arab American groups, "land for peace" did not enter into policymakers' agenda in any meaningful way. Those that wavered on the status quo regarding Israel as a strategic ally were promptly castigated.[42] With nearly unconditional American support, Israel would only negotiate when it was ready to make peace, as it did before the 1978 Camp David Accords.[43] Hence, the agreement between Egypt and Israel would not have been possible without US pressure on Anwar al-Sadat at the behest of Menachem Begin.[44] While encouraging to the pro-Arab lobby, Camp David made Israel supporters very nervous since it signaled willingness on the part of the Arabs, the same people that supposedly wanted to "push Israel into the sea," to make peace.[45] Nevertheless, it was realized that so long as the Jewish state was a close friend of the United States against the Soviet Union, it did not have to negotiate with the Palestinians, a party much weaker than the Egyptians. Incentives for peace with the Palestinians were further diminished since Israel would have had to negotiate over "Judea and Samaria," lands ardently claimed by Zionists of various ideological persuasions.[46] This fact, as etched in American foreign policy and in the minds of elected officials, was the greatest obstacle to the Arab lobby persuading the US government of anything related to the Palestinians, whether it was seeking relief for refugees or favoring land for peace.

American policy toward the Israeli–Palestinian conflict during the 1980s had a lot do with "who maps its specific terrain as it moves along its historically determined coordinates."[47] Specifically, with the rise of Reagan and other hawkish elements to power, Israel followed the lead of its US ally and undertook military solutions to wider political problems. Focusing on how to better clamp down on the leadership of a restless population increasingly identified as terrorists, the Jewish state engaged in various campaigns to ratchet up its hegemony. The 1982 invasion of Lebanon demonstrated this quite well.[48] Israel aimed at annihilating the Palestinian leadership's existence in the region while its American ally was more than willing to help. Accordingly, it was under US military oversight that the head of the Palestinian resistance, Yasser Arafat, departed from Beirut along with his Palestine Liberation Organization (PLO) fighters. This instance showed that while Israel greatly benefited from American power, particularly from advanced weaponry systems and the US turning a blind eye to repeated violations of international laws governing the sovereignty of nation-states like Lebanon, it was also eager to help pursue the goal of eliminating Palestinian organizations from all positions in the Levant. This and other power plays of the 1980s by Israel and its ally made the task of charting a different path in American foreign policy more difficult. Pro-Arab lobbyists for the most part understood that this was the daunting task that lay ahead of them.

Israel's invasion of Lebanon, according to Hussein Ibish, gave Arab American groups a key opportunity to present the US public and policymakers a glimpse into the destructive nature of its occupation of Arab lands.[49] As the "Israelis were going nuts in Lebanon," Arab American leaders tried to discuss the inequality of power in the region.[50] Unlike the June 1967 war, a time prior to the existence of any significant presence by pro-Arab pressure groups, the Jewish state's invasion of Lebanon received attention that was more balanced. Even though, as discussed elsewhere, Israel was favored against the Arab countries in the American psyche, there was at least a voice given to Lebanese suffering as their major population centers were bombed. This was in no small part a key goal of Arab American organizations, which aired pleas for fairness during and after the invasion of Lebanon.[51] So while the public still supported Israel, its portrayal as a fragile protagonist going against a superior Arab foe began to be undermined by the reality on the ground in 1982 Lebanon. While the Arab lobby failed to reverse the course of popular sympathy or policymaker support for Israel, it still managed to present a clearer, albeit underdeveloped, picture of the inequitable situation in the Middle East.[52]

The Lebanon fiasco posed major problems for the Arab lobby as it unleashed divisions that plagued its constituency, particularly as the issues moved beyond the narrow Israeli–Palestinian conflict and into the wider Arab–Israeli conflict. Yvonne Yazbeck Haddad showed how these divisions manifested themselves in activities on Capitol Hill. Hence, whereas some groups called for American support of the Palestinians in Lebanon, others demanded that the US support the Israeli-backed Phalanges, a nationalist element very much opposed to the presence of the PLO in their country.[53] The cleavages discussed earlier by Baroody came into play at once in this specific instance, which split the Arab American community into various factions. From a broader perspective, the 1980s were indeed divisive. Hence, the failure of US policymakers to consider the Palestinian question, a point of unity for pro-Arab groups, meant that the schisms within their constituency were thrust into the forefront. Israel's strategic aims to "divide and conquer" moved beyond the Middle East and extended to Arab Americans, despite their ideological commonalities regarding Zionism and the Israeli–Palestinian conflict.[54]

In general, decisive hindrances overwhelmed Arab American groups during the 1980s. As outlined above, in addition to having to compete with powerful Zionist lobbies even as they were themselves divided, pro-Arab organizations had to overcome rampant impediments to their actions towards US policymakers and throughout the greater socio-political and cultural milieu. Helen Samhan put it best when in 1987 she wrote,

> while today's anti-Arab prejudice has many manifestations, it has not been encouraged by generalized societal prejudice, but by those, including a minority of pro-Israeli organizations and individuals, with the political motive of monopolizing the discussion of the contemporary Middle East in the United States. Especially in the realm of public information and public policy, it has been American Jewish campaigns to protect Israel – on either an organized or spontaneous basis – that have allowed anti-Arab prejudice to grow. For in many instances, protecting Israel has meant discrediting, delegitimizing, and silencing pro-Palestinian work in American schools, political bodies, and the mass media. These efforts have been far reaching enough for the civil liberties of some Arab Americans to be threatened; for acts of violence and harassment to be met with little outrage; and for the recurring exclusion of organized Arab American participation in the political process.[55]

Making a gloomy but accurate statement on the hardships faced by Arab Americans and their allies during the 1980s, Samhan cut to the root of the problem of pro-Arab lobbyists in the US: "political racism" buttressed by exclusion based on their commitment to the Palestinians.[56] The problems Arab Americans faced, however, did not stop at hostility toward their perspectives. They were also handicapped by apathy amongst their ranks when it came to activism. Throughout the history of the Arab American experience in the US, this was attributable to some factors that will only be mentioned here, including: the authoritarian nature of governments throughout the countries of the Middle East and North Africa from which they originated; the privileging in their community of economic achievement over politics, something that may be related to the first issue; the fact that, until the emergence of the likes of AAI and its "Yalla VOTE" campaigns, they had virtually "no vehicle by which to participate in the political process;"[57] and the feeling that they express views too diverse to be represented under a unified umbrella of political organizations.[58] These and other issues had to be overcome, at least on the perceptual level, if Arab Americans were to stand a chance of effectively influencing their government's policies. Their persistence, when combined with other problems discussed above, has proven disastrous for Arab American interests regarding the Israeli–Palestinian conflict in the 1980s. However, by the end of 1987, something changed in the occupied territories of the West Bank and Gaza as the Palestinians began resisting Israel's occupation en masse. What came to be known as the Intifada would not only alter the Israeli–Palestinian conflict, it also engendered a new American foreign policy terrain. This was very much welcomed and harnessed by pro-Arab activists in the United States.

A changing game

All representatives of the pro-Arab lobbying groups under examination supported the Palestinians' right to rebel against occupation as they did from December 1987 until September 1993. Their views regarding the effects of the Intifada on American foreign policy, however, differed. Khalil Jahshan noted, "the impact of the Intifada cannot be overestimated – it was the father and mother of the peace process, a single event that convinced all in the West that we need the two-state solution."[59] The Palestinian uprising indeed permanently changed the prevailing mindset on the conflict.[60] Pro-Arab advocates sought to convey Palestinian agony to an American audience and to use the imagery of resistance to Israeli occupation in order to call for changes in US support for policies that contributed to the Intifada. Writing for an ADC publication during its first year, Don Betz stated:

> in a significant way, the uprising has become a struggle of symbols and stereotypes. Carefully developed and solidly entrenched American perceptions of Israel as the besieged underdog, awash in a boundless sea of menacing Arab and Muslim fanaticism, as the only genuine democracy in that quadrant of the globe, have been challenged by nightly newscasts. The accepted image of an Israeli David bravely defending its existence and honor against a Palestinian and Arab Goliath is being eclipsed by recorded brutal Israeli Army and settler actions in the occupied territories. Empathetic renderings of Palestinians as the victims struggling for self-determination have highlighted both the Western and Israeli-left response to the Intifada.[61]

Propelled in that way to the front and center of the world's consciousness, the Intifada's effects were significant. Jahshan noted that the "Intifada forced the eventual recognition that a political process was necessary as there was no military solution to the Israeli–Palestinian conflict."[62] Furthermore, it would advance unity as the Palestinian struggle involved means and symbols that appealed to both the Arab American community and members of the resistance in the occupied territories.[63] By forcing the reevaluation of conventional wisdom on the Israeli–Palestinian conflict, the Intifada would lead to a permanent change in the approach toward the Middle East. For so long, American policymakers did not question the Israeli occupation over the Palestinians.[64] The Intifada pushed them to be more critical of their strategic ally.

Aside from challenging common perceptions and giving the Palestinians an effective form of collective resistance to Israeli occupation, the Intifada also offered pro-Arab lobbyists in the US new leverage. Hence, "AAI's 1988 campaign for political inclusion and a debate on U.S. Middle East policy was galvanized by the advent of the Palestinian Intifada."[65] Later on, this led Paul Findley to rejoice that the uprising engendered "the making of an American intifada."[66] Without a doubt, the Arab American lobby gained support from a wide constituency because of events in the West Bank and Gaza. Even AIPAC conceded, "we are being challenged. For the first time, anti-Israel forces have organized grassroots support. In the last year, their activity has increased at a rate that would have been unthinkable only a few years ago."[67] Not only did the Intifada strengthen pro-Arab organizations in a matter that caused AIPAC concern, it also created an opening for the opinions of Arab American leaders on the national scene. This space provided a counter-narrative to mainstream and elite support for Israel during a time when the Jewish state was the top priority for US Middle East policy.

Just as the uprising proved that the Palestinians would not be governed by Israel's military, in the US, it brought about increased calls for separate states. A 1988 publication distributed by the AAI led the chorus, when on the front page it demanded "PALESTINE: STATEHOOD NOW!" For most Arab American organizations, the Palestinians were no longer merely "a political problem" to be disposed of but rather a people that have just rights, which "America must come to know."[68] Without such knowledge a solution was not possible, especially when combined with the hard-line stance in favor of the Israelis and against the Palestinians. Pro-Arab groups not only demanded recognition for the Palestinian cause, but also of themselves as being a resource that Americans ought to be familiar with as part of the policy determination process. On numerous occasions, the Arab American lobby aligned its purposes with those of other institutions such as the National Association for the Advancement of Colored People (NAACP), the American Civil Liberties Union (ACLU) and other liberal leaning groups.[69] This was intended to reach across common ground with those organizations and to solidify support for diverse issues from upholding the civil rights of all citizens to extending them to other regions of the globe, particularly the Middle East. As the Intifada raged on, it brought out clear rights violations by an increasingly suppressive occupation.

Consequently, the Intifada helped sponsor policies that sought to offer the Palestinians some relief. For instance, Mary Rose Oakar, a former congress-woman and at the time of this writing, president of the ADC, stated that during the Intifada, she reached out to fellow lawmakers in hope of passing a motion regarding the closure of Palestinian schools by Israel. Oakar appealed to her colleagues by having them "imagine what would happen if American children could not attend their schools" because of mass forced closures.[70] This ultimately led to the authorization of a House resolution that called on Israel to allow schools to reopen.[71] Such an anecdotal example showed that policymakers would listen if they were able to identify with the struggle of the people most affected by their support for Israel.[72] To be sure, this was a minor victory for the pro-Arab side in the US Congress, but it did show a great deal of potential for incremental changes given the right amount of initiative under the proper circumstances. While it was true that American policymakers did not offer the Palestinians any respite outside of calling on Israel to show restraint, the uprising as put across by pro-Arab efforts in the US did plant seeds of change that would later begin to sprout under the appropriate conditions.

During the late 1980s and early 1990s, pro-Arab personnel sought attention for the Intifada by highlighting the unjustness of Israeli occupation not just among lawmakers, but also in the court of public opinion. According to Hussein Ibish, while the Intifada was the

> greatest single event since the founding of the PLO in 1964 to help revitalize the Palestinian identity, it also allowed Arab American groups to capture the symbols and iconography of the Israeli–Palestinian conflict, particularly as it related to the Israeli occupation.[73]

As a result the pro-Arab lobby, especially as represented by the ADC and AAI, became an agent of conveying to Americans the imagery of Palestinians as an unarmed people going up against the heavily armed Israel Defense Forces (IDF). Ibish noted, "this imagery was very effective in making policy arguments."[74] Hence, as newspapers and television screens gave the American public a daily dose of violence in the occupied territories, pro-Arab activists tried to translate what was taking place.[75] Such a position of interpreting the facts of Israeli occupation strengthened their hand in the debate on how to bring about peace in the Middle East. As the Intifada went through various stages by 1989, the Berlin Wall collapsed. This monumental event would lead to momentous changes in the Israeli–Palestinian conflict and gave new optimism to Arab American pressure groups, which were by that time highly involved in advocating for a *just* answer to the Palestinian question.

From the Persian Gulf to the end of the Cold War

Times of trouble, signs of hope

Although enjoying political momentum during the era of the Intifada and the undoing of the Eastern Bloc, the Arab American community suffered a serious setback in August of 1990. Iraq's invasion of Kuwait not only pitted Arabs in the Middle East against one another, it also forced their American kin to choose between two painfully opposed sides.[76] Hence, the Gulf crisis brought the following quandary: do Arab Americans choose the Kuwaiti side, tacitly supporting US action to expel Iraq through military force if necessary? Or do they accept the Iraqi invasion and agree to the illegal occupation and annexation of an Arab country?[77] Taking the Iraqi side would have been even more problematic since Arab Americans could not maintain consistency by condemning Israeli occupation while at the same time embracing the invasion of Kuwait. Conversely, taking Kuwait's side would have had severe consequences such as the decimation of Iraq, the cultural heartland of Arab and Muslim civilization, by overwhelming force. As we now know, irrespective of the position taken by the Arab American leadership, the US-led coalition did manage to remove Iraq from Kuwait. Most of Iraq's military capability was annihilated, as it was assaulted by far superior forces.[78]

After all was said and done, the majority of pro-Arab leaders joined the consensus against Iraq's invasion of Kuwait. However, they were not so quick to throw their support behind the US-led military coalition that included a large contingent of Arab states. This was due to Arab and Muslim American grassroots opposition to war. Still, their elites eventually had no choice but to go along with the actions of their country of allegiance, which began sending troops to Saudi Arabia in earnest shortly after Iraq's invasion. The pro-Arab leadership did not oppose those actions even though there was a glaring double standard of American policy, which immediately condemned and ruthlessly punished Iraq for violating the same UN conventions that Israel had been defying for twenty-seven years at the time of the Persian Gulf crisis. Repeatedly, Arab American groups were placed in an awkward spot. Reflecting on that, Jahshan noted that the Gulf War "was controversial for the community – it divided the Arab American community by exposing the strong nationalist feelings amongst its members."[79] Once again, this demonstrated that when it came to the larger Arab world, which existed outside of the Israeli–Palestinian conflict, divisions existed not only in the Middle East, but in the US as well. Opponents of war were pitted against backers of Kuwaiti sovereignty. That is why the pro-Arab leadership could not speak with a united voice, let alone try to present clear foreign policy planks before US officials.

Furthermore, Jahshan argued that the Gulf crisis presented his community with deep misgivings about political participation in the US. When policymakers committed soldiers in order to repel Iraq's aggression against its neighbors, a majority of constituents supported them.[80] Such popular sentiment gave the pro-Arab lobby a chief incentive to go along with the war. If it did not proffer some backing (or at least silence) toward US action in the Gulf, the people represented by it may have been seen as traitors by an already unsympathetic public. On the flipside, if Arab Americans supported action against Iraq, as they ultimately did, then it would have torn their unity asunder. That was precisely what happened. However, to soften the blow, the largest pro-Arab lobbying organization, the NAAA, at the time headed by Jahshan, gave in to the use of force while expressing "discomfort with war." Through this position, it tried to "keep its constituency happy" by not embracing war or acceding to Iraq's invasion of Kuwait.[81] In the process, however, the NAAA ended up satisfying no one. This was the chief reason behind its decline during the mid-1990s. Jahshan indicated that in addition to the Iraq debacle, the NAAA's ruin was attributable to suspicion by Arab Americans of lobbying, an institution built upon "compromises and corruption" and one that Israel supporters "were better at anyway."[82]

In the midst of the negative consequences that the Gulf crisis had on the Arab American community, there were positive developments as well. Rebecca Abou-Chedid, government relations and policy analyst for the AAI, emphasized that US action in the Gulf brought Americans goodwill from the Kuwaitis.[83] The liberation of their country demonstrated the superpower's resolve to "uphold international justice." However, while Kuwaitis held the US in high esteem, their sentiments did not extend to the Arab American community, which as shown above, split on whether their government ought to take action against Iraq. That was unforgivable to the Kuwaitis, particularly since they were significant patrons of various pro-Arab efforts in the US as well as reliable donors for the Palestinian cause. This would present problems for the Arab American leadership. A few years after the Gulf War, Shain summed up the pro-Arab lobby's troubles when he wrote about the uncertain position of two of its major actors. He stated, "AAI and NAAA, heavily dependent on Gulf connections, maneuvered uneasily between supporting U.S. intervention to restore the government of Kuwait and requiring American 'consistency' toward Israel and the Palestinians."[84] That was a tough place to be in for any advocacy leadership, let alone one marred by disagreements between its followers. In any case, consistency in American policy on Middle East affairs would not magically be waved into existence. It took a series of important events to get change favorable to pro-Arab groups in US foreign policy.

The outcome of the Iraq War brought a key development in that it strengthened American credibility in the Gulf and throughout the world.[85] In many circles, the US was seen as a benevolent actor interested in protecting the security of others. Hence, American power expelled an aggressor country from a considerably weaker neighbor. Meanwhile, according to Ibish, the Gulf War brought attention to the Middle East as a whole, something into which pro-Arab groups understood they had to tap.[86] In conjunction with efforts to link Iraq's invasion to Israeli occupation, the American public began to acquire a better grasp of the totality of the troubled region's affairs. Likewise, giddy about their success in the Persian Gulf, US policymakers felt a renewed sense of effectiveness in global politics, a feeling that would be tremendously enhanced by the beginning of the end of the Soviet Union. However, appreciating the still important role of that rival, the Bush administration took the initiative to call on its counterpart in Moscow to invite various antagonistic parties in the Middle East to Madrid, Spain.

As the Intifada entered its fourth year and by the time the Madrid invitations reached their recipients, the pro-Arab lobby began to take on new life in the aftermath of the Gulf crisis.[87] Talks between Israel and its neighbors involved a great deal of participation by Arab American leaders. Such involvement in the peace process "showed them to be respectable and not terrorists."[88] It was at Madrid that Arab states and Israel met to discuss the possibility of coexistence through future diplomatic engagement. The Arab American community was divided over the negotiations. Some, like AAI president James Zogby, welcomed them while many others were suspicious of peace talks perceived to be stacked so heavily in favor of Israel. For example, Marvin Wingfield, at the time director of education and outreach at ADC, indicated that his organization expressed a "sentiment of suspicion because the negotiations were too open ended and constantly deferred the most central issues to 'final status' negotiations."[89] Still, there was a good deal of support for the pursuit of peace. Against Madrid's critics and in defense of President George Bush's Strategic Peace Initiative Package (SPIP), the groundwork for a future peace process between Israel and its neighbors, Zogby put forth the following.

> To the Israelis, it would offer specific and detailed commitments of international security guarantees, economic cooperation, defense assistance, normalization of relations with the Arab states, and funds for economic development. All would be conditioned, however, on Israel's commitment to withdrawal from the occupied West Bank and Gaza Strip. To the Palestinians, the SPIP would offer, similarly, commitments of independence with international security guarantees, the ability to reunite and reconstruct their national community, economic development assistance, and recognition of their statehood. But they would first have to agree to a phased plan of implementation leading to final-status negotiation with the Israelis.[90]

Although "final status" never came to fruition, the Madrid conference proceeded in some of the ways outlined above. Talks commenced with a number of Arab Americans assisting the various parties. The basic framework of negotiations rested on UNSC resolutions 242 and 338. The invitation to Madrid outlined an interim self-government for the Palestinians.[91] As the conference came to a close, a new reality began to emerge that would forever change the international order: the collapse of the Soviet Union. In addition to the Madrid negotiations, advocates for peace in and out of the Arab American community used this development to pressure US policy toward giving the Palestinians some level of autonomy.

Nearly all pro-Arab lobbyists agreed that the Cold War greatly harmed their interests in the Middle East. Most believed that its end only brought good fortune to the organizations they represented. Jahshan, for instance, lamented the fact that Arab Americans as well as their countries of origin were on the defensive during the Cold War. This was the result of being identified as sympathetic to the communists, especially as Israel was increasingly acknowledged during the Cold War as a staunch American ally by public opinion and policymakers.[92] Events on the world stage confirmed this perception. In the UN, for example, the Soviet Union often took the

Arab side while Israel was supported by the US. Jahshan expressed optimism because the end of the Cold War had brought about a structural change that "no longer forced Arabs into either one corner or the other."[93] It also allowed the US "to focus on small regional conflicts" instead of keeping an eye on its archrival's global activities.[94] This alone gave the pro-Arab voice a better position to be heard since it was no longer drowned out by the deafening cacophony of the East–West rivalry. According to Abou-Chedid, the US could reduce its blanket support of Israel in order to combat the Soviet Union since the "chess game" between the two Cold warriors had ended.[95]

Without a doubt, the end of the Cold War signaled a move beyond the clash of ideology in favor of a new focus. Arab American groups tried to take advantage of that. Christine Gleichert, a Capitol Hill operative of the ADC, saw opportunity since "geographic interests became more varied and the emphasis on ethnic group conflict became more pronounced."[96] Her organization benefited from this shift because the Israeli–Palestinian conflict, one of the ADC's most pressing foreign engagement concerns, would receive more attention from American policymakers who sought a new mission for the US since it no longer was squarely dedicated to combating communism by keeping the Soviet Union in check. Mary Rose Oakar seconded Gleichert's view, adding that Palestinian and Arab Americans in general after the end of the Cold War "would be viewed on their own merits," as opposed to being looked at "as pawns in an ideological rivalry."[97] Likewise, the Palestinian struggle against occupation could no longer be construed as a rebellion against an anti-Soviet US ally. Subsequently, as Rafi Dajani put it, "the end of the Cold War made it easier for the interest of resolving the Israeli–Palestinian conflict to be realized."[98] Hence, what started out as an "American Intifada" of lobbying efforts during the late 1980s and first two years of the 1990s, mirroring the Palestinian uprising in the occupied territories, after the end of the Cold War grew into a productive venture to influence US policy toward a tangible solution to one of the oldest conflicts in history.

During that time, American foreign policy elites began to reckon with a path toward peace in the Middle East that was preferred by the pro-Arab lobby. In the summer of 1992, an issue of *Nota Bene*, a publication of the AAI, celebrated the changing of President Bush's stance on the Israeli–Palestinian conflict by noting

> no American administration has managed to utter the words "Palestinian statehood," but George Bush came about as close as any President before or since Carter in an interview with Middle East Insight. Asked to give his vision of what a Middle East peace might look like, Bush Responded: I'd like to see an area where people come and go in peace, where there is no economic boycott, where people discuss their problems one-on-one; *where the Palestinians are accorded recognition and right of existence, with some designated place to be;*

where Israel's real security demands are guaranteed, not by arms, but by peace agreements.[99]

There was indeed reason to commemorate President Bush's observations, since like other lobbies, pro-Arab groups could only operate within the political parameters outlined by policymakers who themselves have to work inside boundaries set forth by public opinion or risk losing their seats.[100] For an American president to come out and state his support not only for Israel's security but also for the necessity of recognizing Palestinians' national rights was significant, particularly as their existence as a people was dwarfed during the era of the strategic relationship between the US and Israel in the 1980s. Moreover, this provided Arab American organizations more relevance as they proclaimed that their foreign policy goals were not only legitimate, but were also reflected by top officials. On this, Ibish remarked that the pro-Arab lobby wanted to help the US "government get where it was toward the principle of self-determination for the Palestinians in the post-Cold War Madrid era."[101] Zogby added that although "there was a lot of frustration with the peace process, it facilitated the means by which Arab Americans and our friends could weigh in on its outcomes."[102]

While pro-Arab groups experienced great leaps in American policy toward the Israeli–Palestinian conflict after Madrid and the end of the Cold War, there were many pitfalls.[103] Reflecting the growing disunity among their domestic base and between Arab states, some Arab American organizations began fragmenting as their memberships dwindled. Moreover, fallout from the Gulf crisis forced patron states to cut funding to organizations that would have had a unique occasion to influence US policy in the wake of the Madrid peace process and the disintegration of the Eastern Bloc. Exacerbating matters further, what little unity the Arab American community enjoyed in the past had deteriorated, thanks to "the Persian Gulf crisis and to America's foreign policy in the Middle East," which maintained steadfast support for Israel even after the end of the Cold War.[104] However, not all hope was lost for the pro-Arab lobby. By 1993, a newly elected president would capitalize on the gains made previously at Madrid under the direction of his predecessor.[105]

Oslo's impacts

Bill Clinton's efforts at peace through the Oslo meetings signaled another opportunity for the pro-Arab lobby in the United States, particularly concerning the fulfillment of some Palestinian rights. The challenge was to hold Clinton to his pre-Oslo position: "to broaden the circle of peace, recognizing the principles that underlie the peace process: territory for peace, realization of the legitimate rights of the Palestinian people, security for all parties, and full and real peace."[106] Despite that rhetoric, Clinton owed a debt to pro-Israel forces, which were partially responsible for the success of his presidential campaign. Furthermore, the pro-Arab lobby had to compete with Zionist pressure from within the Clinton administration, which had several notable individuals disposed toward the Jewish state, including former US ambassador to Israel Martin Indyk, who was assigned the role of principal advisor to the president on Arab–Israeli issues at the National Security Council. All of this meant that the new phase of peace talks under Clinton's watch favored Israel's security while neglecting the Palestinians. Attempting to alleviate the negative impacts of that, in April 1993, the AAI reported, "after Clinton's election, Arabs and Arab Americans sought to persuade the Administration to repeat [the principles of Palestinian rights] – to reaffirm what had in effect become the Madrid ground rules."[107] And even though he tried to heed that advice, Oslo would have many snags for US evenhandedness, as Clinton was beholden to his electoral benefactors and advisors.

Despite being riddled with hazards, the Oslo period brought American policy closer to facilitating peace between Israel and the Palestinians than ever before as the Declaration of Principles (DOP) outlined a solution.[108] After endorsing that agreement, Israeli Prime Minister Yitzhak Rabin and PLO chairman Yasser Arafat shook hands and the DOP became known as "the handshake" in the parlance of the peace process. President Clinton referred to the agreement between Israelis and Palestinians as the "peace of the brave," which he believed was "within our reach."[109] There was indeed reason for that type of jubilation. For the first time in their history, the Palestinians had gained recognition by the Israelis as a people worthy of self-government.[110] American policy after Madrid was both a catalyst and an expression of that fact, something that would have been unimaginable during the 1980s. Optimism gripped most Arab American pressure groups, many of which were represented at the White House on September 13, 1993. Reflecting on that historic event, Zogby stated "it is significant that Arab Americans were considered a vital part of [the Oslo process]," adding

> we have been working for years to assist our friends and families in the Middle East by trying to foster an honest and fair debate in the United States about the issues facing the region. This day is especially gratifying for those of us who have supported Palestinian statehood in this country because we believe statehood will be the ultimate outcome of this agreement.[111]

However, caution tamed Zogby's buoyancy, as expressed by his pro-Arab cohort.

While Jahshan looked at the handshake as the fulfillment of the Palestinian wish to have a state of their own that recognized Israel on its borders, he took issue with the agreement.[112] "How to get to genuine Palestinian self-government" was a major concern since the DOP was not specific on the concrete results of peace. Particularly vexing was the scope of

Palestinian sovereignty. Would the Palestinian government "assume only bureaucratic functions or would its role be that of a fully functioning state?"[113] Despite these issues, as far as the Arab American lobby was concerned, the DOP allowed better access to the highest levels of the US government. Helen Samhan pondered the occasion with the following.

> As we sat on the White House Lawn, we were very encouraged. It was very interesting that after years at the AAI, the dark cloud above our heads had lifted. Jim [James Zogby] and I believed that this was a turn-around for Arab Americans. We had the opportunity not to be interpreted by our adversaries but rather to represent ourselves. We were no longer untouchables in Washington and our cause was elevated to new heights. Our support of the Palestinians was no longer taboo, there was the understanding that Palestinians have rights and us supporting those rights was no longer viewed as dangerous support of terrorists. Our statehood plank was actually coming into being that day. Arab American groups were treated equally to the pro-Israel groups. We were given equal billing when, for so long, we used to be so unwelcome. After the Oslo peace process, we were actually invited to weigh in on issues having to do with the Palestinians and American foreign policy.[114]

Hence, as American policymakers adopted a more cordial position toward Palestinian aspirations, there was a correlative warming up to groups like the AAI. This suggests that regardless of whether Arab American lobbyists were responsible for *causing* changes in elite perceptions before or after the end of the Cold War, once US energies were dedicated to bringing about peace, they were in a better position to influence policy by adding their voice to an issue with majority public opinion resonance.[115] This was a drastic change from the 1980s when Arab American organizations were shunned in US politics toward the Middle East.

Nevertheless, while most pro-Arab lobbyists were optimistic about the handshake, not everyone was convinced of its value. Nabil Mohamad, organizing director of the ADC, looked at it as another divisive issue for Arab Americans.[116] This was because Oslo's position on the two-state solution was never made clear, except to say that the Palestinians would have an "Interim Self-Government Authority" and an "elected Council" to represent the people of the West Bank and Gaza.[117] Such an arrangement did not engender a Palestinian state. Furthermore, reflecting the opinions of other Arab American leaders, Mohamad observed, "the Oslo negotiations deferred all issues of permanent settlement to some undefined period in the future." This led Palestinian-American scholar Edward Said to remark "those of us who criticized [Oslo] from the start were a tiny minority of Arabs and Jews who grasped its ungenerous, essentially humiliating implications for the Palestinian people."[118] To be sure, Said felt reservations about Oslo since the very beginning. As early as October 1993, he wrote in an AAI publication that the "historical breakthrough" announced recently by the P.L.O. and the Israeli government is a joint decision to signal a new phase of reconciliation between two enemies, but it also leaves Palestinians very much the subordinates, with Israeli [sic] still in charge of East Jerusalem, settlements, sovereignty and the economy.[119]

These issues not only troubled Said but they also affected the Arab American community, as many did not know whether the peace process was a victory or mere capitulation after years of attrition.

From the analysis above, we see that the domestic impacts of the Oslo peace process were threefold. First, it splintered the pro-Arab alliance on the Palestinian issue. There were strong reservations about the nature of peace offered by the handshake. For critics like Said, there was no peace without some concrete and *immediate* relief for and recognition of the Palestinians as a national community deserving of a state.[120] Since such moves were delayed until "final status," the peace process raised many eyebrows. Second, Oslo forced the Palestinians to settle for a small fraction of their ancestral land. This was not something that Arab Americans were onboard with since it meant the end of a dream to reclaim a significant Palestinian homeland in more than just the West Bank and Gaza. Third, Oslo signified a *near* waiver of rights by the PLO leadership on behalf of Palestinians living outside of the West Bank, and Gaza. This was scorned since the refugee issue has been a serious one for the Arab American community and promoters of a comprehensive solution to the Israeli–Palestinian conflict.[121]

Still, the handshake and the ensuing peace process did promote key aims of the pro-Arab lobby. According to Dajani,

> the handshake cemented the idea of a Palestinian nationality and Palestinian nation in the US. It also started people thinking that a Palestinian state was necessary for peace in the Middle East and made it easier in Washington to talk about Palestine and Palestinians in humanizing ways.[122]

No longer were advocates on behalf of the Palestinian cause ignored, they were instead listened to by policymakers and the general public alike.[123] More important than the salutary effect it had on the position of the pro-Arab lobby, Oslo laid the foundation for the two-state solution, an objective not explicitly pursued when negotiations began. Pro-Arab lobbyists were advocating for any solution in vain throughout most of the 1980s when they were throwing their weight behind the land for peace framework. For instance, as early as 1978, Zogby advocated a Palestinian state but "was flatly denied because land for peace lacked support."[124] During the early 1990s, land for peace was not only on the table, it also seemed within reach of implementation as Israelis and Palestinians were setting aside animosity in favor of negotiations. Just as that signaled the end of Israel solely defining the conflict for American audiences, its lobbyists no longer enjoyed unmatched control over the stream of information about the Palestinians. Pro-Arab groups found a niche in US policy because they and the Palestinians on whose behalf they were lobbying were now a basic part of the approach to the Middle East. This was in stark contrast to the early to mid-1980s when the very mention of the Palestinians in Washington was construed as an assault against the strategic alliance between the US and Israel.

In addition to giving them a place at the table of US foreign policy making, Oslo reinvigorated support for pro-Arab lobbyists from a wide variety of actors in civil society, as evidenced by their alliance with moderate Christian leaders.[125] For instance, in a 1995 position, William H. Keeler, president of the National Council of Catholic Bishops, warned of issues that may derail the peace process, including

- Israel's expropriation of Palestinian land.
- Israel's plans for a "Greater Jerusalem."
- Israel's implicit claim to exclusive sovereignty over Jerusalem
- Recent U.S. hedging over the issue of East Jerusalem, which previous administrations have considered occupied territory subject to UN Security Council Resolution 242 and total Israeli withdrawal.
- The failure of U.S. policy to recognize and support Palestinian rights and interests in Jerusalem.[126]

By raising those concerns, Keeler placed himself in the same camp as pro-Arab groups that were protesting similar Israeli violations, which extended well beyond Jerusalem to include the whole of the occupied territories. Other examples of pro-Arab alliances exist after Oslo but will only be noted here.[127]

As the pro-Arab lobby's presence strengthened, new strategies were developed for communicating with policymakers and the public. Ibish stated that "in advocacy, we have pioneered a new style of talking about the" Israeli–Palestinian conflict.

> First, we frame the conflict first and foremost around the American national interest – around framed policy or national interests as defined by the foreign policy establishment in favor of national security. We do not dwell on morality alone, but rather talk about real interests. Second, we try to communicate those interests to policymakers and have had quite a bit of success doing that. We do not only limit our focus to Americans and their policymakers but also expand it to include Israeli and Palestinian leaders – to convince all of them that it is in their best interests to make peace. ... Third, we communicate with the public. We think of ourselves as advocates for the national interests, for our interests as Americans, and inform the public about these interests. Even if policymakers did not agree with us, we would pursue this three-part strategy. Since they do, it makes our work easier.[128]

The understanding that peace was in the interest of all parties concerned could not have become so pedestrian had the political procedure to bring it about not taken place. Hence, Oslo made the task of Arab lobbying, if not easier, then definitely more straightforward. After all, most Americans knew that it was in their national interest to have Palestinian self-determination; the question then was how to help bring it about? As a matter of course, in the domestic arena, pro-Arab lobbyists have always emphasized "the patriotic nature" of their advocacy for Palestinian self-rule.[129] Accordingly, Ibish noted that Arab Americans have come to know that prompting their government on that issue is part of their "civic responsibility."[130] This viewpoint and the strategy outlined above were only possible because the US helped mediate the peace process during the Oslo period as a central part of its interest in the Middle East.

While Oslo allowed the pro-Arab lobby to strengthen not only in its message and tactics, but also by forming notable alliances with likeminded groups, the biggest threat to its prescription for peace was the way in which the issue of terrorism was used by pro-Israel organizations. AAI captured the burden placed on the Palestinian Authority (PA) in the following manner: by asking Arafat to use extremely repressive measures to crack down on terrorism, the Israeli government and its supporters in Washington were violating the "intent of the" Oslo "Declaration" which sought to create a "democratic Palestinian entity" on the West Bank and Gaza Strip. In many ways, what was really going on was that Israel and the US have been encouraging "the kind of police state that they criticize other Arab nations for." This created a situation in which the PA was caught between a "rock and a hard place."[131] Thus, if it cracked down on terrorism by violating human rights, the PA would satisfy Israeli and American desires in one sense while breaching the Oslo Accords – not to mention international conventions – in another. This was an issue that became more acute after the commencement of America's (and Israel's) war on terrorism, as will be discussed later.

Lobbying for peace

Against the mounting tide of rhetoric on terrorism and its state sponsors by Zionist groups, media outlets, and policymakers, pro-Arab lobbyists from all sides of the ideological spectrum agreed on the significance of Oslo and on the need for the Palestinians to have a state at the end of the road. This was the remedy of choice to counter the illegitimate use of violence by factions opposed to the occupation.[132] During the peace process of the 1990s, each pro-Arab organization pursued favorable policy through various means. Jahshan indicated that the NAAA understood the "delicate nature of American policy." On the one hand, it had to look for cues from policymaker preferences. On the other, "with most policymakers siding with Israel, such a task was not easy."[133] An effective strategy discussed by Jahshan was pursuing the two-state solution as something in the joint interests of the Jewish state and the US. This reasoning was built upon the following propositions: "if the US wished to support Israel, and Israel wanted to maintain itself for Jews, then something had to be done with the Palestinians." Although, as shown earlier, during the Cold War, the alliance between Israel and the US was defined as a strategic relationship in opposition to the Soviet Union, the collapse of communism and the forging of the Oslo agreements allowed space for American–Israeli interests to be defined differently, something that the pro-Arab lobby appreciated. Hence, for Jahshan and his organization, the way to influence American foreign policy was to "redefine what was already there." The US was no longer interested in Israel as a Cold War ally, but in the aftermath of the Gulf War and the Madrid peace talks, the Jewish state was expected to uphold stability in a region of instability. The only way to bring that about would be to resolve the Palestinian question and the general Arab–Israeli conflict by starting with the land for peace principle and ending with the two-state solution.[134]

This solution's inception in the post-Cold War peace process meant that the pro-Arab lobby could better focus its efforts on US policy toward the Palestinians. "Arab Americans were in the spotlight of US policymakers as negotiations were taking place under Clinton's statesmanship," which offered members of their leadership more potential for influence.[135] Their aim, as Samhan and others put it, was to ensure that President Clinton was living up to his self-proclaimed "honest broker" position.[136] If there was to be peace at all, reasoned pro-Arab lobbyists, it could only happen once the US dedicated its diplomatic energy in an evenhanded way.[137] Indeed, it was realized, now that the "fig leaf" of the Cold War was lifted and policymakers turned toward resolving troublespots throughout the world, the US could take "more risks" since there was the absence of any viable ideological or military rivalry with another superpower.[138] Arab lobbyists movingly argued that such risks could have paid significant dividends to American self-interest. According to Abou-Chedid, the US has always had the potential to be viewed as a positive force in bringing peace if it were able to "remain engaged in an honest and fair manner."[139] In order to try to convince policymakers of that, pro-Arab lobbyists engaged in all sorts of activity from letter-writing campaigns to publishing talking points to making a presence in the media.[140]

Additionally, pro-Arab groups pursued a strategy of capitalizing on divisions created by Oslo within the lines of pro-Israel elements, which were based on disagreements within the Jewish state about pursuing peace with the Palestinians. For instance, the AAI highlighted differences between Israel's two main political parties at the time. In 1995, it reported "for the first time in the post-'67 era, there is open political warfare over Middle East issues in Washington; but the sides are not Arab and Jewish – they are U.S. supporters of Israel's Labor and Likud parties."[141] Quarrels arose between the two sides over what Israel was willing to "give up" from its 1967 conquest of Palestinian lands. The dispute over those concessions dated back to 1992 when the conservative "Likud refused to concede defeat and function in the role of loyal opposition" to the left of center Labor government. After Madrid's completion, members of the ousted Likud party feared that the new cabinet, headed by Labor Prime Minister Yitzhak Rabin would compromise too much security for peace.[142] Consequently, issues that could not be settled in Tel Aviv were taken to Washington, the town in which the principal broker for peace resided. Supporters of Likud and Labor alike were arguing that their positions were closer to the interests of both Israel and the US. Seeing that, Arab lobbyists entered the ring and tried to exploit pro-Israel differences by advancing their own agenda for American policy, arguing that *they* were acting in the best interests of the United States, which were based on the creation of a "democratic, secular, and viable Palestinian state."[143]

In this regard, pro-Arab groups were no different from other lobbying organizations, which always maintain that their policy planks are in the national interest. From her daily experience on Capitol Hill, Gleichert observed, "the US has to understand the profound impact that [its] policies have on the entire Middle East."[144] Such an understanding would benefit not just people in the region but it would also "help out Arab Americans who suffer from negative perceptions in the US."[145] This is because misguided US policy frequently results in backlash abroad, which is often conveyed to policymakers and their constituents.[146] At that point, Arab Americans and others sharing their affinity are lumped together with those reacting to the US posture on the issue at hand, from the Arab–Israeli conflict and the war in Iraq to the negative depiction of the prophet Muhammad by a Danish cartoonist, to give a few examples.[147] If US policymakers were to acknowledge the pro-Arab points of view on these and other issues, some have argued that policies which inspired anti-American actions would greatly subside, and in turn, negative perception toward Americans of Arab/Muslim origins would diminish with them.[148]

The discussion above demonstrates the clear intersection between foreign policy and domestic attitudes toward those represented by pro-Arab groups. It shows that none of them is able to dedicate its energies solely to the domestic front, but by its very nature, has to try influencing foreign policy, something that has been known all along by seasoned advocates.[149] Although pro-Arab organizations have seen mixed results in *changing* policy, they have been able to pin down the character of the American outlook toward the Middle East and to channel it in ways that maximize their positions and those of their supporters.[150] In the post-Oslo period, American policy was dedicated to finding a solution to the perennial Middle East conflict by bringing both sides to the negotiating table. To do that, the US had to step away from its unfettered support of Israel and recognize the Palestinians' existence as a national community. And even though American policy will forever be criticized for leaning so heavily in favor of Israel, no one can deny the fact that during the post-Oslo period of the 1990s, Palestinians enjoyed recognition in ways unimaginable just ten years earlier.[151] This went so far as to allow the Palestinians a high degree of control over their own affairs.

What did such recognition have to do with international events, particularly the Intifada, the Gulf War, and the end of the Cold War? How did these developments impact domestic efforts to influence American foreign policy? The pro-Arab lobby acted like a recipient and translator of global developments. Although it has a legendary pro-Israel rival, from the late 1980s through the 1990s, it served as a conduit for a message sympathetic to a Palestinian homeland during times of upheaval and change. Later on, the pro-Arab lobby would nourish the seeds of Palestinian sovereignty to such an extent that by the time of George W. Bush's presidency and the 9/11 attacks, the roadmap emerged and *unequivocally* called for the unimaginable, a Palestinian state that exists alongside Israel as part of the official US strategy toward the Middle East. This was not something that any other American administration was ever able to offer the Palestinians. It was an opportunity that would – and should in the future – be seized upon by pro-Arab groups and all others interested in peace.[152]

The pro-Arab lobby in the war on terrorism

Tragedy strikes

By September 11, 2001, many had already declared "the end of the peace process."[153] The Palestinians were undergoing their second year of uprising in the Al-Aqsa Intifada, which started while President Clinton was still in office. After the failure of numerous efforts at peace, the Israeli–Palestinian conflict proved itself unsolvable under the Oslo framework. "Limited autonomy" meant that the Palestinians still had to live under Israeli occupation while the deadline for "final status" had come and gone. One of the principal grievances that al Qa'eda leveled against the United States was the plight of the Palestinians, which in addition to the occupation of Muslim lands by American troops, were among the stated reasons behind 9/11.[154] In the aftermath of the attacks, the affairs of Arab Americans were worsening by the day. On the one hand, they had to prove themselves loyal citizens of their country, while on the other had to assert the justness of their cause regarding the Palestinians, something that international terrorists like Osama bin-Laden claimed as their own. This was an awkward situation for the Arab American leadership. Its lot in many ways seemed worse than it had been during the 1980s.

After 9/11, pro-Arab organizations were swamped with issues that made it nearly impossible for them to focus on lobbying for the facilitation of peace between Israelis and Palestinians. The gains they made over the years were unraveling as everywhere Muslims and Arabs were targeted in what some have viewed as terrorist witch-hunts.[155] Arab American leaders hunkered down in preparation for physical and legal attacks on their community. Their primary concern was the defense of civil liberties.[156] For example, in a press release from its annual convention in 2002, the ADC outlined its objective of "protecting the civil rights and liberties of people of Arab descent, and promoting their interests and concerns" in the "post-September 11 era."[157] Although the organization also advocated "for the rights of the Palestinian people to freedom, equality and self-determination," domestic rights abuses had overwhelmed that goal. To bring attention to them, the ADC had to profess the patriotism of its constituents while pleading for temperance of widespread anger.[158]

With the problems involving their community, most pro-Arab lobbyists tried to seize on the events of 9/11 by articulating moderate perspectives to counter the ones championed by fanatical organizations in the Arab and Muslim parts of the world. According to Rafi Dajani,

> the war against terrorism is a time when we have to remember an important thing. It's an established fact, as numerous surveys have shown, that the issue of Palestine is the number one issue of concern. Since it has been taken up and manipulated by extremists because they know how important it is, resolving the issue is one less tool to recruit or rally people. Resolving it would remove one of the major irritants between Arab/Islamic relations with the United States. We have to remember that if the war on terrorism is also a war to bring democracy, the two-state solution is the way to go. Palestinians have proven themselves capable democrats; their three elections are truly exceptional by Middle East and even world standards. They had three of the fairest elections, even under occupation. A Palestinian state is a prime candidate for being a model for democracy in the Middle East. It would truly serve the stated American interest of bringing democracy to the Middle East.[159]

This position by the former executive director of the ATFP, however, makes assumptions that demand further investigation. It assumes that al Qa'eda is interested in the Palestinian question on its own merits. More importantly, it takes the American narrative of bringing democracy to others seriously. If that was the main aim of the war on terrorism, as had been indicated on several occasions,[160] then the outcome of a Palestinian state as espoused by Arab groups could definitely be worthwhile for policymakers since it would end Israeli occupation and allow a people to rule itself. Nonetheless, such reasoning is precisely what makes advocates like Dajani good at what they do. They take existing expressions of national interest and try to channel them towards their own goals.[161] In this case, the ATFP wants to see an end to conflict through the two-state solution and given the democratic nature of Palestinian politics, such a goal would assist efforts in fighting the war on terrorism. This conceptualization, however, is built upon assumptions that may prove unsustainable. If the US truly respected democracy, then the Hamas victory would not have been such a watershed for the Palestinians. Under such conditions, perhaps Arab American organizations need to humble their mission a bit concerning the two-state solution.

Countering the pro-Israel lobby

Or should they? After all, Bush's roadmap to peace has given the pro-Arab lobby something that most other lobbies could only dream of, *explicit* elite support for their most treasured foreign policy agenda.[162] Such endorsement significantly strengthens a lobby's position. According to Tony Smith, an interest group "becomes a seriously viable political force only when it has an organization whose chief purpose is to influence decisionmakers to adopt policies favorable to the group's interests."[163] As demonstrated by the road-map, US policymakers had already taken up the two-state solution, a policy favorable to Arab American interests. This made pro-Arab lobbying much easier since it directed American diplomacy toward "bringing about a pro-cess for the realization of a Palestinian state."[164] Hence, those interested in that cause simply have to apply pressure in order to accomplish objectives shared by public opinion and policymakers. For the pro-Arab lobby as a whole, this means that it would have to utilize its personnel and resources to hold policymakers to their promise, something clearly in the public interest. The issue, however, is not that simple. It has been demonstrated that the pro-Arab lobby's adversary has Congress in a near vice grip.[165] According to Josh Block of AIPAC, trying to convince Congress of Israel's position "is like pushing at an open door."[166] What was meant by this statement is that since lawmakers share AIPAC's views on many issues concerning Israel, it is easy to work with them in order to pass legislation reaffirming agreement between the two sides. In addition, it is well known that since public opinion tends to favor the Jewish state, Congress members have very little to lose politically by supporting it even against the stated goal of bringing about a Palestinian state. As shown in the last chapter, those that would dissent from toeing the line of what is defined as Israel's security interests suffer harsh consequences.

The strength of the pro-Israel lobby in Congress, however, does not preclude pro-Arab advocates from getting more traction in that body. What needs to be done there as well as in the executive branch is already stated policy, the two-state solution as outlined by the roadmap. In the event that competing with AIPAC becomes difficult at the congressional level, particu-larly concerning other Middle East issues, the pro-Arab lobby could simply inquire into the status of the roadmap. This approach to influencing policy is a powerful tool for several reasons that overlap with what has already been discussed. First, "it allows the pro-Arab lobby a visibility that was not pos-sible in the past."[167] This may be used to articulate specific viewpoints surrounding the two-state solution, such as what a Palestinian state may look like.[168] Second, the roadmap makes access to government officials much easier. Hence, if the Palestinians were to have a state, there would have to be an understanding with policymakers about what is required of it. This is where the Arab American leadership may potentially serve as a liaison between the PA and the US government in much the same way that AIPAC and other pro-Israel groups work on behalf of the Jewish state. Third, "the roadmap allows for a clear path to peace that has incremental steps."[169] Along the way, the pro-Arab lobby has the ability to define those steps as it sees fit.

But even before the roadmap, increases in the Arab and Muslim American population as well as improved contact with their government have allowed a more level playing field, leading some to announce that the "pro-Arab lobby" is "gaining in strength."[170] This has been the case even though since the beginning of the war on terrorism that strength has been harder to recognize as the Arab/Muslim American community faced concerns more immediate than the Israeli–Palestinian conflict. However, in addition to being the cornerstone of US policy toward the conflict, "the two-state solution alone brings the community together in ways that few issues could."[171] The galvanized support for a Palestinian state allows all Americans interested in peace to overlook their differences and to concentrate on pressing US policy toward that end. Just as the pro-Israel lobby has a single issue on which all of its constituting parts agree, the pro-Arab lobby could become more competitive in the same regard by focusing on the two-state solution.

That could result in a chain reaction of Arab and Muslim American concord. As shown earlier, since members of those communities have been divided on US handling of wider international affairs, the focus on the Palestinian question could bring them together, resulting in more energy being dedicated to resolving it. Since public opinion and policymakers support a Palestinian state, the pro-Arab leadership virtually has nothing to lose by advancing the roadmap in US foreign policy. According to Ibish, "advocating for a Palestinian state is one of the few things out there that makes it much easier for Arab Americans to do it from purely a national interest principle."[172] Despite that message's importance, making the case for it has been an area of weakness, as an ATFP publication explained in detail.

> A crucial factor in the success of other American ethnic groups in influencing American foreign policy has been to emphasize the patriotic nature of their advocacy. Jewish Americans, Cubans, Irish, Greeks, Armenians, Iraqis, and other ethnic groups in the US that have sought to influence foreign policy to their own ends have all done so by framing their arguments primarily in terms of the US national interest. To be sure, all policy positions require a moral basis, and the justice of the Palestinian cause and the tragedy of the Palestinian narrative are essential elements to any program of successful advocacy for Palestine.

Nonetheless, the first question Americans want answered is: How is this important to our country? Unfortunately, Palestinian Americans and their supporters have often been exceptionally poor at articulating an answer to this question, and usually do not even attempt to do so. Instead, pro-Palestinian advocacy in the US has typically focused on denunciations of American support for Israel, which, though justified, have at times been strident enough to sound like overt anti-Americanism. This is all the more unfortunate given the obvious powerful arguments that Palestinians can deploy in advocating for an American national interest in creating a Palestinians state. In essence, we must argue that American interests are served by supporting the morally just goal of Palestinian independence and ending the occupation; that Americans can, as the saying goes, "do well by doing good" not in some abstract sense, but simply by applying the logic of existing goals and strategies for US foreign policy in the Middle East articulated by the Administration and accepted by most of the rest of the American political establishment.[173]

While it may be true that Arab Americans have not done a good job of arguing that a Palestinian state was in the US interest, the ATFP's lamentation may have been a bit overstated since the roadmap's explicit call for two states is a relatively recent development. Before it, the Bush administration approached the Israeli–Palestinian conflict with ambivalence. Its predecessor never worked toward "Palestinian statehood" as an outcome of final status negotiations. Instead President Clinton only referred to "mutual recognition" and "limited autonomy" as the outcome of the DOP. The White House did not strive for a two-state solution. In fact, during 1998, pro-Israel forces scolded First Lady Hillary Rodham Clinton for even suggesting Palestinian statehood.[174]

Prior to Oslo, the first Bush administration simply acknowledged the need for a solution to the Middle East conflict, while under Reagan the Palestinians did not have recognition among elite foreign policy circles. In those years, Arab Americans could not have argued that a Palestinian state was in the national interest without policymakers considering that to be the case, as they have stated that it was after the roadmap. Such a position allowed the pro-Arab lobby, its constituents, and allies to have the necessary credibility to make arguments about fulfilling US interests. This has not always been the case and may not remain so in the future. Consequently, the pro-Arab lobby must take the opportunity now to engage in the pluralist conversation about what best serves American aims around the world while at the same time convincing members of its base to better sell the idea of Palestinian statehood to policymakers and the public. That is the central exhortation of the ATFP and other groups interested in a Palestinian state as the cornerstone of US policy.[175]

It is true that the global war on terrorism has made it more difficult for Arab Americans to influence policy, since they have been preoccupied with other issues. But calls for the two-state solution have made lobbying for a Palestinian state less controversial in crucial regards.[176] Pro-Arab lobbyists could use their positions of influence on Palestinian statehood in order to achieve changes in other areas of the political sphere. Simply put, the Arab American leadership would have much more credibility pushing through protections for civil liberties, for instance, if it simultaneously helped secure Palestinian national rights. This is because the outline for a Palestinian state is already in existence and is part of official policy just as much as protecting Arab American civil liberties appeals to the Bill of Rights. In this instance, pro-Arab lobbyists would just as well engage in a foreign issue of domestic significance, the two-state solution, in order to tackle other concerns such as the infringement on their constituents' rights.

The issue at hand here is that of Palestine in a wider context. It is well known that the Palestinian struggle has been a chief marker of how Arabs and even Muslims have been faring throughout the world.[177] To accomplish a Palestinian state through the assistance of American policy would signal that the US has something invested not just in the Middle East, but also in its own population with ties to that region. The officials of the lobbies examined in this chapter understood well that their task to influence foreign policy is at the center of their people's affairs.[178] This is because to be both an Arab/Muslim and an American has always meant that the Middle East was the crux of political action. It was that region after all, which produced the nineteen hijackers that wreaked so much havoc on the US and contributed to the subsequent decline in civil liberties. In such context, even turban-wearing Sikhs who had nothing to do with Arabs or Muslims were gunned down on the streets of US cities.[179] Meanwhile, it was in the Middle East and throughout Islamic lands that so much of American policy operated on a day-to-day basis. Thus, "one cannot speak of [that sphere of the globe] without referring in someway to the US and vice versa."[180] The two have always been inextricably connected. And while the pro-Israel lobby has a very powerful position in that relationship, it is also a reality that in the post-peace process, post-9/11 world, the pro-Arab lobby has a "fundamental place at the table," however diminutive it may appear when compared to its Zionist counterpart.[181]

The position of the pro-Arab lobby rests on numerous conventions of the peace process from Madrid and Oslo to the roadmap and Annapolis.[182] Israel and the Palestinians "have no military option against one another."[183] After all of the violence by both sides, they have to come to the table in order to discuss coexistence. There is already a roadmap out of the cruel turmoil and toward the two-state solution. Pro-Arab lobbyists have to emphasize that as they conduct themselves to influence policy. In many ways, that is exactly what they have been doing.[184] In regards to the Israeli–Palestinian conflict, the "demand side of terrorism," as Shibley Telhami put it, rests to a large extent on the ability of American policy to step back from its unconditional support of Israel.[185] This is where the pro-Arab lobby could appeal to policymakers and the public in the period of the war on terrorism, by guiding their attention to the necessity for a political solution and hence its platform for action. There is no going back. Regardless of how much the pro-Israel lobby works to frustrate the two-state solution, American policy will not revert to the 1980s when it did not even recognize the national existence of the Palestinians.

However, the scenarios today are graver than they were during the concluding years of the Cold War. As the Middle East becomes more destabilized, the result of ambitious American plans at reshaping the region, the Israelis have acted with an eye on what their ally does. Thus, anytime it moves against Hezbollah, Hamas, or any of the handful of groups defined as terrorists by US law,[186] the Jewish state and its advocates justify such actions by (1) making linkages to the war on terrorism, (2) arguing that Israel is doing America's bidding in its immediate sphere of influence, and (3) framing Israel's security interests as US goals. These points are often shared by the majority of policymakers who themselves are under significant pressure by groups like AIPAC. As shown elsewhere, just as during the Cold War, the pro-Israel lobby argued that communism was the common enemy of the US and the Jewish state, in the present, that ideology has been replaced by Islamic fundamentalism and the violence committed by its propagators. In some ways, that transition meant that the pro-Arab lobby has had a very difficult time countering the powerful agenda of pro-Israel groups. In other ways, however, it has potential that never existed before, thanks to the two-state solution and a strategy of emphasizing it as the basis of US policy interests in the Middle East.[187]

Indeed, promoting the founding of a Palestinian state would give American interests after Iraq a boost. Most pro-Arab proponents were very much familiar with that.[188] Ibish put it best when he outlined the dividends from pursuing peace in the following way.

> After the US failure in Iraq and the emergence of Iran as a regional superpower, the US has to recognize the following five aims of the two-state solution. First, without Palestine, there is no other pursuit in the region. The sense that the US presence is a good in the region depends on that. ... And while this will not disband al Qa'eda, nothing else goes so far. Second, solving the Palestinian problem would be a major blow to the terrorists, for whom Palestine is exhibit A in their bill of particulars against the US. ... Third, helping in the founding of a Palestinian state would enhance the US role as a world leader. While we claim sole superpower status in the world, the key to that status is that second tier powers like Russia, the EU, China, India, Brazil, and others go along with us, instead of against us. ... The Palestine issue has been the most politically damaging and the most irretraceable and goes a long way, along with other issues like the Kyoto protocol, to hurt our credibility. The US has to take a huge step in reassuring the world that we are a

responsible world authority. Solving the Palestinian problem would be that huge step. Fourth, billions or trillions of dollars in trade would be added to American companies with the onset of better relations with the Islamic world, whose principal disagreements with us center around the Arab-Israeli conflict, of which the Palestinians are an integral part. Fifth, resolving the ... conflict would do wonders for the promotion of our values. We deal better with other democracies concerning stability, trade, discouraging terrorism, and other issues. ... If we take our value of democracy seriously, then we have to look at the least democratic thing in the Middle East: Israeli occupation. ... If there was a Palestinian state, it would be a new democracy, it would be a friend to the US, if America plays the constructive role outlined in the roadmap and called for by [Arab American] organizations.[189]

This lengthy statement has increasingly become a common position of Arab lobbyists as they try to convey their messages to policymakers and the public. While the issues raised by Ibish primarily appeal to realpolitik interests in the Middle East and throughout the world, there are also moral reasons for a Palestinian state. The dispossession of the Palestinians in 1948,[190] 1967, and their trickling out under the duress of occupation since that time, aside from engendering several humanitarian disasters, has also left the international community, particularly the United States, Israel's closest ally, with the responsibility for a rightful resolution to the conflict. Wingfield noted that this impression has allowed Arab American organizations to "have friends amongst the moral authority in the United States, which includes the Churches for Middle East Peace, for example."[191] Such alliances give the Palestinian cause in the US momentum from a variety of sources. But is the strategic and moral potency of pro-Arab organizations and their associates enough to chip away at the hegemony of pro-Israel pressure groups in the US?

To be sure, the pro-Arab lobby has a long way to go in order to counter the strength of the Israel lobby. According to Jahshan, "the inequality between our side and theirs [i.e. AIPAC] is highly pronounced."[192] In many ways, that disparity has a lot to do with broad support of Israel and its advocates in the proclaimed Judeo-Christian society of the US. While such factors will never fully disappear, what is important is that just as public opinion shifts, policymakers' commitment to peace may also be changed by the situation in the Middle East or the world at large, by constituents, and by pressure groups at any given time. We must remember that American policy moved from a position of denying the Palestinian existence as a national community deserving of a state during the 1980s to embracing "limited autonomy" after the end of the Cold War in the 1990s. In that period, the "US government gave pro-Arab groups as much access as the Zionist lobby."[193] Later, as part of the US-led war on terrorism, the idiom of statehood in the roadmap has given the Palestinian cause a superpower benefactor. However, a major stumbling block to better efforts at pushing for a Palestinian state has been the pro-Israel lobby.[194] In order to overcome that obstacle, those seeking an enlightened pursuit of peace in the Middle East have no choice but to go toe to toe with that powerful lobby and try to dislodge AIPAC from hegemony over policy, particularly at the legislative level. Much work also has to be done at the administrative branch, which does not bow down to pressure as much as Congress. After the 2008 election, if the right administration sat in the White House, it could at the direction of a stronger pro-Arab lobby, execute the two-state policies required to advance the national interest in peace, which has "become an established part of the official American approach" toward the Israeli–Palestinian conflict.[195]

Pro-Arab action, however, will not be given any importance so long as the vital work of various American organizations and their allies, most notably pro-Jewish groups,[196] continues to be overlooked in the literature on lobbying, foreign policy analysis, and in mainstream public discourse.[197] One significant feature of this ignorance is the belief that public opinion alone shapes foreign policy.[198] While, as had been demonstrated earlier, American public opinion toward the two-state solution has corresponded to US policymakers calling for Palestinian self-determination, both are susceptible to a multitude of influences. The Arab lobby has been trying to act as an agent of influence at least since 1967, albeit with ebbs and flows and with mixed results of success and failure. To be certain, its efforts have corresponded to public opinion gradually favoring the two-state solution. Both may have contributed to policymakers favoring negotiations at Madrid and Oslo and ultimately articulating the roadmap. If that is not considered a success of the pro-Arab lobby in the US, then it should at least force academics, journalists, policymakers, and the interested public to investigate Arab American organizations and their partners for peace, which for the most part have been inexcusably left out of serious inquiry.

Conclusion

Looking at the interplay between US foreign policy and domestic pressures, we have to face the fact that public opinion and lobbying groups, like the policymakers they seek to influence, constantly react to international events. It is true that the "Intifada made the Israelis and the rest of the world realize that the Palestinians could not be governed under military occupation."[199] However, the pro-Arab lobby sought to pounce on that fact and to make it a critical nuisance for established support of Israel, which saw its apex during the 1980s under the Reagan administration and the strategic alliance between the US and the Jewish state. Policy change began to take place during the late 1980s and early 1990s because, as the Cold War unraveled, there was a new strategic reality for the Israeli–Palestinian conflict that had to be pointed out not just to the American public, but to its leaders as well. While it would be foolish to deny that structural changes in the international community made change in the US necessary, it is worthwhile to note that the interpretation of those changes had a lot to do with the actors involved, particularly domestic pressure groups vying to influence foreign policy in one direction or another. Indeed, if there ever was any hope for a swing in the pendulum of American policy toward Middle East peace, it stemmed from actions to shape the public and elite levels of policymaking inputs. That has always been a fact that had to be reckoned with in the history of US involvement abroad. While many would agree that the pro-Arab lobby "seeks to present the Arab point of view [and] that America and the Arab countries have many interests in common,"[200] there has to be the acknowledgement, informed by any glance at advocacy practices in the US, that there exists a pivotal moment in history for that lobby. That moment is given life by the fact that stated policy is the same as the wishes of pro-Arab organizations: the "creation of a Palestinian state that lives in peace alongside Israel."[201] Whether the pro-Arab lobby captures that moment and turns the tide in its favor by getting American policy to live up to its promises is not merely up to AIPAC to decide (as many cynics in and outside of the scholarly realm would have us believe), it is also for the pro-Arab lobby and its peace seeking allies to determine.

To most people studying the effects of lobbying on American foreign policy, the pro-Israel lobby has taken the lion's share of analysis while the pro-Arab lobby has been dismissed as its weak caricature.[202] What this chapter has tried to do, however, is not only convey the actors, scope, importance, diversity, functions, struggles, and the history of the pro-Arab lobby, it has also argued that its strength has been greatly increased during the eras of the Intifada, the first Gulf War, Madrid, the collapse of the Soviet Union, Oslo, and later during the wars on terrorism and Iraq as American policy has explicitly called for the two-state solution to the Israeli–Palestinian conflict. Sadly, it is at this vital time that the pro-Arab lobby and the American peace camp are most in need of attention. Regardless of the extent to which they were responsible for the two-state solution, what is important is that such a formula underlies the recognition by American policymakers of the centrality of peace for US interests. These, however, have never been cut and dry. Interest groups of various backgrounds have continually tried to push them to one side or another. For their part, supporters of a Palestinian state have maintained, "the opportunity that exists for peace as articulated by the roadmap is very much in the American national interest."[203] Whether that opportunity is missed or captured depends on the ability of policymakers to allow the US to be an honest broker. That is based on the degree of success realized by the pro-Arab lobby and its sympathizers in the years ahead.

Arab American lobbyists expressed a high degree of optimism about their future in American politics. Jahshan stated the "pattern for the future looks very bright because the Arab American community, and those interested in peace are much more sophisticated today than they were in the past."[204]

Such sophistication, Jahshan argued, has to be put not just toward lobbying, "which is an established, but somewhat outmoded form of political influence," but also toward "think tanks, which have become increasingly important to policy inputs."[205] Like Jahshan, Samhan saw quite a few prospects for pro-Arab efforts but cautioned that the Israel lobby, with its overwhelming financing and political clout, will not be easily overcome. This was also a view shared by Abou-Chedid, who acknowledged that the pro-Arab lobby could do much better, particularly as it is up against a very formidable opponent. What may be done to make the pro-Arab lobby more competitive? Gleichert provided the answer thus: "we need more involvement from Americans from a wide variety of backgrounds, not just Arab Americans," for a just peace in the Middle East. Oakar seconded that sentiment, adding, "increased political awareness at the grassroots goes a long way to help us here in Washington."[206] Ibish concurred, but added that money, time, and other resources are imperative: "if people concerned about the Palestinian cause, whether Arab American or not do not give generously to support what is in the national interest, then it shows that they don't care!"[207] While Timco noted, "political sophistication is crucial," Zogby remarked, "what is needed is better awareness of the many ways to participate in order to ease the Palestinians' suffering."[208] In sum, everyone agreed that heightened involvement, be it in thought production, financial munificence, electoral participation, civic diplomacy, or education, would lead to better political organization, particularly at the "local level," to form an "interested, issue oriented public."[209]

Finally, over a year before the publication of their book, in the conclusion of their working paper on the Israel lobby, Mearsheimer and Walt asked, "can the [pro-Israel] lobby's power be curtailed?" While they outlined the reasons as to why it should be, including the "Iraq debacle, [the] obvious need to rebuild America's image in the Arab and Islamic world, and the recent revelations about AIPAC officials passing U.S. government secrets to Israel," Mearsheimer and Walt concluded that the lobby is not likely to lose power "anytime soon."[210] The reason they gave for this is that groups like "AIPAC and its allies (including Christian Zionists) have no serious opponents in the lobbying world."[211] That conclusion, however, aside from ceding too much ground to the Israel lobby, is not fair to the numerous pro-Arab lobbies and their supporters of all stripes working in Washington and throughout the US. Nor does it do any justice to the fact that they are in a better position because of the American adoption initially of the land for peace framework and ultimately of the two-state solution to address the Palestinian question.[212] This oversight by Mearsheimer and Walt and others like them is understandable given the awe-inspiring power exercised by the pro-Israel lobby. However, parroting that tune without recognition of countervailing trends and potential – aside from bringing hopelessness when confronting the Israeli–Palestinian conflict – obfuscates the truth. That is, the pro-Arab lobby has done an incredible amount of work that has coincided with public opinion and policy changes, and more importantly, "much remains to be done in the era of the roadmap."[213] Although this chapter has attempted a thorough analysis of the pro-Arab lobby, it has only scratched the surface of the kind of inquiry necessary to not only understand the task ahead for supporters of peace through a Palestinian state, but also for developing better strategies in order to induce American policy toward that solution and other prudent pursuits throughout the world.

5 Conclusion and scenarios

Two states versus one

Introduction

As the preceding chapters showed, while public opinion in favor of a Palestinian state and the pro-Arab lobby's peace message have ultimately corresponded to official calls for that solution, the Israel lobby has done everything in its power to stall and alter its outcome.[1] Despite that, looking at the domestic factors operating on American policy from the decline of the Cold War to the global war on terrorism provided the following understanding of the affirmative position toward the two-state solution. First, public opinion *does* matter in the determination of foreign policy. Growing support of a "separate, independent Palestinian nation," the tenet underlying a *viable* two-state solution, has related to the US pursuing that formula. And although sentiment for Palestinian statehood was overshadowed by the American–Israeli "strategic alliance" against the Soviet Union and by the grip that the pro-Israel lobby had on Washington politics during the 1980s, the Intifada, particularly the Arab lobby's attempts to embed its "symbols of resistance" into the public and elite psyches, matched up with the framework for ending the occupation worked out by Oslo (1993) under US sponsorship.[2]

Second, even though changes in the international climate such as the end of the Cold War and the post-Gulf War "New World Order" had significant implications for policymaking,[3] the factors discussed in the foregoing pages had a substantial relationship to the characteristics and intended outcome of American policy toward the Israeli–Palestinian conflict. Thus, *majority* public opinion backing the establishment of a Palestinian state emerged during the era of Oslo, effectively setting the parameters by which policymakers perceived events in the region and acted upon them.[4] Such support related to US pressure on Israel to allow the Palestinians increased autonomy in the occupied territories, as evidenced by President Clinton's brokering for peace. During that time, Arab American groups gained unprecedented levels of access to influence public opinion and policymakers toward their end for a Palestinian state.[5] As previously argued, that offered a fertile policy terrain which engendered the US roadmap in the aftermath of the 9/11 attacks and on the eve of the war to remove Saddam Hussein from power. This showed that there was a robust interplay between international developments and domestic agents acting on foreign policy.

Third, while the pro-Israel lobby remained strong during the periods under examination, it had to adapt to the emerging reality of the Intifada and pro-Arab exploitation of its images and those of the peace process.[6] Moreover, after the end of the Cold War, pro-Israel organizations lost a chief reason in their case for American support of the Jewish state, fighting communism. However, after the collapse of the Soviet Union, groups like the American Israel Public Affairs Committee (AIPAC) lobbied hard to get terrorism to become the new adversary. To their fortune, this put them in the same camp as the neoconservative terror warriors that would take power in the White House a decade after the end of the Cold War, following the 9/11 attacks.[7] Their work paid off as Americans and their policymakers understood that terrorism was both the most serious threat and that it had an Arab (i.e. Islamic, Palestinian) face.[8] Hence, any loss of power in pressuring policy that the pro-Israel lobby may have experienced because of the Intifada's imagery, the fall of communism, and the peace process, was made up for in a spectacular way by the dreadful strikes on the US mainland. Still, the Bush administration, consistent with public opinion and foreign policy elite perceptions, could not sustain the war on terrorism without diplomatic efforts toward a key issue for terrorists, Palestinian torment under an American-backed Israeli occupation, hence an important catalyst for the roadmap and United Nations Security Council (UNSC) resolutions 1397 and 1515. These explicit demands for two states overlapped with the Arab lobby's argument through 9/11 that peace between Israel and the Palestinians would deny terrorists a strategic recruiting tool.[9] This brings us to the fourth point regarding US policy espousal of a Palestinian state. In the era of the roadmap and overwhelming international consensus on it, the pro-Arab lobby currently has a position that most other lobbies could only hope for: popular and policymaker support for their course of action toward the Israeli–Palestinian conflict.

These four points, summarizing what has come before, help conceptualize the problem that will occupy the rest of this chapter. Acknowledging the link between public opinion and foreign policy toward Palestinian statehood, what ought those interested in peace consider if the Israel lobby, which is astronomically more powerful than its pro-Arab counterpart, has done everything in its strength to frustrate the plan for two states? Since the roadmap, which enjoys near-unanimous support, has established that the interests of security and morality demand a Palestinian state, then it is worthwhile to examine that proposal and its relationship to peace. Such a task inevitably leads to the debate on whether the two-state solution practically serves a peaceful end. As it stands, the pro-Israel lobby's actions in that regard are at odds with what it understands to be necessary for Israel to remain a Jewish democracy – Palestinian statehood.[10]

The stakes for Middle East peace are very high.[11] Yet under considerable pressure by Israel's lobby, which benefits from public sympathy for the Jewish state, American policy has failed to realize peace between the Israelis and Palestinians, despite its stated purpose to do so. As shown elsewhere, there are several explanations for that failure. First, policymakers have traditionally followed public opinion insofar as they have supported Israel over the Arabs. And even though they heeded public preference for the pursuit of peace through the two-state solution, they have yet to ensure that Israel would allow for the meaningful existence of a Palestinian state. Second, while the pro-Israel lobby has always professed that its actions are in the US national interest, it has hindered policymakers from pursuing the manifest American goal of Middle East peace.[12] Under direction from AIPAC, pro-Israel groups have attempted to delay peace through the two-state framework, from pressuring the US government into prohibiting dealings with the Palestinian Authority (PA) and other key players in the region, to coaxing President Bush to agree with former Prime Minister Ariel Sharon that Israel would not vacate West Bank settlements.[13] If followed through, that agreement would be the last nail in the coffin of the land for peace process to resolve the Israeli–Palestinian conflict.

Third the pro-Arab lobby has not effectively countered the AIPAC-led Israel lobby to an extent that would curtail its activities against the two-state solution, as proven by the fact that the US has yet to apply *effective* pressure on Israel to keep up its end of the bargain in the negotiations for a workable Palestinian state. American evenhandedness depends on the ability to check pro-Israel lobbyists who blindly follow the Jewish state's hard line, sometimes to a point that makes Israelis themselves uncomfortable.[14] Given all of this, it is likely that the conflict will continue and even escalate as Palestinians struggle against the injustices of dispossession and occupation.

If there was a genuine interest in peace, one of two things would have to happen. Either the Palestinians, in accordance with the roadmap and the UNSC resolutions, would establish a truly sovereign state of territorial integrity without hindrance, *or* Jews and Arabs would have to live on an equal basis in a democratic, secular state that dispenses with religious identity as the determiner of full citizenship. Of these two scenarios, the international community as well as the Israelis and the Palestinians have opted for two states.[15] Through its research on the public opinion of the two sides, the Truman Institute for the Advancement of Peace discovered that

> 68% of the Israelis and 66% of the Palestinians support a mutual recognition of Israel as the state of the Jewish people and Palestine as the state of the Palestinian people after the establishment of an independent Palestinian state and the settlement of all issues in dispute.[16]

However, such a settlement has not been realized years after the Oslo process, the roadmap, and other attempts at peace. This has produced a controversial debate focused on a compelling question that is quickly becoming central to the conversation on peace: one state for Israelis and Palestinians or two states, one for each side? Right now, overwhelming agreement falls on the side of two states, but what if such an outcome was no longer likely, or at least as practical as a one-state solution? In order to address those issues, this chapter will engage in the following three aims. First, it will assess prospects for two states. In particular, it will consider the possibility of a viable Palestinian state after the "end of the peace process"[17] while taking into account the pro-Israel lobby's profound influence on policymakers, who face considerable difficulty in pursuing the two-state solution that their constituents prefer.[18] Second, a substantial portion of this chapter will look at historical and present contentions in favor of one state, considering the apparent futility of creating a Palestinian state in the current context of foreign policymaking.[19] Third, it will consider the role that pro-Arab groups and their allies for peace would have to play if they were to lobby the US government for implementation of the two-state solution *while* keeping the strategic wildcard of the one-state solution in their public relations arsenals.

Prospects for the two-state solution

Oslo's aftermath

Assuming that the peace process and the roadmap ground the framework to which both sides would return if they were to strike a negotiated agreement, what does the future of the Israeli–Palestinian conflict look like? During a 2003 Middle East Policy Council conference symposium on the subject, Khalil Jahshan framed the question this way: "is a two-state solution to the Palestinian problem still viable?" His response, a position shared by many analysts on the future of the peace process is as follows: "theoretically yes, practically No."[20] Jahshan affirmed the viability of the two-state solution because it has always been the option of choice for all involved parties as demonstrated by its international endorsement. However, he was highly skeptical about its likelihood because of facts on the ground, which center on Israel's persistent occupation of lands that would be the foundation of any Palestinian state. Of particular importance for the present analysis is the obduracy of American acquiescence in Israeli settlements, which was taken to new heights when President George W. Bush declared,

> as part of a final peace settlement, Israel must have secure and recognized borders which should emerge from negotiations between the parties, in accordance with U.N. Security Council Resolutions 242 and 338. In light of new realities on the ground, *including already existing major Israeli population centers*, it is unrealistic to expect that the outcome of final status negotiations will be a full and complete return to the

armistice lines of 1949. And all previous efforts to negotiate a two-state solution have reached the same conclusion. It is realistic to expect that any final status agreement will only be achieved on the basis of mutually agreed changes that reflect these realities.[21]

Hence, the US and Israel seem to have concurred that the occupation of territories captured after June 4, 1967 will continue, endangering the prospect for a *contiguous* Palestinian state.[22]

There is good reason to worry that the above agreement would result in a claustrophobic and disjointed Palestinian state. Authoritative maps on Israel's security wall show that Palestinian areas would not only be sliced into dismembered quadrants, they also shed light on the sheer amount of land that would be retained under exclusive Jewish sovereignty.[23] If realized, this would create a Palestinian entity that is anything but a state. Hence, West Bank population centers, particularly Tulkarm, Nablus, Ramallah, East Jerusalem, Jericho, Bethlehem, and Hebron would be disconnected from one another. Under that scenario, President Jimmy Carter concluded that the Palestinians would be "completely surrounded by walls, fences, and Israeli checkpoints, living as prisoners within the small portion of land left to them."[24] Israel would exclusively manage the airspace and control water from the Jordan River and other sources throughout its West Bank highlands. If the "Gaza pullout" forecast anything, it is that the Jewish state would maintain border crossings, restricting products and labor from flowing freely in and out of Palestine.[25] Moreover, the international boycott of the Hamas government has confirmed that the Palestinians may not elect leaders of their choosing. Meanwhile, Israel's devastation of Lebanon and Gaza in its efforts respectively against Hezbollah and Hamas painted a very grim future for any emerging Palestinian state. At any moment, the Jewish state may cripple Palestine. "In such crippled conditions," predicted Virginia Tilley, "no Palestinian government can operate effectively to contain the political fragmentation and extremism that would inevitably result, which suggests dangerous new security risks to Israel."[26]

While the above portrayal offers the worst-case scenario, the two-state solution remains the only acceptable option on the peacemaking table. In order for the US to pursue it in good faith, policymakers must take more direction from those that demand a *just* solution of two states. This will not happen, however, unless there was a fundamental shift in the landscape of US politics, which involves the pro-Israel lobby recognizing the consequences of rejecting Palestinian statehood and *action* by everyone on the fact that resolving the conflict is in the best interests of all sides. Absent that, peace may not come about unless serious changes were made to the power that interest groups exercise over government.[27]

If groups like AIPAC remain entrenched in their position, a workable two-state solution would have to include both vision and courage on the part of policymakers. However, that is easier said than done so long as the Israel lobby continues to stifle "open debate about US interests."[28] What we are left with then is pretty much a continuation of past struggles, a cycle of violence so long as there is no honest effort to resolve the conflict as the US continues "unofficially condoning or abetting the Israeli confiscation and colonization of Palestinian territories."[29] There will be no peace under these conditions, which breach America's interests in the Middle East.

Since standing up to Israel brings dangers to the political health of Capitol Hill and White House officials, there has been a lack of resolve to end the conflict.[30] The Jewish state in these circumstances will maintain its treatment of the Palestinians. In that relationship, American diplomacy will only exacerbate the matter as it attempts to "break down Arab defenses" and to define negotiations in terms acceptable only to Israel and the US.[31] By ignoring its interests among Arab parties, particularly as they pertain to a future Palestinian state, the US would ensure that the Jewish state remains an overwhelming hegemonic presence in the Middle East. That was never a course for stability in any region.[32] Rather, given the disparity in deterrence capabilities between Israel and its neighbors, war will continue to embroil American policy commitments.

This presents a "depressing picture on the ground," particularly as it involves a lack of effort toward peace.[33] In its struggle to defend its citizens against terrorism, Israel has destroyed the PA's infrastructure while killing thousands of civilians, committing a flurry of political assassinations, imprisoning scores of Palestinian leaders, and generally making life unbearable for the people of the West Bank and Gaza. With over 23 percent unemployment in the occupied territories there is little room for hope.[34] The misery of the Palestinians has been conveniently blamed on the global threat after 9/11, terrorism.[35] In the name of fighting it, the US and Israel have exculpated themselves from their parts in derailing the peace process. Since there is no responsibility to be borne on either side, what we have in the present is the AIPAC-led mantra of blaming the Palestinian leadership for the roadmap's failure. From an American–Israeli vantage, at the point that it fails to "rein in the terrorists," any Palestinian government may be sidetracked, isolated, and ultimately destroyed. This was a game played earlier with the regime of Palestine Liberation Organization (PLO) leader Yasser Arafat. As Israeli forces encircled his compound in 2002 and threatened to kill him, the Jewish state's friends in the US advanced Ariel Sharon's portrayal of him as a disappointment in negotiations and ultimately as the chief terrorist.[36] Never acknowledged was the fact that following Israel, American policy took a very hard line stance against the PA and caused it considerable loss of authority among its people.[37] Hence, Arafat could not deliver the peace promised to the Palestinians by the roadmap.[38]

Democracy and terrorism

But what if a viable democratic Palestinian state *did* come into being as called for by the roadmap? Israel's 2006 military campaign against

Hezbollah provided the world with a very grim prophecy of the dangers that may come with that type of solution.[39] Whereas President Bush and other supporters of two states have maintained that they would peacefully coexist, Israel went to war in Lebanon for "harboring" terrorists, the same bloody rift that exists between the Jewish state and the Palestinians.[40] There is nothing to suggest that war would not take place despite the "vision of two states, a secure State of Israel and a viable, peaceful, democratic Palestine."[41] Instead, the Lebanon fiasco gave us the following nightmare scenario for the two-state solution. With its permanent settlements in the West Bank, Israel fortifies itself behind the security wall after taking a significant portion of the 22 percent of land which was supposed to be part of a Palestinian state; the Jewish state constantly detains Palestinians; sometimes it assassinates their leaders; because it controls the ports and airspace in the name of security, the flow of goods and services to the Palestinians, including humanitarian assistance, slows to a trickle; once in a while, Palestinians led by Hamas, Islamic Jihad, or any of the handful of secular organizations such as the Democratic Front for the Liberation of Palestine (DFLP), out of desperation commit a brazen attack against Israeli civilians or soldiers; the Jewish state deems that an act of war and proceeds to destroy much of the new state. If all of that seems farfetched, one only has look at the obliteration of Beirut and Southern Lebanon because Hezbollah kidnapped two soldiers and killed eight others, something that the Ehud Olmert government called "an act of war."[42] On the Palestinian front, by the time a similar declaration was made after the kidnapping of Israeli soldier Galid Shalit,[43] Gaza's infrastructure had been bombed while most members of the Hamas government were jailed.[44]

In short, regardless of how democratic a newly established Palestinian state would be, Israel may seek to destroy it if it felt threatened by any of its factions. After all, the war on terrorism has created dangerous times where any resistance may be construed as an illegal act of aggression. However, illegality would remain the Palestinians' modus operandi so long as Israel does not allow them to have a credible state with a monopoly on violence. Insofar as American policy is concerned, the Palestinians have no way of achieving statehood due to its support of facts on the ground. And as some have pointed out, it seems like all powers involved in the Israeli–Palestinian conflict, particularly the US, are "lacking all conviction" toward the two-state solution.[45] Hence, Israel faces little pressure to give up its control over the Palestinians.[46] Meanwhile, the 2006 invasion of Lebanon showed that rather than being a neutral mediator, the US, in addition to arming the Jewish state, approved its actions as demonstrated by the American refusal to condemn the war. As world opinion and all international actors reproved belligerence in Beirut, Qana, and Tyre, President Bush, backed up by his secretary of state Condoleezza Rice, insisted, "Israel has the right to defend herself."[47] Similarly, the US has refused to call out Israel on its military adventures in the Palestinian territories. Whenever the UNSC sought to condemn the killing of innocent civilians, the United States vetoed such a move while appealing to the doctrine of self-defense on behalf of its ally.[48]

During a time when more children died than combatants, as did in the Hezbollah–Israel war, the argument of self-defense inverted reality to an unimaginable extent.[49] Hence, Hezbollah attacks on military targets were called terrorism while the demolition of Lebanese neighborhoods was understood as part of the Jewish state defending itself.[50] Along with contention over these labels, the violence continued during the thirty days war as Hezbollah reacted to Israeli raids by firing surface-to-surface katyushas. Rather than being seen as self-defense, Israel and the US viewed the Lebanese militia's reaction as the only act of aggression. Little attention was paid to the body count of about ten Lebanese civilians dead for every one Israeli soldier.[51] Despite those figures, in Washington, Democrats often took issue with the Republicans because they have not been pro-Israel enough.[52] The Lebanon example outlined above casts doubt on peace through the two-state solution if Palestine was to follow the same trajectory as Israel's neighbor to the north.

From its inception, a Palestinian state would indeed be in a precarious position. US policymakers must accept some level of blame for that because of "their reckless support of Israel."[53] Emboldened by that backing, some in the Jewish state have gone so far as to pronounce, "it's very clear there is no two-state solution."[54] These declarations are more likely as American policies continue to undermine peace by ostracizing the Palestinian leadership. Despite winning at the ballot box and later expressing its readiness "to accept a two-state solution of the Israeli–Palestinian conflict,"[55] the Hamas government remains on the State Department's terror list.[56]

Buttressed by the US, Israel deprived the Palestinians of democracy or control over their surroundings. It has treated any autonomy gained by them with suspicion at best, and at worst as a breeding ground for terrorism. Hence, when militants blasted holes in the wall separating Gaza from Egypt – an act meant to allow Palestinians to return to their homes or to permit them to buy items necessary for daily life – the blockade was quickly restored after American pressure on Cairo.[57] This demonstrates the fateful intersection between Israeli and US policies toward the Palestinians, whether in the occupied territories or in a future state.

In light of the totality of conflict as outlined above, many issues must be addressed in order for peace to prevail through the two-state solution. Since the Jewish state is perceived in its part of the world as a settler colony, recognizing its existence has been a bitter pill to swallow.[58] Even if it withdrew to the June 4, 1967 borders –in and of itself, this would nearly be impossible so long as the US looks the other way[59] – many Palestinians may still view Israel as an illegitimate entity because of their Nakba (catastrophe) in 1948. Meanwhile, the Jewish democracy that declared its independence during that year is today in danger of becoming neither Jewish nor democratic. Well over 20 percent of its population is non-Jewish. Most of that minority is treated with contempt.[60] Still, at least the Arab Israelis are citizens of the state in which they live and enjoy a high degree of economic well being relative to others.[61] The Palestinians under occupation across the Green Line are citizens of nowhere and may not engage in any political behavior outside of Israel's military jurisdiction. This has been the case since the 1967 war. And as violence has persisted from then onward despite repeated efforts at peace, many have argued that considering the apparent unfeasibility of attaining the two-state solution, Israelis and Palestinians ought to live together under a regime of "truth and reconciliation."[62]

And then there was one state ...

The debate in history

Increasing calls for a one-state solution to the century-long conflict have gained a vociferous place in the discussion on American policy toward the Middle East.[63] As the US has tried to keep Iraq together, many have wondered whether it should pursue one state for Israelis and Palestinians. But is such a solution viable? Tilley put forward the clearest answer to this question, submitting "that the one-state solution is the only viable one and that its obstacles therefore require new thinking and frank discussion."[64] Adding her share to the conversation on the issue, she advanced a groundbreaking position that attempted to overcome the problems with two states discussed so far.

> No deep history of diplomacy or international consensus offers any normative obstacle to a binational or secular-democratic state. The two state-solution itself carries a greater burden of legitimacy, having lacked formal endorsement by the Palestinians until 1988 and by Israel and the United States until 2002. The true obstacles to a one-state solution, then are the views of the two protagonists – their national ideologies, internal politics, and mutual antipathies. Given the psychological burden of a half century of violence, dispossession, mutual fears, and stereotypes, these obstacles are formidable.[65]

While we can agree that the two-state solution has overwhelming obstacles particularly because of the Jewish settlement grid that runs deep into Palestinian territory, one state as a peace proposal has no support among the factors looked at in the previous chapters. Thus, US public opinion support for Israel backs its standing as a state for Jews while most of the pro-Israel and pro-Arab groups are brought together in their opposition to the one-state solution. Rafi Dajani summed it up well when he emphatically stated,

> aside from having no support by the American public, the one-state solution is not supported by the Palestinian people, who want national

expression. Furthermore, the one-state solution has no international support whatsoever, particularly by the principal actors, the US and Israel, who understand that calls for one state completely ignore the *raison d'etre* of Israel as a Jewish haven. Israel itself would strongly fight such a solution, as it has publicly stated that the one-state solution is a backdoor to its destruction—the death of the Jewish state. So, while these one-state people are sitting there arguing for an impractical vision, the Palestinians are going to face more misery and death. Look at Israel, the Arab Israelis are not doing well there at all. In a one state setting, the Christian and Muslim Arabs would be inferior to highly educated, technologically adept, economically well off, and politically dominant Jews.[66]

Like other representatives of the pro-Arab lobby working to pressure US policy toward fulfilling the roadmap, Dajani surmised, "because of all of this, the one-state solution is no where on our table, nor is it on the table of our opposition right down the street [referring to AIPAC]."

Dajani and others offered convincing arguments against the one-state solution. And while its lack of support in the United States, the chief mediator in the conflict, may never be overstated, the violent interactions between Israelis and Palestinians, historically and in the present, have beleaguered any binational proposal. However, this does not mean that the one-state solution may not be considered as the antithesis to forces of exclusivity that have engendered the Israeli–Palestinian conflict. If not that, then at least the one-state solution could serve as a counter-plan to the roadmap, which suffers from a variety of problems. In order to address the characteristics and scope of the one-state solution, we must trace out the arguments favoring it to end the Israeli–Palestinian conflict.

Before and after: Israel and the Nakba

During the 1920s, some advocated cooperation between Arabs and Jews against the grain of ethnic statehood espoused at the time. Their most notable representation was Brit Shalom (Covenant of Peace), an organization of thinkers founded in 1925, which "lobbied domestically and internationally for a binational Arab-Jewish state."[67] It did that throughout the British mandatory period, on the eve of Israel's founding, during years of outright war and rejection between Israel and its Arab neighbors, and continues its work into the present. The following statement by H. M. Kalvaryski captures the mission of Brit Shalom.

Any solution found and put into practice against the will of the Arabs endangers our future. We must recognise the kinship existing between the two branches of the Semitic race, and the duty of both parts to act in accordance with the principle: "that which it would not have the other

branch do unto him, that it should not do unto the other." From this
follow the principles of equality – parity – and of non-domination of
either people by the other. We must find a way of reconciling the two
national movements, the Zionist and the Arab, which seem conflicting
and mutually exclusive, but which are in reality complementary to each
other, and able to live side by side in peace and harmony.[68]

Exemplifying other early conciliatory positions, the one above emphasized
the common roots of both peoples. Though appealing to Jewish identity,
such positions called for the unification of Semites in their shared land. Brit
Shalom in general and Kalvaryski in particular maintained that the diver-
gence between Arab and Jewish nationalisms had been an accident of history
that needed correction. Hence, it was argued that harmony would only be
realized at the point that both recognized their inherent equality on the land,
if not as universal human beings, then at least as Semites. The outcome of
such recognition was that both people would work together for a goal that
serves their collective interests. In order to do that, they would establish a
state that treats all equally in terms of rights and obligations. It was feared
that failure to live up to this image would bring the kind of perils that have
plagued the region. Currently, threats to the Jewish state's security come
from the intensification of Islamic militancy, Arab reactions to what is perceived as an expansionist, ambitious, and bellicose self-proclaimed Western
regime, and the Palestinians themselves, who may burst out of despondency
over assaults on their national existence.[69] Visionaries like Kalvaryski fore-
saw the troubles for an exclusive state and called for Zionism to take a more
accommodating position on the indigenous population.

Such ideas, however, had to overcome strong currents of thought, which
manifested themselves not only in separation, but also in the clash of
national destinies. Commenting on this, and calling for the recognition of a
common peaceful end, Judah Magnes wrote, "our contention is that Arab-
Jewish cooperation is not only necessary for the peace of this part of the
world, but that it is also possible."[70] Magnes faulted the lack of cooperation
between the two sides for the conflict. An examination of their history
reveals that separation between them has been reified internationally. Hence,
before the establishment of Israel, colonial strategy devised in London
sought division in order to control the land, even though such policies led to
the ultimate termination of the mandate, particularly after Britain came
close to defeat at the hands of fascism in World War II. Well before that,
some denounced the idea of a Jewish state as envisioned by Theodor Herzl,
proposed by numerous Zionist Congresses, and sanctioned by the Balfour
Declaration (1917). Magnes wrote "we must once and for all give up on the
idea of a 'Jewish Palestine,'" and argued that "Jews and Arabs ... have each
as much right there, no more and no less, than the other: Equal rights and
equal privileges and equal duties. That is ... the sole ethical basis for [Jewish]
claims there."[71] This sentiment condemned the leading Zionist positions,

particularly those immersed in the colonial thought of the day. Confronting the settler vision concerning natives, Magnes charged, "your Balfour Declaration decrees a Jewish ruling class from the outset. This gift of political primacy to the Jews in Palestine rather than political equality contains the seed of resentment and future conflict."[72]

Magnes sought in his position a long-term commitment to cooperation. He keenly understood the necessity of a safe haven for world Jewry through immigration to Palestine but broke with the imperial politics of his extreme coreligionists in favor of collaboration between Jews and Arabs. This, according to Magnes, was the only way for Jewish survival in any home they were going to have in Palestine. And while Magnes believed that the land had to be "redeemed," that did not mean wrestling it of its inhabitants. Rather, it meant rescuing Arabs and Jews from becoming victims of their designs on it. In this regard, Magnes had a vision of peace that would secure a Jewish home in the Middle East without threatening the people residing there. Unfortunately, the emergent institutionalization of exclusive identities in the 1930s and 1940s blocked that plan from realization.

Despite the mounting tide against cooperation, Magnes had vocal allies, in particular Martin Buber, who on the eve of Israel's "war of independence," declared,

> we aim at a social structure based on the reality of two peoples living together. The foundations of this structure cannot be the traditional ones of majority and minority, but must be different. ... This is what we need and not a "Jewish state"; for any national state in vast hostile surroundings would mean pre-meditated national suicide, and an unstable international basis can never make up for the missing intra-national one. ... The road to be pursued is that of ... agreement ... which, in our opinion, would lead to Jewish-Arab co-operation in the revival of the Middle East, with the Jewish partner concentrated in a strong settlement in Palestine. This co-operation, though necessarily starting out from economic premises, will allow development in accordance with an all-embracing cultural perspective and on the basis of feeling at-oneness, tending to result in a new form of society.[73]

Like Magnes' position, the one advanced by Buber predicted a gloomy existence for Jews if they failed to coexist with their neighbors. However, such predictions subsided since Israel's existence as a Jewish state has gone unchallenged by the international doctrines of the major powers, particularly the United States.[74]

Israel's resilience as a state for Jews is historically indebted to the hard-line Zionist "awakening" well before its independence. Hannah Arendt dubbed this phenomenon the "expression of fanaticism and hysteria" and cautioned against a movement in her name divulging into an orgy of violence. She instead called for moderation and a non-violent solution to the Jewish question. Days before Israel declared its independence and the ensuing Palestinian Nakba, she lamented that within Zionism, "terrorism and the growth of totalitarian methods are silently tolerated and applauded," since many Jews

> are essentially in agreement on the following more or less roughly stated propositions: the moment has now come to get everything or nothing, victory or death; Arab and Jewish claims are irreconcilable and only a military decision can settle the issue; the Arabs, all Arabs, are our enemies and we accept this fact; not only outmoded liberals believe in compromises, only philistines believe in justice, and only *shlemiels* prefer truth and negotiation to propaganda and machine guns; Jewish experience in the last decades – or over the last centuries, or over the last two thousand years – has finally awakened us and taught us to look out for ourselves; this alone is reality, everything else is stupid sentimentality; everybody is against us, Great Britain is anti-Semitic, the United States is imperialist ... in the final analysis we count upon nobody but ourselves; in sum – we are ready to go down fighting, and we will consider anybody who stands in our way a traitor and anything done to hinder us a stab in the back.[75]

Arendt admonished the Jewish leadership away from the brink of, if not national disaster, then an ethical one. Ultimately, like other visionaries of her time, she called for partnership between Jews and Arabs on the land they have to share.[76] The ideas put forward by Arendt and others had institution building as an outcome. An example of this was the formulation of the Association Union, an international lobbying organization calling for a one-state solution.[77] Programs like those sought to move away from ethnic quarrel in favor of nation building and to counterbalance division stemming from the aspirations of two peoples seeking fulfillment in an age of "self-determination." One-state propositions from the 1920s through the 1940s sought to define the nation more inclusively.

In a final effort to move away from what was believed to be impending disaster for the Arab and Jewish communities in Palestine, Arendt issued the following plea.

> The partition of so small a country could at best mean the petrification of the conflict, which would result in arrested development for both peoples; at worst it would signify a temporary stage during which both parties would prepare for further war. The alternative proposition of a federated state, also recently endorsed by Dr. Magnes, is much more realistic, despite the fact that it establishes a common government for two different peoples, it avoids the troublesome majority-minority constellation, which is insoluble by definition. A federated structure, moreover, would have to rest on Jewish-Arab community councils, which would mean that the Jewish-Arab conflict would be resolved on the

lowest and most promising level of proximity and neighborliness. A federated state, finally could be the natural stepping stone for any later, greater federated structure in the Near East and the Mediterranean area. ... It is still not too late.[78]

The goals advocated by Arendt and her comrades were never adopted. At the time Arendt wrote her appeal, Europe was in the midst of recovery from a catastrophic war. The United States was under pressure for an exclusive state for Jews, while the Arabs were preoccupied with fighting to protect their land. The results of those events were cataclysmic to the Palestinians and to the advocates of one state. Israel was born as the state of Jews and banished 750,000 Arabs.[79]

The one-state option, however, did not wither away with Israel's founding. To be sure, the 1948 war and armistice of 1949 changed the political landscape of the Middle East. Still, they did not take away from the binational imagination. After the founding of the PLO and the calamitous 1967 war, the Palestinians themselves endorsed a state in which Arabs and Jews could exercise full and equal rights and liberties.[80] This vision was what they struggled for both before and after Israel's occupation of the West Bank and Gaza. Hence, "the initial platform of the PLO was to establish an independent, democratic, secular state in all of Palestine, in its pre-1948 borders."[81] Such an accomplishment, while evasive for the early proponents of one state, proved impossible, particularly given Israel's military muscle and years of exclusive identity solidification.

Contemporary picture

While the 1993 peace process laid the one-state solution to rest in the official PLO rhetoric, that option has continued to inspire intellectual curiosity, innovation, and debate.[82] In fact, some have noted that given the expansionist and deep-rooted nature of Israel's occupation and the fortification of its dominion over the land, the one-state solution has become inevitable.[83] This is due to a number of factors, including the entrenchment of Jewish settlements in the West Bank, the fact that a military solution is not viable, and the related notion that ethnic cleansing would not bode well for a democratic country like Israel, not to mention the international outrage it would produce.[84] Following in Arendt's footsteps, some have argued that "Israel-Palestine ... was always far too small and sensitive a region to sustain two states" and that "the Jewish state now faces the last act of its own Greek tragedy – the Zionist project to reconstitute a Jewish nation-state in an ancient land already holding an indigenous national society."[85] Those intent on Israel remaining a Jewish state find themselves caught between the one-state solution and that of two states as outlined by the roadmap. However, in the present, the number of dissenters opposed to the consequences of dividing the land continues to grow.

One of the most heartfelt criticisms of the two-state solution came from an Israeli government insider, former deputy mayor of Jerusalem Meron Benvenisti. Reluctantly he mourned, "it is not easy for me to part with my father's dream of a Jewish nation-state. It's hard for me. For most of my life that was my dream too."[86] Benvenisti then directed his attention to the two-state solution.

> The conclusion is that the seemingly rational solution of two states for two nations can't work here. The model of a division into two nation-states is inapplicable. It doesn't reflect the depth of the conflict and doesn't sit with the scale of the entanglement that exists in large parts of the country. You can erect all the walls in the world here but you won't be able to overcome the fact that there is only one aquifer here and the same air that all the streams run into the same sea. You won't be able to overcome the fact that this country will not tolerate a border in its midst. ... There is no choice but to think about western Palestine [Eretz Israel, or the land of Israel] as one geopolitical unit. ... What we have to do is try to reach a situation of personal and collective equality within the framework of one overall regime throughout the country.[87]

Perhaps the most striking feature of the thoughts presented above is that they provide an account of someone who has experienced the hopeless interdependence between his people and the Palestinians. This is something that may not be captured by distant "solutions" and orders, particularly under American hegemony, since most plans put forth by the international community do not have the experience of Benvenisti and others like him, who have lived on the land and could attest first-hand to the futility of separating an apparently indivisible country.

Others like new historian Benny Morris have highlighted the senselessness of separating Arabs and Jews, albeit unenthusiastically. In a *Ha'aretz* interview, Morris agreed to journalist Ari Shavit's proposition that two possibilities exist in light of the reality on the ground in the Israeli–Palestinian conflict, "either a cruel, tragic Zionism, or the foregoing of Zionism."[88] Such a choice means that the only palatable position is to discard mainstream Zionism as it has existed since the founding of Israel. Alternatively, those that wish to maintain a pure Jewish state would have to contend with the following unsavory propositions.

> First of all, the fence [wall] is not built like the Berlin Wall. It's a fence that we will be guarding on either side ... when 2.5 million people live in a closed-off Gaza, it's going to be a human catastrophe. Those people will become even bigger animals than they are today, with the aid of an insane fundamentalist Islam. The pressure at the border will be awful. It's going to be a terrible war. So, if we want to remain alive, we will have to kill and kill and kill. All day, every day. ... If we don't kill, we

will cease to exist. The only thing that concerns me is how to ensure that the boys and men who are going to have to do the killing will be able to return home to their families and be normal human beings.[89]

While coming from someone who has rejected the one-state idea, that position pointed out in grisly detail what the two-state solution, particularly in the era of the "wall," would look like.

To avert that, supporters of the one-state solution point to the follies of maintaining the course on which Israel has set itself after occupying the West Bank and Gaza. Building the wall has ensured that the Jewish state could bypass its negotiating partner altogether. Its imposition on the Palestinians and the grandstanding surrounding it especially by the Israeli right wing – but also by some well-meaning liberals – appear to mimic permanence in the midst of upheaval. Many in the left, particularly in the peace camp, oppose the wall precisely because it gives a false sense of security. It also cajoles Israeli hardliners into thinking that the "Palestinian problem" has finally been dealt with. Pro-Israel groups like AIPAC have been responsible for diffusing such ideas.[90] However, many within Israel itself have expressed indignation at the construction of the wall, as demonstrated by the following statement, which also calls for one state as a more enduring outcome than two states.

> In essence, the binational principle is the deepest antithesis of the wall. The purpose of the wall is to separate, to isolate, to imprison the Palestinians in pens. But the wall imprisons the Israelis, too. It turns Israel into a ghetto. The wall is the greatest despairing solution of the Jewish-Zionist society. It is the last desperate act of those who cannot confront the Palestinian issue. ... In the face of that I say the opposite. I say that we were apparently too forgiving toward Zionism; that the Jews who came here and found a land that wasn't empty adopted a pattern of unrestrained force. ... But that force has played itself out. ... If Israel remains a colonialist state in its character, it will not survive. ... In general, we have to shift to a binational mode of thinking. Maybe in the end we have to create a new, binational Israel, just as a new, multiracial South Africa was created.[91]

This type of thinking demonstrates the necessity for coexistence, the end both Israelis and Palestinians wish for, even though most cling to their national aspirations. By pointing to the concrete case of South Africa, it offers an attainable path to those hoping for a *fair* resolution of the Israeli–Palestinian conflict.

Imprisoning the Palestinians behind the wall is the consequence of separation, a natural outcome of an inherently more powerful state in the midst of a materially less capable people. The disparateness of power between Israel and the Palestinians means that any two-state solution would reflect that reality. Some in the PA have already realized that a state of their own means that they would have to live in perpetual inferiority to Israel. This would continue the outcome of the occupation without the taxing dedication of Israel maintaining its dominion over the Palestinians. In essence, it would be easier for Israel under the internationally mandated two-state solution to control the Palestinians without doing any of the arduous work. Seeing that, Palestinian official Hani al-Masri argued,

> we will have no choice but to abandon the choice of establishing a Palestinian state on the territories occupied in 1967 and revert to the option of establishing a secular, democratic state in the entirety of Palestine where Jews, Muslims and Christians live on equal footing. ... The goal we must pursue, and Israel can't prevent us from pursuing it, lies in dismantling the Palestinian Authority and abandoning Palestinian statehood.[92]

This point of view threatens the existence of Israel's last line of defense, the Palestinians ruled by their own quasi-government. It also extinguishes hope for an Arab Palestine.

Abandoning Palestinian statehood, however, does not have to be mourned any more than discarding the exclusivity of Israel as a Jewish homeland is to be grieved. According to Raja Halwani, "sharing Palestine is not a lesser of two evils. It is a high – indeed, given the conflict, the highest – good."[93] Celebrating the one-state solution as the best possible outcome spells doom for Israeli and Palestinian nationalisms as they have been nurtured for over a century. Paradoxically, it also may allow for the realization of the peace desired by both people. And although the one-state solution seems to be eclipsed from the official framework for peace, some Jews laud its return after a lengthy hiatus. Hence,

> Palestinians are now returning to an earlier, more principled stage of their political development and argument – the PLO solution of a secular, democratic single state in the whole of Palestine; one state that allows equal rights to Jews and Arabs alike. It is ironic that through failing to grasp the nettle which would have enabled them to keep a separate Israeli state in the pre-1967 borders, Israeli leaders have forced a change in Palestinian thinking: "if we are not allowed to live as a free people in 22 per cent of our country, or come to that, even 10 per cent of it, maybe we should go back to fighting to liberate the whole country, for both people to live in peace, as equals."[94]

That type of reasoning represents one of the more powerful positions in the advocacy for one state. It recognizes that Palestinians have much to gain through the principles underlying it and that the only thing they would lose is their vision of a "rump state" which daily, continues to shrink in size and autonomy and therefore in significance and viability.[95] Arguments for one state appear to stem from the realization that Israel may reduce Palestinians to Bantustans reminiscent of the South African apartheid regime or the reservations of Native Americans in the United States. Those arguments gain energy as the Jewish state continues its occupation over the Palestinians and has so far refused to address final status issues based on offers of coexistence by its neighbors.

Meanwhile, in its attempt at severing what Chief of Staff Moshe Ya'alon has dubbed the Palestinian "cancer" from its body, Israel seeks to fragment Palestinian territory and society.[96] By achieving that objective, the Jewish state would have free reign over the Palestinians and could further dictate their struggle to survive as a national community. Furthermore, the policy of limiting the Palestinians to tight enclaves creates a self-fulfilling prophecy of hard-line Zionist thought, which has held that the Arabs cannot be trusted to rule themselves, may never be allowed to live as equals, and therefore must be dominated both for their own good and for Israel's well-being. Such an approach has created conditions whereby the Palestinians, due to "their certain inability to overcome" their "economically doomed" and politically "withering" conditions may resort to violent means both against one another in civil war, and against the Israelis whom they blame for their wretchedness. In such a setting, the wall may be "deemed necessary by the Israeli government to partly contain the simmering unrest certain to arise from the dismembered 'state.'"[97]

Israel's most obstinate position has been on its settlements in the West Bank. Hence,

> To grasp the actual immobility of the Jewish settlements, we need to appreciate not only the grid's physical weight – its size and infrastructure and its impact on the land and on Palestinian society – but also its political weight. The latter includes not only its off-cited [sic] importance to some currents of Zionist imagination but also its less-recognized ties to major state agencies as well as private commercial and industrial investment. These political and economic aspects obviously interplay: evacuating so vast a social infrastructure, including hundreds of thousands of people in full-scale cities would entail huge costs and therefore require a tremendous political will on the part of any Israeli government. But such will is not simply missing in this case: Israeli public policy has for decades been directed into expanding the settlements, through channels more extensive and complicated than most people realize. While occasionally withdrawing a few outposts (with much public fanfare), the Israeli government has actually been funding and building the settlements and working hard to attract settlers to them (doubling their population in the 1990s), for three decades of (supposed) peace talks and at an accelerating pace since the Oslo negotiations began in the early 1990s. Assumptions that this state policy might be

reversed and the settlers withdrawn have gravely underestimated all these dimensions.[98]

That reality means that Israel has one of two options: either, as Baruch Kimmerling called it, "politicide," which entails "a process that has, as its ultimate goal, the dissolution of the Palestinian people's existence as a legitimate social, political, and economic entity," or their absorption into a greater democratic state.[99] Given the tremendous strength of Israel compared to the Palestinians and the Arab states, the politicide option could be put into effect with impunity. However, Israel may only employ it at its own risk given that it would draw massive international protest and open the Jewish state to an explosion of terrorism. In this light, the one-state option appears much less sinister but would signal the death of both Israel's exclusive ethnic identity and the Palestinians' aspirations for a state on their portion of the land.

Despite the trauma that the dissolution of the Jewish state[100] and Palestinian nationalism would bring, Edward Said argued that it might begin the process of healing after years of anguish and violence. Said, however, was never a blind optimist. He recognized, for example, that "the conflict is intractable only to the extent that it was always a contest over the same land by two peoples who believed they had valid title to it and who hoped that the other side would in time give up or go away."[101] That of course never happened. Instead, each side fought for decades only to come to the peace table and negotiate under the US-led international community's guidance. However, those negotiations did not bear fruit. Many complained that this failure was the result of issues that branched out from separating Israelis and Palestinians. Hence, Said observed,

> clearly, a system of privileging Israeli Jews will satisfy neither those who want an entirely homogeneous Jewish state nor those who live there but are not Jewish. ... Israeli Palestinians also feel that they are already in their country, and refuse any talk of moving to a separate Palestinian state, should one come into being. ... It is also evident that as an Arab people ... Palestinians want at all costs to preserve their Arab identity as part of the surrounding Arab and Islamic world. The problem is that Palestinian self-determination in a separate state is unworkable, just as unworkable as the principle of separation between a demographically mixed, irreversibly connected Arab and Jewish population in Israel and the occupied territories. The question, I believe, is not how to devise means for persisting in trying to separate them but to see whether it is possible for them to live together fairly and peacefully.[102]

Like others examined so far, Said thus added his mark to the one-state advocacy. In the final instance, he warned, "Palestinians and Israelis are there to stay." The challenge, however, is how to accomplish "peaceful coexistence and genuine reconciliation. Real self-determination."[103]

Before getting to that, supporters of one state have thoroughly detailed the intractable situation on the ground in Israel and the occupied territories. Currently, "the West Bank holds ... some 141 settlements and some 230,000 Jewish settlers, according to Israeli official figures," while "independent surveys have identified 157 'built-up areas' and dozens of additional outposts."[104] Such information shows a picture of interdependence coupled with hostility as most Israeli settlers carry weapons and have the protection of the IDF while the Palestinians view both with animosity. That is because to Palestinians, the West Bank represents more than just one of the last vestiges of territory left to them by Israel. Even under occupation, its "village culture has indeed assumed an iconic centrality in Palestinian nationalism, which symbolically celebrates their emblematic cultural practices (music, dress, embroidery), and real or supposed values."[105] This connection has always formed the backbone of the Palestinian attachment to the land. In sum, they are not going anywhere unless transferred by force. Tilley wrote, "deep-historical (in some areas, ancient) archipelagos of highland Palestinian peasant villages, with their famous olive and other fruit orchards and artisan industries, are still largely intact in the West Bank highlands (although under grave assault)."[106] When considered through this lens, Palestinians have plenty to lose from a continued occupation that has stripped them of most of their land.

On the other side, Israelis wish to maintain a safe haven for Jews that not only took years and blood to accomplish, but one that also has given them a place to express their identity through democratic means. However, their fear of the Palestinians, while justifiable under present conditions, will only worsen if the current stalemate continues. Israel's policies of domination will only make matters worse. Thus,

> Israel would face a political crisis. Two million disenfranchised (mostly poor) Palestinians embedded in Israeli society would ruin any lingering pretense Israel might make to being a true democracy, and the disenfranchised Palestinian population would be unlikely to tolerate its own exclusion forever. As its own national base disintegrated, it would agitate for political representation, challenging Israeli democracy on its own principles. If the Palestinians did eventually gain the vote, they would combine with 1.5 million Israeli Arabs to compose an ethnic majority – wrecking the Jewishness of the Jewish state. ... Primarily to avert this future, increasing numbers of Jewish Israelis support withdrawing from the settlements and granting Palestinians a state of their own.[107]

However, such a withdrawal is not likely given the seeming permanence of the settlements and because of other reasons discussed above. Since independence, many prominent Israeli figures have explicitly stated their reservations over departure from the occupied territories. This included

Menachem Begin's contention that pulling out would lead to "national suicide," Golda Meir's admonition that calls for withdrawal are "treasonable,"
and Abba Eban's statement that quitting Arab lands brings "a memory of
Auschwitz."[108] In fact, as shown elsewhere, the well known meeting and
subsequent press conference on April 14, 2004 between Bush and Sharon
affirmed keeping West Bank settlements in place.[109] In addition, the two
leaders concurred on maintaining Israel's Jewishness. Although the roadmap's two-state mandate may accomplish that goal, maintaining the settlements
makes it implausible.

Future strategies for the pro-Arab lobby

The AIPAC challenge

After looking at the difficulties confronting the two-state solution and outlining the bulk of debate surrounding its only viable alternative, one state for
Israelis and Palestinians, anyone interested in peace must carefully consider
the following. First, while the pro-Arab lobby supports a Palestinian state as
the end of American policy, it has not effectively countered pro-Israel actions
against the two-state solution. Although this is an obvious point, it has a
major addendum. That is, in addition to showing how a Palestinian state is
in the interest of the US, pro-Arab groups must clearly articulate that the
peaceful substitute to Palestinian statehood would be one state that forces
Israel to cease being an exclusive refuge for Jews. Such a development would
be a far cry from where the international community, American policymakers and public opinion, the pro-Israel lobby, and the pro-Arab lobby
stand on resolving the conflict. Although it may be argued that the more
likely scenario may be a continuation of the bloodshed, the conflict must end
in one way or another since it may escalate to engulf the entire world.[110]
Members of the Quartet behind the UNSC resolutions and the roadmap
outlining a Palestinian state, as well as the Israelis and Palestinians, understand that fact all too well.

The scenarios of conflict include continued strife between Israelis and
Palestinians and the possibility of politicide, the conflict spilling into other
locales, or a resolve to end it given the realities on the ground. Therefore, it
is essential to outline the available approaches to peace, two states as currently authorized by the roadmap, or the one-state solution, which has a
lengthy tradition, albeit with little formal support. Pro-Arab groups are well
positioned to invoke both solutions efficiently since their raison d'être is the
advancement of rights, something that either one state or two would have to
accomplish in order to bring about *genuine* peace.[111]

Second, even if pro-Arab groups fell short in offsetting the pro-Israel
lobby's hindrance of all solutions, they may employ their access to public
opinion and policymakers in a push-pull manner. This would involve Arab
American organizations pulling public opinion toward favoring Palestinian

equality *in* Israel while privately pushing policymakers to honor the US commitment to two states. The struggle for equality in the public discourse may be undertaken by appealing to the Jewish state's rhetoric, and challenging it on its own ethical-political turf. Lest we forget, there is a framework for equality in Israel's Declaration of Establishment, which calls on "the Arab inhabitants of the State of Israel to preserve peace and participate in the upbuilding of the State on the basis of full and equal citizenship and due representation in all its provisional and permanent institutions."[112] The sentiment behind that passage may be appealed to in order to realize the equality of Palestinians as necessary to peace in a single state on the one hand while on the other pressuring policymakers to take serious action toward the two-state solution in order to preserve Israel's Jewish identity.

At this point, it may be argued that pro-Arab organizations in the US already do that. That is not true. In fact, many in the pro-Arab lobby are allergic to any mention of the one-state solution. When asked about it, Hussein Ibish responded in a manner characteristic of the Arab American leadership.

> The one-state "solution" is an unworkable concept. In it, we find virtually no constituency. Its main consequence is stymieing the end to occupation. Its principled political effect is that it shows that these people [the Palestinians] do not want their freedom, rather they want to end Israel. It will be perceived as fundamentally anti-Semitic. It shows that the Arab side cannot reconcile itself, that we have been maximalists from the beginning. It squanders away virtually unanimous support for our position [that of two states] in the US, Russia, the Arab League, Europe, Israel, and among the Palestinians. It also is a solution built upon the same fault lines of sectarian violence that currently shock Iraq as the US tries to keep that country together. Although I see their point of view [that of the supporters of one state], we [the pro-Arab lobby] take a principled stand against it based on these reasons.[113]

While Ibish put forth a compelling case, the one-state solution should not be a taboo, particularly as it pertains to the *strategy* of the pro-Arab lobby, which could be informed by the following formula. Without the roadmap, which in President Bush's words, calls on "us to advance the cause of two states living side by side in peace, and helping both parties eliminate the obstacles that prevent an agreement from being reached,"[114] then the only other solution is that of a country like the United States, which may not "deny to any person within its jurisdiction the equal protection of the laws."[115]

Aside from being a powerful argument to influence Americans toward Palestinian equality with Jews, such a position would force AIPAC and its associates to reckon with what the Israelis themselves have known since 1967: the sustainability of the Jewish state depends on resolving the

Palestinian problem. While many propositions have been advanced toward that end, from politicide to unilateral pullouts, the majority of Israelis support the two-state solution.[116] They do so because of the understanding that it is the only viable option for peace since it avoids calamity to their Jewish state. The pro-Israel lobby will never countenance what its support for Israeli hard-liners has done to suppress chances for peace unless the pro-Arab lobby and its allies use the strategic parlance of the one-state solution. Such action would not only aim to sway policymakers and public opinion, it would also compel AIPAC and its followers to confront the implications of their actions on American policy toward the Jewish state.

This brings us to the third point of foreign policy influence. In lobbying the US government to favor a chief aspiration of Palestinian nationalism, the state of Palestine, Arab American organizations may adopt an approach similar to that of earlier Jewish political activism, which at some level succeeded because it had two extreme elements and a middling one. When the First Zionist Congress convened in Basel, Switzerland in 1898, it brought under one roof an abundance of divergent ideas, which ranged in scope from complete ethnic cleansing to cooperation with the inhabitants.[117] As demonstrated by the one-state thinking outlined above, the idea of coexistence with the Palestinians had quite a bit of currency before Israel's founding and continues to live on today. This was the case, even though the scheme of a Jewish state ultimately triumphed with its independence and had to be recreated to accommodate various strands of Zionism and Judaism throughout the decades of its existence.[118]

The illustration above should not be lost on the pro-Arab lobby. In essence, what the grand Zionist enterprises such as the Yishuv were doing prior to the founding of Israel, was lobbying for inclusive solutions to the problem of Jewish homelessness. The same was true for Zionists who demanded an exclusive enclave to serve as a sanctuary for Jews. In this regard, the Israel pressure groups of the early years had a variety of options on the table that were decidedly competitive because they were mutually exclusive. In short, this is the lesson for the pro-Arab lobby: the likelihood of a Palestinian state would be enhanced if it was presented as the middling element among a variety of options for peace. By unequivocally censuring any pursuit of one state, pro-Arab lobbyists shut down the possibility of creating a policy pincer whereby the evils of extremes on both sides are shunned in favor of doing what is right. Practically speaking, this means the abandonment of the compulsory prohibition on the one-state solution, if not in principled terms, then at least as a tactical matter. Such action will not only increase pro-Arab competitiveness with the Israel lobby by taking a page from the playbook of early Zionism, it would ultimately lead to a stronger likelihood of US policymakers applying pressure on the Jewish state to take appropriate measures and to refrain from hindering a Palestinian state from peacefully existing on its borders through the policy mechanisms already in place.

Fourth, the pro-Arab lobby's weaknesses must never be exaggerated vis-à-vis the pro-Israel lobby. This has been a common mistake of almost everyone involved in the discussion of factors acting on US foreign policy. Even when it has been acknowledged that "there is a growing Arab lobby present in the United States," it was always pointed out that it is nothing comparable to the pro-Israel lobby.[119] While that is true for the most part, as has been detailed throughout the previous chapters, the pro-Arab lobby has a key political weapon against its counterpart, unanimous support for its position on Palestinian statehood. Hence, regarding the message of each lobby, the Arab side has a vital advantage in that its solution to the Israeli–Palestinian conflict is the method of choice for everyone concerned. The pro-Israel lobby has not been able to offer an alternative and has become a casualty of its own devices, which have contributed to a lack of direction in the peace process.

Pro-Arab lobbyists and their friends have an advantage in the sense that they are collectively the only domestic group that "affirms a solution" to the Israeli–Palestinian conflict.[120] Since policymakers and their constituents believe such a development is in the interest of the US, they are more likely to pay attention to a positive solution rather than to those that have sought to delay it. Given the strength of the pro-Israel lobby and the weakness of its pro-Arab competitor, the current lack of resolve in American policy may continue well into the future.[121] However, since most domestic actors on foreign policy making have converged in seeking a resolution to the Israeli–Palestinian conflict, the question is not *whether* policy will reflect those aspirations, but *when* it will do so. Still, in the final instance, this does not say anything about which solution will ultimately end the conflict, two states or one, or something altogether different.

Winners win

Hard work in the late 1980s and 1990s by the pro-Arab lobby and its allies has bequeathed to their political posterity the roadmap in the 2000s, a decisive victory for those interested in peace.[122] At this time, the decision has to be made about what to do with it. Even though to a large extent, the situation between Israelis and Palestinians will take center stage for what will happen next, in regards to American foreign policy, the pro-Arab and pro-Israel lobbies have had a role to play in how the US pursued its interests in the past and how it will do so in the future. This is no small part, since American power will continue to have momentous bearing on global affairs. In its strengthened position, the pro-Arab lobby has to pursue its aim of Palestinian liberation carefully. Although it does not have to beat the pro-Israel lobby at its own game, what it does have to do is "maximize its position given the shape of the US foreign policy terrain."[123]

Right now American policymakers are officially set on having a Palestinian state. However, the belief that Palestinians cannot rule themselves prevents anyone from pressuring the Jewish state to allow for its establishment. Hence, following Israel's lead, public opinion and policymakers, particularly since the election of the Hamas leadership in 2006, have refused to deal with the Palestinians in any serious manner.[124] Quite a bit of effort had to be exerted to bring public opinion and policymakers to that view. In particular, it took years of pro-Israel lobbying to convince a majority in the US that the Jewish state is a vulnerable speck in a turbulent sea of Arabs/Muslims and that the two countries have common enemies, beginning with communism during the Cold War and terrorism after the collapse of the Soviet Union and later the 9/11 attacks. Those points demonstrate how the Israel lobby simply had to work from residual gains and changes in the international environment.

Likewise, the pro-Arab lobby has enjoyed a series of advances that it could capitalize on, but must not mistakenly view them as permanent. Resolving the Israeli–Palestinian conflict with two states, after all, is something that could fizzle out at anytime American policymakers and their constituents are persuaded that it is in their country's interest not to pursue it.[125] This is something that happened during the 1980s. Whereas some Americans began to favor a Palestinian state during the Camp David period of the late 1970s, during the Reagan era of strategic alliance between the US and Israel, that concept was submerged by the renewed perception of communism as a threat.

Coinciding with the pro-Israel lobby's work to convince Americans that Israel is the best ally to defeat that threat in the Middle East, the strategic relationship left little space to maneuver for those interested in peace through a Palestinian state. In that regard, one positive outcome of Zionist efforts in the US significantly contributed to others. Hence, throughout the 1980s, the primary occupation was with how to defer Israel having to deal with the Palestinians for as long as possible. That did not last, however, as the pro-Arab lobby exploited the Intifada against Israeli occupation in order to argue for the necessity of Palestinian self-determination, a principle that would later gain legitimacy. After the collapse of the Soviet Union and the end of the Cold War, the Oslo agreements between Israelis and Palestinians were concretized into limited autonomy with the PLO getting partial rule over some of the occupied territories. US policymakers furthered the diplomatic gains at Oslo with the roadmap. Recounting history in that manner shows that influencing policy is a slow, linear process which takes years to yield desired outcomes. As it concerns prospects for a Palestinian state, the pro-Arab lobby, while far from working in as rigorous a manner as groups like AIPAC, did manage to articulate its position at an opportune time "that brought heightened US attention to peace in the Middle East."[126]

Hence, policymaking has a logic that is both understandable and predictable. While the past cannot be used as an indicator of the future, what is known with some confidence is that much as wealth accumulation takes a certain amount of market capital to begin with – hence "accumulation," not "spontaneous generation" – so too does political power in trying to influence decisions in the foreign policy realm. The potential and growing strength of the pro-Arab lobby has coincided with the development of a solution that takes into account the long-standing aspirations of not just the Palestinians, but of Arab Americans as well. Perhaps this is the reason why many pro-Arab lobbyists were so suspicious of the one-state solution: it ostensibly takes away from the gains that they have made after US acceptance of Palestinian statehood. Thus, while the Arab American Institute (AAI) and the American-Arab Anti-Discrimination Committee (ADC) refuse to take an official position on the one-state solution aside from what could be gleaned from private interviews, because of its potentially divisive nature, the American Task Force on Palestine (ATFP) has strongly condemned it.[127] However, considering the preponderance of issues examined as they pertain to the pro-Arab lobby and the foreign policy milieu in which it operates, we see that advocating one state out of tactical, if not moral concerns, may make it more likely that a proper effort will be made toward a comprehensive solution to the Israeli–Palestinian conflict.

Since that issue is the "number one cause of concern for the Arab American community and unites them like no other," working to resolve it will bring pro-Arab pressure groups more standing among their base, not to mention new allies from the ranks of those interested in peace.[128] At the same time, pushing for the two-state solution will only give the Arab lobby more influence in Beltway politics as it acts to enforce a commitment explicitly stated by policymakers as a vital US interest. Prescriptions viewed in a state's national interests have traditionally been more likely to succeed. And, as Ibish put it, "no one likes to take on a losing issue because there is nothing there for them. Everyone, from policymakers to advocates, likes to be involved in issues that are likely to succeed."[129] While it is not yet known whether the two-state solution will come to fruition, it is a verifiable fact that the US has expressed its interest in bringing it about. However, Ibish's sentiment is also a warning. He noted that "Clinton was humiliated by the outbreak of the second Intifada and the breakdown of the peace process, so Bush wanted nothing to do with it."[130] This ultimately may explain why the Bush administration took a "hands off" approach to the Israeli–Palestinian conflict in its first few months in office. However, that changed after 9/11, even though the outcome of the Bush roadmap did not produce a Palestinian state by 2005, the year in which the two-state agreement was to conclude. In light of that disappointment and the collapse of other peace talks, US policymakers expressed reservations about the likelihood of peace.[131] And while crises in other parts of the world may have a lot to do with the American lack of consideration for a Palestinian state, perhaps a more germane reason is the fact that no one wants to hop on the metaphorical sinking ship that the situation between the Israelis and Palestinians has proved to be.[132]

Regardless of how bleak prospects for peace may appear, the pitch of American policymaking toward the Israeli–Palestinian conflict appears very different than it did during the Cold War. Even though US evenhandedness, a prime goal of the pro-Arab lobby, has not been attained, the fact is that American policy is now more sober toward the necessity of a political solution to the Palestinian problem than it has been previously. America's allies, such as the United Kingdom, a key player in the Quartet, share that sobriety. Sir Nigel Sheinwald, Britain's ambassador to the US, observed, "my government understands the tumultuous nature of a protracted conflict. In addition to doing more for the Palestinians than anybody else, we have Tony Blair over there trying to bring peace between the parties, an outcome that the international community is very much keen on."[133] When combined with American leadership, these efforts may finally pay off in the struggle for a just solution.

From the Cold war zenith of the pro-Israel lobby's power to the growing effectiveness of the pro-Arab voices after the Intifada and the collapse of Soviet communism, American policy has taken great leaps toward the realization of peace in the Middle East. Similarly, the first Gulf War, Madrid, Oslo, the war on terrorism, and the invasion of Iraq, were international events that demanded significant adaptation in the way that pro-Arab and pro-Israel lobbyists pursued their particular ends. All of this points to the fluidity of decision-making concerning foreign affairs, a game in which participants may win or lose depending on how they play "not just at the legislative level, but also in the court of public opinion."[134] Because of its limited resources, it is in the area of public opinion that the pro-Arab lobby has sought to contribute the most influence. Whether in trying to control a part of the discourse on issues pertaining to the Palestinian problem or attempting to whisper in the ears of power during important international crises, pro-Arab pressure groups have tried to make strides that ought to be acknowledged.

Yet unfortunately, because their pro-Israel competitors are so powerful, little attention has been paid to the pro-Arab lobby. This book has tried to remedy that by looking at the possible ways that lobby has sought to inform public opinion and elite perceptions to an extent that shaped foreign policy outcomes. The relationship between inputs and outputs has preoccupied analysts since the dawn of political inquiry. At the input level, it was demonstrated that while all sorts of factors go into convincing policymakers of a particular course of action, the most important ones are public opinion and interest groups, since in any democracy they have considerable bearing on the outcomes of decision-making.[135] Although, as has been shown elsewhere, the executive branch of government is less susceptible to popular and interest group pressures than Congress, the electoral reality means that at some level, both have to keep an eye on their citizens' preferences. These may be articulated in one form or another, but most often, policymakers are apprised of their electorate's pulse through opinion polling and special interest groups.[136]

Often, public opinion and lobbying organizations interact with one another in ways worthy of quite a bit more inquiry than has been offered so far. An example of this comes from an area left largely unexamined by this study, but that nevertheless deserves mention: the effect of the media on public opinion and policymaking on the Israeli–Palestinian conflict. Interest groups in the US understand the key place held by the mass media in influencing political outcomes. The pro-Arab lobby is no exception. For instance, an email from activist Yasmin Hamidi stated the following concerning the sixtieth anniversary of the Palestinian Nakba and Israel's founding.

> Hi all, On Friday, the Arab-American community organized a large rally in front of the U.N. I thought I'd share the AP story on this rally, which ended up running in around 90 papers internationally, including Ha'aretz (homepage), Guardian, IHT, Washington Post, Chicago Tribune, LA Times, Seattle Post Intelligencer, Miami Herald, Houston Chronicle and many others! And just to pat myself on the back, I did the PR. :-) However, I wasn't involved in the bulk of organizing and the core team deserves a tremendous amount of credit for leading an inclusive team effort and working their butts off for weeks and weeks! Also, Hala alumnus Maysoon Zayid spoke at the rally.[137]

There are hundreds of examples like this one, which show the small, yet gradual moves that the pro-Arab lobby takes in order to exercise influence using the news media. Such publicity actions, which admittedly do not in and of themselves produce major shifts, when implemented with direct pressure on policymakers particularly at pivotal times, do eventually contribute to changes in the formulation of decisions. Above all, it must be remembered that what appeared to be baby steps for the pro-Arab lobby in bringing attention to the Intifada during the late 1980s and early 1990s ultimately matched shifts in American policy toward the Israeli–Palestinian conflict. This is the nature of foreign policy influence. Change happens gradually, even if it may appear very minute at the time. This is another lesson of which pro-Arab lobbyists were keenly aware.[138]

Conclusion

As the US finds itself bogged down after years of mayhem from the removal of the Taliban from power in Afghanistan and the ouster and ultimate execution of Saddam Hussein, there needs to be a change in direction.[139] That is only possible by a genuine interest in bringing peace to the Israeli–Palestinian conflict, the end of which would not only relieve two exhausted peoples from war, it may also bring American policy new respect in the wake of several other disasters throughout the region. The US global war on terrorism will ultimately be deemed a cataclysmic failure if necessary action is not taken in order to counter what Jamal Nassar referred to as "the roots" of political violence emanating from deep within the Arab-Islamic world.[140] Such action needs to be wide-ranging and centered not only on the US national interest, but also on what justice demands. If examined in depth, the two may not be that incompatible, particularly as they pertain to the Israeli–Palestinian conflict. In that instance, after all is said and done, US foreign policy has chosen the most suitable, agreed upon, and perhaps the just path to peace, the two-state solution.[141] Time is running out on that solution as every day Israel consolidates its hold on the territorial composition of any future Palestinian state.[142]

The cast examined in this work, including the American public, the pro-Israel lobby, and the pro-Arab lobby, understand in theory what needs to be done by policymakers in order to fulfill not just what is in the US interest, but also what is in the interests of all sides concerned. The international community, particularly the states of the Middle East, North and sub-Saharan Africa, Europe, South and East Asia, many of which have been subject to numerous terrorist attacks, appreciate the high stakes for global security.[143] Since resolving the Palestinian question would effectively remove it from the list of grievances of terrorist organizations like al Qa'eda, all members of the UN wish to see concrete action on that front.[144] Defending the invasion of Iraq, President Bush himself once remarked, "when the Middle East grows in democracy and prosperity and hope, the terrorists will lose their sponsors, lose their recruits, and lose their hopes for turning that region into a base for attacks on America and our allies around the world."[145] Regardless of how we judge his policies, Bush's statement captures an essential truth about the nature of terrorism: the ability to express injustice or aspirations through a genuinely democratic system mitigates the need to resort to violence. The Palestinians must be given an opportunity to put that proposition to the test. In addition, resolving the Israeli–Palestinian conflict would remove one of the most poignant issues that most around the world take with the US.

In the final instance, such a resolution will not be forthcoming anytime soon so long as the pro-Israel lobby continues to operate without more checks from competing groups and individuals, particularly those that make up the pro-Arab lobby. The nature of the pluralist system in which policy decision-making takes place means just that. Unless the system itself is changed by curtailing the actions of lobbying organizations, and hence of democracy as Americans know it, the pro-Israel lobby will continue to prevent the two-state solution as it has done to this point. However, even if such unsavory action was undertaken, since public opinion matters in foreign policymaking, the pro-Israel lobby will continue to use its free speech right to sway the hearts and minds of the masses and their leadership toward favoring the Jewish state. This will inevitably be reflected by policies that privilege Israel, particularly its extremist elements which have so far proven themselves incapable of accepting a Palestinian state.

In the interest of protecting pluralist democracy at the procedural and substantive levels, what needs to happen in order to bring about a Palestinian state is the strengthening of the pro-Israel lobby's rivals. That will not take place unless we at least begin to recognize the role that the pro-Arab lobby has played – and will potentially play in the future – in its attempts to shape American policy toward the Israeli–Palestinian conflict. Once such recognition takes place, change needs to happen within the pro-Arab and pro-peace constituencies as well, particularly toward understanding their efficacy at shaping political outcomes. When President Jimmy Carter was asked about what Arab Americans and everyone interested in peace need to do in order to ensure that their government makes good on its roadmap for a Palestinian state, he replied, "let your voice be heard, don't be timid, stand up for your rights, don't let anybody push you around!"[146] The time for that is now. It is never too late to achieve peace.

Appendix 1
Arab lobby questionnaire

Questionnaire (30–150 minute interviews)

Date:
Organization:
Name and position of interviewee:

Organization information

I know what your organization does, but I would like to hear from you, what are the objectives of your organization?
What has the organization done to bring those about?
What is the organization's position on the Israeli–Palestinian conflict?
What were the organization's reactions to the "handshake"?
According to your organization, what impacts did the handshake have on foreign policy and lobbying efforts?

Foreign policy

According to your organization, what constitutes US national interest in the Israeli–Palestinian conflict?
Does your organization think that there is a difference between US and Israeli interests? Does your organization think that there is a difference between US and Arab interests? According to the organization, how did US interests change after the Cold War?
What, according to the organization, was the impact of the Intifada on US foreign policy?
What, according to the organization, was the impact of the first Persian Gulf war on US foreign policy?

Resolution

According to your organization, what is the best way to resolve the Israeli–Palestinian conflict?

How did the organization arrive at this resolution?

What is the organization's position on the one-state solution?

Public opinion/policymakers

Does your organization shape public opinion?

Does public opinion shape the organization's mission?

How much access has the organization had to American official circles so far?

Are there any impediments to your organization's access to government officials, particularly in the White House and State Department?

Does your organization have regular contact with members of Congress?

How does your organization have access to the media on a regular basis?

Does your organization issue regular communiqués or circulars in order to react to news?

Vis-à-vis other lobbies

According to your organization, why is the Arab lobby weak in Washington when compared to other lobbies?

In your organization's view, why is the Israel lobby so successful?

Miscellaneous:

Is there anything your organization wishes to add?

Source: Khalil M. Marrar, 2006.

Appendix 2
Public opinion polling on Palestinian statehood

Question: Do you favor or oppose the establishment of an independent Palestinian state on the West Bank and the Gaza strip?

Question: [SPLIT SAMPLE] (Do you favor or oppose the establishment of an independent Palestinian state on the West Bank and the Gaza strip?)

Table A2.1

Date	1. Favor	2. Oppose	3. Don't know	4. Refused
6/1/2003	58.11	21.75	18.58	1.57
7/8/2002	44.3	32.26	20.73	2.71
6/23/2002	74.38	18.08	6.46	1.08
5/22/2002	46.56	28.28	23.89	1.28
12/7/1994	81.2	14.62	2.87	1.31
9/10/1993	52.50	25.45	22.05	0.00

[IF OPPOSE, ASK:] If a Palestinian state WERE established, would you be – Very upset, Somewhat upset, Not too upset, or Not upset?

Table A2.2

Date	Not upset	Not too upset	Somewhat upset	Very upset	Don't know
7/8/2002	25.03	36.6	29.14		0.86

Question: [SPLIT SAMPLE] (Do you favor or oppose the establishment of an independent Palestinian state on the West Bank and the Gaza strip?) [IF OPPOSE, ASK:] Do you feel strongly or not strongly about that?

Table A2.3

Date	Yes, feel strongly	No, do not	Don't know
7/8/2002	71	26.97	2.02

Question: Do you favor or oppose the establishment of an independent Palestinian nation within the territories occupied by Israel in the 1967 war?

Table A2.4

Date	Favor	Oppose	Don't know/refused
3/17/1991	42.13	30.49	27.39
10/14/1990	36.24	30.36	33.40

Question: The Palestinians have fought for many years with Israel for the establishment of a Palestinian state. Israel says that such a Palestinian state would be a threat to its security. Do you think the US should favor a Palestinian state or not?

Table A2.5

Date	Yes, should favor	No, should not	Don't know
9/12/1990	33.4	49.19	17.4

Question: (The Palestinians have fought for many years with Israel for the establishment of a Palestinian state. Israel says that such a Palestinian state would be a threat to its security.) Do you feel the US should or should not bring more pressure to bear on Israel to compromise to achieve peace?

Table A2.6

Date	Should	Should not	Don't know
9/12/1990	60.53	30.87	8.6

Question: Should the issue of Israel's occupation of the West Bank, and creation of a Palestinian state there, become part of an overall diplomatic solution to Iraq's invasion of Kuwait, or do you think this should be treated as a separate issue?

Table A2.7

Date	Part of diplomatic solution	A separate issue	Don't know
9/12/1990	9.44	78.39	12.17

Question: Do you favor or oppose the establishment of an independent Palestinian nation within the territories occupied by Israel in the 1967 war?

Table A2.8

Date	Favor	Oppose	Don't know
5/15/1988	30.3	26.51	43.19

Question: [IF HEARD OR READ ABOUT THE SITUATION IN THE MIDDLE EAST, ASK:] As you know, one of the major questions in the Middle East situation concerns the Palestinian people. Do you think a separate, independent Palestinian nation should be established or do you think the Palestinians should continue to live as they do now in Israel and the neighboring Arab nations?

Table A2.9

Date	Establish a separate nation	Continue as they do	Other	No opinion
7/26/1982	41.21	20.94		26.08
3/13/1979	36.92	25.03		25.28
10/11/1977	32.11	26.97		38.29

Table A2.10

In Israel occupied territory (general)	9.02	44
West Bank of the Jordan River	4.1	20
Gaza strip	0.82	4
Sinai Desert/Sinai	0.2	1
Evenly divided between Israel and the Arabs	7.17	35
In Arab territory (general)	3.69	18
In specific Arab nation	2.46	12
Where they are now	8.81	43
Adjacent to Israel	2.05	10
Anywhere they want/They should have their own land	5.53	27
Palestine/Holy Land (general)	3.69	18
In Israel	2.46	12
Middle East (general)	2.66	13
Misc. (keep list)	8.2	40
Don't know	42.21	206

Total N: 488
Date: 10/11/1977

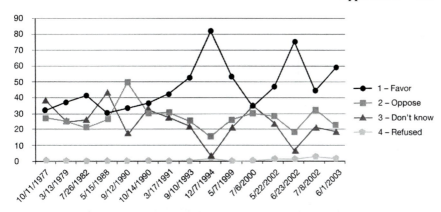

Figure A2 Gallup poll results, 1977–2003
     Source: Gallup Poll, 1977–2003.

Appendix 3
Foreign policy pressure groups

- American-Arab Anti-Discrimination Committee. 4201 Connecticut Ave. NW, Suite 300, Washington, DC 20009. 202-44-2990. Advocacy group for Arabs and Palestinians with 25,000 members. Advocates for a peaceful solution between Palestinians and Israelis. Documents racism toward Arab Americans, provides legal defense, lobbies on civil rights issues. www.adc.org
- American Friends Service Committee (Quakers Mid-Atlantic Region). 4806 York Road, Baltimore, MD 21212. 410-323-7200. This organization espouses non-violence in the Israeli-Palestinian conflict. www.afsc.org
- Americans For Peace Now. 1815 H St. NW, Suite 920, Washington, DC 20006. 202-728-1893. Grassroots group that advocates for Israeli withdrawal from the West Bank and Gaza to safe borders and for an Israeli–Syrian settlement leading to Israeli withdrawal from the Golan Heights. Supports creation of a Palestinian state with certain military restrictions and sharing of Jerusalem. www.peacenow.org
- American Israel Public Affairs Committee, 440 First St. NW, Washington, DC 20001. 202-639-5200. The primary lobby, with a $12 million budget and 60,000 members seeking to influence US policy to strengthen ties to Israel. It moves in step with Israel's government. www.aipac.org
- American Jewish Committee, Jacob Blaustein Building, 165 E. 56th St., New York, NY 10022. 212-751-4000. Promotes interfaith relations, including between Jews and Muslims. www.ajc.org
- American Muslim Council, 1212 New York Ave. NW, Suite 400, Washington, DC 20005. 202-789-2262. Mainly focused on domestic issues, but advocates for an end to terrorism on both sides, an Israeli pullout and a secure state for Palestinians. Holds regular voter registration drives to mobilize American Muslims. www.amconline.org
- American Task Force on Palestine, 815 Connecticut Avenue, Suite 200, Washington, DC 20006. 202-887-0177. Dedicated to bringing about lasting peace and stability in the Middle East by establishing the state of Palestine alongside Israel. www.americantaskforce.org

- American Values (Gary Bauer), 2800 Shirlington Road, Suite 610, Arlington, VA 22206. 703-671-9700. Politically conservative group supports current Israeli government position. www.ouramericanvalues.org
- Anti-Defamation League, Department DJ, 823 United Nations Plaza, New York, NY 10017. 212-885-7700. Defends the interests of Jews worldwide. $50 million budget. Advocates primarily against anti-Semitism but also against racism and bigotry. www.adl.org
- Arab American Action Network. 3148 W. 63rd St., Chicago, IL 60629. 773-436-6060. Grassroots organization Working to improve the quality of life of Arab Americans by building community's capacity to be an active agent for positive social change. www.aaan.org/mission.html
- Arab American Institute, 1600 K St. NW, Suite 601, Washington, DC 20006. 202-429-9210. Secular nonpartisan group focused primarily on encouraging Arab Americans to participate in the political process. www.aaiusa.org
- Association of Arab-American University Graduates, 211 E. 4th St., New York, NY 10009. 212-529-3001. Dedicated to developing, fostering, and promoting educational and cultural information and activities on the Arab world and the Arab American community. www.aaug-asq.org
- B'nai Brith International, 1640 Rhode Island Ave. NW, Washington, DC 20036. 202-857-6511. Advocates support for current Israeli government position on the Middle East conflict. http://bnaibrith.org
- Christian Coalition of America, 499 S. Capitol Street SW, Suite 615, Washington, DC 20003. 202-479-6900. Politically conservative Christian organization supports the position of Israel's government. www.cc.org
- Churches for Middle East Peace, 110 Maryland Ave. NE, #311, Washington, DC 20002. 202-543-1222. Focuses on Washington in the knowledge that sound United States policy is crucial to achieving and maintaining just and stable relationships throughout the Middle East. www.cmep.org
- Presidents Conference. Conference of Presidents of Major Jewish Organizations, 633 Third Ave, New York, NY, 10017. 212-318-6111. Mobilizes support for Israel, educates the public, and coordinates collective action of the American Jewish community. www.conferenceofpresidents.org
- Council on American-Islamic Relations, 453 New Jersey Ave. SE, Washington, DC 20003. 202-488-8787. Advocates an end to Israeli occupation of Palestinian areas and encourages President Bush to meet with American Muslim leaders. It also focuses on defending civil liberties and religious rights of all faiths, particularly Muslims since 9/11. www.cair-net.org
- Electronic Intifada, 1507 E. 53rd St., #500, Chicago, IL 60615. Committed to comprehensive public education on the question of Palestine, the Israeli–Palestinian conflict, and the economic, political, legal, and human dimensions of Israel's occupation of Palestinian territories. http://electronicintifada.net/new.shtml

- Hala Foundation. Hala Salaam Maksoud Foundation for Arab-American Leadership, 815 Connecticut Ave. NW, Suite 200, Washington, DC 20006. 202-438-7297. Dedicated to developing new Arab American leaders. It has a Leadership Training Program designed to create a cadre of highly trained, informed and focused young Arab American professionals equipped to take on the advocacy and organizational efforts required for community leadership. www.halafoundation.org
- International Fellowship of Christians and Jews, 309 W. Washington St., Suite 800, Chicago, IL 60606-3200. 312-641-7200. Ecumenical group encourages understanding between Christians and Jews. www.ifcj.org
- J Street. Americans for Middle East Peace and Security. Washington, DC. Founded to promote meaningful American leadership to end the Arab–Israeli and Palestinian–Israeli conflicts peacefully and diplomatically. www.jstreet.org
- Muslim Public Affairs Council, 110 Maryland Ave. NE, Suite 210, Washington, DC 20002. 202-547-7701. Works for the civil rights of American Muslims, for the integration of Islam into American pluralism, and for a positive, constructive relationship between American Muslims and their representatives. www.mpac.org
- National Conference of Catholic Bishops, 3211 Fourth St. NE, Washington, DC 20017-1194. 202-541-3000. Condemns both Palestinian terrorist actions and Israel's military response. Calls for an immediate ceasefire and international monitors to enforce it. www.nccbuscc.org
- National Council of the Churches of Christ in the USA, 475 Riverside Drive, Room 850, New York, NY 10115. 212-870-2227. Attempts to promote peace in the Middle East through outreach to Christians, Jews, and Muslims in the region. Supports Palestinian state and wants people of all faiths to share Jerusalem. http://ncccusa.org
- Zionist Organization of America, 4 E. 34th St. New York, NY 10016. 212-481-1500. Founded in 1897 to create a Jewish nation in Israel. 50,000 members. Staunchly pro-Israel. www.zoa.org

Source: Khalil M. Marrar, 2008. List not exhaustive. Derived from organizational websites (verbatim language in some cases) and Sumana Chatterjee and Tish Wells, "Groups Involved in the Middle East," from *Knight Ridder/Tribune News Service*, April 14, 2002.

Appendix 4

Settler population and separation map

Table A4

Year	West Bank	Gaza strip	East Jerusalem	Golan Heights	Total
1972	1,182	700	8,649	77	10,608
1983	22,800	900	76,095	6,800	106,595
1985	44,100	1,900	103,900*	8,700	158,700
1989	69,800	3,000	117,100	10,000	199,900
1990	78,600	3,300	135,000	10,600	227,500
1991	90,300	3,800	137,300	11,600	243,000
1992	101,100	4,300	141,000	12,000	258,400
1993	111,600	4,800	152,800	12,600	281,800
1995	133,200	5,300	157,300	13,400	309,200
1996	142,700	5,600	160,400	13,800	322,500
1997	154,400	5,700	161,416	14,300	335,816
1998	163,300	6,100	165,967	14,900	350,267
1999	177,411	6,337	170,123	15,313	369,184
2000	192,976	6,678	172,250	15,955	387,859
2002	214,722	7,277	175,617	16,503	414,119
2003	224,669	7,556	178,601	16,791	427,617
2004	234,487	7,826	181,587	17,265	441,828
2005	258,988	0	184,057	17,793	460,838
2006	268,400	0	n/a	18,105	n/a

Note*1986 Data
Source: Foundation for Middle East Peace, 2006.

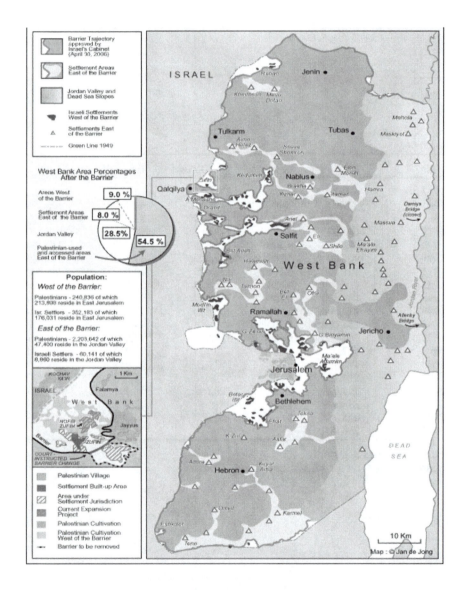

Figure A4 West Bank Separation Barrier – July 2006
Source: Foundation for Middle East Peace, 2006; Jan de Jong, Cartographer.

Appendix 5

Pro-Israel political contributions by election cycle

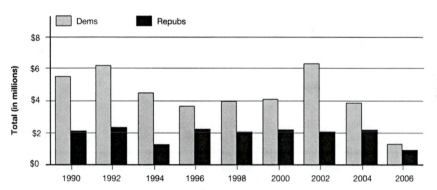

Figure A5.1 Source: Center for Responsible Politics, 2006.

Table A5.1

Election	Total	Individual	PAC	Soft money
2006	$2,330,777	$134,745	$2,196,032	n/a
2004	$6,095,120	$2,924,626	$3,170,494	n/a
2002	$8,426,500	$4,225,899	$2,750,601	$1,450,000
2000	$6,323,292	$3,914,888	$1,923,904	$484,500
1998	$6,105,139	$3,878,058	$2,104,331	$122,750
1996	$5,989,375	$3,422,779	$2,387,880	$178,716
1994	$5,835,357	$3,222,298	$2,378,059	$235,000
1992	$8,630,321	$4,556,341	$4,048,960	$25,020
1990	$7,675,913	$3,576,665	$4,099,248	n/a
Total	$57,411,794	$29,856,299	$25,059,509	$2,495,986

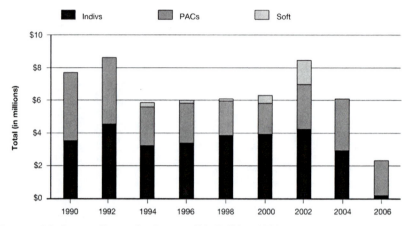

Figure A5.2 Source: Center for Responsible Politics, 2006.

Table A5.2

Election	Donations to Democrats	Donations to Republicans	% to Democrats vs. Republicans
2006	$1,291,668	$940,609	55/40
2004	$3,903,996	$2,190,624	64/36
2002	$6,324,511	$2,098,989	75/25
2000	$4,118,283	$2,204,009	65/35
1998	$3,992,804	$2,112,335	65/35
1996	$3,720,817	$2,268,558	62/38
1994	$4,512,768	$1,317,939	77/23
1992	$6,225,700	$2,391,659	72/28
1990	$5,541,260	$2,134,653	72/28
Total	$39,631,807	$17,659,375	69/31

Appendix 6

Pro-Arab political contributions by election cycle

Table A6

Cycle	Political action committee	Democrats	Republicans	Total
1990	National Assn of Arab-Americans	$1,500	$500	$2,000
1992	National Assn of Arab-Americans	$20,113	$11,500	$31,613
1994	American Muslim Alliance	$0	$500	$500
	National Assn of Arab-Americans	$4,750	$4,996	$9,746
	National Muslims for a Better America	$9,250	$3,000	$12,250
1996	Arab American Leadership PAC	$11,500	$5,500	$17,000
	National Assn of Arab-Americans	$1,000	$125	$1,125
	National Muslims for a Better America	$8,447	$2,500	$10,947
1998	Arab American Leadership PAC	$56,200	$20,850	$77,550
	National Assn of Arab-Americans	$5,000	$1,150	$6,150
	National Muslims for a Better America	$3,000	$2,500	$5,500
2000	American League of Muslims	$0	$0	$147
	Arab American Leadership PAC	$70,829	$27,500	$99,329
	Arab American PAC	$5,499	$6,563	$12,153
	National Assn of Arab-Americans	$2,470	$0	$2,470
2002	American Muslim Institute	$0	$2,000	$2,000
	Arab American Leadership PAC	$3,350	$2,000	$5,350
	Arab American PAC	$1,000	$0	$1,000
	Grand totals	$203,908	$91,184	$296,830

Source: Center for Responsible Politics, 2006.

Appendix 7
Arab American national demographics

Population with Arab ancestry by detailed group: 2000

Detailed group	Arab ancestry alone		Arab ancestry alone or in combination with another ancestry	
	Number	Percent of US population	Number	Percent of US population
Total	850,027[1]	0.30	1,189,731[2]	0.42
Lebanese	244,525	0.09	440,279	0.16
Egyptian	123,489	0.04	142,832	0.05
Syrian	75,517	0.03	142,897	0.05
Palestinian	61,691	0.02	72,112	0.03
Jordanian	36,104	0.01	39,734	0.01
Moroccan	30,352	0.01	38,923	0.01
Iraqi	29,429	0.01	37,714	0.01
"Arab" or "Arabic"	167,166	0.06	205,822	0.07
Other Arab	81,754[3]	0.03	82,337[4]	0.03

Note: Data based on sample. For information on confidentiality protection, sampling error, non-sampling error, and definitions, see www.census.gov/prod/cen2000/doc/sf4.pdf

1 Includes people who reported Arab ancestry only, regardless of whether they reported one or two Arab ancestries.

2 Includes people who reported one or two Arab ancestries and people who reported both an Arab and non-Arab ancestry. The total is less than the sum of the rows because most people reporting two Arab ancestries are tabulated in two categories, but only once in the total. People who reported two Arab ancestries not listed above (e.g. Algerian and Tunisian) are tabulated once in the "Other Arab" category.

3 Includes 68,614 people who reported one Arab ancestry not listed above and 13,140 people who reported two Arab ancestries, whether listed above or not.

4 Represents the number of people who reported one or two Arab ancestries excluding the ancestries listed above. The total of 82,337 includes 68,614 people who reported one Arab ancestry not listed.

Source: U.S. Census Bureau, Census 2000 special tabulation.

Notes

1 US foreign policy and the two-state solution

1 John J. Mearsheimer and Stephen M. Walt, "The Israel Lobby and U.S. Foreign Policy," *Kennedy School of Government Faculty Research Working Paper Series* RWP06-011 (March 2006), p. 15. Mearsheimer and Walt repeated a similar message in their book *The Israel Lobby and U.S. Foreign Policy* (New York: Farrar, Straus and Giroux, 2007), pp. 141–42.

2 Mearsheimer and Walt, "The Israel Lobby and U.S. Foreign Policy," p. 1.

3 See, for example, Cheryl A. Rubenberg, *Israel and the American National Interest: A Critical Examination* (Chicago, IL: University of Illinois Press, 1986), p. 88; and Harry B. Ellis, *The Dilemma of Israel: United States Interests in the Middle East* (Washington, DC: American Enterprise Institute for Public Policy Research, 1970), pp. 51–54. For precursors to the American-Israeli alliance prior to 1967, see John P. Miglietta, *American Alliance Policy in the Middle East, 1945–1992: Iran, Israel, and Saudi Arabia* (New York: Lexington Books, 2002), pp. 105–23. On US Cold War policy, see John Spanier, *American Foreign Policy Since World War II*, 12th ed. (Washington, DC: CQ Press, 1991).

4 According to Karen Puschel, "the very concept, born in the 1980s, of Israel as a 'strategic ally' of the United States, came from a shared sense of alliance between the US and Israel against the Soviet Union and its proxies in the Middle East." See Karen L. Puschel, *US-Israeli Strategic Cooperation in the Post-Cold War Era, An American Perspective* (San Francisco, CA: Westview Press, 1993), p. 3.

5 George W. Bush, "Statement by the President," available from www.whitehouse. gov/news/releases/2004/04/20040414-2.html; Internet; accessed December 28, 2005. For more detail on the two-state solution as a key US interest in the Israeli-Palestinian conflict, see "National Security Strategy of the United States of America," March 16, 2006, available from www.whitehouse.gov/nsc/nss/2006/nss2006.pdf; Internet; accessed March 30, 2006, p. 5.

6 This body preempted the roadmap with its "Arab League Peace Plan" available from www.jewishvirtuallibrary.org/jsource/Peace/arabplan.html; Internet; accessed October 24, 2005. For a brief outline of the Arab League's position on the Israeli-Palestinian conflict, see Khalil M. Marrar, "The Arab League and the Israeli-Palestinian Conflict," in Cheryl A. Rubenberg (ed.), *Encyclopedia of the Israeli-Palestinian Conflict* (New York: Lynne Rienner, forthcoming, 2009).

7 "A Performance-Based Roadmap to a Permanent Two-State Solution to the Israeli-Palestinian Conflict" available from www.state.gov/r/pa/prs/ps/2003/20062. htm; Internet; accessed October 24, 2005.

8 President Carter has authored a work that categorically called for a Palestinian state on the territories occupied in the 1967 war. See Jimmy Carter, *Palestine: Peace not Apartheid* (New York: Simon and Schuster, 2006).

9 Carter risked a tremendous amount of political capital in order to communicate his plans for wider Middle East Peace of which Camp David was only a start. Andrew Young, Carter's representative to the UN, held secret talks about his boss's plans with Zuhdi Tarazi, the chief Palestinian delegate to the UN. See William B. Quandt, *Peace Process: American Diplomacy and the Arab-Israeli Conflict Since 1967* (Washington, DC: Brookings Institution Press, 2005), pp. 445–52.

10 Rashid Khalidi, "The Palestinians Twenty Years After," *MERIP Middle East Report*, no. 146, Twenty Years After (May-June 1987), p. 7. It was not until 1985 that there was any serious effort to recognize the PLO in the US. See Deborah Ehrlich, "New Jewish Agenda Convention Urges Recognition of PLO," *MERIP Reports*, no. 136–37, West Bank, Gaza, Israel: Marching Toward Civil War (October-December 1985), p. 34.

11 The process for the present peace formula has gone through two phases: 1. support for one state (Israel) →Palestinian limited autonomy and 2. increased Palestinian autonomy → support for the two-state solution (Israel and Palestine). The analysis in this book will proceed in a manner mirroring those two phases.

12 "Israel only" refers to the fact that US policy swept the Palestinians under the rubric of its support for the Jewish state. Some echoed the line of conservative pro-Israel lobbyists that believe Arabs living in the occupied territories should merely immigrate to the 22 Arab states. This type of reasoning may be found in works like Benjamin Netanyahu, *The Jerusalem Alternative: Moral Clarity for Ending the Arab-Israeli Conflict* (Green Forest, AR: Balfour Books, 2004) and in Alan Dershowitz, *The Case for Israel* (Hoboken, NJ: John Wiley, 2003).

13 For a synopsis of contemporary arguments for this solution, see Virginia Tilley, *The One-State Solution: A Breakthrough for Peace in the Israeli-Palestinian Deadlock* (Ann Arbor, MI: University of Michigan Press, 2005), Ali Abunimah, *One Country: A Bold Proposal to End the Israeli-Palestinian Impasse* (New York: Metropolitan Books, 2006), and Joel Kovel, *Overcoming Zionism: Creating a Single Democratic State in Israel/Palestine* (London: Pluto Press, 2007).

14 While not matching the strength of the pro-Israel lobby, the pro-Arab lobby has scattered supporters in some circles of government. See, for example, Sam Hodges, "Alabama Statesman Says U.S. Biased against Palestinians," *Washington Report on Middle East Affairs* vol. 19, no. 2 (March 2000). Throughout this work, "lobby," "lobby groups," "lobbyists," "advocates," "pressure groups," and all other related entities will be synonymous with "interest groups." These words may be used interchangeably.

15 See William C. Olson and A. J. R. Groom, *International Relations Then and Now: Origins and Trends in Interpretation* (London: HarperCollins, 1991), Richard Ned Lebow and Thomas Risse-Kappen (eds), *International Relations Theory and the End of the Cold War* (New York: Columbia University Press, 1995), and Michael Barnett and Martha Finnemore, *Rules for the World: International Organizations in Global Politics* (Ithaca, NY: Cornell University Press, 2004).

16 In addition to works referenced above, for that debate from its earliest days, see Martin Buber (ed.), *Towards Union in Palestine: Essays on Zionism and Jewish-Arab Cooperation* (Westport, CT: Greenwood Press, 1972), Judah Magnes and Martin Buber, *Arab-Jewish Unity: Testimony Before the Anglo-American Inquiry Commission for the Ihud (Union) Association* (Westport, CT: Hyperion Press, 1976), and Judah Magnes, *Palestine, Divided or United? The Case for a Binational Palestine Before the United Nations* (Westport, CT: Greenwood Press, 1983). Edward Said revived the idea of one state, appealing to these predecessors in *The*

End of the Peace Process: Oslo and After (New York: Pantheon Press, 2000), p. 321. Also see Naseer Aruri, "Toward a Pluralistic Existence in Palestine/Israel," Naseer Aruri and Muhammad A. Shuraydi (eds), *Revising Culture, Reinventing Peace: The Influence of Edward W. Said* (New York: Olive Branch Press, 2001), pp. 120–33; and Naseer Aruri, *Dishonest Broker: The U.S. Role in Israel and Palestine* (Cambridge, MA: South End Press, 2003), pp. 217–36. In order to achieve the best flow possible, a full discussion on the "nature of the domestic political situation in the US" will be withheld until later chapters. Such discussion will only be optimally comprehendible once public opinion and the two lobbies are examined.

17 Arab Israelis, however, are treated as second-class citizens. See Naseer Aruri, *Occupation: Israel over Palestine* (Belmont, MA: Association of Arab-American University Graduates, 1983), Sabri Jiryis, *The Arabs in Israel* (New York: Monthly Review Press, 1976), Yinon Cohen, *Arab and Jewish Out-Migration from Israel and the Occupied Territories to the U.S.* (Tel Aviv: University of Tel Aviv, 1994), and Ethan Bronner, "After 60 Years, Arabs in Israel Are Outsiders," *New York Times*, May 7, 2008. The contemporary arguments for one state assume that all citizens would be treated equally. See Tilley, *The One-State Solution*, p. 222.

18 Dorothy Stein, "Palestine: The Return of the One-State Solution," *Asian Affairs*, vol. XXXV, no. 3 (November 2004), p. 333.

19 This figure varies based on who is asked and what areas are considered. *The World Fact Book* by the Central Intelligence Agency placed the number at 364,000 in East Jerusalem and the rest of the West Bank as of 2004. The Foundation for Middle East Peace put it at 460,838 in 2006. See CIA, *The World Fact Book*, available from www.odci.gov/cia/publications/factbook/geos/we. html#People; Internet; accessed May 27, 2006; and Appendix 4.

20 Rashid Khalidi, *Resurrecting Empire: Western Footprints and America's Perilous Path in the Middle East* (Boston, MA: Beacon Press, 2004), p. 151. Khalidi also detailed the historical failures of the Palestinians to achieve their state. See Rashid Khalidi, *The Iron Cage: The Story of Palestinian Struggle for Statehood* (Boston, MA: Beacon Press, 2006). *The Iron Cage* advanced the narrative of Khalidi's earlier work, *The Palestinian Identity: The Construction of Modern National Consciousness* (New York: Columbia University Press, 1997). On the general difficulties of the two-state solution, see Daniel Lazare, "The One-State Solution," *The Nation* (November 3, 2003), available from www.thenation.com/doc/ 20031103/lazare; Internet; accessed November 18, 2005.

21 On the settlements' permanence, see Jeffrey Heller, "Sharon Vows to Seek Peace but Big Settlements to Stay," available from www.alertnet.org/thenews/newsdesk/ L01537146.htm; Internet; accessed December 2, 2005. On the conditions that would exist as a result, see Tilley, *The One-State Solution*, pp. 8–9, 181. Bush's strongest supporters in the religious right presented problems for his roadmap with their unwavering support of the settlements. See Howard Fineman, Tamara Lipper, Holly Bailey, and Richard Wolf, "A Very Mixed Marriage," *Newsweek*, vol. 141, no. 22 (June 6, 2003), pp. 34–36. In the post-Ariel Sharon era, Israel continued its claim to large segments of the West Bank. See William Douglas, "Olmert Says Israel 'Cannot Wait for the Palestinians Forever,'" *San Jose Mercury News*, May 24, 2006.

22 Some advocates of a "greater Israel" have even called for the "transfer" of Arabs. See Nur Masalha, *Imperial Israel and the Palestinians: The Politics of Expansion* (London: Pluto Press, 2000), chapters 2–4. It must be emphasized that proponents of ethnic cleansing have always constituted a minority in Israeli society.

23 Tilley, *The One-State Solution*, p. 13.

24 See Appendix 2.

25 When it suits their purposes, some have tried to exaggerate or downplay the influence of the Arab lobby. For two instances, see Maurice Ostroff, "What the

Professors Should have Told Us – But Didn't," available from http://arab-lobby.
blogspot.com/; Internet; accessed November 29, 2007 and Joseph Puder, "The
Arab Lobby Can't Buy Support," *The Bulletin*, September 17, 2007, available
from www.thebulletin.us/site/news.cfm?newsid = 18823821&BRD = 2737&PAG =
461&dept_id = 576361&rfi = 6; Internet; accessed April 7, 2008. The present
work should in no way be construed to support such dubious polemics or others
like them.

26 See, for example, Ken Kollman, "Inviting Friends to Lobby: Interest Groups,
Ideological Bias, and Congressional Committees," *American Journal of Political
Science*, vol. 41, no. 2 (April 1997), pp. 519–44.

27 For one example, see Duncan L. Clark, Daniel B. O'Conner, and Jason D. Ellis,
Send Guns and Money: Security Assistance and US Foreign Policy (Westport, CT:
Praeger, 1997). This work concluded that US strategy, when inspected through the
realm of security assistance, is overly determined by narrowly interested groups
that try to detract from Washington's ability to control policy outcomes.

28 For an outline, see Christopher Hill, *The Changing Politics of Foreign Policy*
(New York: Palgrave Macmillan, 2003).

29 Ole R. Holsti, "Introduction: Beliefs, Perceptions, and Opinions in Policy
Making," in his *Making American Foreign Policy* (New York: Routledge, 2006),
pp. 1–20.

30 See Patrick Callahan, *Logics of American Foreign Policy: Theories of America's
World Role* (New York: Pearson-Longman, 2004), pp. 29–49. The inter-state
analysis of foreign policy is credited to James N. Rosenau, "Pre-theories and
Theories of Foreign Policy," in Barry Farrell (ed.), *Approaches in Comparative
and International Politics* (Evanston, IL: Northwestern University Press, 1966),
pp. 98–99. On the study of state capacity, see Maurice A. East, "Size and Foreign
Policy Behavior: A Test of Two Models," *World Politics*, vol. 25, no. 3 (July
1973), pp. 556–76.

31 See David P. Forsythe, Patrice C. McMahon, and Andrew Wedeman (eds),
American Foreign Policy in a Globalized World (New York: Routledge, 2006), and
Mary Buckley and Robert Singh (eds), *The Bush Doctrine and the War on
Terrorism: Global Responses, Global Consequences* (New York: Routledge, 2006).
Numerous others move beyond the state and the people that compose it. See, for
instance, Robert Axelrod (ed.), *Structure of Decision* (Princeton, NJ: Princeton
University Press, 1976), and William Gudykunst, L. Stewart, and Stella Ting-
Toomey, *Communication, Culture, and Organizational Process* (Beverly Hills, CA:
Sage, 1985). This study is limited to individual, state, and system levels of analysis
since they inevitably involve structural as well as cultural dimensions and are
more manageable in the understanding of American policy in the Israeli–
Palestinian conflict.

32 This emerged in the 1980s. See Charles F. Hermann and Gregory Peacock, "The
Evolution and Future of Theoretical Research in the Comparative Study of
Foreign Policy," in Charles F. Hermann, Charles W. Kegley, Jr., and James N.
Rosenau (eds), *New Directions in the Study of Foreign Policy* (Boston, MA: Allen
and Unwin, 1987), pp. 23–24. For a comprehensive literature review, see Valerie
M. Hudson and Christopher S. Vore, "Foreign Policy Analysis Yesterday, Today,
and Tomorrow," *Mershon International Studies Review*, vol. 39, no. 2 (Oct. 1995),
pp. 209–38.

33 Melvin Small, *Democracy and Diplomacy: The Impact of Domestic Politics on U.
S. Foreign Policy, 1789–1994* (Baltimore, MD: Johns Hopkins University Press,
1996).

34 Khalil M. Marrar, "Ethnic Lobbies," in Hussein Ibish (ed.), *An Arab Guide to
American Politics* (Washington, DC, work in progress, forthcoming, 2009),
p. unknown.

35 Khalil Jahshan, former president of the National Association of Arab Americans and Representative of Association of Arab American University Graduates and Palestine Research and Educational Center, interview by the author, Arlington, VA, March 14, 2006; Nabil Mohamad, organizing director of American-Arab Anti-Discrimination Committee, interview by the author, Washington, DC, March 14, 2006; Christine Gleichert, Capitol Hill lobbyist for American-Arab Anti-Discrimination Committee, interview by the author, Washington, DC, March 15, 2006; Rafi Dajani, former executive director of American Task Force on Palestine, interview by the author, Washington, DC, March 15, 2006; Mary Rose Oakar, former congresswoman from Cleveland, OH, and president of American-Arab Anti-Discrimination Committee, interview by the author, Washington, DC, March 15, 2006; Helen Samhan, former executive director of Arab American Institute Foundation, interview by the author, Washington, DC, March 16, 2006; Rebecca Abou-Chedid, government relations and policy analyst for Arab American Institute, interview by the author, Washington, DC, March 16, 2006; Hussein Ibish, executive director of Hala Foundation, Senior Fellow at American Task Force on Palestine, and former communications director at American-Arab Anti-Discrimination Committee, interview by the author, Washington, DC, November 13, 2006; Marvin Wingfield, director of education and outreach for American-Arab Anti-Discrimination Committee, telephone interview by the author, December 19, 2006; Peter Timco, director of the office of the president, Arab American Institute, telephone interview by the author, April 25, 2008; James Zogby, president and co-founder of Arab American Institute, Co-Founder of Palestine Human Rights Campaign, Co-Founder and Former Executive Director of American-Arab Anti-Discrimination Committee, telephone interview by the author, April 26, 2008.

36 Georges Corm, "Avoiding the Obvious: Arab Perspectives on US Hegemony in the Middle East," *Middle East Report*, no. 208, US Foreign Policy in the Middle East: Critical Assessments (Autumn 1998), p. 24.

37 James A. Baker III and Lee H. Hamilton (co-chairs), *The Iraq Study Group Report*, available from www.usip.org/isg/iraq_study_group_report/report/1206/iraq_study_group_report.pdf; Internet; accessed December 8, 2006.

38 Vaughn P. Shannon, "The Politics of the Middle East Peace Process and the War on Terror," in Patrick Hayden, Tom Lansford, and Robert P. Watson (eds), *America's War on Terror* (Burlington, VT: Ashgate Publishing Company, 2004), p. 81. This type of scholarship descends from a broader corpus of work on decision-making. See, among others, Richard C. Snyder, H. W. Bruck, and Burton Sapin, *Decision Making as an Approach to the Study of International Politics*. Foreign Policy Analysis Project Series no. 3 (Princeton, NJ: Princeton University Press, 1954). Others have benefited from that approach. See, for example, Lester Milbrath, "Interest Groups and Foreign Policy," in James Rosenau (ed.), *Domestic Sources of Foreign Policy* (New York: The Free Press, 1967), Carol S. Greenwald, *Group Power* (New York: Praeger, 1977), Richard W. Gable, "Interest Groups as Policy Shapers," *Annals of the American Academy of Political Science* (September 1958), and Abraham Holzman, *Interest Groups and Lobbying* (New York: Macmillan, 1966).

39 Marie Hojnacki and David C. Kimball, "Organized Interests and the Decision of Whom to Lobby in Congress," *American Political Science Review*, vol. 92, no. 4 (December 1998), pp. 775–90. This is attributable to the *perception* of the international climate, something that has been studied since the 1960s. See Harold Sprout and Margaret Sprout, *The Ecological Perspective on Human Affairs with Special Reference to International Relations* (Princeton, NJ: Princeton University Press, 1965), p. 118. There is a wide variety of scholarship in this vein. See, for example, C. H. Achen, "Mass Political Attitudes and the Survey Response,"

American Political Science Review 69 (1975), pp. 1218–31, Valerie M. Hudson (ed.), *Artificial Intelligence and International Politics* (Boulder, CO: Westview Press, 1991), Graham T. Allison and Morton H. Halperin, "Bureaucratic Politics: A Paradigm and Some Policy Implications," *World Politics* 24 (1972), pp. 40–79, Joseph De Rivera, *The Psychological Dimension of Foreign Policy* (Columbus, OH: C. E. Merrill Publishing Company, 1968), and Martha L. Cottam, *Foreign Policy Decision-Making: The Influence of Cognition* (Boulder, CO: Westview Press, 1986).

40 Abraham Ben-Zvi, *Decade of Transition: Eisenhower, Kennedy, and the Origins of the American-Israeli Alliance* (New York: Colombia University Press, 1998).

41 Patrick J. Haney and Walt Vanderbrush, "The Role of Ethnic Interest Groups in U.S. Foreign Policy: The Case of the Cuban American National Foundation," *International Studies Quarterly*, vol. 43, no. 2 (June 1999), p. 341.

42 This will be outlined in more detail throughout this book.

43 Marie Hojnacki and David C. Kimball, "The Who and How of Organizations' Lobbying Strategies in Committee," *The Journal of Politics*, vol. 61, no. 4 (November 1999), pp. 999–1024.

44 Rosenau, "Introduction: New Directions and Recurrent Questions in the Comparative Study of Foreign Policy," in Hermann, Kegley, and Rosenau (eds), *New Directions in the Study of Foreign Policy*, p. 1. Also see Stephen Andriole, Jonathan Wilkenfeld, and Gerald W. Hopple, "A Framework for the Comparative Analysis of Foreign Policy Behavior," *International Studies Quarterly*, vol. 19, no. 2 (June 1975), pp. 160–98.

45 Valerie Heitshusen, "Interest Group Lobbying and U.S. House Decentralization: Linking Informational Facts to Committee Hearing Appearances," *Political Research Quarterly*, vol. 53, no. 1 (March 2000), pp. 151–76.

46 Examples of this dot the literature landscape. See David Austen-Smith and William H. Riker, "Asymmetric Information and the Coherence of Legislation," *American Political Science Review*, vol. 81, no. 3 (September 1987), pp. 897–918, and "Asymmetric Information and the Coherence of Legislation: A Correction," *American Political Science Review*, vol. 84, no. 1 (March 1990), pp. 243–45. Also see John Mark Hansen, *Gaining Access: Congress and the Farm Lobby, 1919–1981* (Chicago, IL: University of Chicago Press, 1991), Kevin Leyden, "Organized Interests and the Policymaking Process: Explaining Who Testifies at Committee Hearings," paper presented at the Annual Meeting of the Midwest Political Science Association (April 1993), David Austen-Smith and John R. Wright, "Counteractive Lobbying," *American Journal of Political Science*, vol. 38, no. 1 (February 1994), pp. 25–44, and John R. Wright, *Interest Groups and Congress, Lobbying, Contributions, and Influence* (Needham, MA: Allyn and Bacon, 1996).

47 See Reuven Y. Hazan, "Intraparty Politics and Peacemaking in Democratic Societies: Israel's Labor Party and the Middle East Peace Process, 1992–96," *Journal of Peace Research*, vol. 37, no. 3 (May 2000), pp. 363–78, Ian Urbina, "Rogues' Gallery: Who Advises Bush and Gore on the Middle East?," *Middle East Report*, no. 216 (Autumn 2000), pp. 9–12, Paul Kengor, "The Vice President, Secretary of State, and Foreign Policy," *Political Science Quarterly*, vol. 115, no. 2 (Summer 2000), pp. 175–99. On the link between lobbying and aid policies, see Sajal Lahiri and Pascalis Raimondos-Moller, "Lobbying by Ethnic Groups and Aid Allocation," *The Economic Journal*, vol. 110, no. 462, Conference Papers (March 2000), pp. C62–C79.

48 One example looked at coalition building between lobbying groups as it involves shared goals. See Thomas T. Holyoke, "Choosing Battlegrounds: Interest Group Lobbying Across Multiple Venues," *Political Research Quarterly*, vol. 56, no. 3 (September 2003), pp. 325–36.

49 Kathleen Christison, "All Those Old Issues: George W. Bush and the Palestinian-Israeli Conflict," *Journal of Palestine Studies*, vol. 33, no. 2 (Winter 2004), pp. 36–50.
50 For more detail on Christian Zionist lobbying, see Don Wagner, "For Zion's Sake," *Middle East Report*, no. 223 (Summer 2002), pp. 52–57 and Paul Charles Merkley *American Presidents, Religion, and Israel: The Heirs of Cyrus* (Westport, CT: Praeger, 2004).
51 One work that comes to mind when looking at this explanation is James Petras, *The Power of Israel in the United States* (Atlanta, GA: Clarity Press, 2006).
52 William B. Quandt, *Decade of Decisions: American Foreign Policy toward the Arab-Israeli Conflict, 1967–1976* (Berkeley, CA: University of California Press, 1977), p. 20.
53 Interview with James Zogby.
54 Tilley, *The One-State Solution*, p. 92. For a direct example of this, see George Schultz, "The United States and Israel: Partners for Peace and Freedom," *Journal of Palestine Studies*, vol. 14, no. 4 (Summer 1985), pp. 122–28.
55 Fareed Zakaria, "Realism and Domestic Politics," *International Security*, vol. 17 (1992), p. 198, quoted in Hudson and Vore, "Foreign Policy Analysis Yesterday, Today, and Tomorrow," p. 210. Also see Brian Ripley, "Psychology, Foreign Policy, and International Relations Theory," *Political Psychology*, vol. 14 (1993), pp. 403–16.
56 This international politics approach is well established in the study of foreign policy analysis. See James N. Rosenau (ed.), *International Politics and Foreign Policy: A Reader in Research and Theory* (New York: Free Press, 1969).
57 Joseph Massad, "The Persistence of the Palestinian Question," in Begoña Aretxaga, Dennis Dworkin, Joseba Gabilondo, and Joseba Zulaika (eds), *Empire and Terror: Nationalism/Postnationalism in the New Millennium* (Reno, NV: University of Nevada Press, 2005), p. 69.
58 For powerful examples, see works by Mearsheimer and Walt and Paul Findley, *They Dare to Speak Out: People and Institutions Confront Israel's Lobby* (Westport, CT: Lawrence Hill and Company, 1985).
59 Findley, *They Dare to Speak Out*, p. 25. Findley has maintained this position. After a 2006 speech at Illinois State University, he remarked, "Americans have to find a way out of this state of affairs." For coverage of the speech, see Allison Grosz, "Former Congressman Explains Role of Israel in U.S. Policy," *The Daily Vidette*, September 18, 2006, available from www.dailyvidette.com/media/storage/paper420/news/2006/09/18/News/Former.Congressman.Explains.Role.Of.Israel.In.U.s.Policy-2281247.shtml?norewrite200612100211&sourcedomain = www.daily-vidette.com; Internet; accessed December 10, 2006.
60 Findley, *They Dare to Speak Out*, p. 26.
61 For an example, see Patricia Cohen, "A Bitter Spat Over Ideas, Israel and Tenure," *New York Times*, April 12, 2007.
62 Findley, *They Dare to Speak Out*, p. 322.
63 The theory of "prisoners' dilemma" may have a lot of insight to offer here. See William Poundstone, *Prisoner's Dilemma: John von Neumann, Game Theory, and the Puzzle of the Bomb* (New York: Doubleday Press, 1992).
64 This relationship continued through the Gulf War even as Israel sat on the sidelines while the US and its allies sought to expel Iraq from Kuwait. After the Cold War, the strategic alliance was in trouble as the US and Israel no longer had communism as the common enemy. During the George W. Bush presidency, it would take on increased significance as Israel defined itself as an American ally in the "war on terrorism." See Alexander Moens, *The Foreign Policy of George W. Bush: Values, Strategy and Loyalty* (Burlington, VT: Ashgate Publishing Company, 2004), p. 107–8.
65 Rubenberg, *Israel and the American National Interest*, p. 9.
66 Ibid.

67 See, for example, Thomas Ambrosio (ed.), *Ethnic Identity Groups and U.S. Foreign Policy* (Westport, CT: Praeger, 2002), p.p. 143–62, Michael Suleiman (ed.), *U.S. Policy on Palestine from Wilson to Clinton* (Normal, IL: Association of Arab-American University Graduates, 1995), Gabriel Sheffer (ed.), *U.S.-Israeli Relations at the Crossroads* (Portland, OR: Frank Cass, 1997), Robert R. Friedman, "Selling Israel to America," *Journal of Palestine Studies*, vol. 16, no. 4 (Summer 1987), pp. 169–79, Salim Yaqub, *Containing Arab Nationalism: The Eisenhower Doctrine and the Middle East* (Chapel Hill, NC: University of North Carolina Press, 2004), and Mohammed K. Shadid, *The United States and the Palestinians* (New York: St. Martin's Press, 1981), pp. 160–85.

68 Rubenberg, *Israel and the American National Interest*, p. 12.

69 Ibid., p. 13. Also see Tilley, *The One-State Solution*, p. 91. Kissinger was the architect of the framework under which the United States would approach the conflict; see Charles D. Smith, *Palestine and the Arab-Israeli Conflict* (New York: St. Martin's Press, 1988), pp. 222–23. For Kissinger's reflections, see Henry Kissinger, *Does America Need a Foreign Policy: Toward a Diplomacy for the 21st Century* (New York: Simon and Shuster, 2001), pp. 164–96.

70 Rubenberg, *Israel and the American National Interest*, p. 15, emphasis in the original. These features were also observed throughout Findley's *They Dare to Speak Out*.

71 Prior to 9/11, that effort did not take root, particularly as the administrations of George H. W. Bush and Bill Clinton sought to reach out to Muslims and their political leaders, albeit with "some inconsistencies and strains." See Fawaz A. Gerges, *America and Political Islam: Clash of Cultures or Clash of Interests* (New York: Cambridge University Press, 1999), p. 3.

72 See, for example, "NER Interviews: David Horovitz," *Near East Report*, vol. L, no. 7, (May 8, 2006), p. 30.

73 Thomas R. Dye, *Politics in America*, 4th edn (Upper Saddle River, NJ: Prentice-Hall, 2001), p. 294.

74 For more on definitions of a lobby, see US Senate, "Lobbying Disclosure Act Guidance," available from www.senate.gov/legislative/common/briefing/lobby_-disc_briefing.htm#1; Internet; accessed June 15, 2006. Many discussions exist on lobbying in American politics. See, among others, Allan Ciglar and Burdett A. Loomis, *Interest Group Politics*, 2nd ed. (Washington, DC: CQ Press, 1986), Kenneth G. Crawford, *The Pressure Boys: The Inside Story of Lobbying in America* (New York: Arno Press, 1974), Russell W. Howe and Sarah H. Trott, *The Power Peddlers: How Lobbyists Mold America's Foreign Policy* (Garden City, NY: Doubleday and Co., 1977), Dennis S. Ippolito and Thomas G. Walker, *Political Parties, Interest Groups, and Public Policy: Group Influence in American Politics* (Englewood Cliffs, NJ: Prentice-Hall, 1980), H. R. Manhood, *Pressure Groups in American Politics* (New York: Harper and Row, 1967), Bernard C. Cohen, *The Influence of Non-Governmental Groups on Foreign Policy Making* (Boston, MA: World Peace Foundation, 1959), and *The Public's Impact on Foreign Policy* (Boston, MA: Little, Brown, 1973).

75 Interviews with Peter Timco and James Zogby.

76 This literature spans the 1960s to the present. See James Deakin, *The Lobbyists* (Washington, DC: Public Affairs Press, 1966), Lee O'Brien, *American Jewish Organizations and Israel* (Washington, DC: Institute for Palestine Studies, 1986), Abraham Ben-Zvi, *The United States and Israel* (New York: Colombia University Press, 1994), Yossi Melman and Dan Raviv, *Inside the US-Israel Alliance* (New York: Hyperion, 1994), Stephen D. Isaacs and Lee O'Brien, *Jews and American Politics* (New York: Doubleday, 1974).

77 Mearsheimer and Walt, "The Israel Lobby and U.S. Foreign Policy," p. 1.

78 Ibid., pp. 2–7.

79 For example, see Steven Kull, "America's Image in the World," Testimony before House Committee on Foreign Affairs, March 6, 2007, available from www.worldpublicopinion.org/pipa/articles/views_on_countriesregions_bt/326.php?nid = &id = &pnt = 326&lb = btvoc; Internet; accessed May 15, 2007.

80 Zainal Aznam Yusof, "It All Comes Down to the Palestinian Problem," *New Straits Times Press* (Malaysia), July 29, 2006.

81 Mearsheimer and Walt, "The Israel Lobby and U.S. Foreign Policy," pp. 7–12.

82 Ibid., p. 5.

83 Ibid., pp. 15–25.

84 Ibid., pp. 25–39.

85 Among many others, see Michael Massing, "The Storm over the Israel Lobby," *New York Review of Books*, vol. 53, no. 10 (June 8, 2006), David Gergen, "There is No Israel Lobby," *New York Daily News*, March 26, 2006, Ruth R. Wisse "Harvard Attack on 'Israel Lobby' is Actually a Targeting of American Public," *Jewish World Review,* March 23, 2006, Tony Judt, "A Lobby not a Conspiracy," *New York Times*, April 19, 2006, Eliot A. Cohen, "Yes It's Anti-Semitic," *Washington Post*, April 5, 2006, Richard Cohen, "No It's Not Anti-Semitic," *Washington Post*, April 25, 2006, Daniel Levy, "So Pro-Israel It Hurts," *Ha'aretz*, March 24, 2006, and *International Herald Tribune*, April 4, 2006, Noam Chomsky, "The Israel Lobby?" March 28, 2006, available from www.zmag.org/content/showarticle.cfm?ItemID = 9999; Internet; accessed June 14, 2006, Dimitri K. Simes, "Unrealists," *The National Interest*, May 26 2006, Alan Dershowitz, "Debunking the Newest – and Oldest – Jewish Conspiracy: A Reply to the Mearsheimer-Walt 'Working Paper,'" Harvard Law School, April 2006, available from www.ksg.harvard.edu/research/working_papers/dershowitzreply.pdf; Internet; accessed June 14, 2006, Joseph Massad, "Blaming the Lobby," *Al-Ahram Weekly Online*, 23–29 March 2006, available from http://weekly.ahram.org.eg/2006/787/op35.htm; Internet; accessed August 4, 2006, Hussein Ibish, "Is Arab-American Irrelevance Our Goal?" *Daily Star*, Friday, May 19, 2006, and Stephen Zunes, "The Israel Lobby: How Powerful is it Really?" in *Global Politician*, May 24, 2006, available from http://globalpolitician.com/articledes.asp?ID = 1793&cid = 2&sid = 1; Internet; accessed June 14, 2006.

86 Mearsheimer and Walt, *The Israel Lobby and U.S. Foreign Policy*, p. 6.

87 Baker and Hamilton make this clear in *The Iraq Study Group Report.*

88 Ostensible support of Palestinian suicide bombers by Saddam's regime was something that a few believed threatened the Jewish state. See Oliver North, *War Stories: Operation Iraqi Freedom* (Washington, DC: Regnery Publishing, 2003), pp. 208–10.

89 Findley, *They Dare to Speak Out*. Also see Paul Findley, "Congress and the Pro-Israel Lobby," *Journal of Palestine Studies*, vol. 15, no. 1 (Autumn 1985), pp. 104–13. For others that have looked at the interplay between pro-Arab and pro-Israel groups, see Edward Tivnan, *Jewish Political Power and American Foreign Policy* (New York: Simon and Shuster, 1987), M. T. Mehdi, "Arab Americans and Political Images," in Rich Wilbur (ed.), *The Politics of Minority Coalitions: Race Ethnicity and Shared Uncertainties* (New York: Praeger 1996), Yossi Shain, "Arab-Americans at a Crossroads," *Journal of Palestine Studies*, vol. 25, no. 3 (Spring 1996), pp. 46–59, Helen Hatab Samhan, "Politics and Exclusion: The Arab American Experience," *Journal of Palestine Studies*, vol. 16, no. 2 (Winter 1987), pp. 11–28, Saad Ibrahim, "American Domestic Forces and the October War," *Journal of Palestine Studies*, vol. 4, no. 1 (Autumn 1974), pp. 55–81, The Editors, "Palestine and Israel in the US Arena," *Middle East Report*, no. 158, Palestine and Israel in the US Arena (May-June 1989), pp. 4–5 and 42, Ami Arbel and Nimrod Novik, "U.S. Pressure on Israel: Likelihood and Scope," *Journal of Conflict Resolution*, vol. 29, no. 2 (June 1985), pp. 253–82, Marilyn Niemark,

"American Jews and Palestine: The Impact of the Gulf War," *Middle East Report*, no. 175, Palestine and Israel in the New Order (March-April 1992), pp. 19–23.

90 Muriel Asseburg, Dominique Moïsi, Gerd Nonneman, and Stephano Silvestri, "The European Union and the Crisis in the Middle East," in Martin Ortega (ed.), *Chaillot Papers*, (Paris: Institute for Security Studies, July 2003), pp. 34–35.

91 The Israel lobby supports the Jewish state in all of its endeavors even if they are in violation of international law. See Naseer Aruri, *Dishonest Broker*, pp. 198–201.

92 Interview with Khalil Jahshan.

93 Tony Smith, *Foreign Attachments: The Power of Ethnic Groups in the Making of American Foreign Policy* (Cambridge, MA: Harvard University Press, 2000), p. 68.

94 Interview with Helen Samhan.

95 Janice J. Terry, *U.S. Foreign Policy in the Middle East: The Role of Lobbies and Special Interest Groups* (Ann Arbor, MI: Pluto Press, 2005), p. 125. For earlier analyses of the Arab lobby's competitiveness compared to the Israel lobby, see Nabeel A. Khoury, "The Arab Lobby: Problems and Prospects," *Middle East Journal*, vol. 41, no. 3 (Summer 1987), pp. 379–96 and Andrea Barron, "Jewish and Arab Diasporas in the United States and Their Impact on U.S. Middle East Policy," in Yehuda Lukacs and Abdalla M. Battah, (eds), *The Arab-Israeli Conflict: Two Decades of Change* (London: Westview, 1988), pp. 238–59.

96 Attacks on the Palestinians have not decreased their militancy. See Craig S. Smith, "Despite Ties to Hamas, Militants Aren't Following Political Leaders," *New York Times*, July 21, 2006.

97 See Elias T. Nigem, "Arab Americans: Migration, Socioeconomic and Demographic Characteristics," *International Migration Review*, vol. 20, no. 3 (Autumn 1986), pp. 629–49. This thesis was countered by Ali A. Mazrui, "Between the Crescent and the Star Spangled Banner: American Muslims and US Foreign Policy," *International Affairs* (Royal Institute of International Affairs), vol. 72, no. 3, Ethnicity and International Relations (July 1996), pp. 493–506. Although Nigem studied Arab Americans while Mazrui looked at Muslim Americans, the two differ on the extent to which population increases correspond to advocacy.

98 Interview with James Zogby.

99 Interview with Nabil Mohamad.

100 Shain, "Arab-Americans at a Crossroads," p. 52. While these were the specific policy goals of the National Association of Arab Americans (NAAA), they may be generalized to other Arab American lobbying efforts.

101 Take, for instance, the issue of refugees. Recently, a pro-Israel group succeeded in getting Congress to support compensation for Jews that fled from Arab states after the creation of Israel. This move may complicate dealings with Palestinian refugees. See "Let There be Justice for All: America's Israel Lobby Scores another Questionable Victory," *The Economist*, April 10, 2008.

102 Cheryl Rubenberg, *The Palestinians: In Search of a Just Peace* (Boulder, CO: Lynne Rienner, 2003), p. 293. AIPAC will be the focus of the present work.

103 Rubenberg, *The Palestinians*, p. 293.

104 "AIPAC Policy Statement, 1987," in *Journal of Palestine Studies*, vol. 16, no. 4 (Summer 1987), p. 107.

105 Ibid., p. 112.

106 Richard Sobel, *The Impact of Public Opinion on U.S. Foreign Policy Since Vietnam: Constraining the Colossus* (New York: Oxford University Press, 2001), p. 3. How public opinion shapes policy and the extent to which it should continue to be hotly debated. Some, like Benjamin Page and Marshall Bouton, optimistically note that the public is capable of rightly guiding foreign policy. See Benjamin I. Page and Marshall M. Bouton, *The Foreign Policy Disconnect:*

What Americans Want from Our Leaders but Don't Get (Chicago, IL: University of Chicago Press, 2006).

107 See Schuyler H. Foster, *Activism Replaces Isolationism* (Washington, DC: Foxhall, 1983), Frank L. Klingberg, *Cyclical Trends in American Foreign Policy Moods: The Unfolding of America's World Role* (Lanham, MD: University Press of America, 1983), and James A. Stimson, *Public Opinion in America: Moods, Cycles, and Swings* (Boulder, CO: Westview, 1991).

108 *Gallup Poll*, 5/30/2003–6/1/2003. This number has always fluctuated. However, since the Oslo peace process, Americans favoring a two-state solution have generally been part of the majority.

109 For a survey of this type of analysis, see Valerie M. Hudson (ed.), *Culture and Foreign Policy* (Boulder, CO: Lynne Rienner Publishers, 1997).

110 See Kathleen Christison, *Perceptions of Palestine: Their Influence on U.S. Middle East Policy* (Berkeley, CA: University of California Press, 1999) and Douglas Little, *American Orientalism: The United States and the Middle East since 1945* (Chapel Hill, NC: University of North Carolina Press, 2002).

111 Scott M. Davis and Christopher Kline, *The Role of the Public in Foreign Policy Making: An Overview of the Literature* (Washington, DC: Roosevelt Center for American Policy Studies, 1988), Charles W. Kegley, Jr. and Eugene R. Wittkopf, *American Foreign Policy: Patterns and Process*, 4th ed. (New York: St. Martin's Press, 1991), Ole R. Holsti, *Public Opinion and American Foreign Policy* (Ann Arbor, MI: University of Michigan Press, 1996), Vladimer O. Key, *Public Opinion and American Democracy* (New York: Knopf, 1961), William O. Chittick and Keith R. Billinglsy, "The Structure of Elite Foreign Policy Beliefs," *Western Political Quarterly* (1989), and Ronald H. Hinckley, *People, Polls, and Policymakers: American Public Opinion and National Security* (New York: Lexington Books, 1992).

112 Shadid, *The United States and the Palestinians*, pp. 176–77.

113 Interview with James Zogby.

114 Peter Ford, "Why do They Hate Us?" *Christian Science Monitor*, September 27, 2001.

115 Not to mention, the American leadership steered the public away from thinking about the root causes of 9/11. Such inquiry was banished with declarations of "they hate our freedoms" by President Bush and others. See George W. Bush, "Address to a Joint Session of Congress and the American People," September 20, 2001, available from www.whitehouse.gov/news/releases/2001/09/20010920-28.html#; Internet; accessed December 10, 2006. Many vigorously criticized that mindset. For instance, see Tom Regan, "They Hate Our Policies, Not Our Freedom: Pentagon Report Contains Major Criticisms of Administration," *Christian Science Monitor*, November 29, 2004.

116 James Lee Ray, *The Future of American-Israeli Relations* (Lexington, KY: University Press of Kentucky, 1985), p. 56.

117 Nadav Safran, *The United States and Israel* (Cambridge, MA: Harvard University Press, 1963), pp. 270–71.

118 Kathleen Christison, *Perceptions of Palestine: Their Influence on U.S. Middle East Policy* (Berkeley: University of California Press, 1999), pp. 274–75. While this description captured the reality of US policy during the pre-roadmap days, its underlying assumptions still hold true in the present.

119 Sobel, *The Impact of Public Opinion on U.S. Foreign Policy Since Vietnam*, p. 240.

120 There is a vast amount of literature on media coverage and its relationship to public opinion. See James Fallows, *Breaking the News: How the Media Undermine American Democracy* (New York: Pantheon, 1996), Howard Kurtz, *Hot Air: All Talk, All the Time* (New York: Times Books 1996), Michael Janeway, *Republic of Denial: Press, Politics, and Public Life* (New Haven, CT: Yale University Press, 1999), Robert W. McChesney, *The Problem of the Media:*

U.S. Communication Politics in the 21st Century (New York: Monthly Review Foundation, 2004), Norman Solomon and Jeff Cohen, *Behind the Curtain of Mainstream News* (New York: Common Courage, 1997), Bernard C. Cohen, *The Press and Foreign Policy* (Princeton, NJ: Princeton University Press, 1963), Melani McAllister, *Epic Encounters: Culture, Media, and U.S. Interests in the Middle East, 1945–2000* (Berkeley, CA: University of California Press, 2001), Yahya R. Kamalimpour (ed.), *The U.S. Media and the Middle East* (Westport, CT: Greenwood Publishing Group, 1995), Gadi Wolfsfeld, *Media and Political Conflict: News from the Middle East* (Cambridge: Cambridge University Press, 1997), Doreen Kays, *Frogs and Scorpions: Egypt and the Media* (New York: HarperCollins, 1985), Reeva S. Simon, *The Middle East in Crime Fiction: Mysteries, Spy Novels, and Thrillers from 1916 to 1980* (New York: Lilian Barber Press, 1989), Janice J. Terry, *Mistaken Identity: Anti-Arab Stereotypes in Popular Literature* (Washington, DC: Arab American Council, 1985), Jack Shaheen, *Reel Bad Arabs: How Hollywood Vilifies a People* (Northampton, MA: Interlink Publishing Group, Inc. 2001), and *The TV Arab* (Bowling Green, OH: Bowling Green State University Popular Press, 1984).

121 Anatha Guruswami Naidu, *US Policy Towards the Arab-Israeli Conflict* (Atlantic Highlands, NJ: Humanities Press, 1982), p. 64.

122 Ibid., pp. 67–69.

123 For a summary of alternative analysis, see Jerel A. Rosati, Michael W. Ling, and John Creed, "A New Perspective on the Foreign Policy Views of American Opinion in the Cold War and Post-Cold War Eras," *Political Research Quarterly*, vol. 51, no. 2 (June 1998), pp. 461–79.

124 See Appendix 2.

125 Ibid.

126 The periods outlined here guide the approach to the history of the international context of American policy.

127 Puschel, *US-Israeli Strategic Cooperation in the Post-Cold War Era*, p. 65. The three key personality changes are: (1) the replacement of Israeli defense minister Ariel Sharon with Moshe Arens; (2) the succession of Menachem Begin by Yitzhak Shamir; and (3) the resignation of Alexander Haig and the appointment of George Schultz as secretary of state.

128 For an overview, see Jamal R. Nassar and Roger Heacock, *Intifada: Palestine at the Crossroads* (New York: Praeger, 1990).

129 See Yair Evron, "The Invasion of Kuwait and the Gulf War: Dilemmas Facing the Israeli-Iraqi-U.S. Relationship," in David W. Lesch, *The Middle East and the United States: A Historical and Political Reassessment* (Boulder, CO: Westview Press, 1996), pp. 313–22.

130 Rubenberg, "The Bush Administration and the Palestinians: A Reassessment," in Suleiman (ed.), *U.S. Policy on Palestine from Wilson to Clinton*, p. 195.

131 American policymakers saw the end of the Cold War was as a window of opportunity to end the general Arab–Israeli conflict. Hence, after the collapse of the Soviet Union, the Bush administration tried to leverage the outcome of the Madrid talks to address hostilities between Israel and its neighbors. See James Addison Baker and Thomas M. DeFrank, *The Politics of Diplomacy: Revolution, War, and Peace, 1989–1992* (New York: Putnam, 1995), pp. 487–513.

132 "Declaration of Principles," available from www.fmep.org/resources/peace_plans/oslo_accords.html; Internet; accessed October 24, 2005.

133 Joe Stork, "The Clinton Administration and the Palestine Question," in Suleiman (ed.), *U.S. Policy on Palestine from Wilson to Clinton*, p. 223.

134 Robert O. Freedman, "The Bush Administration and the Israeli-Palestinian Conflict: A Preliminary Evaluation," *American Foreign Policy Interests*, vol. 25 (2003), p. 505.

135 For the perceived effects of this policy in the Middle East, see Ibrahim Nafie, "Hands Off Are No Less Bloody," *Al-Ahram Weekly On-Line*, August 30– September 5, 2001, available from http://weekly.ahram.org.eg/2001/549/op1.htm; Internet, accessed December 31, 2005.

136 For an early assessment of the impact of 9/11 on Bush's efforts in the Middle East, see Stephen M. Walt, "Beyond bin Laden: Reshaping U.S. Foreign Policy," *International Security*, vol. 26, no. 3 (Winter 2001/02), pp. 56–78.

137 Freedman, "The Bush Administration and the Israeli-Palestinian Conflict," p. 508.

138 *Gallup Poll*, "Gallup Brain," 1955–2005.

139 See Rashid Khalidi, *The Palestinian Identity: The Construction of Modern National Consciousness* (New York: Columbia University Press, 1997).

140 In a 2007 interview, John Mearsheimer noted that rather than from the pro-Arab lobby, the idea for a Palestinian state "emerged from Israel and from the United States ... in the wake of the first Intifada, which took place in the late 1980s." See James Zogby, "Viewpoint: John Mearsheimer and Stephen Walt," on *Dubai Television*, December 20, 2007.

141 Attempts to influence policy also happen across international forums. For an example, see Helene Cooper, "U.S. Feels Sting of Winning Saudi Help With Other Arabs," *New York Times*, March 30, 2007.

142 While the foreign Arab lobby lies outside the scope of the present analysis, a similar study may account for it by looking at press conferences between American presidents and the heads of Arab governments as they relate to utterances on the Israeli–Palestinian conflict and the two-state solution. Those press conferences may be analyzed through available news outlets and by looking at the federal register of presidential public papers, an invaluable research tool on administrative dealings with and thinking on foreign actors. See National Archives, "Public Papers of the Presidents," available from www.archives.gov/ federal-register/publications/presidential-papers.html#online; Internet; accessed June 19, 2006.

143 NAAA has merged with the Arab-American Anti-Discrimination committee. For an outline of the merger, see *Arabic News*, "Two Arab Organizations Merge, Uncertain on Numbers," December 30, 1999, available from, www.arabicnews. com/ansub/Daily/Day/991230/1999123042.html; Internet; accessed July 31, 2006.

144 Mitchell Bard, "The Israeli and Arab Lobbies," available from www.jew-ishvirtuallibrary.org/jsource/US-Israel/lobby.html; Internet; accessed January 10, 2006.

145 See Appendix 1. There are some issues with interviews. Karen Rasler, William Thompson, and Kathleen Chester, for instance, pointed out that interviews often have research pitfalls, including a lack of acceptable "data reliability" as a result of "source bias, situational circumstances, and temporal inconsistence." While these criticisms were made of interviews with foreign policy officials, they may equally apply to ones conducted with the principals covered in this book. It is hoped that these issues are resolved by combining analysis of interviewee answers with content assessments of publicly stated positions, something that according to Rasler and company, helps alleviate problems in this type of study. See Karen Rasler, William R. Thompson, and Kathleen Chester, "Foreign Policy Makers, Personality Attributes, and Interviews: A Note on Reliability Problems," *International Studies Quarterly*, vol. 24, no. 1 (March 1980), pp. 47–66.

146 Some groups were founded after the end of the Cold War.

147 The ADC and AAI do not officially endorse the two-state solution at the time of this writing. Members of their leadership, however, have worked for a "peaceful resolution" to the Israeli–Palestinian conflict. Interviews with Christine Gleichert, Mary Rose Oakar, Nabil Mohamad, and Peter Timco.

148 Rubenberg, *Israel and the American National Interest*, p. 354. This distinction gave the pro-Israel lobby a level of power that seems out of reach for the foreign registrants of the Arab lobby.
149 This number represents quite a bit of an increase from the 1980s, when Rubenberg placed the number of pro-Israel organizations at thirty-eight. See Rubenberg, *Israel and the American National Interest*, p. 354. Today, there are over fifty-one pro-Israel organizations, according to the Presidents of Major American Jewish Organizations. See www.conferenceofpresidents.org/content. asp?id = 55; Internet; accessed April 19, 2007.
150 Reagan: Elliot Abrams; Bush I: Marc Grossman and Richard Haas; Clinton: Martin Indyk and Dennis Ross; Bush II: Richard Perle, Dov Zakheim, Kenneth Adelman, Lewis "Scooter" Libby, Robert Satloff, Robert Zoellick, Ari Fleischer, James Schlesinger, Joshua Bolten, John Bolton, David Wurmser, Eliot Cohen, and Paul Wolfowitz.
151 Baker and Hamilton, *Iraq Study Group Report*.
152 Interview with James Zogby.

2 Public opinion and foreign policy perception

1 Robert H. Trice, "Foreign Policy Interest Groups, Mass Public Opinion and the Arab-Israeli Dispute," *Western Political Quarterly*, vol. 31, no. 2 (June 1978), p. 238. Although Trice was interested in the role of the media, studying public opinion as informed by electronic and print outlets will subsume analyzing their roles in shaping sentiment. Public opinion has many sources of influence, particularly from interest groups.
2 See, for example, Steven A. Shull, *Presidential Policy Making: An End of Century Assessment* (Armonk, NY: M. E. Sharpe, 1999), Edward N. Kearny, *Dimensions of the Modern Presidency* (St. Louis, MO: Forum Press, 1981), Steven W. Hook, *U.S. Foreign Policy: The Paradox of World Power* (Washington, DC: CQ Press, 2005), Jeffrey E. Cohen, "Presidential Rhetoric and the Public Agenda," *American Journal of Political Science*, vol. 39, no. 1 (February 1995), pp. 87–107, Robert Y. Shapiro and Benjamin I. Page, "Foreign Policy and the Rational Public," *The Journal of Conflict Resolution*, vol. 32, no. 2 (June 1988), pp. 211–57, George C. Edwards III and Tami Swenson, "Who Rallies: The Anatomy of a Rally Event," *The Journal of Politics*, vol. 59, no. 1 (February 1997), pp. 200–212, Ronald H. Hinckley, "Public Attitudes toward Key Foreign Policy Events," *The Journal of Conflict Resolution*, vol. 32, no. 2 (June 1988), pp. 295–318, Benjamin I. Page and Robert Shapiro, "Effects of Public Opinion on Policy," *American Political Science Review*, vol. 77, no. 1 (March 1983), pp. 175–90, Benjamin I. Page and Jason Barabas, "Foreign Policy Gaps between Citizens and Leaders," *International Studies Quarterly*, vol. 44, no. 2 (September 2000), pp. 339–64, and Alan D. Monroe, "Public Opinion and Public Policy, 1980–93," *The Public Opinion Quarterly*, vol. 62, no. 1 (Spring 1998), pp. 6–28.
3 All public opinion data below came from Gallup polls. For variance in public opinion support of the two-state solution, see Appendix 2.
4 On the "strategic relationship," see Karen L. Puschel, *US-Israeli Strategic Cooperation in the Post-Cold War Era, An American Perspective* (San Francisco, CA: Westview Press, 1993), pp. 2–5.
5 According to Hussein Ibish, "the invasion of Kuwait by Iraq could have been more easily condemned had the US taken a consistent policy on the Palestine question." This was a point emphatically made by pro-Arab pressure groups at the time of the Gulf crisis. Hussein Ibish, executive director of the Hala Foundation, senior fellow at the American Task Force on Palestine, and former

communications director at American-Arab Anti-Discrimination Committee, interview by the author, Washington, DC, November 13, 2006.

6 For more on this, see Richard K. Herrmann, "The Middle East and the New World Order: Rethinking U.S. Political Strategy after the Gulf War," *International Security*, vol. 16, no. 2 (Autumn 1991), pp. 42–75.

7 For analyses of the media's effects on public opinion and political decisions, see Mark J. Rozell, *Media Power, Media Politics* (Lanham, MD: Rowman and Littlefield, 2003), Doris Graber, *Media Power in Politics* (Washington, DC: CQ Press, 2000), Benjamin I. Page, "The Mass Media as Political Actors," *Political Science and Politics*, vol. 29, no. 1 (March 1996), pp. 20–24, and Donald L. Jordan, "Newspaper Effects on Policy Preferences," *The Public Opinion Quarterly*, vol. 57, no. 2 (Summer 1993), pp. 191–204. George Edwards and Dan Wood looked at the interplay between the branches of government and the media. See George C. Edwards III and B. Dan Wood, "Who Influences Whom? The President, Congress, and the Media," *American Political Science Review*, vol. 93, no. 2 (June 1999), pp. 327–44.

8 Helen Samhan, executive director of the Arab American Institute Foundation, interview by the author, Washington, DC, March 16, 2006.

9 For that debate, see Ole R. Holsti, *Public Opinion and American Foreign Policy*, revised edition (Ann Arbor, MI: University of Michigan Press, 2004), Philip J. Powlick and Andrew J. Katz, "Defining the American Public Opinion/Foreign Policy Nexus," *Mershon International Studies Review*, vol. 42, no. 1 (May 1998), pp. 29–61, Philip J. Powlick, "The Sources of Public Opinion for American Foreign Policy Officials," *International Studies Quarterly*, vol. 39, no. 4 (December 1995), pp. 427–51, Benjamin I. Page, Robert Y. Shapiro, and Glenn R. Dempsey, "What Moves Public Opinion," *American Political Science Review*, vol. 81, no. 1 (March 1987), pp. 23–44, Miroslav Nincic, "A Sensible Public: New Perspectives on Popular Opinion and Foreign Policy," *The Journal of Conflict Resolution*, vol. 36, no. 4 (December 1992), pp. 772–89, and Philip J. Powlick, "The Attitudinal Bases for Responsiveness to Public Opinion among American Foreign Policy Officials," *The Journal of Conflict Resolution*, vol. 35, no. 4 (December 1991), pp. 611–41.

10 See Benjamin I. Page, "Democratic Responsiveness? Untangling the Links between Public Opinion and Policy," *Political Science and Politics*, vol. 27, no. 1 (March 1994), pp. 25–29, B. Dan Wood and Jeffrey S. Peake, "The Dynamics of Foreign Policy Agenda Setting," *The American Political Sciences Review*, vol. 92, no. 1 (March 1998), pp. 173–84, Robert W. Oldendick and Barbara Ann Bardes, "Mass and Elite Foreign Policy Opinions," *The Public Opinion Quarterly*, vol. 46, no. 3 (Autumn 1982), pp. 368–82, and Thomas Risse-Kappen, "Public Opinion, Domestic Structure, and Foreign Policy in Liberal Democracies," *World Politics*, vol. 43, no. 4 (July 1991), pp. 479–512.

11 James Zogby, president and co-founder of Arab American Institute, co-founder of Palestine Human Rights Campaign, co-founder and former executive director of American-Arab Anti-Discrimination Committee, telephone interview by the author, April 26, 2008.

12 Mohammed K. Shadid, *The United States and the Palestinians* (New York: St. Martin's Press, 1981), pp. 13–14. For the historical context and personalities of the relationship explored by Shadid, see Naseer Aruri, "The United States and Palestine: Reagan's Legacy to Bush," *Journal of Palestine Studies*, vol. 18, no. 3 (Spring 1989), pp. 3–21, Donald Neff, "U.S. Policy and the Palestinian Refugees," *Journal of Palestine Studies*, vol. 18, no. 1, Special Issue: Palestine 1948 (Autumn 1988), pp. 96–111, Naseer H. Aruri and Fouad Moghrabi, "The Reagan Middle East Initiative," *Journal of Palestine Studies*, vol. 12, no. 2 (Winter 1983), pp. 10–30, Richard Falk, "Stalemate and Stagnation: United States Policy in the Near East. An Interview with Richard Falk," *Journal of Palestine Studies*, vol. 8, no. 1

(Autumn 1978), pp. 85–89, Stephen G. Walker, "The Interface between Beliefs and Behavior: Henry Kissinger's Operational Code and the Vietnam War," *The Journal of Conflict Resolution*, vol. 21, no. 1 (March 1977), pp. 129–68, Charles Malik, "Continuity of US Policy," *Journal of Palestine Studies*, vol. 4, no. 1 (Autumn 1974), pp. 159–62, Ole Holsti, "The 'Operational Code' Approach to the Study of Political Leaders: John Foster Dulles' Philosophical and Instrumental Beliefs," *Canadian Journal of Political Science/Revue Canadienne de science politique*, vol. 3, no. 1 (March 1970), pp. 123–57, and Inis L. Claude, Jr., "The United Nations, the United States, and the Maintenance of Peace," *International Organization*, vol. 23, no. 3, The United States and International Organization: The Changing Setting (Summer 1969), pp. 621–36.

13 For a first-rate analysis, see Edward W. Said, *Orientalism* (New York: Vintage Books, 1979).
14 Douglas Little, *American Orientalism: The United States and the Middle East since 1945* (Chapel Hill, NC: University of North Carolina Press, 2002), p. 11.
15 Of course, the US has always been suspicious of Third World nationalisms as exemplified by the Palestinians seeking to cast off Western (i.e. Israeli) hegemony. See David D. Newsom, *The Imperial Mantle: The United States, Decolonization, and the Third World* (Bloomington, IN: Indiana University Press, 2001).
16 *Gallup Poll*, 10/30/1986–11/12/1986.
17 Puschel, *US-Israeli Strategic Cooperation in the Post-Cold War Era*, pp. 3–5.
18 While it may be argued that Saudi Arabia and other Gulf monarchies were staunchly anti-Soviet, this was often not something that the American public perceived, the result of numerous factors, most notably, pro-Israel efforts at painting the Arab states with a wide stroke of anti-Americanism and calling for increased US support of the Jewish state. See Trice, "Foreign Policy Interest Groups," for an early assessment.
19 *Gallup Poll*, 11/13/1985–11/14/1985.
20 See, for example, *Gallup Poll*, 9/20/1986–11/18/1986.
21 *Gallup Poll*, 9/20/1986–11/18/1986.
22 For more on this, see Jerry Lembcke, *The Spitting Image: The Myth, Memory, and the Legacy of Vietnam* (New York: New York University Press, 1998).
23 *Gallup Poll*, 10/30/1986–11/12/1986.
24 Khalil Jahshan, former president of National Association of Arab Americans and representative of Association of Arab American University Graduates and Palestine Research and Educational Center, interview by the author, Arlington, VA, March 14, 2006.
25 According to Gene Sharp, 85 percent of the resistance involved nonviolent means. See Gene Sharp "The Intifada and Nonviolent Struggle," *Journal of Palestine Studies*, vol. 19, no. 1 (Autumn 1989), p. 6. For the link between television news and public opinion, see Donald L. Jordan and Benjamin I. Page, "Shaping Foreign Policy Opinions: The Role of TV News," *The Journal of Conflict Resolution*, vol. 36, no. 2 (June 1992), pp. 227–41.
26 According to critical scholarship produced during the late 1980s, this was just a myth propagated by Israeli historians. For instance, see Nur-eldeen Masalha, "On Recent Hebrew and Israeli Sources for the Palestinian Exodus, 1947–49," *Journal of Palestine Studies*, vol. 18, no. 1, Special Issue: Palestine 1948 (Autumn 1988), pp. 121–37.
27 *Gallup Poll*, 2/4/1988.
28 *Gallup Poll*, 5/13/1988–5/15/1988.
29 Alvin Richman, "A Report: American Attitudes Toward Israeli-Palestinian Relations in the Wake of the Uprising," *The Public Opinion Quarterly*, vol. 53, no. 3 (Autumn 1989), p. 415.

30 Ibrahim Abu-Lughod, "On Achieving Independence," in Jamal Nassar and Roger Heacock (eds), *Intifada: Palestine at the Crossroads* (New York: Praeger, 1990), pp. 3–4.
31 For a glimpse into the domestic portrayal of the Intifada by Arab American groups, see John Kifner, "New Pride for Palestinian-Americans," *New York Times*, December 12, 1988, "Syracuse Coalition Supports Palestinian State," *The Post-Standard*, December 21, 1988, Walter Goodman, "Review/Television; The Palestinian View, Between Bookends," *New York Times*, September 6, 1989, and Chris Hedges, "Palestinians Struggling to Rebuild their Lives," *New York Times*, October 4, 1990. This will be discussed in more depth elsewhere.
32 Richman, "A Report: American Attitudes Toward Israeli-Palestinian Relations in the Wake of the Uprising," p. 421. For an in depth analysis of those and other trends, see Eytan Gilboa, *American Public Opinion toward Israel and the Arab-Israeli Conflict* (Lexington, MA: Lexington Books, 1986).
33 *Gallup Poll*, 3/13/1979. For the 1988 poll, see *Gallup Poll*, 5/13/1988–5/15/1988.
34 *Gallup Poll*, 5/13/1988–5/15/1988.
35 These are the results of *Gallup Poll*, 1/17/1978: "Which of the plans listed on this card would you prefer with regard to the Palestinians – They should have a separate, independent nation on the West Bank of the Jordan River in the area that was formerly Jordan but is now occupied by Israel; they should have a state on the West Bank of the Jordan River that is not totally independent and is linked with Jordan; or they should go on living as they are now in Israel and in the existing Arab nations? Just read off your answer by the letter. [Answers:] They should have a separate, independent nation on the West Bank of the Jordan River in the area that was formerly Jordan but is now occupied by Israel (11.67 percent); They should have a state on the West Bank of the Jordan River that is not totally independent and is linked with Jordan (10.60 percent); They should go on living as they are now in Israel and in the existing Arab nations (14.75 percent); No Opinion (11.59 percent); Don't know (0.00 percent), No answer/not applicable (51.39 percent)."
Compare those results to *Gallup Poll*, 3/28/1978: "Which of the plans listed on this card would you prefer with regard to the Palestinians – They should have a separate, independent nation on the West Bank of the Jordan River in the area that was formerly Jordan but is now occupied by Israel; they should have a state on the West Bank of the Jordan River that is not totally independent and is linked with Jordan; or they should go on living as they are now in Israel and in the existing Arab nations? Just read off your answer by letter. [Answers:] They should have a separate, independent nation on the West Bank of the Jordan River in the area that was formerly Jordan but is now occupied by Israel (29.99 percent); They should have a state on the West Bank of the Jordan River that is not totally independent and is linked with Jordan (23.00 percent); The should go on living as they are now in Israel and in the existing Arab nations (20.78 percent); Don't know (25.92 percent); No answer (0.32 percent).
36 "Memorandum of Understanding between the Government of the United States and the Government of Israel On Strategic Cooperation," in Puschel, *US-Israeli Strategic Cooperation in the Post-Cold War Era*, p. 178.
37 *Gallup Poll*, 7/23/1982–7/26/1982.
38 Interviews with Hussein Ibish and James Zogby.
39 *Gallup Poll*, 9/20/1986–11/18/1986.
40 For a synopsis of public opinion toward the Israeli-Palestinian conflict during the early 1980s and before, see Editors, "Americans' Attitudes Toward the Middle East," *Journal of Palestine Studies*, vol. 12, no. 3 (Spring 1983), pp. 134–46, Fouad Moghrabi, "American Public Opinion and the Palestine Question," *Journal of Palestine Studies*, vol. 15, no. 2 (Winter 1986), pp. 56–75, and Michael

Suleiman, "Development of Public Opinion on the Palestine Question," *Journal of Palestine Studies*, vol. 13, no. 3 (Spring 1984), pp. 87–116.

41 Douglas Foyle nicely outlined the link between public opinion and foreign policymakers. See Douglas C. Foyle, "Public Opinion and Foreign Policy: Elite Beliefs as a Mediating Variable," *International Studies Quarterly*, vol. 41, no. 1 (March 1997), pp. 141–69.

42 This is something that continued to generate debate well after the end of Bush's presidency since some questioned his commitment to Israel or worse, saw him as being too pro-Arab. See Samuel Segev, "The Arab-Israeli Conflict under President Bush," in Meena Bose and Rosanna Perotti (eds), *From Cold War to New World Order: The Foreign Policy of George H. W. Bush* (Westport, CT: Praeger, 2002), pp. 113–26.

43 The Soviet Union also made changes in its approach towards the USA. See Jeffrey T. Checkel, *Ideas and International Political Change: Soviet/Russian Behavior and the End of the Cold War* (New Haven, CT: Yale University Press, 1997), pp. 77–79.

44 For a few excellent analyses on this topic, see Richard Ned LeBow and Thomas Risse-Kappen (eds), *International Relations Theory and the End of the Cold War* (New York: Columbia University Press, 1995), Fraser Cameron, *US Foreign Policy After the Cold War* (New York: Routledge, 2002), and Michael J. Hogan (ed.), *The End of the Cold War: Its Meaning and Implications* (Cambridge: Cambridge University Press, 1992).

45 See United Nations Security Council Resolution 660 (New York, August 2, 1990), available from www.un.org/documents/scres.htm; Internet; accessed August 21, 2005.

46 *Gallup Poll*, 11/8/1990–11/11/1990.

47 Khalil Jahshan; Nabil Mohamad, organizing director of American-Arab Anti-Discrimination Committee, interview by the author, Washington, DC, March 14, 2006; Christine Gleichert, Capitol Hill lobbyist for American-Arab Anti-Discrimination Committee, interview by the author, Washington, DC, March 15, 2006; Rafi Dajani, former executive director of American Task Force on Palestine, interview by the author, Washington, DC, March 15, 2006; Mary Rose Oakar, former congresswoman from Cleveland, OH, and president of American-Arab Anti-Discrimination Committee, interview by the author, Washington, DC, March 15, 2006; Helen Samhan, executive director of Arab American Institute Foundation, interview by the author, Washington, DC, March 16, 2006; Rebecca Abou-Chedid, government relations and policy analyst for Arab American Institute, interview by the author, Washington, DC, March 16, 2006; Hussein Ibish; Marvin Wingfield, director of education and outreach for American-Arab Anti-Discrimination Committee, telephone interview by the author, December 19, 2006.

48 *Gallup Poll*, 10/19/1990–10/16/1990.

49 *Gallup Poll*, 10/23/1990–11/15/1990. Support for Israel in this poll was considerably lower than before the Gulf crisis. In 1989 for example, when asked, "in the Middle East situation, are your sympathies more with the Israelis or more with the Palestinian Arabs?" the percentage of Americans who chose Israel was 50.27, while a meager 13.57 percent chose the Palestinians. See *Gallup Poll*, 8/10/1989–8/13/1989.

50 The Palestinians continued to support Saddam Hussein after the end of the Gulf War. See Sabra Chartrand, "After the War: The West Bank Palestinians Still Revere Hussein as their Savior," *New York Times*, March 4, 1991.

51 A few days after the invasion of Kuwait, President Hussein called for the withdrawal of Israel from the Palestinian territories and the end of all other occupation in exchange for removing his troops from the tiny Gulf nation. See Xinhua

Newswire, "US Rejects Iraq's 'Peace Initiative' on Gulf Crisis," available from *Xinhua General Overseas News Service*, August 12, 1990.

52 According to Ghada Talhami, just as many Palestinians in Kuwait resisted the Iraqi occupation. See Ghada Hashem Talhami, *Palestinian Refugees: Pawns to Political Actors* (New York: Nova Science Publishers, 2003), pp. 114–21.

53 *Gallup Poll*, 10/16/1990–10/19/1990.

54 See Leon T. Hadar, "High Noon in Washington: The Shootout over the Loan Guarantees," *Journal of Palestine Studies*, vol. 21, no. 2 (Winter 1992), pp. 72–87, and Sheldon L. Richman, "The Economic Impact of the Israeli Loan Guarantees," *Journal of Palestine Studies*, vol. 21, no. 2 (Winter 1992), pp. 88–95.

55 There were some exceptions. See Clyde R. Mark, "Israel: U.S. Foreign Assistance," *CRS Issue Brief for Congress* (April 26, 2005), and Jim Drinkard, "Legislator Warns Israel on Expansion of Settlements," available from *Associated Press*, June 27, 1990.

56 For one such instance involving the confrontation between President Bush and pro-Israel groups, see Andrew Rosenthal, "Bush Acts to Calm Israel Aid Uproar," *New York Times*, September 21, 1991.

57 *Gallup Poll*, 10/11/1990–10/14/1990.

58 *Gallup Poll*, 9/11/1990–9/12/1990 and 4/5/1990–4/6/1990.

59 *Gallup Poll*, 10/11/1990–10/14/1990.

60 *Gallup Poll*, 11/8/1990–11/11/1990.

61 *Gallup Poll*, 1/11/1991–1/13/1991.

62 These attacks caused more harm from panic than from their effectiveness. See Carol S. Fullerton, George Brandt, and Robert Ursano, "Chemical and Biological Silent Agents of Terror," in Robert J. Ursano and Ann E. Norwood (eds), *Emotional Aftermath of the Persian Gulf War: Veterans, Families, Communities, and Nations* (Washington, DC: American Psychiatric Press, Inc., 1996), pp. 128–30.

63 *Gallup Poll*, 1/23/1991–1/26/1991.

64 *Gallup Poll*, 2/15/1991.

65 *Gallup Poll*, 2/15/1991.

66 *Gallup Poll*, 3/14/1991–3/17/1991.

67 *Gallup Poll*, 3/14/1991–3/17/1991.

68 According to Hussein Ibish, this gave pro-Arab groups some level of confidence in the United States' ability to resolve the Israeli-Palestinian conflict. Interview with Hussein Ibish.

69 Little, *American Orientalism*, p. 3.

70 For a glimpse into the region's developments preceding the Gulf War, particularly between the Iraq and the Palestinians, see Yezid Sayigh, *Armed Struggle and the Search for State: The Palestinian National Movement, 1949–1993* (London: Oxford University Press, 1999), p. 638–45.

71 *Gallup Poll*, 7/18/1991–7/21/1991.

72 Interview with Khalil Jahshan.

73 *Gallup Poll*, 8/8/1991–8/11/1991. Paradoxically, five months earlier in a poll exemplifying American skepticism about prospects for peace, a majority of Americans said that both sides would not live up to their respective ends of the bargain. See *Gallup Poll*, 3/14/1991–3/17/1991.

74 Interview with Hussein Ibish.

75 *Gallup Poll*, 8/8/1991–8/11/1991.

76 *Gallup Poll*, 9/26/1991–9/29/1991.

77 Interview with James Zogby.

78 *Gallup Poll*, 9/26/1991–9/29/1991.

79 To trace the evolution of this, see Samuel Segev, "Turning a Page in the Middle East," *American Foreign Policy Interests*, 23 (2001), pp. 71–86, Xingping Kang

and Yongjiang Zhao, "The Violence-Plagued Peace Process: Predicament, Prospect, and Test for U.S. Middle East Policy," *American Foreign Policy Interests*, 23 (2001), pp. 357–68, Fouad Ajami, "Home Base," *The New Republic* (June 4, 2001), p. 62, Jeffrey W. Legro, "Whence American Internationalism," *International Organization*, vol. 54, no. 2 (Spring 2000), pp. 253–89, Sam Hodges, "Alabama Statesman Says U.S. Biased Against Palestinians," *Washington Report on Middle East Affairs* vol. 19, no. 2 (March 2000), pp. 21–23, Kathleen Christison, "Bound by a Frame of Reference, Part II: U.S. Policy and the Palestinians, 1948–88," *Journal of Palestine Studies*, vol. 27, no. 3 (Spring 1998), pp. 20–34, and "Bound by a Frame of Reference, Part III: U.S. Policy and the Palestinians, 1988–98," *Journal of Palestine Studies*, vol. 27, no. 4 (Summer 1998), pp. 53–64.

80 *Gallup Poll*, 1/28/1993–1/29/1993.
81 For more on the post-communist context, see James M. Scott, *After the End: Making U.S. Foreign Policy in the Post-Cold War World* (Durham, NC: Duke University Press, 1998).
82 Interviews with Hussein Ibish and Peter Timco. Peter Timco, director of the office of the president, Arab American Institute, telephone interview by the author, April 25, 2008.
83 Interview with James Zogby.
84 *Gallup Poll*, 9/10/1993–9/12/1993. Before the collapse of the Soviet Union, 42.13 percent of Americans favored "the establishment of an Independent Palestinian nation within the territories occupied by Israel in the 1967 war." See *Gallup Poll*, 3/14/1991–3/17/1991.
85 *Gallup Poll*, 9/10/1993–9/12/1993.
86 Still, many called for caution. See Kathleen Christison, "Splitting the Difference: The Palestinian-Israeli Policy of James Baker," *Journal of Palestine Studies*, vol. 24, no. 1 (Autumn 1994), pp. 39–50, Donald Neff, "The Clinton Administration and UN Resolution 242," *Journal of Palestine Studies*, vol. 23, no. 2 (Winter 1994), pp. 20–30, Leon T. Hadar, "Clinton's Tilt," *Journal of Palestine Studies*, vol. 22, no. 4 (Summer 1993), pp. 62–72, Bernard Lewis, "Rethinking the Middle East," *Foreign Affairs* (Fall 1992), p. 99, and Joe Stork and Rashid Khalidi, "Washington's Game Plan in the Middle East," *Middle East Report*, no. 164/165, Intifada Year Three (May-August 1990), pp. 9–11.
87 This is not meant to be an accusation of penury. The United States has spent billions on the Middle East, particularly where Israel is concerned. For the relationship between public opinion and aid to the Jewish state until 1990, see A. F. K. Organski, *The $36 Billion Bargain: U.S. Aid to Israel and American Public Opinion* (New York: Columbia University Press, 1990).
88 *Gallup Poll*, 9/10/1993–9/12/1993.
89 See for example, Martin Gilens, *Why Americans Hate Welfare: Race, Media, and the Politics of Anti-Poverty Policy* (Chicago, IL: University of Chicago Press, 1999).
90 *Gallup Poll*, 9/10/1993–9/12/1993.
91 *Gallup Poll*, 9/10/1993–9/12/1993.
92 *Gallup Poll*, 1/6/1994–1/8/1994.
93 *Gallup Poll*, 10/7/1994–10/25/1994. This number soars to nearly 86 percent. See *Gallup Poll*, 10/26/1994–12/7/1994.
94 *Gallup Poll*, 10/7/1994–10/25/1994 and 10/26/1994–12/7/1994.
95 *Gallup Poll*, 9/29/1995–9/30/1995.
96 Such a mood was reflected in other areas of US foreign policy. See, for example, Jeffrey A. Frankel and Peter R. Orszag (eds), *American Economic Policy in the 1990s* (Cambridge, MA: MIT Press, 2002), pp. 213–14.
97 *Gallup Poll*, 8/12/1997–8/13/1997.
98 *Gallup Poll*, 8/12/1997–8/13/1997.

99 After 9/11, Fareed Zakaria argued that support for Israel might have contributed to the terrorist attacks. See Fareed Zakaria, "The Politics of Rage: Why do They Hate Us?" *Newsweek*, October 15, 2001.

100 *Gallup Poll*, 8/12/1997–8/13/1997.

101 This is something that James Lindsay warned about in the early 1990s. See James M. Lindsay, "Congress and Diplomacy," in Randall B. Ripley and James M. Lindsay (eds), *Congress Resurgent: Foreign and Defense Policy on Capitol Hill* (Ann Arbor, MI: University of Michigan Press, 1993), p. 280.

102 Ibid.

103 See Appendix 4.

104 For more on this, see Noam Chomsky, *The Fateful Triangle: The United States, Israel and the Palestinians* (London: Pluto Press, 1999).

105 *Gallup Poll*, 5/8/1998–5/10/1998.

106 Such inconsistencies have led some to argue for maintaining foreign policy "responsibility in the hands of an expert minority" because of "the complexity of foreign affairs and the slight attention paid to external events by the citizens of liberal democracies." Miles Kahler, *Liberalization and Foreign Policy* (New York: Columbia University Press, 1997), p. 5. Also see Robert A. Dahl, *On Democracy* (New Haven, CT: Yale University Press, 1988), pp. 69–79.

107 *Gallup Poll*, 5/8/1998–5/10/1998. The poll found 49.02 percent of Americans believed that to be the case.

108 *Gallup Poll*, 5/7/1999–5/9/1999.

109 *Gallup Poll*, 5/7/1999–5/9/1999. This was the question in the survey: "Do you favor or oppose the establishment of an independent Palestinian state on the West Bank and the Gaza strip? [Answers] Favor (53.17 percent); Oppose (25.81 percent); Don't know/refused (21.01 percent)."

110 *Gallup Poll*, 5/7/1999 and 7/25/1999. A slightly higher percentage of respondents thought that economic aid to Israel should be maintained than those that thought it should be decreased or altogether eliminated.

111 *Gallup Poll*, 7/23/1999–7/25/1999. This was also expressed later. See *Gallup Poll*, 1/25/2000–1/26–2000.

112 *Gallup Poll*, 1/25/2000–1/26/2000.

113 *Gallup Poll*, 7/6/2000–7/9/2000.

114 Interview with Hussein Ibish.

115 *Gallup Poll*, 10/9/2000–10/15/2000.

116 B'Tselem, the Israeli Center for Human Rights in the Occupied Territories, "Statistics on Fatalities," available from www.btselem.org/english/statistics/Casualties.asp; Internet; accessed December 30, 2007.

117 *Gallup Poll*, 2/1/2001–2/4/2001. This was one of the first polls taken since President George W. Bush took office.

118 For this in perspective, see Clayton E. Swisher, *The Truth about Camp David: The Untold Story about the Collapse of the Middle East Peace Process* (New York: Nation Books, 2004).

119 As the 2006 Lebanon war demonstrated, some evangelists welcomed instability in the region since it brought Armageddon closer to realization. For an analysis on Israel's place in the policy perceptions of the religious right, see David D. Kirkpatrick, "For Evangelicals, Supporting Israel is 'God's Foreign Policy,'" *New York Times*, November 14, 2006.

120 They were also his greatest supporters as the country's political elites slid into polarization. See Gary C. Jacobson, *A Divider, Not a Uniter: George W. Bush and the American People* (New York: Pearson-Longman, 2007), pp. 151–55.

121 The power of this group has been growing in American politics since the late 1970s. At least two contemporary works move beyond the person of President Bush and discuss the political role of the religious right in America. See John

Micklethawait and Adrian Wooldridge, *The Right Nation: Conservative Power in America* (New York: Penguin Press, 2004), and Harold Perkin, "American Fundamentalism and the Selling of God," in David Marquand and Ronald L. Nettler (eds), *Religion and Democracy* (Boston, MA: Blackwell Publishers, 2000), pp. 79–89. The analyses contained in both works were influential on the discussion to follow.

122 Jeremy D. Mayer, "Christian Fundamentalists and Public Opinion Toward the Middle East: Israel's New Best Friends?" *Social Science Quarterly*, vol. 84, no. 3 (September 2004), pp. 695–712.

123 See A. James Rudin, *Israel for Christians: Understanding Modern Israel* (Philadelphia, PA: Fortress Press, 1983).

124 Ibid., p. 62.

125 In a 2002 public opinion poll, 20 percent identified their support for Israel with any religious cause. See *Gallup Poll*, 4/22/2002–4/24/2002.

126 See Jeffrey Heller, "Sharon Vows to Seek Peace but Big Settlements to Stay," available from www.alertnet.org/thenews/newsdesk/L01537146.htm; Internet; accessed December 2, 2005. The same understanding applied between Bush and Sharon's successor, Prime Minister Ehud Olmert.

127 Vaughn P. Shannon, *Balancing Act: US Foreign Policy and the Arab-Israeli Conflict* (Burlington, VT: Ashgate Publishing Company, 2003), p. 110.

128 A Christian Zionist is someone for whom it is "a requirement of faith to prefer the blessing of Israel above all passing things. Doing this, he believes, cannot, by definition, ever be incompatible with the will of God." See Paul Charles Merkley, *Christian Attitudes Towards the State of Israel* (Montreal: McGill-Queen's University Press, 2001), p. 218. Of course, there is a substantial debate on this and other issues. See Alexander Moens, *The Foreign Policy of George W. Bush: Values, Strategy and Loyalty* (Burlington, VT: Ashgate Publishing Company, 2004), particularly p. 17. For a review of Christian politics in US foreign policy before George W. Bush, see Clyde Wilcox, *Onward Christian Soldiers? The Religious Right in American Politics* (Boulder, CO: Westview Press, 2000), p. 89.

129 Virginia Tilley, *The One-State Solution: A Breakthrough for Peace in the Israeli-Palestinian Deadlock* (Ann Arbor, MI: University of Michigan Press, 2005), p. 93. For an excellent assessment of Palestinian Islamist terrorism in reaction to the Israeli occupation, see John L. Esposito, *Unholy War: Terror in the Name of Islam* (New York: Oxford University Press, 2003), pp. 94–102.

130 For the Bush administration's general policy, see Colin Campbell, *The George W. Bush Presidency: Appraisals and Prospects* (Washington, DC: CQ Press, 2004).

131 United Nations Security Council Resolution 1397 (New York, March 12, 2002), available from http://domino.un.org/unispal.nsf/0/4721362dd7ba3dea85256b7b00 536c7f?OpenDocument; Internet; accessed August 21, 2005. However, Tilley pointed out that Israel's West Bank settlements were accepted by the Bush–Sharon understanding, a condition for Sharon's lack of opposition to the resolution and the strategic reasoning behind the building of the wall. See Tilley, *The One-State Solution*, p. 123.

132 Without Resolution 1397, Resolution 242 only called for the return of territories occupied by Israel to the Arab states. Resolution 1515 reiterated 1397 but added the roadmap as its basis.

133 The roadmap received a solid defense in an interview with National Security Advisor Condoleezza Rice. See "Dr. Condoleezza Rice Discusses the Roadmap for Peace in the Middle East," June 3, 2003, available from www.whitehouse.gov/ news/releases/2003/06/20030603-6.html; Internet; accessed January 9, 2007.

134 *Gallup Poll*, 9/14/2001–9/15/2001.

135 See *Gallup Poll*, 9/14/2001–9/15/2001 and 10/19/2001–10/21/2001.
136 *Gallup Poll*, 2/4/2002–2/6/2002.
137 *Gallup Poll*, 2/4/2002–2/6/2002.
138 *Gallup Poll*, 4/5/2002–4/7/2002.
139 *Gallup Poll*, 4/5/2002–4/7/2002.
140 Against public opinion, this was something that President Bush recanted through the understanding on settlements he reached with Prime Minister Ariel Sharon. See Heller, "Sharon Vows to Seek Peace but Big Settlements to Stay."
141 *Gallup Poll*, 4/5/2002–4/7/2002.
142 *Gallup Poll*, 6/21/2002–6/23/2002. The Palestinian Authority stopping suicide bombings against Israel qualified the poll question.
143 Matt Kelley, "Afghan War May Guide Iraq Planning," available from *Associated Press*, October 6, 2002.
144 *Gallup Poll*, 6/21/2002–6/23/2002.
145 John J. Mearsheimer and Stephen M. Walt, "The Israel Lobby and U.S. Foreign Policy," *Kennedy School of Government Faculty Research Working Paper Series* RWP06–011 (March 2006), pp. 31–35.
146 *Gallup Poll*, 9/2/2002–9/4/2002 and 2/3/2003–2/6/2003.
147 *Gallup Poll*, 3/29/2003–3/30/2003.
148 Military experts were among the first to point this out. See, for example, Williamson Murray and Robert H. Scales, Jr., *The Iraq War: A Military History* (Cambridge, MA: Harvard University Press, 2003), p. 39.
149 Despite its 2005 withdrawal, Israel has engaged in air and ground operations against Gaza. For one example, see Illene R. Prusher, "Israel's Gaza Balancing Act," *Christian Science Monitor*, July 3, 2006.
150 This was one of the many reasons given by Bush and British Prime Minister Tony Blair for the Iraq War. See Laura Chernaik, *Social and Virtual Space: Science Fiction, Transnationalism, and the American New Right* (Cranbury, NJ: Rosemont Publishing, 2005), pp. 185–87.
151 There was the belief at the highest level of command that Iraq possessed such weapons. For that and other issues surrounding intelligence before and during the war on terror, see George Tenet, *At the Center of the Storm: My Years at the CIA* (New York: HarperCollins, 2007).
152 For these, see Douglas Feith, *War and Decision: Inside the Pentagon at the Dawn of the War on Terrorism* (New York: HarperCollins, 2008).
153 *Gallup Poll*, 5/19/2003–5/21/2003.
154 For an account of these developments and the ensuing nation building, see Paul L. Bremmer III and Malcolm McConnell, *My Year in Iraq: The Struggle to Build a Future of Hope* (New York: Simon and Schuster, 2006).
155 *Gallup Poll*, 5/19/2003–5/21/2003.
156 There were many issues involved in this disillusionment, all of which centered on the US failure in the Middle East and elsewhere. See Clyde R. Mark, "Israeli-United States Relations," *CRS Issue Brief for Congress* (November 9, 2004), Dierdre Mullan and Carol Rittner, "Do Good Fences Make Good Neighbors?" *American Foreign Policy Interests*, 26 (2004), pp. 477–84, Adam Nagourney, "Clinton Assails Bush as Democrats Open Convention," *New York Times*, July 27, 2004, Anne Bayefsky, "Israel, the United Nations, and the Road Map," *American Foreign Policy Interests*, 24 (2003), pp. 373–94, Robert O. Freedman, "The Bush Administration and the Israeli-Palestinian Conflict: A Preliminary Evaluation," *American Foreign Policy Interests*, 25 (2003), pp. 505–11, Robert G. Kaiser, "Bush and Sharon Nearly Identical on Mideast Policy," *Washington Post*, February 9, 2003, and Michael Lind, "Distorting U.S. Foreign Policy: The Israel Lobby and American Power," *Washington Report on Middle East Affairs*

(May 2002), available from www.thirdworldtraveler.com/Israel/Israel_Lobby_US. html; Internet; accessed December 25, 2005.

157 *Gallup Poll*, 5/30/2003–6/1/2003.

158 It is possible that the public was generally moving toward religious explanations for world events, which is the reason for the election of Bush in the first place. Still, the poll was significant in that it showed clear evidence of the increasing link between religion and American Middle East policy. Some have considered that divisive. See Jacobson, *A Divider, Not a Uniter*, pp. 151–57.

159 *Gallup Poll*, 5/30/2003–6/1/2003.

160 On how this may take place, see Shibley Telhami and Jon Krosnick, "U.S. Public Attitudes Toward Israel: A Study of the Attentive and Issue Publics," in Gabriel Sheffer (ed.), *U.S.-Israeli Relations at the Crossroads* (Portland, OR: Frank Cass, 1997), pp. 109–10.

161 *Gallup Poll*, 6/12/2003–6/15/2003.

162 *Gallup Poll*, 10/10/2003–10/12/2003.

163 Some reported 655,000 deaths. See Sarah Boseley, "655,000 Iraqis Killed Since Invasion," *Guardian*, October 11, 2006.

164 *Gallup Poll*, 2/9/2004–2/12/2004.

165 *Gallup Poll*, 9/24/2004–9/26/2004.

166 *Gallup Poll*, 9/24/2004–9/26/2004.

167 AIPAC sought to exploit the new government's leanings toward Israel. See American Israel Public Affairs Committee, "AIPAC Statement on 2004 Election Results," AIPAC press release, November 3, 2004.

168 *Gallup Poll*, 2/7/2005–2/10/2005.

169 *Zogby International*, 7/6/2003–7/9/2003.

170 For the opinion of Israelis and Palestinians, see Harry S. Truman Institute for the Advancement of Peace, "Majority Support among Palestinians and Israelis for the Road Map and for Mutual Recognition," available from http://truman. huji.ac.il/polls.asp; Internet; accessed July 2, 2006.

171 Tanya Reinhart, *Israel/Palestine: How to End the War of 1948* (New York: Seven Stories Press, 2002), pp. 55–56.

172 For the policy outcomes, see William B. Quandt, "U.S. Policy Toward the Arab-Israeli Conflict," in William B. Quandt (ed.), *The Middle East: Ten Years after Camp David* (Washington, DC: Brookings Institution Press, 1988).

173 The roles of the pro-Israel and pro-Arab lobbies in this development will be examined later.

174 For a variety of assessments, see Francis Fukuyama, "After Neoconservatism," *New York Times Magazine*, February 19, 2006, p. 62, Martin Peretz, "The Politics of Churlishness," *The New Republic* (April 11, 2005), pp. 20–23, James Kitfield, "Daring and Costly, The Bush Record: Foreign Affairs," *National Journal*, vol. 36, no. 28 (July 10, 2004), pp. 2158–68, John Nichols, "Taking Sides," *The Nation*, 277 (October 6, 2003), pp. 6–7, and Stephen M. Walt, "Beyond bin Laden," *International Security*, vol. 26, no. 3 (Winter 2001/02), pp. 56–78.

175 Tilley, *The One-State Solution*, p. 123.

3 The effects of the pro-Israel lobby

1 "Pro-Israel" groups are not homogeneous in their ideologies or aims. Organizations such as Americans for Peace Now, the Israel Policy Forum, the Jewish Alliance for Justice and Peace, and J Street have on numerous occasions opposed groups like the American Israel Public Affairs Committee. However, this chapter will focus on the pro-Israel lobby as directed by the American Israel Public Affairs Committee to help channel American foreign policy in ways that

are synonymous with Israeli policies concerning land for peace and the two-state solution. For an excellent outline of contemporary pro-Israel lobbying efforts, see Glenn Frankel, "A Beautiful Friendship," *Washington Post*, July 16, 2006.

2 Paul Findley, "Paul Findley: Congress and the Pro-Israel Lobby," *Journal of Palestine Studies*, vol. 15, no. 1 (Autumn 1985), p. 107. For a short history of AIPAC's influence, see David Schoenbaum, *The United States and the State of Israel* (New York: Oxford University Press, 1993), pp. 4–6. Of course, some would condemn an inquiry like the present one as conspiracy theory. See Daniel Pipes, *The Hidden Hand: Middle East Fears of Conspiracy* (New York: St. Martin's Press, 1996). For a response to such condemnation see John J. Mearsheimer and Stephen M. Walt, *The Israel Lobby and U.S. Foreign Policy* (New York: Farrar, Straus and Giroux, 2007), pp. 12–13. Like the work done by Mearsheimer and Walt, everything stated in this chapter is part of the public record.

3 Paul Findley, *They Dare to Speak Out: People and Institutions Confront Israel's Lobby* (Westport, CT: Lawrence Hill and Company, 1985), p. 180. This mission has a long history in the USA. See Odeh Abu Rudeneh, "The Jewish Factor in US Politics," *Journal of Palestine Studies*, vol. 1, no. 4 (Summer 1972), pp. 92–107, Eric Rouleau, "US-Israel Relations," *Journal of Palestine Studies*, vol. 6, no. 4 (Summer 1977), pp. 169–77, Nadav Safran, *The United States and Israel* (Cambridge, MA: Harvard University Press, 1963), pp. 270–92 and James Lee Ray, *The Future of American-Israeli Relations* (Lexington, KY: University Press of Kentucky, 1985), pp. 5–22. Naturally, some long ago have maintained that the Israel lobby did not possess the power attributed to it. See Hyman Bookbinder, "The Pro-Israel Lobby Does Not Dictate US Mideast Policy," in Bob Anderson and Janelle Rohr (eds), *Israel: Opposing Viewpoints* (San Diego, CA: Greenhaven Press, 1989), pp. 121–27.

4 For an assessment of that influence on American government and society during the early Reagan years, see Alfred M. Lilienthal, *The Zionist Connection II* (New Brunswick, NJ: North American Publishers, 1982). For more details on Reagan's Middle East policies, see George Lenczowski, *American Presidents and the Middle East* (Durham, NC: Duke University Press, 1990), p. 212–79. On the increase of AIPAC's strength during the Reagan years, see Douglas Franks, "U.S.-Israeli Free Trade Agreement: Aid to Israel Takes New Form," *Journal of Palestine Studies*, vol. 14, no. 2, Special Issue: The Palestinians in Israel and the Occupied Territories (Winter 1985), pp. 169–71, Ibrahim I. Ibrahim, "The American-Israeli Alliance: Raison d'etat Revisited," *Journal of Palestine Studies*, vol. 15, no. 3 (Spring 1986), pp. 17–29, and Kathleen Christison, *Perceptions of Palestine: Their Influence on U.S. Middle East Policy* (Berkeley, CA: University of California Press, 1999), pp. 219–23.

5 Letter excerpted from "Israel in the US Senate," *Journal of Palestine Studies*, vol. 4, no. 4 (Summer 1975), pp. 167–69. Many attribute that letter to the efforts of AIPAC. See Ray, *The Future of American-Israeli Relations*, p. 28.

6 Israeli settlement activity commenced after the war in June 1967. See Gershom Gorenberg, *The Accidental Empire: Israel and the Birth of the Settlements, 1967–1977* (New York: Times Books, 2006), and Appendix 4.

7 David K. Shipler, "On Middle East Policy, A Major Influence," *New York Times*, July 6, 1987.

8 Karen L. Puschel, *US-Israeli Strategic Cooperation in the Post-Cold War Era: An American Perspective* (San Francisco, CA: Westview Press, 1993), p. 3.

9 Thomas A. Dine, "The Revolution in U.S.-Israel Relations," *Journal of Palestine Studies*, vol. 15, no. 4 (Summer 1986), p. 138. This "revolution" would lead Paul Findley to comment, "AIPAC has effectively gained control of virtually all of Capitol Hill's actions on Middle East policy." See Findley, *They Dare to Speak Out*, p. 25.

10 During that year, Robert Trice surmised that Arab American pressure groups' "impact on most aspects of U.S. Miuddle East policy remains negligible." Robert H. Trice, "Domestic Interest Groups and the Arab-Israeli Conflict," in Abdul Aziz Said, *Ethnicity and U.S. Foreign Policy* (New York: Greenwood Publishing Group, 1981), p. 123.

11 Dine, "The Revolution in U.S.-Israel Relations," p. 135.

12 For a sample of literature on US policy from Ford to the first Bush administration, see Edward Sheehan, "Step by Step in the Middle East," *Journal of Palestine Studies*, vol. 5, no. 3/4 (Spring 1976), pp. 3–53, Ghassan Bishara, "The Middle East Arms Package: A Survey of the Congressional Debates," *Journal of Palestine Studies*, vol. 7, no. 4 (Summer 1978), pp. 67–78, Nancy Jo Nelson, "The Zionist Organizational Structure," *Journal of Palestine Studies*, vol. 10, no. 1 (Autumn 1980), pp. 80–93, Michael Adams, "America, Zionism, and the Prospects for Peace," *Journal of Palestine Studies*, vol. 19, no. 1 (Autumn 1989), pp. 32–45, Walid Khalidi, "The Half-Empty Glass of Middle East Peace," *Journal of Palestine Studies*, vol. 19, no. 3 (Spring 1990), pp. 14–38, Geoffrey Aronson, "Questioning Sacred Cows," *Journal of Palestine Studies*, vol. 19, no. 3 (Spring 1990), pp. 111–16, Jonathan Marcus, "Discordant Voices: The US Jewish Community and Israel during the 1980s," *International Affairs*, vol. 66, no. 3 (July 1990), pp. 545–58, Kathleen Christison, "The 'Fuller Report,'" *Journal of Palestine Studies*, vol. 19, no. 4 (Summer 1990), pp. 106–11, Lyn Teo Simarki "The Rhetoric of Reassurance at AIPAC's 31st Annual Policy Conference," *Journal of Palestine Studies*, vol. 20, no. 1 (Autumn 1990), pp. 92–100, Sharif S. Elmusa, "Shorter Notices," *Journal of Palestine Studies*, vol. 20, no. 3 (Spring 1991), pp. 130–32, Leon T. Hadar, "Was It All Worth It?" *Journal of Palestine Studies*, vol. 20, no. 4 (Summer 1991), pp. 124–32, Edward W. Said, "Reflections on Twenty Years of Palestinian History," *Journal of Palestine Studies*, vol. 20, no. 4 (Summer 1991), pp. 5–22, and Leon T. Hadar, "The Last Days of Likud: The American-Israeli Big Chill," *Journal of Palestine Studies*, vol. 21, no. 4 (Summer 1992), pp. 80–94.

13 As mentioned in the introductory chapter of this book, because of its strength in the pro-Israel camp, AIPAC will serve as the bellwether of all other pro-Jewish state pressure groups affecting foreign policy. Since its founding in the 1950s, AIPAC has been considered the most powerful purveyor of Israel's diplomatic position in the US. See Isaac Alteras, *Eisenhower and Israel: U.S.-Israel Relations, 1953–1960* (Gainesville, FL: University of Florida Press, 1993), p. 288. In addition, some view AIPAC as "the most important organization affecting America's relationship with Israel." See Robert Pear and Richard L. Berke, "Pro-Israel Group Exerts Quiet Might as it Rallies Supporters in Congress," *New York Times*, July 7, 1987. AIPAC has boasted about that on its website. See www.aipac. org/index.cfm; Internet; accessed July 11, 2006.

14 Josh Block, AIPAC media affairs executive, has denied attempts to set up interviews with members of his organization.

15 Cheryl A. Rubenberg, *Israel and the American National Interest, A Critical Examination* (Chicago, IL: University of Illinois Press, 1986), p. 354.

16 The American policy elite internalized that shared culture. For example, see Richard B. Cheney, "Policy Conference 2006 Closing Plenary Leadership Perspective: The U.S.-Israel Relationship," March 6, 2006, available from www. aipac.org/Publications/SpeechesByPolicymakers/Cheney-PC-2006.pdf; Internet; accessed May 1, 2007.

17 Steven L. Spiegel, *The Other Arab-Israeli Conflict: Making America's Middle East Policy, From Truman to Reagan* (Chicago, IL: University of Chicago Press, 1985), p. 390.

18 Ibid.

19 "Memorandum of Understanding between the Government of the United States and the Government of Israel on Strategic Cooperation," in Puschel, *US-Israeli Strategic Cooperation in the Post-Cold War Era*, p. 178. For more on the Israel–US relationship after the Memorandum, see Joe Stork, "Israel as a Strategic Asset," *MERIP Reports*, no. 105, Reagan Targets the Middle East (May 1982), pp. 3–13+32.

20 Not every Jewish organization agreed with AIPAC's mission. For weaknesses in the intra-Jewish alliance in America, see Robert Pear, "Leaders of 3 U.S. Jewish Groups Take Issue with Pro-Israel Lobby," *New York Times*, October 18, 1988.

21 President Reagan counted on AIPAC to gain support in Congress for his Lebanon mission. See Henry Paolucci, *Iran, Israel, and the United States* (Whitestone, NY: Griffon House Publications, 1991), p. 29.

22 For a history, see Rashid Khalidi, *Under Siege: P.L.O. Decisionmaking During the 1982 War* (New York: Columbia University Press, 1986).

23 The US intervened during fallout from the Lebanon invasion. See Thomas L. Friedman, "Marines' View of Beirut Mission: To 'Hunker Down and Bunker In,'" *New York Times*, December 2, 1983.

24 For details, see Joyce M. Davis, *Martyrs: Innocence, Vengeance, and Despair in the Middle East* (New York: Palgrave, 2003), pp. 34, 81–83, 156.

25 Robert Friedman blasted the lack of concern for Palestinian suffering. Robert I. Friedman, "Selling Israel to America," *Journal of Palestine Studies*, vol. 16, no. 4 (Summer 1987), pp. 169–79. Years later, some have bemoaned the disregard of ethical considerations in US policy. For instance, see Mark Lewis Delmar, "Americans Accept Decline of Moral Standing," *The Times Union*, May 20, 2004.

26 See Sheila Ryan, "Israel's Invasion of Lebanon: Background to the Crisis," *Journal of Palestine Studies*, vol. 11, no. 4, Special Issue: The War in Lebanon (Summer 1982), pp. 23–37, and Yoram Peri, "Israel in Lebanon-One Year Later," *Journal of Palestine Studies*, vol. 13, no. 1 (Autumn 1983), pp. 190–96.

27 Richard H. Curtiss, *Stealth PACs: Lobbying Congress for Control of U.S. Middle East Policy*, 4th ed. (Washington, DC: The American Educational Trust, 1996), pp. vi–vii, emphasis added. For figures of pro-Israel political contributions after 1988, see Appendix 5.

28 See, for instance, Mitchell Geoffrey Bard, *The Water's Edge and Beyond: Defining the Limits of Domestic Influence on United States Middle East Policy* (New Brunswick, NJ: Transaction Publishers, 1991).

29 William B. Quandt, *Decade of Decisions: American Foreign Policy toward the Arab-Israeli Conflict, 1967–1976* (Berkeley, CA: University of California Press, 1977), p. 19.

30 For the outcome of the vehement opposition to a Palestinian state, see Jimmy Carter, *Palestine: Peace not Apartheid* (New York: Simon and Schuster, 2006).

31 "AIPAC Policy Statement, 1987," *Journal of Palestine Studies*, vol. 16, no. 4 (Summer 1987), p. 107.

32 Quandt, *Decade of Decisions*, p. 20.

33 Mohammed K. Shadid, *The United States and the Palestinians* (New York: St. Martin's Press, 1981), p. 165.

34 The scope of the pro-Israel lobby is much more complex in the present. See Emad Mekay, "The Compelling Lobby: According to a Recent Study, the Israel Lobby in the US Dictates Washington's Middle East Policy," *Al-Ahram Weekly On-Line*, March 23–29, 2006, available from http://weekly.ahram.org.eg/2006/787/in2.htm; Internet; accessed August 4, 2006.

35 Shadid, *The United States and the Palestinians*, p. 168.

36 Ibid., p. 174. While pro-Israel PACs have in the past given more money to Democrats than Republicans, they have balanced their contributions over time, perhaps reflecting increasing sympathy from and alliance with the political right in America. See Appendix 5. For an excellent analysis on the relationship between

the pro-Israel lobby and Jewish American politics, see Ofira Seliktar, *Divided We Stand: American Jews, Israel, and the Peace Process* (Westport, CT: Praeger, 2002). For an example of the alliance between the Republican Party and Israel supporters, see Dick Morris, "True Friends of Israel Cannot Let the Dems Take Power," *The Hill*, July 26, 2006, available from http://thehill.com/dick-morris/true-friends-of-israel-cannot-let-the-dems-take-power-2006-07-26.html; Internet; accessed April 18, 2008.

37 Findley, *They Dare to Speak Out*, p. 25.
38 See Lev Grinberg, "Post-Mortem for the Ashkenazi Left," in Dan Leon (ed.), *Who's Left in Israel? Radical Political Alternatives for the Future of Israel* (Portland, OR: Sussex Academic Press, 2004), p. 91.
39 Findley, *They Dare to Speak Out*, p. 26.
40 Ibid., p. 27.
41 Norman G. Finkelstein, *Image and Reality of the Israel-Palestine Conflict* (London: Verso, 2001), pp. 158–65.
42 For details of the Reagan plan, see Naseer H. Aruri and Fouad M. Moughrabi, "The Reagan Middle East Initiative," *Journal of Palestine Studies*, vol. 12, no. 2 (Winter 1983), pp. 10–30.
43 Paolucci, *Iran, Israel, and the United States*, p. 29.
44 Findley, *They Dare to Speak Out*, p. 35.
45 Although Egypt and Jordan have been recipients of quite a bit of US economic aid, American policy has resoundingly supported Israel against the Arab states in diplomatic and military affairs. See Edward W. Said and David Barsamian, *Culture and Resistance: Conversations with Edward W. Said* (Boston, MA: South End Press, 2003), pp. 105–7.
46 Findley, *They Dare to Speak Out*, p. 129.
47 Ibid., p. 315.
48 Seth P. Tillman, "United States Middle East Policy: Theory and Practice," *American-Arab Affairs*, no. 4 (Spring 1983), pp. 9–10. Tillman was a senior member of the professional staff of the Senate Foreign Affairs Committee, an aide to Senator William J. Fulbright, and an expert on the US role in the Israeli–Palestinian conflict.
49 Rubenberg, *Israel and the American National Interest*, pp. 3–4.
50 Finkelstein, *Image and Reality of the Israel-Palestine Conflict*, p. 167. For a military history of that war, see Simon Dunstan, *The Yom Kippur War 1973: The Sinai* (Oxford: Osprey Publishing, 2003).
51 Khalil Jahshan, former president of National Association of Arab Americans and representative of Association of Arab American University Graduates and Palestine Research and Educational Center, interview by the author, Arlington, VA, March 14, 2006, Hussein Ibish, executive director of Hala Foundation, senior fellow at American Task Force on Palestine, former communications director at American-Arab Anti-Discrimination Committee, interview by the author, Washington, DC, November 13, 2006, and James Zogby, president and co-founder of Arab American Institute, co-founder of Palestine Human Rights Campaign, co-founder and former executive director of American-Arab Anti-Discrimination Committee, telephone interview by the author, April 26, 2008. This development is discussed in further detail elsewhere.
52 David Pollock, "The American Response to the Intifada," in Robert O. Freedman (ed.), *The Intifada and its Impact on Israel, the Arab World, and the Superpowers* (Gainesville, FL: Florida International University Press, 1991), p. 120. For an excerpt of Baker's speech, see Cheryl A. Rubenberg, "The Bush Administration and the Palestinians: A Reassessment," in Michael Suleiman (ed.), *U.S. Policy on Palestine from Wilson to Clinton* (Normal, IL: Association of Arab-American University Graduates, 1995), p. 200.

53 This was the case despite increased Jewish American support for that solution, particularly in the aftermath of the first Gulf War. See Marilyn Neimark, "American Jews and Palestine: The Impact of the Gulf War," *Middle East Report*, no. 175, Palestine and Israel in the New World Order (March 1992), p. 20.

54 See Deborah J. Gerner, *One Land, Two Peoples: The Conflict over Palestine*, 2nd ed. (Boulder, CO: Westview Press, 1994), pp. 146–57 and John P. Miglietta, *American Alliance Policy in the Middle East, 1945–1992, Iran, Israel, and Saudi Arabia* (New York: Lexington Books, 2002), pp. 149–52.

55 See Abraham Ben-Zvi, *The United States and Israel: The Limits of the Special Relationship* (New York: Columbia University Press, 1993), p. 204.

56 Zbigniew Brzezinski, *Second Chance: Three Presidents and the Crisis of American Superpower* (New York: Basic Books, 2007), pp. 76–78. The former National Security Advisor to President Carter noted that without genuine peace, the USA was perceived as doing Israel's bidding, which brought back memories of British imperialism in the Middle East.

57 For how this chill unfolded, see Leon T. Hadar, "Thawing the American-Israeli Chill," *Journal of Palestine Studies*, vol. 22, no. 2 (Winter 1993), pp. 78–89.

58 See "The Madrid Peace Conference," *Journal of Palestine Studies*, vol. 21, no. 2 (Winter 1992), pp. 117–49.

59 For an in-depth discussion of this and other Madrid-related issues, see William B. Quandt, *Peace Process: American Diplomacy and the Arab-Israeli Conflict Since 1967*, 3rd ed (Washington, DC: Brookings Institution Press, 2005), pp. 290–319.

60 See Denny Ryder and Ali Omar, *Opening Pandora's Box* (Baltimore, MD: Publish America, 2004), p. 313.

61 This applied to Israel's foreign policy. When it came to disagreements about domestic affairs, such as the nature of the Jewish state, the Israelis often yielded to pressure emanating from the USA. See Neimark, "American Jews and Palestine," pp. 19–20.

62 Edward W. Said, *The Politics of Dispossession: The Struggle for Palestinian Self-Determination, 1969–1994* (New York: Vintage Books, 1995), pp. 100–106.

63 See Tanya Reinhart, *Israel/Palestine: How to End the 1948 War* (St. Paul, MN: Seven Stories Press, 2002), p. 14.

64 For staunch criticism of the peace process, see Edward W. Said, *Peace and its Discontents: Essays on Palestine in the Middle East Peace Process* (New York: Vintage Books, 1995).

65 Joe Stork, "The Clinton Administration and the Palestine Question," in Suleiman (ed.), *U.S. Policy on Palestine from Wilson to Clinton*, p. 242.

66 Curtiss, *Stealth PACs*, p. 206.

67 As early as 1991, the decision was made to create the "Christians' Israel Public Action Campaign" (CIPAC) in order to coordinate tactics with AIPAC. See Paul Charles Merkley, *Christian Attitudes towards the State of Israel* (Montreal: McGill-Queen's University Press, 2001), p. 182. For more on the links between the Israel lobby and the evangelical community, see See Bill Berkowitz, "Christian Right Steps Up Pro-Israel Lobby," available from *Inter Press Service*, July 26, 2006. The rightward shift of Jewish Americans is, of course, disputable. See Paul Charles Merkley, *American Presidents, Religion, and Israel: The Heirs of Cyrus* (Westport, CT: Praeger, 2004), p. 175.

68 "The Talk of the Town," *The New Yorker*, June 17, 1996. Also excerpted in Curtiss, *Stealth PACs*, p. 238.

69 Reflecting this, pro-Israel groups gave money to the Republican Party in larger numbers. See Appendix 5. On the broader conservative reemergence, see William C. Berman, *America's Right Turn: From Nixon to Clinton* (Baltimore, MD: Johns Hopkins University Press), 1998.

70 For example, in 1997 the neoconservative outfit Project for the New American Century complained, "American foreign and defense policy is adrift." See Project for the New American Century, "Statement of Principles," June 3, 1997, available from www.newamericancentury.org/statementofprinciples.htm; Internet; accessed January 11, 2007.

71 See Robert Booth Fowler, Laura Olson, and Allen Hertzke, *Religion and Politics in America: Faith, Culture, and Strategic Choices* (Boulder, CO: Westview Press, 1999), pp. 75–84.

72 Mearsheimer and Walt, *The Israel Lobby and U.S. Foreign Policy*, pp. 168–69.

73 Charles Lipson, "American Support for Israel: History, Sources, Limits," in Gabriel Sheffer (ed.), *U.S.-Israeli Relations at the Crossroads* (Portland, OR: Frank Cass, 1997), p. 129. Lipson, however, disagreed that AIPAC alone was responsible for the overwhelming support of Israel. Rather, he argued that AIPAC lobbying is "necessary," but not "sufficient." See p. 144. This is something that the author of the present work agrees with.

74 This strategy worked. Hence, the last time the US provided high technology military goods to an Arab state on par with Israel was the sale of AWACS aircraft to Saudi Arabia in 1981. President Reagan had to defend that action, as demonstrated by his numerous public utterances and letters to policymakers. For example, see Ronald Reagan, "Letter to the Speaker of the House of Representatives and the President of the Senate on the Sale of AWACS Aircraft to Saudi Arabia," June 18, 1986, available from www.reagan.utexas.edu/archives/speeches/1986/61886e.htm; Internet; accessed January 11, 2007. For the interplay between pro-Israel and pro-Arab pressure groups on the issue, see Nicholas Laham, *Selling AWACS to Saudi Arabia: The Reagan Administration and the Balancing of America's Competing Interests in the Middle East* (New York: Greenwood Publishing Group, 2002), pp. 60–67.

75 See Appendix 2.

76 Quoted in Tony Smith, *Foreign Attachments: The Power of Ethnic Groups in the Making of American Foreign Policy* (Cambridge, MA: Harvard University Press, 2000), pp. 123–24.

77 In addition to special interest groups, this is a valuable way for pro-Israel forces to disseminate their message. See Mearsheimer and Walt, *The Israel Lobby and U.S. Foreign Policy*, pp. 175–85. Scholars need to do more on the influence of think tanks on foreign policy. For a fine example of a think tank production, see Mitchell G. Bard, *Myth and Facts: A Guide to the Arab-Israeli Conflict* (Chevy Chase, MD: American-Israeli Cooperative Enterprise, 2001).

78 Robert Satloff, "Shifting Sands," *New Republic*, June 1, 1998.

79 Cheryl Rubenberg considered think tanks to be the most important element of the pro-Israel lobby. See Cheryl Rubenberg, *The Palestinians: In Search of a Just Peace* (Boulder, CO: Lynne Rienner, 2003), pp. 293–94.

80 Robert Satloff, "U.S., Israel Still Need Each Other," *Newsday*, October 14, 1998.

81 For the broader use of that label, see Alexander Cockburn and Jeffrey St. Clair (eds), *The Politics of Anti-Semitism* (Edinburgh: AK Press, 2003).

82 See Marc H. Ellis, "Edward Said and the Future of the Jewish People," in Naseer Aruri and Muhammad A. Shuraydi (eds), *Revising Culture, Reinventing Peace: The Influence of Edward W. Said* (New York: Olive Branch Press, 2001), p. 43. On the exploitation of anti-Semitism, see Norman G. Finkelstein, *The Holocaust Industry: Reflections on the Exploitation of Jewish Suffering* (New York: Verso, 2000), and his *Beyond Chutzpah: On the Misuse of Anti-Semitism and the Abuse of History* (Berkeley, CA: University of California Press, 2005).

83 See, for example, Patricia Cohen, "Outspoken Political Scientist Denied Tenure at DePaul," *New York Times*, June 11, 2007. For a characteristic reaction of the Israel lobby, see Anti-Defamation League, "ADL Reacts to DePaul's Denial of

Tenure to Prof. Norman Finkelstein," press release available from www.adl.org/
PresRele/Mise_00/5071_00.htm; Internet; accessed June 11, 2007.

84 For a history of his presidency, see Larry J. Sabato (ed.), *The Sixth Year Itch: The
Rise and Fall of the George W. Bush Presidency* (New York: Pearson-Longman, 2008).

85 See the first and second "Gore–Bush Debates," on October 1 and October 11,
2000, available from www.debates.org/; Internet; accessed July 6, 2006.

86 For the effects of the second Intifada on Palestinian society, see Nathan J. Brown,
Palestinian Politics after the Oslo Accords: Resuming Arab Palestine (Berkeley,
CA: University of California Press, 2003), pp. 244–54. As will be discussed later,
that Intifada made stifling Palestinian statehood by the pro-Israel lobby easier
while making it harder for pro-Arab pressure groups to hold US policymakers
accountable for their official positions on the two-state solution. Interview with
Hussein Ibish.

87 Naseer H. Aruri, *Dishonest Broker: The U.S. Role in Israel and Palestine*
(Cambridge, MA: South End Press, 2003), p. 198.

88 Throughout the global war on terrorism, the White House extensively used that
phrase. For example, see George W. Bush, "Executive Order of Alien Unlawful
Enemy Combatants by Military Commission," February 14, 2007, available from
www.whitehouse.gov/news/releases/2007/02/20070214-15.html; Internet; accessed
May 1, 2007.

89 This was something that instantly provided Israel justification for grave violations
against Palestinian rights. See Micheline Ishay, "Globalization and the New
Realism of Human Rights," in Manfred B. Steger (ed.), *Rethinking Globalism*
(New York: Rowman and Littlefield, 2004), p. 139. Also, it was no surprise that
Palestinian organizations made up nearly 20 percent of the US list of foreign ter-
rorist organizations. See Office of the Coordinator for Counterterrorism, "2001
Report on Foreign Terrorist Organizations," October 5, 2001, available from
www.state.gov/s/ct/rls/rpt/fto/2001/5258.htm; accessed May 1, 2007.

90 For example, see "Iraqi-Palestinian Parallels," *Near East Report*, vol. XLVII, no.
5 (March 17, 2003), p. 18.

91 Vaughn P. Shannon, *Balancing Act: US Foreign Policy and the Arab-Israeli
Conflict* (Burlington, VT: Ashgate Publishing Company, 2003), p. 110.

92 See George Tenet, "The Tenet Plan: Israeli-Palestinian Ceasefire and Security
Plan," June 13, 2001; available from www.yale.edu/lawweb/avalon/mideast/
mid023.htm; Internet; accessed July 6, 2006.

93 Israeli and AIPAC interests, however, sometimes clashed. For a recent instance of that,
see Ori Nir, "Israelis Want AIPAC-Backed Bill Softened," *Forward*, March 10, 2006.
For an in depth discussion of Jewish-Israel lobby relations, see Stephen Schwartz, *Is it
Good for the Jews? The Crisis of America's Israel Lobby* (New York: Doubleday, 2006).

94 Quoted in Thomas Ambrosio, "Legitimate Influence or Parochial Capture?
Conclusions on Ethnic Identity Groups and the Formulation of U.S. Foreign
Policy," in Thomas Ambrosio (ed.), *Ethnic Identity Groups and U.S. Foreign
Policy* (Westport, CT: Praeger), p. 203.

95 Ibid., p. 210.

96 James Bennet, "Israeli Troops Close to Arafat Headquarters," *New York Times*,
October 2, 2002.

97 Ambrosio, "Legitimate Influence or Parochial Capture?" in Ambrosio (ed.),
Ethnic Identity Groups and U.S. Foreign Policy, p. 210.

98 Ibid., p. 211.

99 Numerous proclamations expressed American support of Israel against
terrorism. See, for example, House Concurrent Resolution 280, "Expressing
Solidarity with Israel in the Fight Against Terrorism," December 5, 2001, available
from www.jewishvirtuallibrary.org/jsource/US-Israel/Con280.html; Internet; accessed
April 7, 2008.

100 George W. Bush, "Address to a Joint Session of Congress and the American People," September 20, 2001, available from www.whitehouse.gov/news/releases/2001/09/20010920-28.html#; Internet; accessed April 15, 2006.
101 See Chapter 2.
102 In the age of the war on terrorism, Americans viewed Israel less as an oppressor of the Palestinians and more as their victim. That development was not instantaneous, however. The pro-Israel lobby worked throughout the 1990s to substitute Palestinian terrorism for the old communist enemy to rally US support. For its part, American policy moved in directions that made advocacy against terrorist organizations more effective. See Paul R. Pillar, *Terrorism and U.S. Foreign Policy* (Washington, DC: Brookings Institution Press, 2001), pp. 26–29.
103 Naseer H. Aruri, *Dishonest Broker*, p. 199.
104 Even though Palestinians have their own Islamist groups, a distinction must be made between their nationalist struggle and the international platform of groups like al-Qa'eda. See Yaroslav Trofimov, *Faith At War: A Journey on the Frontlines of Islam, from Baghdad to Timbuktu* (New York: Henry Holt and Company, 2005).
105 Rashid Khalidi, *Resurrecting Empire: Western Footprints and America's Perilous Path in the Middle East* (Boston, MA: Beacon Press), pp. 145–46.
106 For an excellent position against occupation from within the context of the American national interest, see Laurie E. King-Irani, "Awakening the American Political Debate on Israel and Palestine," in Alan Curtis (ed.), *Patriotism, Democracy, and Common Sense: Restoring America's Promise at Home and Abroad* (New York: Rowman and Littlefield, 2004), pp. 229–37.
107 See Appendix 4 for increases in the settler population.
108 Israeli governments under prime ministers Ehud Barak, Ariel Sharon, and Ehud Olmert subscribed to that view. See As'ad Ghanem, "A New Phase in Israel's Approach to the Palestinian Question: A Solution Based on the Concept of a Joint Entity Cannot be Ruled Out," *Palestine-Israel Journal of Politics Economics and Culture*, vol. 13, no. 2 (2006), p. 37.
109 See Kenneth R. Bazinet, "Mideast Sides Get Earful: Powell Describes U.S. Vision of 2 Peaceful States," *New York Daily News*, November 20, 2001.
110 Ibid. For the scope of Israeli settlements, see Appendix 4.
111 George W. Bush, "President Bush Calls for New Palestinian Leadership," June 24, 2002, available from www.whitehouse.gov/news/releases/2002/06/20020624-3.html; Internet; accessed July 6, 2006.
112 For a couple of examples, see Yossef Bodansky, *The Secret History of the Iraq War* (New York: HarperCollins, 2004), pp. 107 and 315–18, and Robert J. Pauly, Jr. and Tom Lansford, *Strategic Preemption: US Foreign Policy and the Second Iraq War* (Burlington, VT: Ashgate Publishing Company, 2005), pp. 51, 139.
113 However, information is slowly trickling out from former White House officials. For instance, see Douglas Feith, *War and Decision: Inside the Pentagon at the Dawn of the War on Terrorism* (New York: HarperCollins, 2008).
114 On the precarious existence of Palestinians throughout the Arab world, see Ghada Hashem Talhami, *Palestinian Refugees: Pawns to Political Actors* (New York: Nova Science Publishers), pp. 77–128.
115 "Iraqi-Palestinian Parallels," *Near East Report*, p. 18.
116 There is a longstanding alliance between the Israeli right wing and AIPAC. See David Hirst, *The Gun and the Olive Branch: The Roots of Violence in the Middle East* (New York: Nation Books), pp. 37–57.
117 Secretary of State Colin Powell, "Colin Powell's Speech to the American Israel Public Affairs Committee," March 31, 2003, available from www.guardian.co.uk/israel/Story/0,926276,00.html; Internet; accessed July 6, 2006.
118 "Members of Congress Circulate Letter on Israeli-Palestinian 'Roadmap,'" *Near East Report*, vol. XLVII, no. 7 (April 14, 2003), p. 25.

119 "Sideline Arafat," *Near East Report*, vol. XLVII, no. 10 (May 26, 2003), p. 39.

120 This has gained increased recognition. For example, see Robert Pape, *Dying to Win: The Strategic Logic of Suicide Terrorism* (New York: Random House, 2006).

121 "Disarm and Destroy," *Near East Report*, vol. XLVII, no. 10 (May 26, 2003), pp. 39, 42.

122 "Key House Panel Supports Bush's June 24th Criteria," *Near East Report*, vol. XLVII, no. 10 (May 26, 2003), p. 39. While the wording of that title made it seem as if AIPAC shared President Bush's vision on Palestinian statehood, its actions showed little agreement with the administration, particularly on Israeli settlements and occupation.

123 Interview with James Zogby.

124 See, for example, "Congress says 'Road Map' Should Stick to Bush Vision," *Near East Report*, vol. XLVII, no. 8 (April 28, 2003), p. 31.

125 "Abu Mazen's Test," *Near East Report*, vol. XLVII, no. 11 (June 9, 2003), p. 43.

126 "Road Map Reality," *Near East Report*, vol. XLVII, no. 9 (May 12, 2003), p. 35. For a similar position, see "Bush Says Key to Peace Process is Fighting Terror," *Near East Report*, vol. XLVII, no. 14 (August 11, 2003), p. 63.

127 For a report on AIPAC's position on the two-state solution, see Ron Kampeas, "New Initiative: Not AIPAC Competitor," *Jewish News of Greater Phoenix Online*, vol. 59, no. 5 (October 20, 2006), available from www.jewishaz.com/issues/story.mv?061020+aipac; Internet; accessed January 13, 2007.

128 Keith B. Richburg, "U.N. Court Rejects West Bank Barrier, Israel Says Security Fence Will Stay," *Washington Post*, July 10, 2004.

129 "Obstacle to Terrorism," *Near East Report*, vol. XLVII, no. 14 (July 28, 2003), p. 57.

130 Virginia Tilley, *The One-State Solution: A Breakthrough for Peace in the Israeli-Palestinian Deadlock* (Ann Arbor: University of Michigan Press, 2005), p. 5. This may explain factional fighting between Hamas and Fatah.

131 For what this scenario might look like, see Steven Erlanger, "Israel Continues Airstrikes Against Hamas, as Rival Palestinian Factions Battle in Gaza," *New York Times*, May 19, 2007. For its broader impacts on Israel and the Palestinians, see Sylvain Cypel, *Walled: Israeli Society at an Impasse* (New York: Other Press, 2007).

132 For two examples among many others, See "Syria Sanctions Bill Gains Support on Capitol Hill," and "Shared Concern: U.S., Israeli Lawmakers Meet to Highlight Iran's Nuclear Ambitions," *Near East Report*, vol. XLVII, no. 16 (September 22, 2003), p. 71.

133 For a seminal journalistic analysis, see Bob Woodward, *State of Denial: Bush at War, Part III* (New York: Simon and Schuster, 2006).

134 See Efraim Karsh and Inari Rautsi, *Saddam Hussein: A Political Biography* (New York: Grove Press, 2003), pp. 209–11.

135 Some policymakers have deemed the violence in Iraq as "a violent civil war." See Russell D. Feingold, "Remarks on the Feingold-Reid Amendment As Prepared for Delivery from the Senate Floor," May 16, 2007, available from www.commondreams.org/news2007/0516-05.htm; Internet; accessed May 22, 2007.

136 On how the removal of the Iraqi regime primarily served Israel's interests, see Mearsheimer and Walt, "The Israel Lobby and U.S. Foreign Policy," *Kennedy School of Government Faculty Research Working Paper Series* RWP06-011 (March 2006), p. 31.

137 For more on the one-state solution, see Tilley, *The One-State Solution*, Ali Abunimah, *One Country: A Bold Proposal to End the Israeli-Palestinian Impasse* (New York: Metropolitan Books, 2006), and Joel Kovel, *Overcoming Zionism: Creating a Single Democratic State in Israel/Palestine* (London: Pluto Press, 2007).

138 "Appalling Idea," *Near East Report*, vol. XLVII, no. 19 (November 3, 2003), p. 85.
139 For the original vision of Gaza disengagement, see Prime Minister Ariel Sharon, "Landmark Address," *Near East Report*, vol. XLVIII, no. 1 (January 12, 2004), p. 2.
140 Noted in "Historic Agreement Forged," *Near East Report*, vol. XLVIII, no. 8 (April 26, 2004), p. 30.
141 Ibid. It is noteworthy here that this may include Iran after the US deemed its Revolutionary Guard as "a specially designated global terrorist." See Robin Wright, "Iranian Unit to Be Labeled 'Terrorist,' U.S. Moving Against Revolutionary Guard," *Washington Post*, August 15, 2007. Some have noted that war on Iran has already commenced. See Andrew Cockburn, "Democrats Okay Funds for Covert Ops, Secret Bush 'Finding' Widens War on Iran," *Counterpunch*, May 2, 2008, available from www.counterpunch.org/andrew05022008.html; Internet; accessed May 4, 2008.
142 The summer 2006 invasion of Lebanon provided the world with a salient example. Pro-Arab advocates viewed that war as an ominous move in the context of the global war on terrorism. Interviews with Hussein Ibish and James Zogby. Also see Bana Hajj, "War in Lebanon and War on Terror," *Washington Report on Middle East Affairs* (December 2006), pp. 57–58.
143 See, for example, "Double Standard," *Near East Report*, vol. XLVIII, no. 18 (October 11, 2004), p. 75.
144 Quoted in "Dollars and Sense," *Near East Report*, vol. XLVIII, no. 14 (August 2, 2004), p. 57.
145 See Noam Chomsky, "The Israel Lobby?" March 28, 2006, available from www.zmag.org/content/showarticle.cfm?ItemID = 9999; Internet; accessed June 14, 2006 and Joseph Massad, "Blaming the Lobby," *Al-Ahram Weekly On-Line*, March 23–29, 2006, available from http://weekly.ahram.org.eg/2006/787/op35.htm; Internet; accessed August 4, 2006.
146 President Bush, "Principles for Peace," *Near East Report*, vol. XLIX, no. 5 (March 7, 2005), p.18.
147 Janice Terry aptly notes, "lobbies serve to reinforce predetermined policies, particularly because …U.S. foreign policy is remarkably consistent under both Republican and Democratic administrations." See Janice J. Terry, *U.S. Foreign Policy in the Middle East: The Role of Lobbies and Special Interest Groups* (Ann Arbor, MI: Pluto Press, 2005), p. 29.
148 Taken from Rubenberg, *Israel and the American National Interest*, p. 15. Also see Findley, *They Dare to Speak Out*, p. 25 and John T. Tierney, "Interest Group Involvement in Congressional Foreign and Defense Policy," in Randall B. Ripley and James M. Lindsay (eds), *Congress Resurgent: Foreign and Defense Policy on Capitol Hill* (Ann Arbor, MI: University of Michigan Press, 1993), p. 94.
149 For a list of the organizations represented by the Presidents Conference, see Conference of Presidents of Major American Jewish Organizations, "Member Organizations," available from www.conferenceofpresidents.org/Members.pdf; Internet; accessed July 6, 2006.
150 Conference of Presidents of Major American Jewish Organizations, "American Jewish Leaders Issue Major Statement on Disengagement," August 16, 2005, available from www.conferenceofpresidents.org/disengagementaug.pdf; Internet; accessed July 13, 2006.

4 The effects and potential of the pro-Arab lobby

1 See Yossi Shain, "Arab Americans at a Crossroads," *Journal of Palestine Studies*, vol. 25, no. 3 (Spring 1996), pp. 46–59 and Helen Hatab Samhan, "Politics and Exclusion: The Arab American Experience," *Journal of Palestine Studies*, vol. 16, no. 2 (Winter 1987).

2 Khalil M. Marrar, telephone conversation with anonymous pro-Arab lobbying source, March 7, 2006.
3 Saad Ibrahim, "American Domestic Forces and the October War," *Journal of Palestine Studies*, vol. 4, no. 1 (Autumn 1974), p. 55.
4 Ibid.
5 Thomas R. Dye, *Politics in America*, 4th ed. (Upper Saddle River, NJ: Prentice Hall, 2001), p. 294. Of course, we have to remember that as far as the letter of the law is concerned, the US government has different classifications for the variety of political activity engaged in by pressure groups. These are based primarily on two factors: (1) where/how groups get funding and constituency, and (2) the type of political activities to which they dedicate themselves. Regulations governing lobbies are part of the United States Internal Revenue Service, Section 501(c) (3) Organizations, available from www.irs.gov/publications/p557/ch03.html#d0e7391; Internet; accessed January 14, 2007.
6 Quoted in Jeffrey H. Birnbaum, *The Lobbyist: How Influence Peddlers Get Their Way in Washington* (New York: Times Books, 1992), p. 13.
7 For a list of domestic pro-Arab lobbies, see Appendix 3. The foreign Arab lobby, mainly composed of state entities, was important insofar as it allowed the Palestinians to express their position in elite American politics regarding the two-state solution. Its aims on Palestinian statehood were similar to those of the domestic lobby.
8 For one example among thousands, see James J. Zogby, "The Lingering Image of Arafat," *Washington Post*, October 21, 1995. In this instance, the leader of the Arab American Institute attempted to shape opinion by critiquing Arafat's portrayal in his meeting with a major American newspaper. For a television example of pro-Arab lobbyists trying influence policy, see Mary Rose Oakar on "Mideast Lawsuit," *The O'Reilly Factor*, July 25, 2006, available from www.foxnews.com/video2/launchPage.html?072506/072506_oreilly_oakar&Mideast%20Lawsuit&OReilly_Factor&An%20Arab-American%20group%20sues%20the%20U.S.%20gov%27t%20over%20Mideast%20violence&World&-1&Mideast%20Lawsuit&Video%20Launch%20Page; Internet; accessed July 28, 2006.
9 This is also true in the administrative branch. For example, see David Rothkopf, *Running the World: The Inside Story of the National Security Council and the Architects of American Power* (New York: Public Affairs, 2006), pp. 6–8.
10 Angela Brittingham and G. Patricia de la Cruz, "We the People of Arab Ancestry in the United States," Census 2000 Special Reports, March 2005, available from www.census.gov/prod/2005pubs/censr-21.pdf; Internet; accessed May 19, 2007. For a specific breakdown by nationality, see Appendix 7.
11 Electronic communications do not have to be responses to particular queries. Pro-Arab websites, such as Electronic Intifada, present a wealth of information on the Israeli–Palestinian conflict. See Electronic Intifada, "About EI," available from http://electronicintifada.net/v2/aboutEI.shtml; Internet; accessed May 5, 2008.
12 For instance, see Sara Bakhshian, "Dershowitz Debates Israel-Palestinian Issue," November 17, 2006, available from www.jewishjournal.com/home/preview.php?id = 16809; Internet; accessed June 4, 2007.
13 While the domestic role of the petroleum industry is well established, this chapter will not examine it in any depth since, as Janice Terry reminded us, it "has had virtually no success in" regard to securing a "more balanced approach to the Arab-Israeli conflict." See Janice J. Terry, *U.S. Foreign Policy in the Middle East: The Role of Lobbies and Special Interest Groups* (Ann Arbor, MI: Pluto Press, 2005), p. 58.
14 The one recent exception to this is Janice Terry's work, noted above. For an earlier example, see Nabeel A. Khoury, "The Arab Lobby: Problems and Prospects," *Middle East Journal*, vol. 41, no. 3 (Summer 1987).

15 Although the focus of this chapter is on secular ethno-national pro-Arab organizations, we must never underemphasize the importance of organizations like the
Council on American-Islamic Relations for lobbying US policymakers and public
opinion on behalf of Palestinian rights. For one example among a vast showcase
of others, see CAIR, "Thank Those in Congress Who Did Not Vote for Pro-Israel
Resolutions," May 3, 2002, available from www.cair.com/default.asp?Page =
articleView&id = 110&theType = Aal; Internet; accessed January 14, 2007. It
would be very interesting for future inquiry to study the impacts that religion-
oriented groups have had on US policy throughout the history of the Israeli–
Palestinian conflict and particularly under the Bush administration's preference
for faith-based organizations. While that preference's effects have largely involved
benefits for Christian charity organizations in the USA, groups like CAIR may
have enjoyed significant access to the factors acting on policy during a time when
many Americans took a great deal of interest in Islam and Muslims after
September 11, 2001. CAIR filled that need quite well since its mission "is to
enhance understanding of Islam, encourage dialogue, protect civil liberties,
empower American Muslims, and build coalitions that promote justice and
mutual understanding." See CAIR, "What's CAIR's Vision and Mission?" available from www.cair.com/default.asp?Page = About; Internet; accessed January 14,
2007.
16 ARAMCO is only "defunct" as a domestic US actor since it still exists as an oil
business association in Saudi Arabia under its new name Saudi Aramco. For
more on what that group does, see Saudi Aramco, "Who We Are," available from
www.saudiaramco.com/bvsm/JSP/content/channelDetail.jsp?BV_SessionID   =
@@@@0380322060.1168761664@@@@&BV_EngineID = cccfaddjljmfjfgcefe-
ceefdfnkdfhl.0&datetime = 01%2F14%2F07+11%3A01%3A04&SA.channelID
=-11681; accessed January 14, 2007.
17 Hussein Ibish, executive director of Hala Foundation, senior fellow at American
Task Force on Palestine, and former communications director at American-Arab
Anti-Discrimination Committee, interview by the author, Washington, DC,
November 13, 2006.
18 Press conferences between American and foreign officials for issues relevant to
lobbying on behalf of the two-state solution are a strong indicator of where concerns by both sides lie. For the importance of the function of press conferences in
foreign policy, see Barbara Hinckley, *Less Than Meets the Eye: Foreign Policy
Making and the Myth of the Assertive Congress* (Chicago, IL: University of
Chicago Press, 1994), p. 185.
19 The domestic Arab lobby prints literature from single-page pamphlets to books.
Outside of the USA, printing presses with a variety of purposes continue to
emerge as political and economic development takes root. For instance, Dubai-
based Kaleem Books has recently published its first novel by Hassouna Al
Mosbahi, *Hikaya Tunisiyya* (Dubai: Kaleem Books, 2008). That work of modern
Arabic social fiction aims at audiences worldwide and demonstrates outreach
abilities beyond the Middle East. There are other examples too numerous to detail here.
20 See Appendix 1 for interview questions.
21 President George W. Bush, "President Discusses Roadmap for Peace in the
Middle East," March 14, 2003, available from www.whitehouse.gov/news/releases/
2003/03/20030314-4.html; Internet; accessed March 16, 2006. American support
for a Palestinian state used to be an unfulfilled dream of some pro-Arab organizations. See Jim Zogby and Joe Stork, "Jim Zogby: 'They Control the Hill, but
We've Got a Lot of Positions Around the Hill,'" *MERIP Middle East Report*, no.
146, Twenty Years After (May-June 1987), p. 25.
22 "Memorandum of Understanding between the Government of the United States
and the Government of Israel On Strategic Cooperation," in Karen L. Puschel,

US-Israeli Strategic Cooperation in the Post-Cold War Era, An American Perspective (San Francisco, CA: Westview Press, 1993), p. 178.

23 At the 2007 meeting of the Southern Political Science Association, panel chair Kyle Christensen of West Virginia University pointed out that while these interviews "were golden – the kind of stuff you could not get anywhere else," he cautioned of biases by professional pro-Arab advocates, who may embellish their influence. However, the response to that criticism, as it remains now, was that if anything, pro-Arab lobbyists, consistent with the scholarly literature on the issue, underplayed their role in shaping US foreign policy and exalted the pro-Israel lobby in that regard. That however, misses the point of this book, even as it concedes that international factors and the pro-Israel lobby have played a significant role in the determination of US policy toward the Middle East. The purpose of this inquiry all along has been to examine how *other* domestic factors matter as well, particularly the role of public opinion support for Palestinian statehood and the concurrent potential of the pro-Arab lobby. Southern Political Science Association Conference, "Panel on U.S. Foreign Policy and Conflict Management," New Orleans, LA, January 3–7, 2007.

24 According to Khalil Jahshan, NAAA merged with ADC in the mid-1990s. Khalil Jahshan, former president of National Association of Arab Americans and representative of Association of Arab American University Graduates and Palestine Research and Educational Center, interview by the author, Arlington, VA, March 14, 2006.

25 Arab American Institute, "Palestinians are a People," informational flyer, 1992.

26 Quoted in Steven L. Spiegel, *The Other Arab-Israeli Conflict: Making America's Middle East Policy, From Truman to Reagan* (Chicago, IL: University of Chicago Press, 1985), p. 8. This position was also expressed by Rafi Dajani, who explained, "there is no Arab lobby – there should not be an Arab lobby because it lumps all Arabs together. We are unhappy when that happens since it would be a disservice to our differing goals. What we could have is an umbrella organization that brings Arab interests together." Rafi Dajani, former executive director of American Task Force on Palestine, interview by the author, Washington, DC, March 15, 2006. For analysis of Arab American demographic trends by the mid-1980s, see Elias T. Nigem, "Arab Americans: Migration, Socioeconomic, and Demographic Characteristics," *International Migration Review*, vol. 20, no. 3 (Autumn 1986), pp. 629–49.

27 Elizabeth Stephens, *US Policy Toward Israel: The Role of Political Culture in Defining the "Special Relationship"* (Brighton: Sussex Academic Press, 2006), pp. 34–40.

28 James Lee Ray, *The Future of American-Israeli Relations* (Lexington, KY: University Press of Kentucky, 1985), p. 30.

29 See Appendix 5 and Appendix 6. For analysis, see Center for Responsive Politics, "Pro-Israel and Pro-Arab Interests: The Money," available from www.opensecrets. org/news/pro-israel.pro-arab/index.asp; Internet; accessed August 13, 2006.

30 Shain, "Arab Americans at a Crossroads," p. 46.

31 Interviewees of the pro-Arab organizations expressed this unanimously.

32 As quoted in Spiegel, *The Other Arab-Israeli Conflict*, p. 8 and noted earlier.

33 For details of early efforts to express Palestinian concerns in the USA, see Fawaz Turki, "The Passions of Exile: The Palestine Congress of North America," *Journal of Palestine Studies*, vol. 9, no. 4 (Summer 1980), pp. 17–43.

34 Ibrahim, "American Domestic Forces and the October War," p. 63.

35 Interview with Khalil Jahshan.

36 Ibrahim, "American Domestic Forces and the October War," p. 64. For the interplay between the NAAA and other Arab American groups, see Michael W. Suleiman, "Arab Americans and the Political Process," in Ernst N. McCarus

(ed.), *The Development of Arab-American Identity* (Ann Arbor: University of Michigan Press, 1994), pp. 37–60. For an outline of pro-Arab activities during the 1970s, see "Pushing the Arab Cause in America," *Time*, June 23, 1975.

37 For more on this, see Yezid Saigh and Avi Shlaim (eds), *The Cold War and the Middle East* (Oxford: Oxford University Press, 1997). For perceptions of Arab Americans, see Samhan, "Politics and Exclusion," pp. 11–28.

38 Beverley Milton-Edwards and Peter Hinchcliffe, *Conflicts in the Middle East since 1945*, 2nd edn (New York: Routledge, 2003), p. 38.

39 Association of Arab American University Graduates, *The First Decade: 1967–1977* (Washington, DC: Tammuz, 1977), section on "Activities and growth," no page number.

40 See Alexander George and Robert Keohane, "The Concept of National Interests: Uses and Limitations," in Alexander George (ed.), *Presidential Decisionmaking in Foreign Policy: The Effective Use of Information and Advice* (Boulder, CO: Westview Press, 1980), pp. 217–37. For further analysis on this, especially after the collapse of Soviet communism, see Jerel A. Rosati, Michael W. Link, and John Creed "A New Perspective on the Foreign Policy Views of American Opinion Leaders in the Cold War and Post-Cold War Eras," *Political Research Quarterly*, vol. 51, no. 2 (June 1998), pp. 461–79.

41 For a history of the "strategic context" of the American–Israeli relationship before and after the Cold War, see Bernard Reich, *Securing the Covenant: United States-Israel Relations after the Cold War* (Westport, CT: Greenwood Press, 1995), pp. 35–64. For an assessment of how policymakers perceived the Palestine question under Reagan, see Walid al-Khalidi, "The Palestine Issue Forty Years after Partition: Reflections on the Past and Perspectives on the Future," *Bulletin (British Society for Middle East Studies)*, vol. 14, no. 2 (1987), pp. 123–35.

42 Paul Findley, *They Dare to Speak Out: People and Institutions Confront Israel's Lobby* (Westport, CT: Lawrence Hill and Company, 1985), p. 315.

43 See "Illusions about America," *Journal of Palestine Studies*, vol. 7, no. 1 (Autumn 1988), pp. 175–78.

44 Sadat's negotiations with Israel happened at the request of Secretary of State Henry Kissinger. See Laura Zittrain Eisenberg and Neil Caplan, *Negotiating Arab-Israeli Peace: Patterns, Problems, Possibilities* (Indianapolis, IN: Indiana University Press, 1998), pp. 30–32.

45 "Credible" Arab peace proposals have always caused Israel supporters in Washington fear during the Reagan era because they may have pressured the Jewish state into concessions that most of its leaders refused to make. This carried over into the term of Reagan's vice president and successor, George H. W. Bush. See "The New U.S. Administration," *Journal of Palestine Studies*, vol. 18, no. 2 (Winter 1989), p. 169.

46 This was studied by Ami Arbel and Nimrod Novik, "U.S. Pressure on Israel: Likelihood and Scope," *The Journal of Conflict Resolution*, vol. 29, no. 2 (June 1985), pp. 253–82.

47 Beshara Doumani, "They Dare to Speak Out: People and Institutions Confront Israel's Lobby," book review, in *MERIP Middle East Report*, no. 140, Terrorism and Intervention (May-June 1986), p. 36.

48 For American perspectives on this, see "The Palestine Problem in Public Debate," *Journal of Palestine Studies*, vol. 13, no. 4 (Summer 1984), pp. 187–98. For a history of the Palestinian role in that war, see Rashid Khalidi, *Under Siege: P.L.O. Decisionmaking During the 1982 War* (New York: Columbia University Press, 1986).

49 Interview with Hussein Ibish. This view was seconded by Peter Timco, director of the Office of the President, Arab American Institute, telephone Interview by the author, April 25, 2008.

50 Interview with Hussein Ibish.
51 For example, a series of commercials called for cutting aid to Israel in light of the Lebanon invasion. See W. Dale Nelson, "Arab Lobby Uses Commercials to Blast Aid to Israel," available from *Associated Press*, December 17, 1982.
52 Ibid.
53 Yvonne Yazbeck Haddad, "Maintaining the Faith of the Fathers: Dilemmas of Religious Identity in the Christian and Muslim Arab-American Communities," in McCarus (ed.), *The Development of Arab-American Identity*, pp. 80–81. The Phalanges were responsible for the Sabra and Shatila massacres. For a brief outline of lobbying efforts against Palestinian meddling in Lebanon, see C. L. Gates, "The Lebanese Lobby in the U.S.," *MERIP Reports*, no. 73 (December 1978), pp. 17–19. That was discomfiting for the Arab American leadership.
54 This strategy has a lengthy history that dates back to well before 1948. See Efraim Karsh and P. R. Kumaraswamy (eds), *Israel, the Hashemites and the Palestinians: The Fateful Triangle* (London: Routledge, 2003).
55 Samhan, "Politics and Exclusion," pp. 11–12.
56 Ibid.
57 James Zogby, president and co-founder of Arab American Institute, co-founder of Palestine Human Rights Campaign, co-founder and former executive director of American-Arab Anti-Discrimination Committee, telephone interview by the author, April 26, 2008.
   For more on Yalla VOTE, see "About Yalla Vote," available from www.yallavote. org/; Internet; accessed April 30, 2008.
58 Interviews with Hussein Ibish and Khalil Jahshan.
59 Interview with Khalil Jahshan. When the Intifada was in full swing, opinions varied widely on the pursuit of peace in the Middle East. See, for example, Eqbal Ahmad, Jeanne Butterfield, Noam Chomsky, Denis F. Doyon, Deena Hurwitz, Shiela Ryan, and James Zogby, "Middle East Peace Priorities in the US: Seven Perspectives," *Middle East Report*, no. 158, Palestine and Israel in the US Arena (May-June 1989), pp. 6–11.
60 For a variety of perspectives on that, see Jamal R. Nassar and Roger Heacock (eds), *Intifada: Palestine at the Crossroads* (New York: Praeger, 1990).
61 Don Betz, "Introduction to the Uprising in Cartoons: North American Political Cartoonists Look at the Palestinian Uprising," *ADC Issue Paper*, no. 21 (December 9, 1988), p. 1.
62 Interview with Khalil Jahshan.
63 This was something in which even extremist Palestinian groups were interested. See Shaul Mishal and Avraham Sela, *The Palestinian Hamas: Vision, Violence, and Coexistence* (New York: Columbia University Press, 2000), p. 102. The most powerful symbol was of youths braving violence. See Brian K. Barber, "What has Become of the 'Children of the Stone?'" *Palestine-Israel Journal*, vol. VI, no. 4, (1999/2000), pp. 7–15.
64 Richard Falk, "U.S. Foreign Policy in the Middle East," in Hooshang Amirahamdi (ed.), *The United States and the Middle East: A Search for New Perspectives* (Albany, NY: SUNY Press, 1993), p. 72.
65 Arab American Institute, "Ending the Deadly Silence, the Arab American Institute at Work – Opening an American Debate on Palestinian Rights" (1990), p. 1.
66 Ibid.
67 AIPAC Memorandum from Edward C. Levy, Jr., President Thomas A. Dine, Executive Director, August 3, 1988. AIPAC was also concerned about the prominence of pro-Arab positions in American universities. See Cheryl A. Rubenberg, *Israel and the American National Interest, A Critical Examination* (Chicago: University of Illinois Press, 1986), p. 336. Volumes may be dedicated to explaining the roles of pro-Arab and pro-Israel academics in shaping public and elite opinions.

68 Arab American Institute, "Palestine Lives" (1988), p. 1.
69 These include Jewish American groups as well, particularly the Israel Policy Forum and Brit Tzedek v'Shalom. See Nathan Guttman, "Dovish Groups Mull Mega-Merger in Bid to Build Peace Powerhouse," *The Jewish Daily Forward*, May 30, 2007, available from www.forward.com/articles/dovish-groups-mull-mega-merger-in-bid-to-build-pea/; Internet; accessed June 6, 2007, and Delinda C. Hanley, "Israeli Elections and Palestinian Prospects," *Washington Report on Middle East Affairs* (January/February 2003), pp. 68–70.
70 Mary Rose Oakar, former congresswoman from Cleveland, OH, and president of American-Arab Anti-Discrimination Committee, interview by the author, Washington, DC, March 15, 2006.
71 See House Resolution 2508, Section 2001, "Palestinian Schools and Universities in the West Bank and Gaza Strip," 1991, available from http://thomas.loc.gov/cgi-bin/query/F?c102:2:./temp/~mdbsM5Q2cG:e514886: Internet; accessed April 20, 2007. The resolution stated the following: "the United States Congress understands that all Palestinian schools and universities in the West Bank and Gaza Strip will be opened at an early date, and expresses the hope that they will remain open, and will be respected and regarded by all parties as places of learning."
72 Interview with Mary Rose Oakar.
73 Interview with Hussein Ibish.
74 Ibid.
75 This was not the first attempt to bring attention to violence against people in the West Bank and Gaza. See for example, Livia Rokach, *Israel's Sacred Terrorism*, 3rd edn (Washington, DC: AAUG Press, 1986).
76 Interviews with Khalil Jahshan and Helen Samhan. Helen Samhan, executive director of Arab American Institute Foundation, interview by the author, Washington, DC, March 16, 2006.
77 Most interviewees posed those questions in some form.
78 For a history of the Persian Gulf crisis, see Suzanne J. Murdico, *The Gulf War* (New York: The Rosen Group, 2004).
79 Interview with Khalil Jahshan.
80 The public, however, wanted its leaders to exhaust the diplomatic options. See Gerald F. Seib and Michel McQueen, "Poll Finds Americans Feel Hawkish Toward Iraq but Would Grant Some Concessions to Avoid War," *Wall Street Journal*, December 13, 1990.
81 Interview with Khalil Jahshan.
82 Ibid.
83 Rebecca Abou-Chedid, government relations and policy analyst for Arab American Institute, interview by the author, Washington, DC, March 16, 2006.
84 Shain, "Arab Americans at a Crossroads," p. 54.
85 Hussein Ibish and Khalil Jahshan saw this as a positive development to bring peace to the Israeli–Palestinian conflict. Interviews with Khalil Jahshan and Hussein Ibish.
86 Interview with Hussein Ibish.
87 Well after the end of the Cold War, however, groups like AIPAC still tried to "slip into their 'cold warrior' suits," according to an AAI criticism. See Arab American Institute, "Israel's Cold War," *Nota Bene* (March 1993), p. 4.
88 Interview with Hussein Ibish.
89 Marvin Wingfield, director of education and outreach for American-Arab Anti-Discrimination Committee, telephone interview by the Author, December 19, 2006.
90 James Zogby, "New Thinking for Israeli-Palestinian Peace," AAI Publication (1991), pp. 17–18.

91 See "Letter of Invitation to Madrid Peace Conference," October 30, 1991, available from www.jewishvirtuallibrary.org/jsource/Peace/madrid.html; Internet; accessed July 15, 2006.
92 Interview with Khalil Jahshan.
93 Ibid.
94 Interview with Helen Samhan.
95 Interview with Rebecca Abou-Chedid.
96 Christine Gleichert, Capitol Hill lobbyist for American-Arab Anti-Discrimination Committee, interview by the author, Washington, DC, March 15, 2006.
97 Interview with Mary Rose Oakar.
98 Interview with Rafi Dajani.
99 Arab American Institute, "Bush on Palestinian Rights," *Nota Bene* (June 1992), p. 4, emphasis in the original.
100 Interview with Hussein Ibish. Also see Richard Sobel, *The Impact of Public Opinion on U.S. Foreign Policy Since Vietnam: Constraining the Colossus* (New York: Oxford University Press, 2001), p. 5.
101 Interview with Hussein Ibish.
102 Interview with James Zogby. Peter Timco shared that sentiment.
103 Pro-Arab lobbyists also gained currency outside of the US, notably among Israeli and Palestinian officials. See James J. Zogby, "Israeli Impediments Cripple Commerce," *Washington Times*, March 31, 1996 for an example of how the Arab American Institute president directly appealed issues surrounding Israeli occupation to both sides of the conflict.
104 Interview with Khalil Jahshan.
105 Since his candidacy for president, then Arkansas governor Bill Clinton had a negative record on issues of concern to the pro-Arab lobby. Consequently, in July 1992, the AAI expressed concern about Clinton's campaign having "no reason to open its doors to 'the Arab lobby.'" See Arab American Institute, "Anti-Semitism Revisited," *Nota Bene* (July 1992), p. 4. Clinton's attitude toward the pro-Arab lobby, however, did not keep it from actively pursuing favorable policy on the eve of the 1992 election season. According to the AAI, "in the months leading up to the Democratic and Republican conventions, Arab Americans participated in and helped shape the national debate over U.S. Middle East policy." See Arab American Institute, "An AAI Summary," *Politics, Peace and the Presidency, Challenge '92* (Summer 1992), p. 3.
106 Quoted in Arab American Institute, "The Untold Story," *Nota Bene* (April 1993), p. 1.
107 Ibid.
108 For that document, see "Declaration of Principles on Interim Self-Government Arrangements," available from www.jewishvirtuallibrary.org/jsource/Peace/dop.html; Internet; accessed January 27, 2006.
109 "1993: Rabin and Arafat Shake on Peace Deal," September 13, 1993, available from http://news.bbc.co.uk/onthisday/hi/dates/stories/september/13/newsid_30530 00/3053733.stm; Internet; accessed July 24, 2006.
110 Interview with Hussein Ibish.
111 Arab American Institute, "Arab Americans Witness Signing of Historic Peace Accord, Meet with Clinton," *AAI Issues* (Summer 1993), p. 1. At the time, Zogby's positive sentiments were as guarded as the rest of the pro-Arab leadership. Interview with James Zogby.
112 Interview with Khalil Jahshan.
113 Ibid.
114 Interview with Helen Samhan.
115 See Appendix 2.

116 Nabil Mohamad, organizing director of American-Arab Anti-Discrimination Committee, interview by the author, Washington, DC, March 14, 2006.
117 "Declaration of Principles," Article I.
118 Edward W. Said, *The End of the Peace Process: Oslo and After* (New York: Pantheon Books, 1999), p. 109.
119 Edward W. Said, "A Troubling Accord," *Nota Bene*, The Peace Accord – A Special Edition (October 1993), p. 1. This commentary was originally published in *The Nation*, September 20, 1993.
120 At the time, Zogby shared that concern. Interview with James Zogby.
121 For an analysis of the DOP's relationship to refugees, see Ghada Hashem Talhami, *Palestinian Refugees: Pawns to Political Actors* (New York: Nova Science Publishers, 2003), pp. 181–83, 190–203. For the position of Arab American activists, see Ali Abunimah and Hussein Ibish, "The Palestinian Right of Return," *ADC Issue Paper* 30 (2001).
122 Interview with Rafi Dajani. This was also echoed during interviews with Hussein Ibish, James Zogby, and Peter Timco.
123 However, Gallup polling only showed slight shifts in public opinion concerning sympathy towards Arabs. See Chapter 2 and *Gallup Poll*, 8/12/1997–8/13/1997.
124 Interview with James Zogby.
125 Interview with Marvin Wingfield.
126 Quoted in Arab American Institute, "Jerusalem and the Politics of Obstruction," *Nota Bene* (April/May 1995), p. 2. Jerusalem has been a constant issue of concern for the Arab American leadership. In a keynote address at ADC's 2000 convention, Walid Khalidi declared

> uniquely in Jerusalem, the spiritual and material, the religious and the secular, the political and the symbolic, the utopian and the geopolitic [sic?], the territorial and the psychological, the mystical and the palpable merge and interact with one another, over the centuries, and millennia, to inform the core definitions of the cultural and national identities of the protagonists involved.
> (See Walid Khalidi, "Our Jerusalem: Separate and Joint," keynote address, ADC's 17th National Convention, June 11, 2000)

127 In addition to the aforementioned NAACP and the ACLU, Arab Americans enjoyed support on their platforms from various Jewish American groups such as Jewish Voice for Peace, an organization founded three years after Oslo. For its background, see Jewish Voice for Peace, "JVP History," available from www.jewishvoiceforpeace.org/publish/article_29.shtml; Internet; accessed July 28, 2006. In the present, pro-Arab groups like the ATFP continue to "build alliances with partners who share" their goals. See American Task Force on Palestine, "Strategic Plan," October 2004, available from www.americantaskforce.org/pdfs/strategy.pdf; Internet; accessed December 21, 2006.
128 Interview with Hussein Ibish.
129 American Task Force on Palestine, "Strategies for Advocating Palestinian Statehood," available from www.americantaskforce.org/pdfs/advocacy_strategy.pdf; Internet; accessed December 21, 2006.
130 Interview with Hussein Ibish.
131 Arab American Institute, "The Rock and the Hard Place," *Nota Bene* (April/May 1995), pp. 4–5.
132 Interview with Hussein Ibish.
133 Interview with Khalil Jahshan.
134 Interviews with Khalil Jahshan, Hussein Ibish, Peter Timco, and James Zogby.

135 Interviews with Helen Samhan, Nabil Mohamad, Christine Gleichert, and James Zogby.
136 Pro-Arab organizations issued numerous calls for US policymakers to be that. For one instance, see Arab American Institute, "Mutual Commitments, One-Sided Attention," *Nota Bene* (January/February 1996), p. 3. The Arab American lobby boasted of its access to the White House during the 1990s. For example, see Arab American Institute, "White House Overtures for Policy Input: President Clinton Hosts Second Arab American Leadership Delegation," *Issues* (Summer 1996), pp. 1–2, and Arab American Institute, "Leadership Meets with Secretary Albright, 42 Groups Endorse Statement of Concern," *Issues* (Spring 1997), pp. 1, 8.
137 American Task Force on Palestine, "Strategies for Advocating Palestinian Statehood," and interview with Helen Samhan.
138 Interviews with Khalil Jahshan and Helen Samhan.
139 Interview with Rebecca Abou-Chedid.
140 Interview with Hussein Ibish.
141 Arab American Institute, "Labor-Likud in DC, Too," *Nota Bene* (Summer 1995), p. 1.
142 The Likud party leadership tried to undo the issues negotiated by Oslo, particularly surrounding Jerusalem. See James J. Zogby, "Likud Uses City as Wedge Issue," *Washington Times*, February 21, 1996.
143 Interview with Hussein Ibish. This remained a constant theme of pro-Arab lobbying efforts. For example, see American Task Force on Palestine, "Two States: Palestine Alongside Israel, Peace in the Middle East, Freedom for Palestine, Security for America," informational flyer, 2006.
144 Interview with Christine Gleichert.
145 Ibid.
146 Arab American leaders have understood quite well the negative effects of the mainstream media on their causes. For one poignant example, see Arab American Institute, "A Tale of Two Killings: Observations of Media Bias in Reports of Palestinian and Israeli Deaths," informational flyer, 2001.
147 For the intersection between Israel, the Danish cartoons, and Western countries including the USA, see Manfred Gerstenfel, "The Mohammed-Cartoon Controversy, Israel, and the Jews: A Case Study," in Jerusalem Center for Public Affairs, *Post-Holocaust and Anti-Semitism*, no. 43 (April 4, 2006), available from www.jcpa.org/phas/phas-043-gerstenfeld.htm; Internet; accessed January 21, 2007.
148 In conversations with pro-Arab activists, there was unanimous agreement that the lot of Arab Americans depends on US–Middle East interactions.
149 This came out in the interviews with James Zogby and Peter Timco.
150 Interviews with Khalil Jahshan, Helen Samhan, Christine Gleichert, Rebecca Abou-Chedid, and Rafi Dajani.
151 Interviews with Hussein Ibish and Khalil Jahshan
152 This includes organizations such as Americans for Peace Now, who have on numerous occasions worked with Arab American groups in support of the roadmap. For an example, see Americans for Peace Now, "Joint AAI/APN Poll: Jewish and Arab Americans Overwhelmingly Support Two-State Solution, U.S. Engagement; Bush Gets Low Marks," available from www.peacenow.org/pr.asp? rid = &cid = 3738; Internet; accessed June 6, 2007.
153 While Edward Said coined this phrase, countless others mourned the sentiment it expressed. For a set of Palestinian reflections on conflict and peace, see Kathleen Christison, *The Wound of Dispossession: Telling the Palestinian Story* (Santa Fe, NM: Sunlit Hills Press, 2001).
154 Osama bin Laden, "Speech to the American People," *Al Jazeera*, October 29, 2004, and Adam Gadahn, "Message to President Bush," *As Sahab*, May 29, 2007.

155 Jonathan Randal, *Osama: The Making of a Terrorist* (London: I. B. Tauris, 2004), p. 22.
156 This was a chief concern of Arab American groups before 9/11. See Hussein Ibish and Laila Al-Qatami (eds), *1998–2000 Report on Hate Crimes and Discrimination Against Arab Americans* (Washington, DC: ADC Research Institute, 2001), available from www.adc.org/hatecrimes/pdf/1998-2000.pdf; Internet; accessed April 7, 2008.
157 American-Arab Anti-Discrimination Committee, "ADC Resolutions Adopted at the 2002 National Convention," press release, June 15, 2002, available from www.adc.org/index.php?id = 352&no_cache = 1&sword_list[] = adc&sword_list[] = reso; Internet; Accessed March 15, 2006.
158 For some examples, see ADC Research Institute, "Arab Americans," an insert in the *Washington Times*, February 10, 2004, Casey Kasem, "Arab Americans: Making a Difference," informational flyer, 2005, and Arab American Institute, "Leading the Way," informational flyer, 2005. Still, the Palestinian question will remain on the political platform of ADC. See American-Arab Anti-Discrimination Committee, "2005 ADC Board Resolutions," October 11, 2005, available from www.adc.org/index.php?id = 2524&no_cache = 1&sword_list[] = adc&sword_list[] = res; Internet; accessed March 15, 2006.
159 Interview with Rafi Dajani. The grievous conditions after the election of Hamas cast doubt on the viability of Palestinian democracy. See Ibrahim Barzak and Sarah el Deeb, "Bloody Gaza Street Battles Edging Closer to Civil War," *The Star-Ledger*, May 17, 2007.
160 See, for example, President George W. Bush, "President Bush Discusses Importance of Democracy in Middle East: Remarks by the President on Winston Churchill and the War on Terror in the Library of Congress," February 4, 2004, available from www.whitehouse.gov/news/releases/2004/02/20040204-4. html; Internet; accessed December 22, 2006.
161 This was also exhibited by Rebecca Abou-Chedid, who stated, "Arabs and Americans have a common interest in stopping terrorism since Arab states have long been targeted by terrorist organizations." Interview with Rebecca Abou-Chedid.
162 Interviews with Khalil Jahshan, Nabil Mohamad, Christine Gleichert, Rafi Dajani, Mary Rose Oakar, Helen Samhan, Rebecca Abou-Chedid, Hussein Ibish, Marvin Wingfield, Peter Timco, and James Zogby.
163 Tony Smith, *Foreign Attachments: The Power of Ethnic Groups in the Making of American Foreign Policy* (Cambridge, MA: Harvard University Press, 2000), p. 109. Also, see Terry, *U.S. Foreign Policy in the Middle East*, p. 29 for a similar position.
164 Interview with Hussein Ibish.
165 AIPAC's influence has been well documented by John J. Mearsheimer and Stephen M. Walt, *The Israel Lobby and U.S. Foreign Policy* (New York: Farrar, Straus and Giroux, 2007), and "The Israel Lobby and U.S. Foreign Policy," *Kennedy School of Government Faculty Research Working Paper Series* RWP06–011 (March 2006).
166 Quoted in Glenn Frankel, "A Beautiful Friendship," *Washington Post*, July 16, 2006.
167 Interviews with Christine Gleichert and Rafi Dajani.
168 This is already something that groups like the ATFP have in place. See American Task Force on Palestine, "A Vision for the State of Palestine," available from www.americantaskforce.org/pdfs/advocacy_strategy.pdf; Internet; accessed December 22, 2006 and ATFP's "Official Policy Document," available from www.americantaskforce.org/pdfs/policy.pdf; Internet; accessed December 22, 2006.

169 Interview with Rafi Dajani.
170 Laura Chatfield and Carmen Gentile, "Pro-Arab Lobby Gaining in Strength in U.S.," from *United Press International*, June 20, 2001.
171 Interview with Mary Rose Oakar.
172 Interview with Hussein Ibish.
173 ATFP, "Strategies for Advocating Palestinian Statehood," in Hussein Ibish and Saliba Sarsar (eds), *Principles and Pragmatism: Key Documents from the American Task Force on Palestine* (Washington, DC: American Task Force on Palestine, October 2006), pp. 22–23.
174 Robert Satloff, "Shifting Sands," *New Republic*, June 1, 1998. For the disconnect between US policy and Hillary Clinton's words, see Marilyn Henry and Jay Bushinsky, "Hillary Clinton Says Palestinians Deserve an Independent State," *Jerusalem Post*, May 8, 1998 and Rachel Zabarkes Friedman, "Senator Israel: Hillary Runs from her Past," *National Review*, May 25, 2005.
175 Interviews with Rafi Dajani and Hussein Ibish.
176 Despite pro-Israel pressure, a Palestinian state remains in the interests of all parties. This allows ATFP and its allies to exercise influence on American policy. See Jerome Slater, "Muting the Alarm over the Israeli-Palestinian Conflict," *International Security*, vol. 32, no. 2 (Fall 2007), pp. 84–85.
177 For that narrative, see Sari Nusseibeh, *Once Upon a Country: A Palestinian Life* (New York: Farrar, Straus and Giroux, 2007).
178 Interviews with Khalil Jahshan, Nabil Mohamad, Christine Gleichert, Rafi Dajani, Mary Rose Oakar, Helen Samhan, Rebecca Abou-Chedid, Hussein Ibish, Marvin Wingfield, Peter Timco, and James Zogby.
179 Cable News Network, "Hate Crime Reports up in Wake of Terrorist Attacks," available from http://archives.cnn.com/2001/US/09/16/gen.hate.crimes/; Internet; accessed December 22, 2006.
180 Interview with Khalil Jahshan.
181 Interview with Hussein Ibish.
182 For one example, see Arab American Institute, "AAI Countdown: March 25, 2008-vol. 9, #11, A Regular Update from the Arab American Institute, 223 Days Until Election 2008!" available from www.aaiusa.org/countdown/3519/pandering-for-the-promised-land; Internet; accessed April 7, 2008.
183 Interview with Khalil Jahshan.
184 Interview with Hussein Ibish.
185 Shibley Telhami, *The Stakes: America in the Middle East, Consequences of Power and the Choice for Peace* (Boulder, CO: Westview Press, 2004), pp. 13–14.
186 Office of Counterterrorism, "Foreign Terrorist Organizations (FTOs), Fact Sheet, October 11, 2005," available from www.state.gov/s/ct/rls/fs/37191.htm; Internet; accessed July 30, 2006.
187 Worried about that, some have sought to exaggerate the strength of pro-Arab forces. For an example, see David Forman, "Opinion: The Arab Lobby Grows," *Jerusalem Post*, May 10, 2007.
188 Interviews with Khalil Jahshan, Nabil Mohamad, Christine Gleichert, Rafi Dajani, Mary Rose Oakar, Helen Samhan, Rebecca Abou-Chedid, Hussein Ibish, Marvin Wingfield, Peter Timco, and James Zogby.
189 Interview with Hussein Ibish.
190 For a primary account of the Palestinian problem during that time, see Pablo de Azcárate, *Mission in Palestine, 1948–52* (Washington, DC: Middle East Institute, 1966).
191 Interview with Marvin Wingfield. For more on this, see Duncan L. Clarke and Eric Flohr, "Christian Churches and the Palestine Question," *Journal of Palestine Studies*, vol. 21, no. 4 (Summer 1992), pp. 67–79.
192 Interview with Khalil Jahshan.

193 Ibid.
194 Mearsheimer and Walt made that clear in their work. See Mearsheimer and Walt, *Israel Lobby and U.S. Foreign Policy*, pp. 204–12.
195 Interview with Hussein Ibish.
196 This includes J Street, which identifies itself as "pro-peace" and "pro-Israel," a 501 (c) 4 group dedicated to opposing AIPAC's influence in Congress. See www.jstreet.org/about/about-us; Internet; accessed April 16, 2008.
197 Even many of the people interviewed for the data in this book undersold their effectiveness and potential in Washington politics.
198 For a notable example, see Mark N. Katz, "Policy Watch: Where is the Arab Lobby?" from *United Press International*, July 1, 2006.
199 Interview with Hussein Ibish.
200 Interview with Khalil Jahshan.
201 Interview with Hussein Ibish.
202 This was summed up best by Mearsheimer and Walt, who argued, "pro-Arab interest groups are weak to non-existent [making the pro-Israel] lobby's task even easier. Mearsheimer and Walt, "The Israel Lobby and U.S. Foreign Policy," p. 15. In their book, they softened their position, noting, "pro-Arab organizations are ... no match for the major groups that make up the Israel lobby." Mearsheimer and Walt, *Israel Lobby and U.S. Foreign Policy*, p. 141.
203 Interview with Hussein Ibish.
204 Interview with Khalil Jahshan. The fact that there is a pro-Arab lobby today is a far cry from the past. Janice Terry gave an anecdote about Egyptian President Gamal Abdul Nasser asking an aide who lived in the USA, "What is a lobby?" Clearly, the pro-Arab lobby, foreign or domestic, knows better in the present. See Terry, *U.S. Foreign Policy in the Middle East*, p. 50.
205 For a seminal set of works on this issue, see James G. McGann (ed.), *Think Tanks and Policy Advice in the US: Academics, Advisors, and Advocates* (Oxford: Routledge, 2007).
206 Interview with Mary Rose Oakar.
207 Interview with Hussein Ibish.
208 Interviews with Peter Timco and James Zogby.
209 Interviews with Nabil Mohamad, Rafi Dajani, and Marvin Wingfield.
210 Mearsheimer and Walt, "The Israel Lobby and U.S. Foreign Policy," p. 39.
211 Ibid.
212 Months after the Annapolis Conference, the USA maintained calls for a Palestinian state. See Ashraf Khalil, "Cheney Says a Palestinian State is 'Long Overdue,'" in *Los Angeles Times*, March 24, 2008.
213 Interview with Hussein Ibish.

5 Conclusion and scenarios: two states versus one

1 As mentioned elsewhere, some pro-Israel groups, in addition to advocating the two-state solution, seek to redefine what it means to be "pro-Israel." For one example, see Spencer Ackerman, "Reframing the Israel Debate: New PAC Forms to Support Two-State Solution Candidates," *Washington Independent*, available from www.washingtonindependent.com/view/reframing-the-israel; Internet; accessed April 25, 2008.
2 Hussein Ibish, executive director of the Hala Foundation, senior fellow at American Task Force on Palestine, and former communications director at American-Arab Anti-Discrimination Committee, interview by the author, Washington, DC, November 13, 2006.
3 John Stockwell, *The Praetorian Guard: The U.S. Role in the New World Order* (Cambridge, MA: South End Press, 1991).

4 See Appendix 2. For public opinion's role, see Richard Sobel, *The Impact of Public Opinion on U.S. Foreign Policy Since Vietnam: Constraining the Colossus* (New York: Oxford University Press, 2001).

5 Khalil Jahshan, former president of National Association of Arab Americans and representative of Association of Arab American University Graduates and Palestine Research and Educational Center, interview by the author, Arlington, VA, March 14, 2006; Nabil Mohamad, organizing director of American-Arab Anti-Discrimination Committee, interview by the author, Washington, DC, March 14, 2006; Christine Gleichert, Capitol Hill lobbyist for American-Arab Anti-Discrimination Committee, interview by the author, Washington, DC, March 15, 2006; Rafi Dajani, former executive director of American Task Force on Palestine, interview by the author, Washington, DC, March 15, 2006; Mary Rose Oakar, former congresswoman from Cleveland, OH, and president of American-Arab Anti-Discrimination Committee, interview by the author, Washington, DC, March 15, 2006; Helen Samhan, executive director of Arab American Institute Foundation, interview by the author, Washington, DC, March 16, 2006; Rebecca Abou-Chedid, government relations and policy analyst for Arab American Institute, interview by the author, Washington, DC, March 16, 2006; Hussein Ibish; Marvin Wingfield, director of education and outreach for American-Arab Anti-Discrimination Committee, telephone interview by the author, December 19, 2006; Peter Timco, director of the Office of the President, Arab American Institute, telephone interview by the author, April 25, 2008; James Zogby, president and co-founder of Arab American Institute, co-founder of Palestine Human Rights Campaign, co-founder and former executive director of American-Arab Anti-Discrimination Committee, telephone interview by the author, April 26, 2008.

6 For instance, ceremonies of Palestinian leaders shaking hands with the Israeli government went a long way in showing that support for the Palestinians was not as virulent as the Israel lobby made it out to be. Interviews with Khalil Jahshan, Helen Samhan, Hussein Ibish, and James Zogby.

7 In general, pro-Israel groups began courting Republicans and the right in the years leading up to the war on terrorism, as demonstrated by their increased campaign contributions. See Appendix 6.

8 After all, the nineteen hijackers of 9/11 were all Arab and Muslim, the same ethno-religious characteristics shared by the majority of Palestinians.

9 Interview with Hussein Ibish.

10 In a unified voice of the Israel lobby, the Presidents Conference has supported Gaza disengagement but has not gone so far as to back US policy toward a Palestinian state. See Conference of Presidents of Major American Jewish Organizations, "American Jewish Leaders Issue Major Statement on Disengagement," August 16, 2005, available from www.conferenceofpresidents. org/disengagementaug.pdf; Internet; accessed July 13, 2006.

11 See Shibley Telhami, *The Stakes: America in the Middle East, Consequences of Power and the Choice for Peace* (Boulder, CO: Westview Press, 2004), pp. 95–100, and James Zogby, "The Stakes Have Never Been Higher: The Need to Debate U.S. Mideast Policy in the 2008 Election," *Washington Watch*, March 3, 2008.

12 It is well known that pro-Israel lobbyists draft resolutions in Congress to ensure their policy preferences. See Ari Berman, "AIPAC's Hold," *The Nation*, August 4, 2006, available from www.thenation.com/doc/20060814/aipacs_hold; Internet; accessed August 5, 2006.

13 Prime Minister Ehud Olmert has affirmed this agreement. See Donald Macintyre, "Olmert Says West Bank Settlements Will Stay," *Independent*, February 8, 2006. However, some, like Hussein Ibish, disagree with those that say the US has agreed to keep the settlements in place, pointing to President Bush's meeting with

Mahmoud Abbas, which restated their agreement to a Palestinian state with only minor, multilateral territorial alterations. See "President Welcomes Palestinian President Abbas to the White House," October 20, 2005, available from www. whitehouse.gov/news/releases/2005/10/20051020.html; Internet; accessed December 23, 2006. Bush reaffirmed that agreement months prior to leaving office. See "President Bush Meets with President Abbas of the Palestinian Authority," April 24, 2008, available from www.whitehouse.gov/news/releases/2008/04/20080424-10.html; Internet; accessed May 6, 2008.

14 For example, see Ori Nir, "Israelis Want AIPAC-Backed Bill Softened," *Forward*, March 10, 2006. Also, see Esther Kaplan, "The Jewish Divide on Israel," *The Nation*, July 12, 2004. An official of the Jewish United Fund once remarked

> AIPAC has to be stopped ... most of us [Jews] are afraid of what would happen if we showed division in the face of so much adversary throughout the world [including], anti-Semitism in Europe and throughout the world, violence and hostility from Islamic fundamentalists, Palestinian terrorism, and so on.
>
> (Khalil M. Marrar, conversation with anonymous official of the Jewish United Fund, Chicago, IL, June 5, 2007)

15 Ali Abunimah has maintained, "based on what has been happening recently and the history of the two people, it doesn't look like we are going to have two states anytime soon." Ali Abunimah, conversation with the author, Chicago, IL, March 5, 2008.

16 Harry S. Truman Institute for the Advancement of Peace, "Overwhelming Majority Among Israelis and Palestinians for Negotiated Rather than Unilateral Further Disengagements," available from http://truman.huji.ac.il/upload/PressRelease-15-240306English.doc; Internet; accessed December 28, 2006. Similar majorities exist within the Arab and Jewish American communities. See Americans for Peace Now, "Joint AAI/APN Poll: Jewish and Arab Americans Overwhelmingly Support Two-State Solution, U.S. Engagement; Bush Gets Low Marks," available from www.peacenow.org/pr.asp?rid = &cid = 3738; Internet; accessed June 6, 2007.

17 This phrase comes from Edward Said's *The End of the Peace Process: Oslo and After* (New York: Pantheon Press, 2000).

18 See Appendix 2.

19 The section on the one-state solution benefits from Virginia Tilley's *The One-State Solution*, one of the finest books written on the subject. Tilley, *The One-State Solution: A Breakthrough for Peace in the Israeli-Palestinian Deadlock* (Ann Arbor, MI: University of Michigan Press, 2005). For equally compelling arguments in favor of the one-state, see Ali Abunimah, *One Country: A Bold Proposal to End the Israeli-Palestinian Impasse* (New York: Metropolitan Books, 2006) and Joel Kovel, *Overcoming Zionism: Creating a Single Democratic State in Israel/ Palestine* (London: Pluto Press, 2007).

20 Stephen P. Cohen, Michael C. Hudson, Nathan Guttman, and Khalil E. Jahshan, "Is a Two-State Solution Still Viable?" *Middle East Policy*, vol. X, no. 2 (Summer 2003), p. 10. Zogby repeated that point. Interview with James Zogby.

21 George W. Bush, "President Bush Commends Israeli Prime Minister Sharon's Plan," April 14, 2004, available from www.whitehouse.gov/news/releases/2004/04/ 20040414-4.html#; Internet; accessed May 20, 2005, emphasis added. Some have argued that Bush's proclamation has hidden appendages. See Glenn Kessler, "Israelis Claim Secret Agreement with U.S., Americans Insist No Deal Made on Settlement Growth," *Washington Post*, April 24, 2008.

22 In talks with the Palestinians, Bush continued to deny that this agreement would have any impact on their territorial integrity. See Khaled Abu Toameh, "Palestine

Can't Be Swiss Cheese," *Jerusalem Post*, January 10, 2008, and Sheryl Gay Stolberg, "Bush Meets Abbas, but Palestinians Criticize Plans for Trip," *New York Times*, April 25, 2008.

23 For a preview, see Appendix 4.

24 Jimmy Carter, *Palestine: Peace not Apartheid* (New York: Simon and Schuster, 2006), p. 215. For a review of Carter's work on the two-state solution by a key one-state supporter, see Ali Abunimah, "Jimmy Carter's Book: A Palestinian View," *Wall Street Journal*, December 26, 2006.

25 Some have noted that the situation in Gaza is the worst it has been since Israel began its occupation. See "Gaza Humanitarian Situation 'Worst Since 1967,'" *Belfast Telegraph*, March 6, 2008, available from www.belfasttelegraph.co.uk/breaking-news/world/middle-east/article3493041.ece; Internet; accessed March 8, 2008.

26 Tilley, *The One-State Solution*, p. 5. This prediction may have come to realization as Israel found itself under attack in the midst of fighting – bordering on civil war – in Gaza between rival factions Hamas and Fatah. See Isabel Kershner, "Israeli Army Strikes Cell in Northern Gaza as Palestinian Factional Fighting Persists," *New York Times*, May 20, 2007.

27 Even after the Jack Abramoff scandal, Congress has discarded any changes to business as usual. See "Lobbying Reform Abandoned: After Abramoff Scandal Left Front Page, Congress Cooled on Ethics Reform," *The Tennesan*, August 4, 2006, available from www.rctimes.com/apps/pbcs.dll/article?AID = /20060806/OPINION01/608060344/1007/MTCN0305; Internet; accessed August 7, 2006.

28 John J. Mearsheimer and Stephen M. Walt, "The Israel Lobby and U.S. Foreign Policy," *Kennedy School of Government Faculty Research Working Paper Series* RWP06–011 (March 2006), p. 41. See their book, *The Israel Lobby and U.S. Foreign Policy* (New York: Farrar, Straus and Giroux, 2007), p. 168, for a similar message.

29 Carter, *Palestine*, p. 215.

30 A US senator speaking on condition of anonymity indicated that this would only be prevented if pro-Arab groups "gave supporters of the Palestinian cause more cover." Khalil M. Marrar, conversation with US senator, Washington, DC, March 15, 2006.

31 Ghada Hashem Talhami, *Syria and the Palestinians: The Clash of Nationalisms* (Miami, FL: University of Florida Press, 2001), p. 202.

32 Mearsheimer and Walt, "The Israel Lobby and U.S. Foreign Policy," pp. 5–7. Also see John J. Mearsheimer, "Back to the Future: Instability in Europe after the Cold War," *International Security*, vol. 15, no. 1 (Summer 1990), pp. 5–56.

33 Smaen Areikat, Zeinah Salahi, and Khaled Elgindy, "Is a Two-State Solution Still Possible?" Speech before the Johns Hopkins School of Advanced International Studies, April 28, 2005, available from www.mideasti.org/articles/doc372.html; Internet; accessed August 7, 2006.

34 James R. Kunder, "U.S. Policy Toward the Palestinians," *CQ Congressional Testimony*, March 2, 2004.

35 Office of the Press Secretary, "President Discusses Middle East Peace with Prime Minister Sharon," July 29, 2003, available from www.whitehouse.gov/news/releases/2003/07/20030729-2.html; Internet; accessed December 27, 2006.

36 Israel's actions caused widespread outrage in the Arab/Islamic world. See Hani Shukrallah, Sana Kamal, Mona Zaide, Marlin Dick, and Cengiz Candar, "The Street Reacts to Operation Defensive Shield: Snapshots from the Middle East," *Journal of Palestine Studies*, vol. 31, no. 4 (Summer 2002), pp. 44–65.

37 Of course, the PLO led government ultimately lost power because of its own doing. Rather than signaling Palestinians' embrace for the Islamists, Hamas's victory in early 2006 was a rejection of PLO corruption. See "Abbas Considers Election Call to End Impasse with Hamas," *CBC News*, December 9, 2006,

available from www.cbc.ca/world/story/2006/12/09/fatah-hamas.html; Internet; accessed December 27, 2006.

38 For a history of Palestinian failures on that end, see Rashid Khalidi, *Iron Cage: The Story of Palestinian Struggle for Statehood* (Boston, MA: Beacon Press, 2006).

39 For superb insight into the connection between the Lebanon war, US interests, and the larger Arab–Israeli conflict, see Seymour Hersh, "Watching Lebanon: Washington's Interests in Israel's War," *New Yorker*, August 21, 2006.

40 Much scholarship has examined this democratic peace position. See, among others, Dean V. Babst, "A Force For Peace," *Industrial Research* (1972), pp. 55–58, Steve Chan, "Mirror, Mirror On The Wall ... Are Democratic States More Pacific?" *Journal of Conflict Resolution*, 28 (1984), pp. 617–48, William J. Dixon, "Democracy and the Management of International Conflict," *Journal of Conflict Resolution*, 37 (1993), pp. 42–68, Michael W. Doyle, "Kant, Liberal Legacies and Foreign Affairs Part I," *Philosophy and Public Affairs*, vol. 12, no. 3 (1983), pp. 323–53, and "Michael Doyle on the Democratic Peace," *International Security*, 19 (1995), pp. 184–184, Nils Petter Gleditsch, "Democracy and Peace," *Journal of Peace Research*, 29 (1992), pp. 369–76, Immanuel Kant, *Perpetual Peace* (New York: The Library of Liberal Arts, 1957), Charles W. Kegley, Jr., "The Neoidealist Moment in International Studies? Realist Myths and the New International Realities," *International Studies Quarterly*, 37 (1993), pp. 131–46, David A. Lake, "Powerful Pacifists: Democratic States and War," *American Political Science Review*, 86 (1992), pp. 24–37, Christopher Layne, "Kant or Cant: The Myth of the Democratic Peace," *International Security*, 19 (1994), pp. 5–49, Edward D. Mansfield and Jack Snyder, "Democratization and War," *Foreign Affairs*, 74 (1995), pp. 79–97, Alex Mintz and Nehmia Geva, "Why Don't Democracies Fight Each Other? An Experimental Study," *Journal of Conflict Resolution*, 37 (1993), pp. 484–503, Clifton T. Morgan and Valerie L. Schwebach, "Take Two Democracies and Call Me in the Morning: A Prescription for Peace?" in *International Interactions*, 17 (1992), pp. 305–20, Nicholas G. Onuf and Thomas J. Johnson, "Peace in the Liberal World: Does Democracy Matter?" in Charles W. Kegley, Jr. (ed.), *Controversies in International Relations Theory: Realism and the Neoliberal Challenge* (New York: St. Martin's Press, 1995), pp. 179–98, John M. Owen, "How Liberalism Produces Peace," *International Security*, vol. 19, no. 2 (1994), and *Liberal Peace, Liberal War: American Politics and International Security* (Ithaca, NY: Cornell University Press, 1998), James Lee Ray, *Democracy and International Politics: An Evaluation of the Democratic Peace Proposition* (Columbia, SC: University of South Carolina Press, 1995), and Volker Rittberger, "On the Peace Capacity of Democracies: Reflections on the Political Theory of Peace," *Law and State*, 39 (1989), pp. 40–57.

41 George W. Bush, "Roadmap for Peace in the Middle East: Israeli/Palestinian Reciprocal Action, Quartet Support" July 16, 2003, available from www.state.gov/r/pa/ei/rls/22520.htm; Internet; accessed August 8, 2006.

42 Quoted in Laura King and Vita Bekker, "Israel Strikes Lebanon after Militants Capture 2 Soldiers," *Los Angeles Times*, July 13, 2006.

43 In addition to the kidnapping of Galid Shalit, Hamas also killed two soldiers. See Joshua Mitnick, "Hamas Kidnaps Soldier, Kills Two; Tel Aviv Warns of Gaza Attack," *Washington Times*, June 26, 2006.

44 For an example of the carnage, see Sarah el Deeb, "23 Killed in Gaza, Deadliest Day There Since Israel Withdrew Last Year," available from *Associated Press*, July 27, 2006.

45 Tilley *The One-State Solution*, p. 89.

46 Interviews with Hussein Ibish and James Zogby.

47 Peter Baker, "U.S. Urges Restraint By Israel; Democratic Government Seen Facing Jeopardy in Lebanon," *Washington Post*, July 14, 2006. Of course,

Hezbollah committed grievous crimes against Israel. See Human Rights Watch, "Lebanon: Hezbollah Rocket Attacks on Haifa Designed to Kill Civilians – Anti-Personnel Ball Bearings Meant to Harm 'Soft' Targets," July 18, 2006, available from http://hrw.org/english/docs/2006/07/18/lebano13760.htm; Internet; accessed January 28, 2007.

48 For a recent example, see Warren Hoge, "U.S. Vetoes Security Council Resolution Assailing Israel for Attacks," *New York Times*, November 12, 2006.

49 Jim Clancy, "Italy Willing to Lead United Nations Forces in Southern Lebanon," on *Your World Today*, August 21, 2006, available from http://transcripts.cnn.com/TRANSCRIPTS/0608/21/ywt.01.html; Internet; accessed December 28, 2006.

50 For an example of this rhetoric at the highest levels of US government, see House Committee on Intelligence, "Key Findings of Congressional Delegation to the Middle East," July 21–25, 2006.

51 In a conversation about Israel's invasion of Lebanon, Norman Finkelstein pointed that out during discussion of the Human Rights Watch condemnation of Hezbollah. Norman G. Finkelstein, professor of political science at DePaul University, conversation with the author, Chicago, IL, October 25, 2006. See Human Rights Watch, "Israel/Lebanon: Hezbollah Must End Attacks on Civilians," August 5, 2006, available from http://hrw.org/english/docs/2006/08/05/lebano13921.htm; Internet; accessed December 28, 2006.

52 This was demonstrated by the Democratic party's boycott of Iraqi Prime Minister Nouri al-Maliki upon his visit to Washington. See Rick Klein, "Democrats Set an Agenda They Can Agree On," *Boston Globe*, August 4, 2006. For an assessment of support for Israel in American electoral politics, see Hilary Leila Kreieger, "Obama: Pro-Israel Needn't be Pro-Likud," *Jerusalem Post*, February 25, 2008.

53 Interview with James Zogby.

54 Tovah Lazaroff, "Elon: Two-State Solution Dead," *Jerusalem Post*, March 5, 2006.

55 Quoted in Mohammed Daraghmeh, "Hamas Official Says Group Ready for 'Two-State' Solution with Israel," from *Associated Press*, April 7, 2006. Hamas has repeatedly made such statements. See Ethan Bronner, "Carter Says Hamas and Syria Are Open to Peace," *New York Times*, April 22, 2008.

56 Office of the Coordinator for Counterterrorism, "Foreign Terrorist Organizations," April 8, 2008, available from www.state.gov/s/ct/rls/fs/08/103392.htm; Internet; accessed May 5, 2008.

57 For two instances, see Ashraf Sweilam, "Police Reinforce Gaza-Egypt Border After Palestinian Militants Blast Hole in Wall," available from *Associated Press*, June 29, 2006 and Bret Stephens, "The Gaza Breakout," *Wall Street Journal*, January 29, 2008. For a report on the siege of Gaza after the Israeli "pullout," see Gisha Legal Center for Freedom of Movement, "Disengaged Occupiers: The Legal Status of Gaza," January 17, 2007, available from www.gisha.org/english/reports/Report_for_the_website.pdf; Internet; accessed January 26, 2007.

58 Nadia Abu El-Haj, *Facts on the Ground: Archaeological Practice and Territorial Self-fashioning* (Chicago, IL: University of Chicago Press, 2002), p. 5.

59 Withdrawal would also entail the "the evacuation of Jewish settlements, something that would cause near civil war conditions in Israel." Interview with James Zogby.

60 Sabri Jiryis, *The Arabs in Israel* (New York: Monthly Review Press, 1976). Little has changed since the 1970s when Jiryis wrote his work. See Ethan Bronner, "After 60 Years, Arabs in Israel Are Outsiders," *New York Times*, May 7, 2008.

61 See Mehran Kamrava, *The Modern Middle East: A Political History Since the First World War* (Berkeley: University of California Press, 2005), pp. 312–14.

62 This was the title of a piece by Edward Said in one of the largest Arab newspapers. For the English version, see Edward W. Said, "Truth and Reconciliation," *Al-Ahram Weekly On-Line*, January 14–20, 1999, available from http://weekly.

ahram.org.eg/1999/412/op2.htm; Internet; accessed January 28, 2007. It also appears in Said's *The End of the Peace Process*, pp. 312–21.

63 Although the most of the Arab American leadership does not take the one-state solution seriously, and the Israel lobby views it with disdain, the issue still raises intellectual curiosity by all sides concerned. Interview with Hussein Ibish.

64 Tilley, *The One-State Solution*, p. 13.

65 Ibid., p. 209.

66 Interview with Rafi Dajani. Hussein Ibish seconded Dajani's points while James Zogby argued, "instead of far off solutions, what we have to think about now is how to mitigate the suffering of the Palestinian people." Interviews with Hussein Ibish and James Zogby.

67 Tilley, *The One-State Solution*, p. 214.

68 H. M. Kalvaryski, excerpted in "The History of the Original Brit Shalom, Founded 1925," (date unknown), available from www.britshalom.org/background. htm; Internet; accessed October 11, 2005.

69 Tilley, *The One-State Solution*, pp. 6–7; pp. 86 and 93 discuss Islamist terrorism in more depth.

70 Judah Magnes, quoted in *Official Records of the Second Session of the General Assembly*, Supplement no. 11, United Nations Special Committee on Palestine, Report of the General Assembly, Volume III, Oral Evidence Presented at Public Meeting (Lake Success, NY, July 14, 1947), available from http://domino.un.org/ UNISPAL.NSF/0/8677dc1263a21f1385256e93006a50d3?OpenDocument; Internet; accessed October 11, 2005.

71 Magnes, quoted in Brit Shalom, available from www.britshalom.org/background. htm; Internet; accessed April 22, 2007.

72 Excerpted in Tilley, *The One-State Solution*, pp. 214–15.

73 Martin Buber, quoted in Yossi Schwartz, "Israel/Palestine: Two States or One Bi-National State," available from www.marxist.com/MiddleEast/israel_binational_state.html; Internet; accessed April 22, 2007.

74 The only international challenge to Israel's exclusive Jewish identity came from UN conferences on racism to which Israel retorted with charges of anti-Semitism for being singled out. For an example, see Chaim Herzog, "Response to Zionism is Racism Resolution," available from www.jewishvirtuallibrary.org/jsource/UN/ herzogsp.html; Internet; accessed October 12, 2005. The UN has condemned Zionism as racism in General Assembly Resolution 3379, November 10, 1975, available from www.jewishvirtuallibrary.org/jsource/UN/unga3379.html; Internet; accessed October 12, 2005. In 1991, it repealed Resolution 3379. See General Assembly Resolution 46/86, December 16, 1991, available from www.jewishvirtuallibrary. org/jsource/UN/unga46_86.html; Internet; accessed May 6, 2008.

75 Hannah Arendt, "To Save the Jewish Homeland: There is Still Time," *Commentary* (May 1948), p. 400.

76 Ibid., p. 403. One of the most famous Jews, Albert Einstein, wrote "I would much rather see reasonable agreement with the Arabs on the basis of living together in peace than the creation of a Jewish state." See Albert Einstein, *Ideas and Opinions* (New York: Crown Publishers, 1954), p. 190.

77 Buber, "Program of the Ichud," excepted in Tilley, *The One-State Solution*, pp. 235–36

78 Hannah Arendt, "To Save the Jewish Homeland," Tilley, *The One-State Solution*, pp. 238–39.

79 Norman G. Finkelstein, *Image and Reality of the Israel-Palestine Conflict* (London: Verso, 2001), pp. 62–63.

80 The Palestinian Declaration of Independence eventually outlined this. See "Declaration of Independence," November 15, 1988, available from www.palestine-net.com/ politics/indep.html; Internet; accessed June 11, 2007.

81 Samir Awad, "Background to the 'Peace Process,'" *Socialism and Democracy*, issue 38, vol. 19, no. 2, available from www.sdonline.org/32/peace_process.htm; Internet; accessed October 12, 2005.
82 Ibid.
83 Ali Abunimah, "One Country: A Bold Proposal to End the Israeli-Palestinian Impasse," speech for Students for Justice in Palestine, DePaul University, Chicago, IL, March 5, 2008.
84 Tilley, *The One-State Solution*, pp. 9–17, 86–87.
85 Ibid., pp. 86–87.
86 Meron Benvenisti, quoted in Tilley, *The One-State Solution*, p. 185.
87 Ibid. The original source for this is Meron Benvenisti, quoted in Association for One Democratic State in Palestine/Israel, "Is the 'Two State Solution' Still a Viable and Desirable Solution to the Israeli-Palestinian Conflict," available from www.one-democratic-state.org/articles/shavit-hanegbi-benvenisti.html; Internet; accessed April 22, 2007.
88 Ari Shavit, "Survival of the Fittest," *Ha'aretz*, January 9, 2004.
89 Arnon Soffer, quoted in Tilley, *The One-State Solution*, p. 187. Originally quoted in Paul de Rooij, "The Carnivores and the Ivy League Apologist: The Voices of Sharon's Little Helpers," *Counterpunch*, December 9, 2004, available from www.counterpunch.org/rooij12092004.html; Internet; accessed May 4, 2008.
90 "Obstacle to Terrorism," *Near East Report*, vol. XLVII, no. 14 (July 28, 2003), p. 57.
91 Haim Hanegbi, quoted in Tilley, *The One-State Solution*, p. 187. The original source for this is Haim Hanegbi, quoted in Association for One Democratic State in Palestine/Israel, "Is the 'Two State Solution' Still a Viable and Desirable Solution to the Israeli-Palestinian Conflict," available from www.one-democratic-state.org/articles/shavit-hanegbi-benvenisti.html; Internet; accessed April 22, 2007.
92 Hani al-Masri, quoted in Tilley, *The One-State Solution*, pp. 188–89. The original source for this is Khalid Amayreh, "Controversial Move," *Al-Ahram Weekly On-Line*, January 15–21, 2004, available from http://weekly.ahram.org.eg/2004/673/re1.htm; Internet; accessed April 22, 2007.
93 Raja Halwani, quoted in Tilley, *The One-State Solution*, p. 190.
94 Haim Bresheeth, quoted in Tilley, *The One-State Solution*, pp. 191–92. This may also be found in Haim Bresheeth, "Two-States, Too Little, Too Late," *Al-Ahram Weekly On-Line*, March 11–17, 2004, available from http://weekly.ahram.org.eg/2004/681/op61.htm; Internet; accessed April 22, 2007.
95 See Appendix 4.
96 Baruch Kimmerling, *Politicide: Ariel Sharon's War Against the Palestinians* (New York: Verso, 2003), p. 165.
97 Tilley, *The One-State Solution*, p. 29.
98 Ibid., p. 20.
99 Kimmerling, *Politicide*, pp. 3–4. Kimmerling noted that this policy is the *status quo ante*.
100 According to some new research, Israel would not lose its Jewish character, even if the Palestinians were absorbed into the state. See Bennett Zimmerman, Roberta Seid, Michael L. Wise, and Yoram Ettinger, "The Fourth Way: An Integrated Strategy to Strengthen Israel's Unilateral Political and Security Options – A New Demographic, Electoral, and Political Paradigm for Israel," produced by American-Israel Demographic Research Group, January 21, 2007, available from www.pademographics.com/4th%20Way%20Israel%20Summary%20Januar%2021%202007.doc; Internet; accessed January 30, 2007.
101 Said, *The End of the Peace Process*, p. 314.
102 Ibid., pp. 315–16.
103 Ibid., p. 321.

104 Tilley, *The One-State Solution*, p. 25. Also, see Appendix 4.
105 Tilley, *The One-State Solution*, p. 32.
106 Ibid.
107 Ibid., p. 74.
108 Quoted in Tilley, *The One-State Solution*, p. 166.
109 Tilley, *The One-State Solution*, p. 123.
110 As had been established, many strands of global terrorism feed off of the Israeli–Palestinian conflict. Despite it being well documented, this overwhelmingly accepted suggestion has its critics. See, for example, the argument of Israeli ambassador to the UN, Dore Gold, in *Hatred's Kingdom: How Saudi Arabia Supports the New Global Terrorism* (Washington, DC: Regnery Publishing, 2003), pp. 9–10. Gold argued,

> of course, achieving a peace settlement between Israel and the Palestinians is a highly desirable goal. But resolving that conflict would not be a panacea. To focus solely on this conflict is to ignore the real motivating forces behind terrorism against the West.

While most of those forces relate back to Saudi Arabian Wahhabi and Salafi extremism, Gold does not deny the importance of the Palestinian problem to the recruitment of terrorists.
111 We must remember that groups like the American-Arab Anti-Discrimination Committee, the Arab American Institute, and the Hala Foundation deal with the following issues in order of priority: ensuring the civil liberties of Arab Americans; demanding respect for human rights by calling on the US government to support the peaceful transition to democracy in the Middle East; and pushing American policy toward honoring its commitment to the establishment of a Palestinian state. Therefore, if they turned some of their attention toward the "one-state option," they would simply have to bring to bear on US foreign policy their missions of protecting civil and human rights for all people, Arabs and Jews. All interviewees went into length about their organizations' missions. Interviews with Khalil Jahshan, Nabil Mohamad, Christine Gleichert, Rafi Dajani, Mary Rose Oakar, Helen Samhan, Rebecca Abou-Chedid, Hussein Ibish, Marvin Wingfield, Peter Timco, and James Zogby.
112 See "The Declaration of the Establishment of the State of Israel" May 14, 1948, available from www.mfa.gov.il/MFA/Peace%20Process/Guide%20to%20the%20Peace%20Process/Declaration%20of%20Establishment%20of%20State%20of%20Israel; Internet; accessed June 11, 2007.
113 Interview with Hussein Ibish.
114 George W. Bush, "President Bush Meets with British Prime Minister Tony Blair," December 7, 2006, available from www.whitehouse.gov/news/releases/2006/12/20061207-1.html; Internet; accessed December 30, 2006.
115 Amendment XIV, *US Constitution*, available from www.archives.gov/national-archives-experience/charters/constitution_amendments_11-27.html; Internet; accessed June 22, 2005.
116 Harry S. Truman Institute for the Advancement of Peace, "Overwhelming Majority Among Israelis and Palestinians for Negotiated Rather than Unilateral Further Disengagements," available from http://truman.huji.ac.il/upload/PressRelease-15-240306English.doc; Internet; accessed December 28, 2006.
117 Michael Berkowitz, *Zionist Culture and West European Jewry Before the First World War* (Chapel Hill, NC: University of North Carolina Press, 1996), pp. 8–10.
118 For more on this, see Howard Wettstein (ed.), *Diasporas and Exiles: Varieties of Jewish Identity* (Berkeley, CA: University of California Press, 2002).

119 Vaughn P. Shannon, *Balancing Act: US Foreign Policy and the Arab-Israeli Conflict* (Burlington, VT: Ashgate Publishing Company, 2003), pp. 7–8, 129.
120 Interview with Hussein Ibish.
121 John J. Mearsheimer and Stephen M. Walt, *The Israel Lobby and U.S. Foreign Policy* (New York: Farrar, Straus and Giroux, 2007), pp. 112, 141–42, 144.
122 James Zogby stated, "the two-state solution is a good step forward, but much remains to be done." Interview with James Zogby.
123 Interview with Hussein Ibish.
124 Nevertheless, in the beginning of 2008, a majority of Israelis favored negotiations with Hamas. See Yossi Verter, "Poll: Most Israelis Back Direct Talks with Hamas on Shalit," *Ha'aretz*, February 27, 2008.
125 Mearsheimer and Walt declared that the two-state solution "is now largely forgotten." See Mearsheimer and Walt, *The Israel Lobby and U.S. Foreign Policy*, p. 204.
126 Interview with Khalil Jahshan.
127 Interviews with Khalil Jahshan, Nabil Mohamad, Christine Gleichert, Rafi Dajani, Mary Rose Oakar, Helen Samhan, Rebecca Abou-Chedid, Hussein Ibish, Marvin Wingfield, Peter Timco, and James Zogby.
128 Interview with Khalil Jahshan.
129 Interview with Hussein Ibish.
130 Ibid.
131 Secretary of State Condoleezza Rice has stated "the window for the two-state solution is not open forever … it's gotten narrower and narrower over time." Quoted in Anne Gearan, "Rice: Israelis and Palestinians Must Agree on Final Borders," available from *Associated Press*, May 1, 2008.
132 Interview with Hussein Ibish.
133 Sir Nigel Sheinwald, British ambassador to the United States, conversation with the author at the Chicago Council on Foreign Relations, Chicago, IL, April 25, 2008.
134 Interview with Christine Gleichert.
135 Sobel, *The Impact of Public Opinion on U.S. Foreign Policy Since Vietnam*, p. 5.
136 Milton C. Cummings, Jr. and David Wise, *Democracy Under Pressure: An Introduction to the American Political System*, 10th ed. (Boston, MA: Thomson Publishers, 2007), chapters 6 and 7.
137 Yasmin Hamidi, Arab American activist, email to the author, May 18, 2008. For the referenced story, see Verena Dobnik, "Palestinian-Americans Mark 60 Years Displaced," *Chicago Tribune*, May 16, 2008.
138 Interviews with Khalil Jahshan, Hussein Ibish, Helen Samhan, and James Zogby.
139 Many criticized US action in those cases. For a scathing example, see Michael Mann, *Incoherent Empire* (New York: Verso, 2003).
140 Jamal R. Nassar, *Globalization and Terrorism: The Migration of Dreams and Nightmares* (New York: Rowman and Littlefield, 2004), chapters 2 and 5.
141 Interview with Hussein Ibish. Zogby noted that this also might be the "path of least resistance." Interview with James Zogby.
142 Isabel Kershner, "Abbas and Olmert Struggle to Move Talks Forward," *New York Times*, February 20, 2008. Also see Appendix 4.
143 Sir Nigel Sheinwald seconded this point. Conversation with Sir Nigel Sheinwald.
144 UN officials at the highest level have expressed support for two states. In particular, see a confidential report by the UN's under-secretary-general, special coordinator for Middle East Peace, personal representative of the secretary-general to the Palestine Liberation Organization and the Palestinian Authority, and envoy to the Quartet, Alvaro de Soto, "End of Mission Report," May 2007, available from http://image.guardian.co.uk/sys-files/Guardian/documents/2007/

06/12/DeSotoReport.pdf; Internet; accessed June 13, 2007. On page 5, de Soto wrote, "I am guided by what I believe the UN should be doing in furtherance of the goal of a two State solution in which Israel's existence and security are assured and legitimate Palestinian aspirations for end of occupation and state-hood are made a reality."

145 George W. Bush, "President Addresses Nation, Discusses Iraq, War on Terror," June 28, 2005, available from www.whitehouse.gov/news/releases/2005/06/20050628-7.html; Internet; accessed December 30, 2006.

146 Jimmy Carter, question by the author, Chicago, IL, April 30, 2008.

Bibliography

"1993: Rabin and Arafat Shake on Peace Deal," September 13, 1993, available from http://news.bbc.co.uk/onthisday/hi/dates/stories/september/13/newsid_3053000/3053733.stm; Internet; accessed July 24, 2006.

"A Performance-Based Roadmap to a Permanent Two-State Solution to the Israeli-Palestinian Conflict" available from www.state.gov/r/pa/prs/ps/2003/20062.htm; Internet; accessed October 24, 2005.

"Abbas Considers Election Call to End Impasse with Hamas," *CBC News*, December 9, 2006, available from www.cbc.ca/world/story/2006/12/09/fatah-hamas.html; Internet; accessed December 27, 2006.

Abou-Chedid, Rebecca, government relations and policy analyst for Arab American Institute. Interview by the author, Washington, DC, March 16, 2006.

Abu El-Haj, Nadia. *Facts on the Ground: Archaeological Practice and Territorial Self-fashioning* (Chicago: University of Chicago Press, 2002).

———. "Abu Mazen's Test," in *Near East Report*, vol. XLVII, no. 11 (June 9, 2003), p. 43.

Abu Toameh, Khaled. "Palestine Can't be Swiss Cheese," *Jerusalem Post*, January 10, 2008.

Abunimah, Ali. Conversation with the author, Chicago, IL, March 5, 2008.

———. "One Country: A Bold Proposal to End the Israeli-Palestinian Impasse," speech for Students for Justice in Palestine, DePaul University, Chicago, IL, March 5, 2008.

———. "Jimmy Carter's Book: A Palestinian View," *Wall Street Journal*, December 26, 2006.

———. *One Country: A Bold Proposal to End the Israeli-Palestinian Impasse* (New York: Metropolitan Books, 2006).

Abunimah, Ali and Hussein Ibish. "The Palestinian Right of Return," *ADC Issue Paper* 30 (2001).

Abu Rudeneh, Odeh. "The Jewish Factor in US Politics," *Journal of Palestine Studies*, vol. 1, no. 4 (Summer 1972), pp. 92–107.

Ackerman, Spencer. "Reframing the Israel Debate: New PAC Forms to Support Two-State Solution Candidates," in *The Washington Independent*, available from www.washingtonindependent.com/view/reframing-the-israel; Internet; accessed April 25, 2008.

Achen, C. H. "Mass Political Attitudes and the Survey Response," *American Political Science Review* 69 (1975), pp. 1218–31.

Adams, Michael. "America, Zionism, and the Prospects for Peace," *Journal of Palestine Studies*, vol. 19, no. 1 (Autumn 1989), pp. 32–45.

Ahmad, Eqbal, Jeanne Butterfield, Noam Chomsky, Denis F. Doyon, Deena Hurwitz, Shiela Ryan, and James Zogby. "Middle East Peace Priorities in the US: Seven Perspectives," *Middle East Report*, no. 158, Palestine and Israel in the US Arena (May-June 1989), pp. 6–11.

Ahrari, Mohammed (ed.). *Ethnic Groups and U.S. Foreign Policy* (New York: Greenwood Press, 1987).

Ajami, Fouad. "Home Base," *The New Republic* (June 4, 2001), p. 62.

Al Mosbahi, Hassouna. *Hikaya Tunisiyya* (Dubai: Kaleem Books, 2008).

Aldrich, John H., John L. Sullivan, and Eugene Borgida. "Foreign Affairs and Issue Voting: Do Presidential Candidates 'Waltz Before A Blind Audience'?" *American Political Science Review*, vol. 83, no. 1 (March 1989), pp. 123–41.

Allison, Graham T. *The Essence of Decision: Explaining the Cuban Missile Crisis* (Glenview, IL: Scott Foresman and Company, 1971).

Almond, Gabriel A. *The American People and Foreign Policy* (New York: Praeger, 1950).

Alshamisi, Ibrahim Abdulla. *A Perspective on United States Policy Toward the Arab Gulf Countries and Iraq* (Carlisle Barracks, PA: U.S. Army War College, 2005).

Alteras, Isaac. *Eisenhower and Israel: U.S.-Israel Relations, 1953–1960* (Gainesville, FL: University of Florida Press, 1993).

Amayreh, Khalid. "Controversial Move," *Al-Ahram Weekly On-Line*, January 15–21, 2004, available from http://weekly.ahram.org.eg/2004/673/re1.htm; Internet; accessed April 22, 2007.

American-Arab Anti-Discrimination Committee. "2005 ADC Board Resolutions," October 11, 2005, available from www.adc.org/index.php?id = 2524&no_cache = 1&sword_list[] = adc&sword_list[] = res; Internet; accessed March 15, 2006.

——. "ADC Resolutions Adopted at the 2002 National Convention," press release, June 15, 2002, available from www.adc.org/index.php?id = 352&no_cache = 1&sword_list[] = adc&sword_list[] = reso; Internet; accessed March 15, 2006.

American-Arab Anti-Discrimination Committee Research Institute. "Arab Americans," an insert in the *Washington Times*, February 10, 2004.

American Israel Public Affairs Committee (AIPAC). "AIPAC Statement on 2004 Election Results," AIPAC press release, November 3, 2004.

——. "AIPAC Policy Statement, 1987," *Journal of Palestine Studies*, vol. 16, no. 4 (Summer 1987).

——. "Appalling Idea," *Near East Report*, vol. XLVII, no. 19 (November 3, 2003), p. 85.

——. "Bush Says Key to Peace Process is Fighting Terror," *Near East Report*, vol. XLVII, no. 14 (August 11, 2003), p. 63.

——. "Congress says 'Road Map' Should Stick to Bush Vision," *Near East Report*, vol. XLVII, no. 8 (April 28, 2003), pp. 31.

——. "Disarm and Destroy," *Near East Report*, vol. XLVII, no. 10 (May 26, 2003), pp. 39, 42.

——. "Dollars and Sense," *Near East Report*, vol. XLVIII, no. 14 (August 2, 2004), p. 57.

——. "Double Standard," *Near East Report*, vol. XLVIII, no. 18 (October 11, 2004), p. 75.

——. "Historic Agreement Forged," *Near East Report*, vol. XLVIII, no. 8 (April 26, 2004), p. 30.

——. "Iraqi-Palestinian Parallels," *Near East Report*, vol. XLVII, no. 5 (March 17, 2003), p. 18.

——. "Key House Panel Supports Bush's June 24th Criteria," *Near East Report*, vol. XLVII, no. 10 (May 26, 2003), p. 39.

——. "Members of Congress Circulate Letter on Israeli-Palestinian 'Roadmap,'" *Near East Report*, vol. XLVII, no. 7, (April 14, 2003), p. 25.

——. Memorandum from Edward C. Levy, Jr., President Thomas A. Dine, Executive Director, August 3, 1988.

——. "NER Interviews: David Horovitz," *Near East Report*, vol. L, no. 7, (May 8, 2006), p. 30.

——. "Obstacle to Terrorism," *Near East Report*, vol. XLVII, no. 14 (July 28, 2003), p. 57.

——. "Road Map Reality," *Near East Report*, vol. XLVII, no. 9 (May 12, 2003), p. 35.

——. Rodeo, Kiandra. Activist for Bethlehem Group. Email to the author, December 26, 2006.

——. "Shared Concern: U.S., Israeli Lawmakers Meet to Highlight Iran's Nuclear Ambitions," *Near East Report*, vol. XLVII, no. 16 (September 22, 2003), p. 71.

——. "Sideline Arafat," *Near East Report*, vol. XLVII, no. 10 (May 26, 2003), p. 39.

——. "Syria Sanctions Bill Gains Support on Capitol Hill," *Near East Report*, vol. XLVII, no. 16 (September 22, 2003), p. 71.

American Task Force on Palestine. "ATFP Statement on Dismissal of Rafi Dajani," March 9, 2008, available from http://aatimesnews.blogspot.com/2008/03/atfp-statement-on-dismissal-of-rafi.html; Internet; accessed May 5, 2008.

——. "A Vision for the State of Palestine," available from www.americantaskforce.org/pdfs/advocacy_strategy.pdf; Internet; accessed December 22, 2006.

——. "Official Policy Document," available from www.americantaskforce.org/pdfs/policy.pdf; Internet; accessed December 22, 2006.

——. "Two States: Palestine Alongside Israel, Peace in the Middle East, Freedom for Palestine, Security for America," informational flyer, 2006.

——. "Strategies for Advocating Palestinian Statehood," available from www.americantaskforce.org/pdfs/advocacy_strategy.pdf; Internet; accessed December 21, 2006.

——. "Strategic Plan," October 2004, available from www.americantaskforce.org/pdfs/strategy.pdf; Internet; accessed December 21, 2006.

Americans for Peace Now. "Joint AAI/APN Poll: Jewish and Arab Americans Overwhelmingly Support Two-State Solution, U.S. Engagement; Bush Gets Low Marks," available from www.peacenow.org/pr.asp?rid = &cid = 3738; Internet; accessed June 6, 2007.

Ambrosio, Thomas (ed.). *Ethnic Identity Groups and U.S. Foreign Policy* (Westport, CT: Praeger, 2002).

Amirahamdi, Hooshang (ed.). *The United States and the Middle East: A Search for New Perspectives* (Albany, NY: SUNY Press, 1993).

Anderson, Bob and Janelle Rohr (eds), *Israel: Opposing Viewpoints* (San Diego, CA: Greenhaven Press, 1989).

Andriole, Stephen, Jonathan Wilkenfeld, and Gerald W. Hopple. "A Framework for the Comparative Analysis of Foreign Policy Behavior," *International Studies Quarterly*, vol. 19, no. 2 (June 1975), pp. 160–98.

Anti-Defamation League. "ADL Reacts to DePaul's Denial of Tenure to Prof. Norman Finkelstein," press release available from www.adl.org/PresRele/Mise_00/5071_00.htm; Internet; accessed June 11, 2007.

Apter, David E. (ed.). *Ideology and its Discontents* (New York: Free Press, 1964).

Arab American Institute. "A Tale of Two Killings: Observations of Media Bias in Reports of Palestinian and Israeli Deaths," informational flyer, 2001.

——. "AAI Countdown: March 25, 2008-vol. 9, #11, A Regular Update from the Arab American Institute, 223 Days Until Election 2008!" available from www.

aaiusa.org/countdown/3519/pandering-for-the-promised-land;   Internet;   accessed April 7, 2008.
——. "An AAI Summary," in *Politics, Peace and the Presidency, Challenge '92* (Summer 1992), p. 3.
——. "Anti-Semitism Revisited," *Nota Bene* (July 1992), p. 4.
——. "Arab Americans Witness Signing of Historic Peace Accord, Meet with Clinton," *AAI Issues* (Summer 1993), p. 1.
——. "Bush on Palestinian Rights," *Nota Bene* (June 1992), p. 4.
——. "Ending the Deadly Silence, the Arab American Institute at Work – Opening an American Debate on Palestinian Rights," (1990).
——. "Israel's Cold War," *Nota Bene* (March 1993), p. 4.
——. "Jerusalem and the Politics of Obstruction," *Nota Bene* (April/May 1995), p. 2.
——. "Labor-Likud in DC, Too," *Nota Bene* (Summer 1995), pp. 1–2.
——. "Leadership Meets with Secretary Albright, 42 Groups Endorse Statement of Concern," *Issues* (Spring 1997), pp. 1 and 8.
——. "Leading the Way," informational flyer, 2005.
——. "Mutual Commitments, One-Sided Attention," *Nota Bene* (January/February 1996), p. 3.
——. "Palestine Lives" (1988).
——. "Palestinians are a People," informational flyer, 1992.
——. "The Rock and the Hard Place," *Nota Bene* (April/May 1995), pp. 4–5.
——. "The Untold Story," *Nota Bene* (April 1993), p. 1.
——. "White House Overtures for Policy Input: President Clinton Hosts Second Arab American Leadership Delegation," *Issues* (Summer 1996), pp. 1–2.
Arabic News. "Two Arab Organizations Merge, Uncertain on Numbers," December 30, 1999, available from www.arabicnews.com/ansub/Daily/Day/991230/1999123042.html; Internet; accessed July 31, 2006.
Arbel, Ami and Nimrod Novik, "U.S. Pressure on Israel: Likelihood and Scope," *Journal of Conflict Resolution*, vol. 29, no. 2 (June 1985), pp. 253–82.
Areikat, Smaen, Zeinah Salahi, and Khaled Elgindy. "Is a Two-State Solution Still Possible?" Speech before the Johns Hopkins School of Advanced International Studies, April 28, 2005, available from www.mideasti.org/articles/doc372.html; Internet; accessed August 7, 2006.
Arendt, Hannah. "To Save the Jewish Homeland: There is Still Time," *Commentary* (May 1948), pp. 400–403.
Aretxaga, Begoña, Dennis Dworkin, Joseba Gabilondo, and Joseba Zulaika (eds), *Empire and Terror: Nationalism/Postnationalism in the New Millennium* (Reno, NV: University of Nevada Press, 2005).
Aronson, Geoffrey. "Questioning Sacred Cows," *Journal of Palestine Studies*, vol. 19, no. 3 (Spring 1990), pp. 111–16.
Aruri, Naseer. *Occupation: Israel over Palestine* (Belmont, MA: Association of Arab-American University Graduates, 1983).
——. "The United States and Palestine: Reagan's Legacy to Bush," *Journal of Palestine Studies*, vol. 18, no. 3 (Spring 1989), pp. 3–21.
——. "Toward a Pluralistic Existence in Palestine/Israel," in Naseer Aruri and Muhammad A. Shuraydi (eds), *Revising Culture, Reinventing Peace: The Influence of Edward W. Said* (New York: Olive Branch Press, 2001), pp. 120–33.
Aruri, Naseer H. and Fouad Moghrabi. "The Reagan Middle East Initiative," *Journal of Palestine Studies*, vol. 12, no. 2 (Winter 1983), pp. 10–30.

Aruri, Naseer and Muhammad A. Shuraydi. *Dishonest Broker: The U.S. Role in Israel and Palestine* (Cambridge, MA: South End Press, 2003), pp. 217–36.

Aruri, Naseer and Muhammad A. Shuraydi (eds). *Revising Culture, Reinventing Peace: The Influence of Edward W. Said* (New York: Olive Branch Press, 2001).

Asseburg, Muriel, Dominique Moïsi, Gerd Nonneman, and Stephano Silvestri. "The European Union and the Crisis in the Middle East," in Martin Ortega (ed.), *Chaillot Papers*, (Paris: Institute for Security Studies, July 2003).

Association of Arab American University Graduates. *The First Decade: 1967–1977* (Washington, DC: Tammuz, 1977).

Atwan, Ahmad. *The Influence of AIPAC on U.S. Foreign Policy: An Analysis of the Debate and the U.S.-PLO Dialogue* (dissertation at Oxford, 1998).

Austen-Smith, David and William H. Riker. "Asymmetric Information and the Coherence of Legislation," *American Political Science Review*, vol. 81, no. 3 (September 1987), pp. 897–918.

——. "Asymmetric Information and the Coherence of Legislation: A Correction," *American Political Science Review*, vol. 84, no. 1 (March 1990), pp. 243–45.

Austen-Smith, David and John R. Wright. "Counteractive Lobbying," *American Journal of Political Science*, vol. 38, no. 1 (February 1994), pp. 25–44.

Awad, Samir. "Background to the 'Peace Process,'" *Socialism and Democracy*, issue 38, vol. 19, no. 2, available from www.sdonline.org/32/peace_process.htm; Internet; accessed October 12, 2005.

Axelrod, Robert (ed.). *Structure of Decision* (Princeton, NJ: Princeton University Press, 1976).

B'Tselem. The Israeli Center for Human Rights in the Occupied Territories. "Statistics on Fatalities," available from www.btselem.org/english/statistics/Casualties.asp; Internet; accessed December 30, 2007.

Babst, Dean V. "A Force For Peace," *Industrial Research* (1972), pp. 55–58.

Baker, James Addison and Thomas M. DeFrank. *The Politics of Diplomacy: Revolution, War, and Peace, 1989–1992* (New York: Putnam, 1995).

Baker III, James A. and Lee H. Hamilton (co-chairs), *The Iraq Study Group Report*, available from www.usip.org/isg/iraq_study_group_report/report/1206/iraq_study_group_report.pdf; Internet; accessed December 8, 2006.

Baker, Peter. "U.S. Urges Restraint By Israel; Democratic Government Seen Facing Jeopardy in Lebanon," *Washington Post*, July 14, 2006.

Bakhshian, Sara. "Dershowitz Debates Israel-Palestinian Issue," November 17, 2006, available from www.jewishjournal.com/home/preview.php?id = 16809; Internet; accessed June 4, 2007.

Barber, Brian K. "What has Become of the 'Children of the Stone?'" *Palestine-Israel Journal*, vol. VI, no. 4, (1999/2000), pp. 7–15.

Bard, Mitchell Geoffrey. *Myth and Facts: A Guide to the Arab-Israeli Conflict* (Chevy Chase, MD: American-Israeli Cooperative Enterprise, 2001).

——. *The Water's Edge and Beyond: Defining the Limits of Domestic Influence on United States Middle East Policy* (New Brunswick, NJ: Transaction Publishers, 1991).

Barnett, Michael and Martha Finnemore. *Rules for the World: International Organizations in Global Politics* (Ithaca, NY: Cornell University Press, 2004).

Barzak, Ibrahim and Sarah el Deeb. "Bloody Gaza Street Battles Edging Closer to Civil War," *Star-Ledger*, May 17, 2007.

Bayefsky, Anne. "Israel, the United Nations, and the Road Map," *American Foreign Policy Interests*, 24 (2003), pp. 373–94.

Bazinet, Kenneth R. "Mideast Sides Get Earful: Powell Describes U.S. Vision of 2 Peaceful States," *New York Daily News*, November 20, 2001.

Ben-Zvi, Abraham. *Decade of Transition: Eisenhower, Kennedy, and the Origins of the American-Israeli Alliance* (New York: Colombia University Press, 1998).

——. *The United States and Israel* (New York: Colombia University Press, 1994).

Bennet, James. "Israeli Troops Close to Arafat Headquarters," *New York Times*, October 2, 2002.

Bennis, Phyllis. *Before and After: U.S. Foreign Policy and the War on Terrorism* (New York: Olive Branch Press, 2003).

Benvenisti, Meron. Quoted in Association for One Democratic State in Palestine/Israel, "Is the 'Two State Solution' Still a Viable and Desirable Solution to the Israeli-Palestinian Conflict," available from www.one-democratic-state.org/articles/shavit-hanegbi-benvenisti.html; Internet; accessed April 22, 2007.

Berkowitz, Bill. "Christian Right Steps Up Pro-Israel Lobby," available from *Inter Press Service*, July 26, 2006.

Berkowitz, Michael. *Zionist Culture and West European Jewry Before the First World War* (Chapel Hill, NC: University of North Carolina Press, 1996).

Berman, Ari. "AIPAC's Hold," *The Nation*, August 4, 2006, available from www.thenation.com/doc/20060814/aipacs_hold; Internet; accessed August 5, 2006.

Berman, William C. *America's Right Turn: From Nixon to Clinton* (Baltimore, MD: Johns Hopkins University Press, 1998).

Betz, Don. "Introduction to the Uprising in Cartoons: North American Political Cartoonists Look at the Palestinian Uprising" *ADC Issue Paper*, no. 21 (December 9, 1988).

Bin Laden, Osama. "Speech to the American People," *Al Jazeera*, October 29, 2004.

Birnbaum, Jeffrey H. *The Lobbyist: How Influence Peddlers Get Their Way in Washington* (New York: Times Books, 1992).

Bishara, Ghassan. "The Middle East Arms Package: A Survey of the Congressional Debates," *Journal of Palestine Studies*, vol. 7, no. 4 (Summer 1978), pp. 67–78.

Bodansky, Yossef. *The Secret History of the Iraq War* (New York: HarperCollins Books, 2004).

Bose, Meena and Rosanna Perotti (eds). *From Cold War to New World Order: The Foreign Policy of George H. W. Bush* (Westport, CT: Praeger Press, 2002).

Boseley, Sarah. "655,000 Iraqis Killed Since Invasion," *Guardian*, October 11, 2006.

Bremmer III, L. Paul and Malcolm McConnell. *My Year in Iraq: The Struggle to Build a Future of Hope* (New York: Simon and Schuster, 2006).

Brittingham, Angela and G. Patricia de la Cruz. "We the People of Arab Ancestry in the United States." Census 2000 Special Reports, March 2005, available from www.census.gov/prod/2005pubs/censr-21.pdf; Internet; accessed May 19, 2007.

Bronner, Ethan. "After 60 Years, Arabs in Israel Are Outsiders," *New York Times*, May 7, 2008.

——. "Carter Says Hamas and Syria Are Open to Peace," *New York Times*, April 22, 2008.

Brown, Nathan J. *Palestinian Politics after the Oslo Accords: Resuming Arab Palestine* (Berkeley, CA: University of California Press, 2003).

Brzezinski, Zbigniew. *Second Chance: Three Presidents and the Crisis of American Superpower* (New York: Basic Books, 2007).

Buber, Martin (ed.). *Towards Union in Palestine: Essays on Zionism and Jewish-Arab Cooperation* (Westport, CT: Greenwood Press, 1972).

Buckley, Mary and Robert Singh (eds). *The Bush Doctrine and the War on Terrorism: Global Responses, Global Consequences* (New York: Routledge, 2006).

Bush, George W. "Address to a Joint Session of Congress and the American People," September 20, 2001, available from www.whitehouse.gov/news/releases/2001/09/20010920-28.html#; Internet; accessed April 15, 2006.

——. "Executive Order of Alien Unlawful Enemy Combatants by Military Commission," February 14, 2007, available from www.whitehouse.gov/news/releases/2007/02/20070214-15.html; Internet; accessed May 1, 2007.

——. "President Addresses Nation, Discusses Iraq, War on Terror," June 28, 2005, available from www.whitehouse.gov/news/releases/2005/06/20050628-7.html; Internet; accessed December 30, 2006.

——. "President Bush Calls for New Palestinian Leadership," June 24, 2002, available from www.whitehouse.gov/news/releases/2002/06/20020624-3.html; Internet; accessed July 6, 2006.

——. "President Bush Discusses Importance of Democracy in Middle East: Remarks by the President on Winston Churchill and the War on Terror in the Library of Congress," February 4, 2004, available from www.whitehouse.gov/news/releases/2004/02/20040204-4.html; Internet; accessed December 22, 2006.

——. "President Discusses Roadmap for Peace in the Middle East," March 14, 2003, available from www.whitehouse.gov/news/releases/2003/03/20030314-4.html; Internet; accessed March 16, 2006.

——. "Principles for Peace," *Near East Report*, vol. XLIX, no. 5 (March 7, 2005), p.18.

——. "Roadmap for Peace in the Middle East: Israeli/Palestinian Reciprocal Action, Quartet Support" July 16, 2003, available from www.state.gov/r/pa/ei/rls/22520.htm; Internet; accessed August 8, 2006.

——. "Statement by the President," available from www.whitehouse.gov/news/releases/2004/04/20040414-2.html; Internet; accessed December 28, 2005.

Callahan, Patrick. *Logics of American Foreign Policy: Theories of America's World Role* (New York: Pearson-Longman, 2004).

Cameron, Fraser. *US Foreign Policy After the Cold War* (New York: Routledge, 2002).

Campbell, Colin. *The George W. Bush Presidency: Appraisals and Prospects* (Washington, DC: CQ Press, 2004).

Carter, Jimmy. *Palestine: Peace not Apartheid* (New York: Simon and Schuster, 2006).

——. Question by the author, Chicago, IL, April 30, 2008.

Carter, John J. *Covert Operations as a Tool of Presidential Foreign Policy from 1800–1920: Foreign Policy in the Shadows* (Lewiston, NY: Edwin Mellen Press, 2000).

Center for Responsive Politics. "Arab-American and Muslim PAC Contributions, 1989–2002," available from www.opensecrets.org/news/pro-israel.pro-arab/pro-arab.asp; Internet; accessed August 13, 2006.

——. "Pro-Israel: Long Term Contribution Trends," available from www.opensecrets.org/industries/indus.asp?Ind = Q05; Internet; accessed August 13, 2006.

——. "Pro-Israel and Pro-Arab Interests: The Money," available from www.opensecrets.org/news/pro-israel.pro-arab/index.asp; Internet; accessed August 13, 2006.

Central Intelligence Agency. *The World Fact Book*, available from www.odci.gov/cia/publications/factbook/; Internet; accessed May 27, 2006.

Chan, Steve. "Mirror, Mirror On The Wall … Are Democratic States More Pacific?" *Journal of Conflict Resolution*, vol. 28 (1984), pp. 617–48.

Chartrand, Sabra. "After the War: The West Bank Palestinians Still Revere Hussein as their Savior," *New York Times*, March 4, 1991.

Chatfield, Laura and Carmen Gentile. "Pro-Arab Lobby Gaining in Strength in U.S.," *United Press International*, June 20, 2001.

Chatterjee, Sumana and Tish Wells. "Groups Involved in the Middle East," *Knight Ridder/Tribune News Service*, April 14, 2002.

Checkel, Jeffrey T. *Ideas and International Political Change: Soviet/Russian Behavior and the End of the Cold War* (New Haven, CT: Yale University Press, 1997).

Cheney, Richard B. "Policy Conference 2006 Closing Plenary Leadership Perspective: The U.S.-Israel Relationship," March 6, 2006, available from www.aipac.org/Publications/SpeechesByPolicymakers/Cheney-PC-2006.pdf; Internet; accessed May 1, 2007.

Chernaik, Laura. *Social and Virtual Space: Science Fiction, Transnationalism, and the American New Right* (Cranbury, NJ: Rosemont Publishing, 2005).

Chittick, William O. and Keith R. Billingsly. "The Structure of Elite Foreign Policy Beliefs," *Western Political Quarterly* (1989).

Chomsky, Noam. *The Fateful Triangle: The United States, Israel and the Palestinians* (London: Pluto Press, 1999).

——. "The Israel Lobby?" March 28, 2006, available from www.zmag.org/content/showarticle.cfm?ItemID = 9999; Internet; accessed June 14, 2006.

Chomsky, Noam and Carlos Peregrín Otero. *Language and Politics* (Oakland, CA: AK Press, 2004), pp. 185–203.

Christison, Kathleen. "All Those Old Issues: George W. Bush and the Palestinian-Israeli Conflict," *Journal of Palestine Studies*, vol. 33, no. 2 (Winter 2004), pp. 36–50.

——. "Bound by a Frame of Reference, Part II: U.S. Policy and the Palestinians, 1948–88," *Journal of Palestine Studies*, vol. 27, no. 3 (Spring 1998), pp. 20–34.

——. "Bound by a Frame of Reference, Part III: U.S. Policy and the Palestinians, 1988–98," *Journal of Palestine Studies*, vol. 27, no. 4 (Summer 1998), pp. 53–64.

——. *Perceptions of Palestine: Their Influence on U.S. Middle East Policy* (Berkeley, CA: University of California Press, 1999).

——. "Splitting the Difference: The Palestinian-Israeli Policy of James Baker," *Journal of Palestine Studies*, vol. 24, no. 1 (Autumn 1994), pp. 39–50.

——. "The 'Fuller Report,'" *Journal of Palestine Studies*, vol. 19, no. 4 (Summer 1990), pp. 106–11.

——. *The Wound of Dispossession: Telling the Palestinian Story* (Santa Fe, NM: Sunlit Hills Press, 2001).

Ciglar, Allan and Burdett A. Loomis. *Interest Group Politics*, 2nd ed. (Washington, DC: CQ Press, 1986).

Clancy, Jim. "Italy Willing to Lead United Nations Forces in Southern Lebanon," on *Your World Today*, August 21, 2006, available from http://transcripts.cnn.com/TRANSCRIPTS/0608/21/ywt.01.html; Internet; accessed December 28, 2006.

Clark, Duncan L., Daniel B. O'Conner, and Jason D. Ellis. *Send Guns and Money: Security Assistance and US Foreign Policy* (Westport, CT: Praeger, 1997).

Clarke, Duncan L. and Eric Flohr. "Christian Churches and the Palestine Question," *Journal of Palestine Studies*, vol. 21, no. 4 (Summer 1992), pp. 67–79.

Claude, Jr., Inis L. "The United Nations, the United States, and the Maintenance of Peace," *International Organization*, vol. 23, no. 3, The United States and International Organization: The Changing Setting (Summer 1969), pp. 621–36.

Cobban, Helen. *The Superpowers and the Syrian-Israeli Conflict* (Washington, DC: Praeger, 1991).

Cockburn, Alexander and Jeffrey St. Clair (eds). *The Politics of Anti-Semitism* (Edinburgh: AK Press, 2003).

Cockburn, Andrew. "Democrats Okay Funds for Covert Ops, Secret Bush 'Finding' Widens War on Iran," *Counterpunch*, May 2, 2008, available from www.counterpunch. org/andrew05022008.html; Internet; accessed May 4, 2008.

Cohen, Bernard C. *The Influence of Non-Governmental Groups on Foreign Policy Making* (Boston, MA: World Peace Foundation, 1959).

——. *The Press and Foreign Policy* (Princeton, NJ: Princeton University Press, 1963).

——. *The Public's Impact on Foreign Policy* (Boston, MA: Little, Brown, 1973).

Cohen, Eliot A. "Yes It's Anti-Semitic," *Washington Post*, April 5, 2006.

Cohen, Jeffrey E. "Presidential Rhetoric and the Public Agenda," *American Journal of Political Science*, vol. 39, no. 1 (February 1995), pp. 87–107.

Cohen, Patricia. "A Bitter Spat Over Ideas, Israel and Tenure," *New York Times*, April 12, 2007.

——. "Outspoken Political Scientist Denied Tenure at DePaul," *New York Times*, June 11, 2007.

Cohen, Richard. "No It's Not Anti-Semitic," *Washington Post*, April 25, 2006.

Cohen, Stephen P, Michael C. Hudson, Nathan Guttman, and Khalil E. Jahshan. "Is a Two-State Solution Still Viable?" *Middle East Policy*, vol. X, no. 2 (Summer 2003), p. 10.

Cohen, Yinon. *Arab and Jewish Out-Migration from Israel and the Occupied Territories to the U.S.* (Tel Aviv, Israel: University of Tel Aviv, 1994).

Conference of Presidents of Major American Jewish Organizations. "American Jewish Leaders Issue Major Statement on Disengagement," August 16, 2005, available from www.conferenceofpresidents.org/disengagementaug.pdf; Internet; accessed July 13, 2006.

——. "Member Organizations," available from www.conferenceofpresidents.org/ Members.pdf; Internet; accessed July 6, 2006.

Cooper, Helene. "U.S. Feels Sting of Winning Saudi Help With Other Arabs," *New York Times*, March 30, 2007.

Corm, Georges. "Avoiding the Obvious: Arab Perspectives on US Hegemony in the Middle East," *Middle East Report*, no. 208, US Foreign Policy in the Middle East: Critical Assessments (Autumn 1998), pp. 23–25.

Cottam, Martha L. *Foreign Policy Decision-Making: The Influence of Cognition* (Boulder, CO: Westview Press, 1986).

Council on American-Islamic Relations. "Thank Those in Congress Who Did Not Vote for Pro-Israel Resolutions," May 3, 2002, available from www.cair.com/ default.asp?Page = articleView&id = 110&theType = Aal; Internet; accessed January 14, 2007.

——. "What's CAIR's Vision and Mission?" available from www.cair.com/default. asp?Page = About; Internet; accessed January 14, 2007.

Crawford, Kenneth G. *The Pressure Boys: The Inside Story of Lobbying in America* (New York: Arno Press, 1974).

Cummings, Jr., Milton C., and David Wise. *Democracy Under Pressure: An Introduction to the American Political System*, 10th ed. (Boston, MA: Thomson Publishers, 2007), chapters 6 and 7.

Curtis, Alan (ed.). *Patriotism, Democracy, and Common Sense: Restoring America's Promise at Home and Abroad* (New York: Rowman and Littlefield, 2004).

Curtiss, Richard H. *Stealth PACs: Lobbying Congress for Control of U.S. Middle East Policy*, 4th ed. (Washington, DC: The American Educational Trust, 1996).

Cypel, Sylvain. *Walled: Israeli Society at an Impasse* (New York: Other Press, 2007).

Dahl, Robert. *A Preface to Democratic Theory* (Chicago: University of Chicago Press, 1956).

——. *On Democracy* (New Haven, CT: Yale University Press, 1988).

Dajani, Rafi, former executive director of American Task Force on Palestine, Interview by the author, Washington, DC, March 15, 2006.

Daraghmeh, Mohammed. "Hamas Official Says Group Ready for 'Two-State' Solution with Israel," available from *Associated Press*, April 7, 2006.

Davis, Joyce M. *Martyrs: Innocence, Vengeance, and Despair in the Middle East* (New York: Palgrave, 2003).

Davis, Scott M., and Christopher Kline. *The Role of the Public in Foreign Policy Making: An Overview of the Literature* (Washington, DC: Roosevelt Center for American Policy Studies, 1988).

De Azcárate, Pablo. *Mission in Palestine, 1948–52* (Washington, DC: The Middle East Institute, 1966).

De Rivera, Joseph. *The Psychological Dimension of Foreign Policy* (Columbus, OH: C. E. Merrill Publishing Company, 1968).

De Rooij, Paul. "The Carnivores and the Ivy League Apologist: The Voices of Sharon's Little Helpers," *Counterpunch*, December 9, 2004, available from www. counterpunch.org/rooij12092004.html; Internet; accessed May 4, 2008.

De Soto, Alvaro. "End of Mission Report," May 2007, available from http://image. guardian.co.uk/sys-files/Guardian/documents/2007/06/12/DeSotoReport.pdf; Internet; accessed June 13, 2007.

Deakin, James. *The Lobbyists* (Washington, DC: Public Affairs Press, 1966).

"Declaration of Independence." November 15, 1988, available from www.palestine-net.com/politics/indep.html; Internet; accessed June 11, 2007.

"Declaration of Principles," available from www.fmep.org/resources/peace_plans/oslo_accords.html; Internet; accessed October 24, 2005.

"Declaration of Principles on Interim Self-Government Arrangements," available from www.jewishvirtuallibrary.org/jsource/Peace/dop.html; Internet; accessed January 27, 2006.

Delmar, Mark Lewis. "Americans Accept Decline of Moral Standing," *The Times Union*, May 20, 2004.

Dershowitz, Alan. "Debunking the Newest – and Oldest – Jewish Conspiracy: A Reply to the Mearsheimer-Walt 'Working Paper,'" Harvard Law School, April 2006, available from www.ksg.harvard.edu/research/working_papers/dershowitzreply.pdf; Internet; accessed June 14, 2006.

——. *The Case for Israel* (Hoboken, NJ: John Wiley, 2003).

Dine, Thomas A. "The Revolution in U.S.-Israel Relations," *Journal of Palestine Studies*, vol. 15, no. 4 (Summer 1986), p. 138.

Dixon, William J. "Democracy and the Management of International Conflict," *Journal of Conflict Resolution*, vol. 37 (1993), pp. 42–68.

Dobnik, Verena. "Palestinian-Americans Mark 60 Years Displaced," *Chicago Tribune*, May 16, 2008.

Douglas, William. "Olmert Says Israel 'Cannot Wait for the Palestinians Forever,'" *San Jose Mercury News*, May 24, 2006.

Doumani, Beshara. "They Dare to Speak Out: People and Institutions Confront Israel's Lobby," book review, *MERIP Middle East Report*, no. 140, Terrorism and Intervention (May-June 1986), p. 36.

Doyle, Michael W. "Kant, Liberal Legacies and Foreign Affairs Part I," *Philosophy and Public Affairs*, vol. 12, no. 3 (1983), pp. 323–53.

———. "Michael Doyle on the Democratic Peace," *International Security*, vol. 19 (1995), pp. 180–184.

Drinkard, Jim. "Legislator Warns Israel on Expansion of Settlements," available from *Associated Press*, June 27, 1990.

Dunstan, Simon. *The Yom Kippur War 1973: The Sinai* (Oxford: Osprey Publishing, 2003).

Dye, Thomas R. *Politics in America*, 4th ed. (Upper Saddle River, NJ: Prentice Hall, 2001).

East, Maurice A. "Size and Foreign Policy Behavior: A Test of Two Models," *World Politics*, vol. 25, no. 3 (July 1973), pp. 556–76.

East, Maurice A., Stephen A. Salmore, and Charles F. Hermann (eds). *Why Nations Act* (Beverly Hills, CA: Sage, 1978).

Editors. "Americans' Attitudes toward the Middle East," *Journal of Palestine Studies*, vol. 12, no. 3 (Spring 1983), pp. 134–46.

Editors. "Palestine and Israel in the US Arena," *Middle East Report*, no. 158, Palestine and Israel in the US Arena (May-June 1989), pp. 4–5+42.

Edwards III, George C. and B. Dan Wood. "Who Influences Whom? The President, Congress, and the Media," *American Political Science Review*, vol. 93, no. 2 (June 1999), pp. 327–44.

Edwards III, George C. and Tami Swenson. "Who Rallies: The Anatomy of a Rally Event," *The Journal of Politics*, vol. 59, no. 1 (February 1997), pp. 200–212.

Ehrlich, Deborah. "New Jewish Agenda Convention Urges Recognition of PLO," *MERIP Reports*, no. 136–37, West Bank, Gaza, Israel: Marching Toward Civil War (October-December 1985).

Einstein, Albert. *Ideas and Opinions* (New York: Crown Publishers, 1954).

Eisenberg, Laura Zittrain and Neil Caplan. *Negotiating Arab-Israeli Peace: Patterns, Problems, Possibilities* (Indianapolis, IN: Indiana University Press, 1998).

El Deeb, Sarah. "23 Killed in Gaza, Deadliest Day There Since Israel Withdrew Last Year." available from *Associated Press*, July 27, 2006.

Electronic Intifada. "About EI," available from http://electronicintifada.net/v2/aboutEI.shtml; Internet; accessed May 5, 2008.

Ellis, Harry B. *The Dilemma of Israel: United States Interests in the Middle East* (Washington, DC: American Enterprise Institute for Public Policy Research, 1970).

Elmusa, Sharif. S. "Shorter Notices," *Journal of Palestine Studies*, vol. 20, no. 3 (Spring 1991), pp. 130–32.

Erlanger, Steven. "Israel Continues Airstrikes Against Hamas, as Rival Palestinian Factions Battle in Gaza," *New York Times*, May 19, 2007.

Esposito, John L. *Unholy War: Terror in the Name of Islam* (New York: Oxford University Press, 2003).

Falk, Richard. "Stalemate and Stagnation: United States Policy in the Near East. An Interview with Richard Falk," *Journal of Palestine Studies*, vol. 8, no. 1 (Autumn 1978), pp. 85–89.

Falkowski, Lawrence S. (ed.). *Psychological Models in International Politics* (Boulder, CO: Westview Press, 1979).

Fallows, James. *Breaking the News: How the Media Undermine American Democracy* (New York: Pantheon, 1996).

Farrell, Barry (ed.). *Approaches in Comparative and International Politics* (Evanston, IL: Northwestern University Press, 1966).

Feingold, Russell D. "Remarks on the Feingold-Reid Amendment As Prepared for Delivery from the Senate Floor," May 16, 2007, available from www.commondreams. org/news2007/0516-05.htm; Internet; accessed May 22, 2007.

Feith, Douglas. *War and Decision: Inside the Pentagon at the Dawn of the War on Terrorism* (New York: HarperCollins Books, 2008).

Findley, Paul. "Congress and the Pro-Israel Lobby," *Journal of Palestine Studies*, vol. 15, no. 1 (Autumn 1985), pp. 104–13.

——. *They Dare to Speak Out: People and Institutions Confront Israel's Lobby* (Westport, CT: Lawrence Hill and Company, 1985).

Fineman, Howard, Tamara Lipper, Holly Bailey, and Richard Wolf. "A Very Mixed Marriage," *Newsweek*, vol. 141, issue 22 (June 6, 2003), pp. 34–36.

Finkelstein, Norman G. *Beyond Chutzpah: On the Misuse of Anti-Semitism and the Abuse of History* (Berkeley, CA: University of California Press, 2005).

——. *Image and Reality of the Israel-Palestine Conflict* (London: Verso, 2001).

——. Professor of Political Science at DePaul University, conversation with the author, Chicago, IL, October 25, 2006.

——. *The Holocaust Industry: Reflections on the Exploitation of Jewish Suffering* (New York: Verso, 2000).

Ford, Peter. "Why do They Hate Us?" *Christian Science Monitor*, September 27, 2001.

Forman, David. "Opinion: The Arab Lobby Grows," *Jerusalem Post*, May 10, 2007.

Forsythe, David P., Patrice C. McMahon, and Andrew Wedeman (eds). *American Foreign Policy in a Globalized World* (New York: Routledge, 2006).

Foster, Schuyler H. *Activism Replaces Isolationism* (Washington, DC: Foxhall, 1983).

Foundation for Middle East Peace. "Israel Settler Population 1972–2006," available from www.fmep.org/settlement_info/stats_data/settler_populations/Israeli_settler_ population_in_occupied_territories.html; Internet; accessed March 25, 2008.

——. "West Bank Separation Barrier – July 2006," by Jan de Jong, cartographer, available from www.fmep.org/maps/map_data/west_bank/west_bank_separation_ba rrier-july2006.pdf; Internet; accessed March 25, 2008.

Fowler, Robert Booth, Laura Olson, and Allen Hertzke. *Religion and Politics in America: Faith, Culture, and Strategic Choices* (Boulder, CO: Westview Press, 1999), pp. 75–84.

Foyle, Douglas C. "Public Opinion and Foreign Policy: Elite Beliefs as a Mediating Variable," *International Studies Quarterly*, vol. 41, no. 1 (March 1997), pp. 141–69.

Frankel, Glenn. "A Beautiful Friendship," *Washington Post*, July 16, 2006.

Frankel, Jeffrey A. and Peter R. Orszag (eds). *American Economic Policy in the 1990s* (Cambridge, MA: MIT Press, 2002).

Franks, Douglas. "U.S.-Israeli Free Trade Agreement: Aid to Israel Takes New Form," *Journal of Palestine Studies*, vol. 14, no. 2, Special Issue: The Palestinians in Israel and the Occupied Territories (Winter 1985), pp. 169–71.

Freedman, Robert O. "The Bush Administration and the Israeli-Palestinian Conflict: A Preliminary Evaluation," *American Foreign Policy Interests*, vol. 25 (2003), pp. 505–11.

Freedman, Robert O. (ed.). *The Intifada and its Impact on Israel, the Arab World, and the Superpowers* (Gainesville, FL: Florida International University Press, 1991).

Friedman, Rachel Zabarkes. "Senator Israel: Hillary Runs from her Past," *National Review*, May 25, 2005.

Friedman, Robert R. "Selling Israel to America," *Journal of Palestine Studies*, vol. 16, no. 4 (Summer 1987), pp. 169–79.

Friedman, Thomas L. "Marines' View of Beirut Mission: To 'Hunker Down and Bunker In,'" *New York Times*, December 2, 1983.

Fukuyama, Francis. "After Neoconservatism," *New York Times Magazine*, February 19, 2006.

Gable, Richard W. "Interest Groups as Policy Shapers," *Annals of the American Academy of Political Science* (September 1958).

Gadahn, Adam. "Message to President Bush," *As Sahab*, May 29, 2007.

Gaenslen, Fritz. "Culture and Decision Making in China, Japan, Russia, and the United States," *World Politics*, vol. 39, no. 1 (October 1986), pp. 78–103.

Gallup Poll. "Gallup Brain," 1955–2005.

Gates, C. L. "The Lebanese Lobby in the U.S.," *MERIP Reports*, no. 73 (December 1978), pp, 17–19.

"Gaza Humanitarian Situation 'Worst Since 1967,'" *Belfast Telegraph*, March 6, 2008, available from www.belfasttelegraph.co.uk/breaking-news/world/middle-east/article3493041.ece; Internet; accesses March 8, 2008.

Gearan, Anne. "Rice: Israelis and Palestinians Must Agree on Final Borders," *Associated Press*, May 1, 2008.

Geertz, Clifford. *The Interpretation of Cultures* (New York: Basic Books, 1973).

General Assembly of the UN. Resolution 46/86. December 16, 1991, available from www.jewishvirtuallibrary.org/jsource/UN/unga46_86.html; Internet; accessed May 6, 2008.

——. Resolution 3379. November 10, 1975, available from www.jewishvirtuallibrary.org/jsource/UN/unga3379.html; Internet; accessed October 12, 2005.

George, Alexander. "The 'Operational Code': A Neglected Approach to the Study of Political Leaders and Decision-making," *International Studies Quarterly*, 13 (1969), pp. 190–222.

George, Alexander (ed.). *Presidential Decisionmaking in Foreign Policy: The Effective Use of Information and Advice* (Boulder, CO: Westview Press, 1980).

Gergen, David. "There is No Israel Lobby," *New York Daily News*, March 26, 2006.

Gerges, Fawaz A. *America and Political Islam: Clash of Cultures or Clash of Interests* (New York: Cambridge University Press, 1999).

Gerner, Deborah J. *One Land, Two Peoples: The Conflict over Palestine*, 2nd ed. (Boulder, CO: Westview Press, 1994).

Gerstenfel, Manfred. "The Mohammed-Cartoon Controversy, Israel, and the Jews: A Case Study," in Jerusalem Center for Public Affairs, *Post-Holocaust and Anti-Semitism*, no. 43 (April 4, 2006), available from www.jcpa.org/phas/phas-043-gerstenfeld.htm; Internet; accessed January 21, 2007.

Ghanem, As'ad. "A New Phase in Israel's Approach to the Palestinian Question: A Solution Based on the Concept of a Joint Entity Cannot be Ruled Out," *Palestine-Israel Journal of Politics Economics and Culture*, vol. 13, no. 2 (2006), pp. 35–41.

Gilboa, Eytan. *American Public Opinion toward Israel and the Arab-Israeli Conflict* (Lexington, MA: Lexington Books, 1986).

Gilens, Martin. *Why Americans Hate Welfare: Race, Media, and the Politics of Anti-Poverty Policy* (Chicago, IL: University of Chicago Press, 1999).

Gisha Legal Center for Freedom of Movement. "Disengaged Occupiers: The Legal Status of Gaza," January 17, 2007, available from www.gisha.org/english/reports/Report_for_the_website.pdf; Internet; accessed January 26, 2007.

Gleditsch, Nils Petter. "Democracy and Peace," *Journal of Peace Research*, vol. 29 (1992), pp. 369–76.

Gleichert, Christine. Capitol Hill lobbyist for American-Arab Anti-Discrimination Committee. Interview by the author, Washington, DC, March 15, 2006.

Gold, Dore. *Hatred's Kingdom: How Saudi Arabia Supports the New Global Terrorism* (Washington, DC: Regnery Publishing, 2003).

Goodman, Walter. "Review/Television; The Palestinian View, Between Bookends," *New York Times*, September 6, 1989.

"Gore-Bush Debates," on October 1 and October 11, 2000, available from www.debates.org/; Internet; accessed July 6, 2006.

Gorenberg, Gershom. *The Accidental Empire: Israel and the Birth of the Settlements, 1967–1977* (New York: Times Books, 2006).

Graber, Doris. *Media Power in Politics* (Washington, DC: CQ Press, 2000).

Grammy, Abbas P. and Kaye C. Bragg. *United States–Third World Relations in the New World Order* (New York: Nova Science Publishers, 1996).

Greenwald, Carol S. *Group Power* (New York: Praeger, 1977).

Grosz, Allison. "Former Congressman Explains Role of Israel in U.S. Policy," *The Daily Vidette*, September 18, 2006, available from www.dailyvidette.com/media/storage/paper420/news/2006/09/18/News/Former.Congressman.Explains.Role.Of.Isr ael.In.U.s.Policy-2281247.shtml?norewrite200612100211&sourcedomain = www.dailyvidette.com; Internet; accessed December 10, 2006.

Gudykunst, William, L. Stewart, and Stella Ting-Toomey. *Communication, Culture, and Organizational Process* (Beverly Hills, CA: Sage, 1985).

Guttman, Nathan. "Dovish Groups Mull Mega-Merger in Bid to Build Peace Powerhouse," *The Jewish Daily Forward*, May 30, 2007, available from www.forw ard.com/articles/dovish-groups-mull-mega-merger-in-bid-to-build-pea/;   Internet; accessed June 6, 2007.

Hadar, Leon T. "Clinton's Tilt," *Journal of Palestine Studies*, vol. 22, no. 4 (Summer 1993), pp. 62–72.

——. "High Noon in Washington: The Shootout over the Loan Guarantees," *Journal of Palestine Studies*, vol. 21, no. 2 (Winter 1992), pp. 72–87.

——. "Thawing the American-Israeli Chill," *Journal of Palestine Studies*, vol. 22, no. 2 (Winter 1993), pp. 78–89.

——. "The Last Days of Likud: The American-Israeli Big Chill," *Journal of Palestine Studies*, vol. 21, no. 4 (Summer 1992), pp. 80–94.

——. "Was It All Worth It?" *Journal of Palestine Studies*, vol. 20, no. 4 (Summer 1991), pp. 124–32.

Hajj, Bana. "War in Lebanon and War on Terror," *Washington Report on Middle East Affairs* (December 2006), pp. 57–58.

Halperin, Morton H. *Bureaucratic Politics and Foreign Policy* (Washington, DC: Brookings Institution Press, 1974).

Halperin, Morton H. and Arnold Kanter (eds). *Readings in American Foreign Policy: A Bureaucratic Perspective* (Boston, MA: Little, Brown, 1973).

Hamidi, Yasmin, Arab-American activist, email to the author, May 18, 2008.

Hanegbi, Haim. Quoted in Association for One Democratic State in Palestine/Israel, "Is the 'Two State Solution' Still a Viable and Desirable Solution to the Israeli-Palestinian Conflict?" available from www.one-democratic-state.org/articles/shavit-hanegbi-benvenisti.html; Internet; accessed April 22, 2007.

Haney, Patrick J. and Walt Vanderbrush. "The Role of Ethnic Interest Groups in U.S. Foreign Policy: The Case of the Cuban American National Foundation," *International Studies Quarterly*, vol. 43, no. 2 (June 1999), pp. 341–61.

Hanley, Delinda C. "Israeli Elections and Palestinian Prospects," *Washington Report on Middle East Affairs* (January/February 2003), pp. 68–70.

Hansen, John Mark. *Gaining Access: Congress and the Farm Lobby, 1919–1981* (Chicago, IL: University of Chicago Press, 1991).

Harry S. Truman Institute for the Advancement of Peace. "Majority Support among Palestinians and Israelis for the Road Map and for Mutual Recognition," available from http://truman.huji.ac.il/polls.asp; Internet; accessed July 2, 2006.

Hayden, Patrick, Tom Lansford, and Robert P. Watson (eds). *America's War on Terror* (Burlington, VT: Ashgate Publishing Company, 2004).

Hazan, Reuven Y. "Intraparty Politics and Peacemaking in Democratic Societies: Israel's Labor Party and the Middle East Peace Process, 1992–96" *Journal of Peace Research*, vol. 37, no. 3 (May 2000), pp. 363–78.

Hedges, Chris. "Palestinians Struggling to Rebuild their Lives," *New York Times*, October 4, 1990.

Heitshusen, Valerie. "Interest Group Lobbying and U.S. House Decentralization: Linking Informational Facts to Committee Hearing Appearances," *Political Research Quarterly*, vol. 53, no. 1 (March 2000), pp. 151–76.

Heller, Jeffrey. "Sharon Vows to Seek Peace but Big Settlements to Stay," available from www.alertnet.org/thenews/newsdesk/L01537146.htm; Internet; accessed December 2, 2005.

Henry, Marilyn and Jay Bushinsky. "Hillary Clinton Says Palestinians Deserve an Independent State," *Jerusalem Post*, May 8, 1998.

Hermann, Charles F., Charles W. Kegley, Jr., and James N. Rosenau (eds). *New Directions in the Study of Foreign Policy* (Boston, MA: Allen and Unwin, 1987).

Hermann, Margaret G. "Explaining Foreign Policy behavior Using Personal Characteristics of Political Leaders," *International Studies Quarterly*, 24 (1980), pp. 7–46.

Hermann, Margaret G (ed.). *A Psychological Examination of Political Leaders* (New York: The Free Press, 1977).

Hermann, Margaret G. and Charles W. Kegley Jr., "Rethinking Democracy and International Peace: Perspectives from Political Psychology," *International Studies Quarterly*, 39 (1995), pp. 511–33.

Herrmann, Richard K. "The Middle East and the New World Order: Rethinking U.S. Political Strategy after the Gulf War," *International Security*, vol. 16, no. 2 (Autumn 1991), pp. 42–75.

Hersh, Seymour. "Watching Lebanon: Washington's Interests in Israel's War," *New Yorker*, August 21, 2006.

Herzog, Chaim. "Response to Zionism is Racism Resolution," available from www.jewishvirtuallibrary.org/jsource/UN/herzogsp.html; Internet; accessed October 12, 2005.

Hill, Christopher. *The Changing Politics of Foreign Policy* (New York: Palgrave Macmillan, 2003).

Hilsman, Roger. *To Move a Nation* (New York: Doubleday Press, 1967).

Hinckley, Barbara. *Less Than Meets the Eye: Foreign Policy Making and the Myth of the Assertive Congress* (Chicago, IL: University of Chicago Press, 1994).

Hinckley, Ronald H. *People, Polls, and Policymakers: American Public Opinion and National Security* (New York: Lexington Books, 1992).

——. "Public Attitudes toward Key Foreign Policy Events," *Journal of Conflict Resolution*, vol. 32, no. 2 (June 1988), pp. 295–318.

Hirst, David. *The Gun and the Olive Branch: The Roots of Violence in the Middle East* (New York: Nation Books).

Hodges, Sam. "Alabama Statesman Says U.S. Biased against Palestinians," *Washington Report on Middle East Affairs*, vol. 19, no. 2 (March 2000), pp. 21–23.

Hojnacki, Marie and David C. Kimball. "Organized Interests and the Decision of Whom to Lobby in Congress," *American Political Science Review*, vol. 92, no. 4 (December 1998), pp. 775–90.

——. "The Who and How of Organizations' Lobbying Strategies in Committee," *Journal of Politics*, vol. 61, no. 4 (November 1999), pp. 999–1024.

Hogan, Michael J. (ed.). *America in the World: The Historiography of American Foreign Relations Since 1941* (New York: Cambridge University Press, 1995).

——. *The End of the Cold War: Its Meaning and Implications* (Cambridge: Cambridge University Press, 1992).

Hoge, Warren. "U.S. Vetoes Security Council Resolution Assailing Israel for Attacks," *New York Times*, November 12, 2006.

Holsti, Ole R. *Making American Foreign Policy* (New York: Routledge, 2006).

——. *Public Opinion and American Foreign Policy* (Ann Arbor, MI: University of Michigan Press, 1996).

——. *Public Opinion and American Foreign Policy*, revised ed. (Ann Arbor, MI: University of Michigan Press, 2004).

——. "The 'Operational Code' as An Approach to the Analysis of Belief Systems," final report to the National Science Foundation (Durham, NC: Duke University Press, 1977).

——. "The 'Operational Code' Approach to the Study of Political Leaders: John Foster Dulles' Philosophical and Instrumental Beliefs," *Canadian Journal of Political Science/Revue Canadienne de science politique*, vol. 3, no. 1 (March 1970), pp. 123–57.

Holyoke, Thomas T. "Choosing Battlegrounds: Interest Group Lobbying Across Multiple Venues," *Political Research Quarterly*, vol. 56, no. 3 (September 2003), pp. 325–36.

Holzman, Abraham. *Interest Groups and Lobbying* (New York: Macmillan, 1966).

Hook, Steven W. *U.S. Foreign Policy: The Paradox of World Power* (Washington, DC: CQ Press, 2005).

Hopple, G. W. (ed.). *Biopolitics, Political Psychology, and International Politics* (New York: St. Martin's Press, 1982).

House Committee on Intelligence. "Key Findings of Congressional Delegation to the Middle East," July 21–25, 2006.

House Concurrent Resolution 280. "Expressing Solidarity with Israel in the Fight Against Terrorism," December 5, 2001, available from www.jewishvirtuallibrary. org/jsource/US-Israel/Con280.html; Internet; accessed April 7, 2008.

House Resolution 2508, section 2001. "Palestinian Schools and Universities in the West Bank and Gaza Strip," 1991, available from http://thomas.loc.gov/cgi-bin/ query/F?c102:2:./temp/~mdbsM5Q2cG:e514886; Internet; accessed April 20, 2007.

Howe, Russell W. and Sarah H. Trott. *The Power Peddlers: How Lobbyists Mold America's Foreign Policy* (Garden City, NY: Doubleday and Co., 1977).

Hudson, Valerie M. (ed.). *Artificial Intelligence and International Politics* (Boulder, CO: Westview Press, 1991).

Hudson, Valerie M. (ed.). *Culture and Foreign Policy* (Boulder, CO: Lynne Rienner, 1997).

Hudson, Valerie M. and Christopher S. Vore. "Foreign Policy Analysis Yesterday, Today, and Tomorrow," *Mershon International Studies Review*, vol. 39, no. 2 (October 1995), pp. 209–38.

Human Rights Watch. "Israel/Lebanon: Hezbollah Must End Attacks on Civilians," August 5, 2006, available from http://hrw.org/english/docs/2006/08/05/lebano13921. htm; Internet; accessed December 28, 2006.

——. "Lebanon: Hezbollah Rocket Attacks on Haifa Designed to Kill Civilians – Anti-Personnel Ball Bearings Meant to Harm 'Soft' Targets," July 18, 2006, available from http:// hrw.org/english/docs/2006/07/18/lebano13760.htm; Internet; accessed January 28, 2007.

Huntington, Samuel. "Strategic Planning and the Political Process," *Foreign Affairs* vol. 38, no. 2 (1960), pp. 285–99.

Hymans, Jacques E. C. *The Psychology of Nuclear Proliferation: Identity, Emotions, and Foreign Policy* (Cambridge: Cambridge University Press, 2006).

Ibish, Hussein. Executive director of the Hala Foundation, senior fellow at American Task Force on Palestine, and former communications director at American-Arab Anti-Discrimination Committee. Interview by the author, Washington, DC, November 13, 2006.

——. "Is Arab-American Irrelevance Our Goal?" *Daily Star*, Friday, May 19, 2006.

Ibish, Hussein (ed.). *An Arab Guide to American Politics* (Washington, DC, work in progress, forthcoming, 2009).

Ibish, Hussein and Laila Al-Qatami (eds). *1998–2000 Report on Hate Crimes and Discrimination Against Arab Americans* (Washington, DC: ADC Research Institute, 2001), available from www.adc.org/hatecrimes/pdf/1998-2000.pdf; Internet; accessed April 7, 2008.

Ibish, Hussein and Saliba Sarsar (eds). *Principles and Pragmatism: Key Documents from the American Task Force on Palestine* (Washington, DC: American Task Force on Palestine, October 2006).

Ibrahim, Ibrahim I. "The American-Israeli Alliance: Raison d'etat Revisited," *Journal of Palestine Studies*, vol. 15, no. 3 (Spring 1986), pp. 17–29.

Ibrahim, Saad. "American Domestic Forces and the October War," *Journal of Palestine Studies*, vol. 4, no. 1 (Autumn 1974), pp. 55–81.

"Illusions about America," *Journal of Palestine Studies*, vol. 7, no. 1 (Autumn 1988), pp. 175–78.

Ippolito, Dennis S. and Thomas G. Walker. *Political Parties, Interest Groups, and Public Policy: Group Influence in American Politics* (Englewood Cliffs, NJ: Prentice-Hall, 1980).

Isaacs, Stephen D. and Lee O'Brien. *Jews and American Politics* (New York: Doubleday, 1974).

J Street. "About Us," available from www.jstreet.org/about/about-us; Internet; accessed April 16, 2008.

Jacobson, Gary C. *A Divider, Not a Uniter: George W. Bush and the American People* (New York: Pearson-Longman, 2007).

Janeway, Michael. *Republic of Denial: Press, Politics, and Public Life* (New Haven, CT: Yale University Press, 1999).

Jahshan, Khalil, former president of National Association of Arab Americans and representative of Association of Arab American University Graduates and Palestine Research and Educational Center. Interview by the author, Arlington, VA, March 14, 2006.

Jewish Virtual Library, available from www.jewishvirtuallibrary.org/jsource/index. html; Internet; accessed November 18, 2005.

Jewish Voice for Peace. "JVP History," available from www.jewishvoiceforpeace.org/publish/article_29.shtml; Internet; accessed July 28, 2006.

Jiryis, Sabri. *The Arabs in Israel* (New York: Monthly Review Press, 1976).

Jordan, Donald L. "Newspaper Effects on Policy Preferences," *Public Opinion Quarterly*, vol. 57, no. 2 (Summer 1993), pp. 191–204.

Jordan, Donald L. and Benjamin I. Page. "Shaping Foreign Policy Opinions: The Role of TV News," *Journal of Conflict Resolution*, vol. 36, no. 2 (June 1992), pp. 227–41.

Judt, Tony. "A Lobby not a Conspiracy," *New York Times*, April 19, 2006.

Kahler, Miles. *Liberalization and Foreign Policy* (New York: Columbia University Press, 1997).

Kaiser, Robert G. "Bush and Sharon Nearly Identical on Mideast Policy," *Washington Post*, February 9, 2003.

Kalvaryski, H. M. Excerpted in "The History of the Original Brit Shalom, Founded 1925" (date unknown), available from www.britshalom.org/background.htm; Internet; accessed October 11, 2005.

Kamalimpour, Yahya R. (ed.). *The U.S. Media and the Middle East* (Westport, CT: Greenwood Publishing Group, 1995).

Kampeas, Ron. "New Initiative: Not AIPAC Competitor," *Jewish News of Greater Phoenix Online*, vol. 59, no. 5 (October 20, 2006), available from www.jewishaz.com/issues/story.mv?061020+aipac; Internet; accessed January 13, 2007.

Kamrava, Mehran. *The Modern Middle East: A Political History Since the First World War* (Berkeley, CA: University of California Press, 2005).

Kang, Xingping and Yongjiang Zhao. "The Violence-Plagued Peace Process: Predicament, Prospect, and Test for U.S. Middle East Policy," *American Foreign Policy Interests*, 23 (2001), pp. 357–68.

Kant, Immanuel. *Perpetual Peace* (New York: The Library of Liberal Arts, 1957).

Kaplan, Esther. "The Jewish Divide on Israel," *The Nation*, July 12, 2004.

Karsh, Efraim and Inari Rautsi, *Saddam Hussein: A Political Biography* (New York: Grove Press, 2003).

Karsh, Efraim and P. R. Kumaraswamy (eds). *Israel, the Hashemites and the Palestinians: The Fateful Triangle* (London: Routledge, 2003).

Kasem, Casey. "Arab Americans: Making a Difference," informational flyer, 2005.

Katz, Mark N. "Policy Watch: Where is the Arab Lobby?" from *United Press International*, July 1, 2006.

Kays, Doreen. *Frogs and Scorpions: Egypt and the Media* (New York: HarperCollins, 1985).

Kearny, Edward N. *Dimensions of the Modern Presidency* (St. Louis, MO: Forum Press, 1981).

Kegley, Jr., Charles W. "The Neoidealist Moment in International Studies? Realist Myths and the New International Realities," *International Studies Quarterly*, 37 (1993), pp. 131–46.

——. *Controversies in International Relations Theory: Realism and the Neoliberal Challenge* (New York: St. Martin's Press, 1995).

Kegley, Jr., Charles W., and Eugene R. Wittkopf. *American Foreign Policy: Patterns and Process*, 4th ed. (New York: St. Martin's Press, 1991).

Kelley, Matt. "Afghan War May Guide Iraq Planning," from *Associated Press*, October 6, 2002.

Kengor, Paul. "The Vice President, Secretary of State, and Foreign Policy," *Political Science Quarterly*, vol. 115, no. 2 (Summer 2000), pp. 175–99.

Kershner, Isabel. "Abbas and Olmert Struggle to Move Talks Forward," *New York Times*, February 20, 2008.

——. "Israeli Army Strikes Cell in Northern Gaza as Palestinian Factional Fighting Persists," *New York Times*, May 20, 2007.

Kessler, Glenn. "Israelis Claim Secret Agreement with U.S., Americans Insist No Deal Made on Settlement Growth," *Washington Post*, April 24, 2008.

Key, Vladimer O. *Public Opinion and American Democracy* (New York: Knopf, 1961).

Khalidi, Rashid. *Resurrecting Empire: Western Footprints and America's Perilous Path in the Middle East* (Boston, MA: Beacon Press, 2004).

——. *The Iron Cage: The Story of Palestinian Struggle for Statehood* (Boston, MA: Beacon Press, 2006).

——. *The Palestinian Identity: The Construction of Modern National Consciousness* (New York: Columbia University Press, 1997).

——. "The Palestinians Twenty Years After," *MERIP Middle East Report*, no. 146, Twenty Years After (May-June 1987).

——. *Under Siege: P.L.O. Decisionmaking During the 1982 War* (New York: Columbia University Press, 1986).

Khalidi, Walid. "Our Jerusalem: Separate and Joint," keynote address, ADC's 17th National Convention, June 11, 2000.

——. "The Half-Empty Glass of Middle East Peace," *Journal of Palestine Studies*, vol. 19, no. 3 (Spring 1990), pp. 14–38.

——. "The Palestine Issue Forty Years after Partition: Reflections on the Past and Perspectives on the Future," *Bulletin (British Society for Middle East Studies)*, vol. 14, no. 2 (1987), pp. 123–35.

Khalil, Ashraf. "Cheney Says a Palestinian State is 'Long Overdue,'" *Los Angeles Times*, March 24, 2008.

Khoury, Nabeel A. "The Arab Lobby: Problems and Prospects," *Middle East Journal*, vol. 41, no. 3 (Summer 1987), pp. 379–96.

Kifner, John. "New Pride for Palestinian-Americans," *New York Times*, December 12, 1988.

Kimmerling, Baruch. *Politicide: Ariel Sharon's War Against the Palestinians* (New York: Verso, 2003).

King, Laura and Vita Bekker. "Israel Strikes Lebanon after Militants Capture 2 Soldiers," *Los Angeles Times*, July 13, 2006.

Kirkpatrick, David D. "For Evangelicals, Supporting Israel is 'God's Foreign Policy,'" *New York Times*, November 14, 2006.

Kissinger, Henry. *Does America Need a Foreign Policy?: Toward a Diplomacy for the 21st Century* (New York: Simon and Shuster, 2001).

Kitfield, James. "Daring and Costly: The Bush Record: Foreign Affairs," *National Journal*, vol. 36, no. 28 (July 10, 2004), pp. 2158–68.

Klein, Rick. "Democrats Set an Agenda They Can Agree On," *Boston Globe*, August 4, 2006.

Klingberg, Frank L. *Cyclical Trends in American Foreign Policy Moods: The Unfolding of America's World Role* (Lanham, MD: University Press of America, 1983).

Koh, Harold Hongju. *The National Security Constitution: Sharing Power After the Iran-Contra Affair* (New Haven, CT: Yale University Press, 1990).

Kollman, Ken. "Inviting Friends to Lobby: Interest Groups, Ideological Bias, and Congressional Committees," *American Journal of Political Science*, vol. 41, no. 2 (April 1997), pp. 519–44.

Kovel, Joel. *Overcoming Zionism: Creating a Single Democratic State in Israel/ Palestine* (London: Pluto Press, 2007).

Kowert, Paul. *Groupthink or Deadlock: When do Leaders Learn from Their Advisors?* (Albany, NY: SUNY Press, 2002).

Kreiger, Hilary Leila. "Obama: Pro-Israel Needn't be Pro-Likud," *Jerusalem Post*, February 25, 2008.

Kull, Steven. "America's Image in the World," Testimony before House Committee on Foreign Affairs, March 6, 2007, available from www.worldpublicopinion.org/ pipa/articles/views_on_countriesregions_bt/326.php?nid = &id = &pnt = 326&lb = btvoc; Internet; accessed May 15, 2007.

Kunder, James R. "U.S. Policy Toward the Palestinians," *CQ Congressional Testimony*, March 2, 2006.

Kurtz, Howard. *Hot Air: All Talk, All the Time* (New York: Times Books, 1996).

Laham, Nicholas. *Selling AWACS to Saudi Arabia: The Reagan Administration and the Balancing of America's Competing Interests in the Middle East* (New York: Greenwood Publishing Group, 2002).

Lahiri, Sajal and Pascalis Raimondos-Moller. "Lobbying by Ethnic Groups and Aid Allocation," *Economic Journal*, vol. 110, no. 462, Conference Papers (March 2000), pp. C62-C79.

Lake, David A. "Powerful Pacifists: Democratic States and War," *American Political Science Review*, 86 (1992), pp. 24–37.

Layne, Christopher. "Kant or Cant: The Myth of the Democratic Peace," *International Security*, 19 (1994), pp. 5–49.

Lazare, Daniel. "The One-State Solution," *The Nation* (November 3, 2003), available from www.thenation.com/doc/20031103/lazare; Internet; accessed November 18, 2005.

Lazaroff, Tovah. "Elon: Two-State Solution Dead," *Jerusalem Post*, March 5, 2006.

"Let There be Justice for All: America's Israel Lobby Scores another Questionable Victory," *Economist*, April 10, 2008.

League of Arab States. "Arab League Peace Plan," available from www.jew- ishvirtuallibrary.org/jsource/Peace/arabplan.html; Internet; accessed October 24, 2005.

Leana, C. R. "A Partial Test of Janus' Groupthink Model: Effects of Group Cohesiveness and Leader Behavior on Defective Decision Making," *Journal of Management*, 111 (1975), pp. 5–17.

Lebovic, James H. "Capabilities in Context: National Attributes and Foreign Policy in the Middle East," *Journal of Peace Research*, vol. 22, no. 1 (March 1985), pp. 47–67.

LeBow, Richard Ned and Thomas Risse-Kappen (eds). *International Relations Theory and the End of the Cold War* (New York: Columbia University Press, 1995).

Legro, Jeffrey W. "Whence American Internationalism," *International Organization*, vol. 54, no. 2 (Spring 2000), pp. 253–89.

Leites, Nathan. *The Operational Code of the Politburo* (New York: McGraw-Hill, 1951).

Lembcke, Jerry. *The Spitting Image: The Myth, Memory, and the Legacy of Vietnam* (New York: New York University Press, 1998).

Lenczowski, George. *American Presidents and the Middle East* (Durham, NC: Duke University Press, 1990).

Leon, Dan (ed.). *Who's Left in Israel? Radical Political Alternatives for the Future of Israel* (Portland, OR: Sussex Academic Press, 2004).

Lerner, Daniel and Harold D. Lasswell (eds). *The Policy Sciences* (Stanford, CA: Stanford University Press, 1951).

Lesch, David W. *The Middle East and the United States: A Historical and Political Reassessment* (Boulder, CO: Westview Press, 1996).

"Letter of Invitation to Madrid Peace Conference," October 30, 1991, available from www.jewishvirtuallibrary.org/jsource/Peace/madrid.html; Internet; accessed July 15, 2006.

Levine, Robert A. *Culture, Behavior, and Personality* (Chicago, IL: Aldine, 1973).

Levy, Daniel. "So Pro-Israel It Hurts," *Ha'aretz*, March 24, 2006 and *International Herald Tribune*, April 4, 2006.

Levy, Jack S. "Prospect Theory, Rational Choice, and International Relations," *International Studies Quarterly*, vol. 41, no. 1 (1997), pp. 87–112.

Lewis, Bernard. "Rethinking the Middle East," *Foreign Affairs* (Fall 1992), p. 99.

Leyden, Kevin. "Organized Interests and the Policymaking Process: Explaining Who Testifies at Committee Hearings," paper presented at the Annual Meeting of the Midwest Political Science Association (April 1993).

Lilienthal, Alfred M. *The Zionist Connection II* (New Brunswick, NJ: North American Publishers, 1982).

Lind, Michael. "Distorting U.S. Foreign Policy: The Israel Lobby and American Power," *Washington Report on Middle East Affairs* (May 2002), available from www.thirdworldtraveler.com/Israel/Israel_Lobby_US.html; Internet; accessed December 25, 2005.

Little, Douglas. *American Orientalism: The United States and the Middle East since 1945* (Chapel Hill, NC: University of North Carolina Press, 2002).

"Lobbying Reform Abandoned: After Abramoff Scandal Left Front Page, Congress Cooled on Ethics Reform," *The Tennesan*, August 4, 2006, available from www.rctimes.com/apps/pbcs.dll/article?AID = /20060806/OPINION01/608060344/1007/MTCN0305; Internet; accessed August 7, 2006.

Loomis, Burdett A. *Interest Group Politics*, 2nd ed. (Washington, DC: CQ Press, 1986).

Lukacs, Yehuda and Abdalla M. Battah (eds). *The Arab-Israeli Conflict: Two Decades of Change* (London: Westview, 1988), pp. 238–59.

Macintyre, Donald. "Olmert Says West Bank Settlements Will Stay," *Independent*, February 8, 2006.

Magnes, Judah. *Palestine, Divided or United? The Case for a Bi-national Palestine Before the United Nations* (Westport, CT: Greenwood Press, 1983).

——. Quoted in *Brit Shalom*, available from www.britshalom.org/background.htm; Internet; accessed April 22, 2007.

——. Quoted in *Official Records Of The Second Session Of The General Assembly*, Supplement no. 11, United Nations Special Committee On Palestine, Report Of The General Assembly, Volume III, Oral Evidence Presented At Public Meeting (Lake Success, NY, July 14, 1947), available from http://domino.un.org/UNISPAL.NSF/0/8677dc1263a21f1385256e93006a50d3?OpenDocument; Internet; accessed October 11, 2005.

Magnes, Judah and Martin Buber. *Arab-Jewish Unity: Testimony Before the Anglo-American Inquiry Commission for the Ihud (Union) Association* (Westport, CT: Hyperion Press, 1976).

Malik, Charles. "Continuity of US Policy," *Journal of Palestine Studies*, vol. 4, no. 1 (Autumn 1974), pp. 159–62.

Manhood, H. R. *Pressure Groups in American Politics* (New York: Harper and Row, 1967).

Mann, Michael. *Incoherent Empire* (New York: Verso, 2003).

Mansfield, Edward D. and Jack Snyder. "Democratization and War," *Foreign Affairs*, vol. 74 (1995), pp. 79–97.

Marcus, Amy Dockser. *Jerusalem 1913: The Origins of the Arab-Israeli Conflict* (New York: Penguin Press, 2007).

Marcus, Jonathan. "Discordant Voices: The US Jewish Community and Israel during the 1980s," *International Affairs*, vol. 66, no. 3 (July 1990), pp. 545–58.

Mark, Clyde R. "Israel: U.S. Foreign Assistance," *CRS Issue Brief for Congress* (April 26, 2005).

——. "Israeli-United States Relations," *CRS Issue Brief for Congress* (November 9, 2004).

Marquand, David and Ronald L. Nettler (eds). *Religion and Democracy* (Boston, MA: Blackwell Publishers, 2000).

Marrar, Khalil M. Conversation with anonymous official of the Jewish United Fund, Chicago, IL, June 5, 2007.

——. Conversation with US Senator, Washington, DC, March 15, 2006.

——. Telephone conversation with anonymous pro-Arab lobbying source, March 7, 2006.

Masalha, Nur-eldeen. *Imperial Israel and the Palestinians: The Politics of Expansion* (London: Pluto Press, 2000).

——. "On Recent Hebrew and Israeli Sources for the Palestinian Exodus, 1947–49," *Journal of Palestine Studies*, vol. 18, no. 1, Special Issue: Palestine 1948 (Autumn 1988), pp. 121–37.

Massad, Joseph. "Blaming the Lobby," *Al-Ahram Weekly On-Line*, March 23–29, 2006, available from http://weekly.ahram.org.eg/2006/787/op35.htm; Internet; accessed August 4, 2006.

Massing, Michael. "The Storm over the Israel Lobby," *New York Review of Books*, vol. 53, no. 10 (June 8, 2006).

Mayer, Jeremy D. "Christian Fundamentalists and Public Opinion Toward the Middle East: Israel's New Best Friends?" *Social Science Quarterly*, vol. 84, no. 3 (September 2004), pp. 695–712.

Mazrui, Ali A. "Between the Crescent and the Star Spangled Banner: American Muslims and US Foreign Policy," *International Affairs* (Royal Institute of International Affairs), vol. 72, no. 3, Ethnicity and International Relations (July 1996), pp. 493–506.

McAllister, Melani. *Epic Encounters: Culture, Media, and U.S. Interests in the Middle East, 1945–2000* (Berkeley, CA: University of California Press, 2001).

McCarus, Ernst N. (ed.). *The Development of Arab-American Identity* (Ann Arbor, MI: University of Michigan Press, 1994).

McCauley, Martin. *Russia, America and the Cold War, 1949–1991* (New York: Longman, 1998), pp. 28–30, 46, 81.

McChesney, Robert W. *The Problem of the Media: U.S. Communication Politics in the 21st Century* (New York: Monthly Review Foundation, 2004).

McGann, James G. *Think Tanks and Policy Advice in the US: Academics, Advisors, and Advocates* (London: Routledge, 2007).

McGraw, Kathleen M., Milton Lodge, and Jeffrey M. Jones. "The Pandering Politicians of Suspicious Minds," *The Journal of Politics*, vol. 4, no. 2 (May 2002), pp. 362–83.

Mearsheimer, John J. "Back to the Future: Instability in Europe after the Cold War," *International Security*, vol. 15, no. 1 (Summer 1990), pp. 5–56.

Mearsheimer, John J. and Stephen M. Walt, "The Israel Lobby and U.S. Foreign Policy," *Kennedy School of Government Faculty Research Working Paper Series* RWP06-011 (March 2006).

———. *The Israel Lobby and U.S. Foreign Policy* (New York: Farrar, Straus and Giroux, 2007).

Mekay, Emad. "The Compelling Lobby: According to a Recent Study, the Israel Lobby in the US Dictates Washington's Middle East Policy," *Al-Ahram Weekly On-Line*, March 23–29, 2006, available from http://weekly.ahram.org.eg/2006/787/in2.htm; Internet; accessed August 4, 2006.

Melman, Yossi and Dan Raviv. *Inside the US-Israel Alliance* (New York: Hyperion, 1994).

Merkley, Paul Charles. *American Presidents, Religion, and Israel: The Heirs of Cyrus* (Westport, CT: Praeger, 2004).

———. *Christian Attitudes towards the State of Israel* (Ithaca, NY: McGill-Queen's University Press, 2001).

Mezrich, J. J., S. Frysinger, and R. Slivjanovski. "Dynamic Representation of Multivariate Time Series Data," *Journal of the American Statistical Association*, vol. 79, no. 385 (March 1984), pp. 34–40.

Miglietta, John P. *American Alliance Policy in the Middle East, 1945–1992, Iran, Israel, and Saudi Arabia* (New York: Lexington Books, 2002).

Micklethawait, John and Adrian Wooldridge. *The Right Nation: Conservative Power in America* (New York: Penguin Press, 2004).

Milton-Edwards, Beverley and Peter Hinchcliffe. *Conflicts in the Middle East since 1945*, 2nd ed. (New York: Routledge, 2003).

Mintz, Alex and Nehmia Geva. "Why Don't Democracies Fight Each Other? An Experimental Study," *Journal of Conflict Resolution*, vol. 37 (1993), pp. 484–503.

Mishal, Shaul and Avraham Sela. *The Palestinian Hamas: Vision, Violence, and Coexistence* (New York: Columbia University Press, 2000).

Mitnick, Joshua. "Hamas Kidnaps Soldier, Kills Two; Tel Aviv Warns of Gaza Attack," *Washington Times*, June 26, 2006.

Moens, Alexander. *The Foreign Policy of George W. Bush: Values, Strategy and Loyalty* (Burlington, VT: Ashgate Publishing Company, 2004).

Moghrabi, Fouad. "American Public Opinion and the Palestine Question," *Journal of Palestine Studies*, vol. 15, no. 2 (Winter 1986), pp. 56–75.

Mohamad, Nabil. Organizing director of American-Arab Anti-Discrimination Committee. Interview by the author, Washington, DC, March 14, 2006.

Monroe, Alan D. "Public Opinion and Public Policy, 1980–93," *Public Opinion Quarterly*, vol. 62, no. 1 (Spring 1998), pp. 6–28.

Moon, Bruce E. "Consensus or Compliance? Foreign-Policy Change and External Dependence," *International Organization*, vol. 39, no. 2 (Spring 1985), pp. 297–329.

Morgan, Clifton T. and Valerie L. Schwebach. "Take Two Democracies and Call Me in the Morning: A Prescription for Peace?" *International Interactions*, 17 (1992), pp. 305–20.

Morris, Dick. "True Friends of Israel Cannot Let the Dems Take Power," *The Hill*, July 26, 2006, available from http://thehill.com/dick-morris/true-friends-of-israel-cannot-let-the-dems-take-power-2006-7-26.html; Internet; accessed April 18, 2008.

Mullan, Dierdre and Carol Rittner. "Do Good Fences Make Good Neighbors?" *American Foreign Policy Interests*, 26 (2004), pp. 477–84.

Murdico, Suzanne J. *The Gulf War* (New York: The Rosen Group, 2004).

Murray, Williamson and Robert H. Scales, Jr. *The Iraq War: A Military History* (Cambridge, MA: Harvard University Press, 2003).

Nafie, Ibrahim. "Hands Off are No Less Bloody," *Al-Ahram Weekly On-Line*, August 30–September 5, 2001, available from http://weekly.ahram.org.eg/2001/549/op1.htm; Internet, accessed December 31, 2005.

Nagourney, Adam. "Clinton Assails Bush as Democrats Open Convention," *New York Times*, July 27, 2004.

Naidu, Anatha Guruswami. *US Policy Towards the Arab-Israeli Conflict* (Atlantic Highlands, NJ: Humanities Press, 1982).

Nassar, Jamal R. *Globalization and Terrorism: The Migration of Dreams and Nightmares* (New York: Rowman and Littlefield, 2004).

Nassar, Jamal R. and Roger Heacock (eds). *Intifada: Palestine at the Crossroads* (New York: Praeger, 1990).

National Archives, "Public Papers of the Presidents," available from www.archives.gov/federal-register/publications/presidential-papers.html#online; Internet; accessed June 19, 2006.

"National Security Strategy of the United States of America," March 16, 2006, available from www.whitehouse.gov/nsc/nss/2006/nss2006.pdf; Internet; accessed March 30, 2006.

NBC4. "Bethlehem Group Re-Enacts Walk of Mary, Joseph at White House," December 23, 2006, available from www.nbc4.com/print/10599195/detail.html; Internet; accessed December 30, 2006.

Neff, Donald. "The Clinton Administration and UN Resolution 242," *Journal of Palestine Studies*, vol. 23, no. 2 (Winter 1994), pp. 20–30.

——. "U.S. Policy and the Palestinian Refugees," *Journal of Palestine Studies*, vol. 18, no. 1, Special Issue: Palestine 1948 (Autumn 1988), pp. 96–111.

Nelson, Nancy Jo. "The Zionist Organizational Structure," *Journal of Palestine Studies*, vol. 10, no. 1 (Autumn 1980), pp. 80–93.

Nelson, W. Dale. "Arab Lobby Uses Commercials to Blast Aid to Israel," available from *Associated Press*, December 17, 1982.

Netanyahu, Benjamin. *The Jerusalem Alternative: Moral Clarity for Ending the Arab-Israeli Conflict* (Green Forest, AR: Balfour Books, 2004).

Neustadt, Richard E. *Alliance Politics* (New York: Columbia University Press, 1970).

Newsom, David D. *The Imperial Mantle: The United States, Decolonization, and the Third World* (Bloomington, IN: Indiana University Press, 2001).

Nichols, John. "Taking Sides," *The Nation*, 277 (October 6, 2003), pp. 6–7.

Niemark, Marilyn. "American Jews and Palestine: The Impact of the Gulf War," *Middle East Report*, no. 175, Palestine and Israel in the New Order (March-April 1992), pp. 19–23.

Nigem, Elias T. "Arab Americans: Migration, Socioeconomic and Demographic Characteristics," *International Migration Review*, vol. 20, no. 3 (Autumn 1986), pp. 629–49.

Nincic, Miroslav. "A Sensible Public: New Perspectives on Popular Opinion and Foreign Policy," *The Journal of Conflict Resolution*, vol. 36, no. 4 (December 1992), pp. 772–89.

Nir, Ori. "Israelis Want AIPAC-Backed Bill Softened," *Forward*, March 10, 2006.

North, Oliver. *War Stories: Operation Iraqi Freedom* (Washington, DC: Regnery Publishing, 2003).

Nusseibeh, Sari. *Once Upon a Country: A Palestinian Life* (New York: Farrar, Straus and Giroux, 2007).

O'Brien, Lee. *American Jewish Organizations and Israel* (Washington, DC: Institute for Palestine Studies, 1986).

Oakar, Mary Rose. Former congresswoman from Cleveland, OH, and president of American-Arab Anti-Discrimination Committee, Interview by the author, Washington, DC, March 15, 2006.

——. "Mideast Lawsuit," in *The O'Reilly Factor*, July 25, 2006, available from www. foxnews.com/video2/launchPage.html?072506/072506_oreilly_oakar&Mideast%20 Lawsuit&OReilly_Factor&An%20Arab-American%20group%20sues%20the%20U. S.%20gov%27t%20over%20Mideast%20violence&World&-1&Mideast%20Lawsuit &Video%20Launch%20Page; Internet; accessed July 28, 2006.

Office of Counterterrorism. "Foreign Terrorist Organizations (FTOs), Fact Sheet", October 11, 2005, available from www.state.gov/s/ct/rls/fs/37191.htm; Internet; accessed July 30, 2006.

Office of the Coordinator for Counterterrorism. "2001 Report on Foreign Terrorist Organizations," October 5, 2001, available from www.state.gov/s/ct/rls/rpt/fto/2001/ 5258.htm; Internet; accessed May 1, 2007.

——. "Foreign Terrorist Organizations," April 8, 2008, available from www.state.gov/ s/ct/rls/fs/08/103392.htm; Internet; accessed May 5, 2008.

Office of the Press Secretary. "President Discusses Middle East Peace with Prime Minister Sharon," July 29, 2003, available from www.whitehouse.gov/news/releases/ 2003/07/20030729-2.html; Internet; accessed December 27, 2006.

Oldendick, Robert W. and Barbara Ann Bardes. "Mass and Elite Foreign Policy Opinions," *Public Opinion Quarterly*, vol. 46, no. 3 (Autumn 1982), pp. 368–82.

Olson, William C. and A. J. R. Groom. *International Relations Then and Now: Origins and Trends in Interpretation* (London: HarperCollins, 1991).

Onuf, Nicholas G. and Thomas J. Johnson. "Peace in the Liberal World: Does Democracy Matter?" In Charles W. Kegley, Jr. (ed.) *Controversies in International Relations Theory: Realism and the Neoliberal Challenge*, New York: St. Martin's Press, 1995, pp. 179–98.

Organski, A. F. K. *The $36 Billion Bargain: U.S. Aid to Israel and American Public Opinion* (New York: Columbia University Press, 1990).

Ostroff, Maurice. "What the Professors Should have Told Us – But Didn't," available from http://arab-lobby.blogspot.com/; Internet; accessed November 29, 2007.

Owen, John M. "How Liberalism Produces Peace," *International Security* vol. 19, no. 2 (1994).

——. *Liberal Peace, Liberal War: American Politics and International Security* (Ithaca, NY: Cornell University Press, 1998).

Page, Benjamin I. "Democratic Responsiveness? Untangling the Links between Public Opinion and Policy," *Political Science and Politics*, vol. 27, no. 1 (March 1994), pp. 25–29.

——. "The Mass Media as Political Actors," *Political Science and Politics*, vol. 29, no. 1 (March 1996), pp. 20–24.

Page, Benjamin I. and Jason Barabas. "Foreign Policy Gaps between Citizens and Leaders," *International Studies Quarterly*, vol. 44, no. 2 (September 2000), pp. 339–64.

Page, Benjamin I. and Marshall M. Bouton. *The Foreign Policy Disconnect: What Americans Want from Our Leaders but Don't Get* (Chicago, IL: University of Chicago Press, 2006).

Page, Benjamin I. and Robert Shapiro. "Effects of Public Opinion on Policy," *American Political Science Review*, vol. 77, no. 1 (March 1983), pp. 175–90.

Page, Benjamin I., Robert Y. Shapiro, and Glenn R. Dempsey. "What Moves Public Opinion," *American Political Science Review*, vol. 81, no. 1 (March 1987), pp. 23–44.

Paolucci, Henry. *Iran, Israel, and the United States* (Whitestone, NY: Griffon House Publications, 1991).

Pape, Robert. *Dying to Win: The Strategic Logic of Suicide Terrorism* (New York: Random House Trade Books, 2006).

Pauly, Jr., Robert J. and Tom Lansford. *Strategic Preemption: US Foreign Policy and the Second Iraq War* (Burlington, VT: Ashgate Publishing Company, 2005).

Pear, Robert. "Leaders of 3 U.S. Jewish Groups Take Issue With Pro-Israel Lobby," *New York Times*, October 18, 1988.

Pear, Robert and Richard L. Berke. "Pro-Israel Group Exerts Quiet Might as it Rallies Supporters in Congress," *New York Times*, July 7, 1987.

Peretz, Martin. "The Politics of Churlishness," *The New Republic* (April 11, 2005), pp. 20–23.

Peri, Yoram. "Israel in Lebanon – One Year Later," *Journal of Palestine Studies*, vol. 13, no. 1 (Autumn 1983), pp. 190–96.

Petras, James. *The Power of Israel in the United States* (Atlanta, GA: Clarity Press, 2006).

Pillar, Paul R. *Terrorism and U.S. Foreign Policy* (Washington, DC: Brookings Institution Press, 2001).

Pipes, Daniel. *The Hidden Hand: Middle East Fears of Conspiracy* (New York: St. Martin's Press, 1996).

Plocker, Sever. *Dollarization in Israel-Palestine* (Washington, DC: Saban Center for Middle East Policy at the Brookings Institution, 2005).

Poundstone, William. *Prisoner's Dilemma: John von Neumann, Game Theory, and the Puzzle of the Bomb* (New York: Doubleday Press, 1992).

Powell, Colin. "Colin Powell's Speech to the American Israel Public Affairs Committee," March 31, 2003, available from www.guardian.co.uk/israel/Story/0,926276,00.html; Internet; accessed July 6, 2006.

Powlick, Philip J. "The Attitudinal Bases for Responsiveness to Public Opinion among American Foreign Policy Officials," *Journal of Conflict Resolution*, vol. 35, no. 4 (December 1991), pp. 611–41.

——. "The Sources of Public Opinion for American Foreign Policy Officials," *International Studies Quarterly*, vol. 39, no. 4 (December 1995), pp. 427–51.

Powlick, Philip J. and Andrew J. Katz. "Defining the American Public Opinion/Foreign Policy Nexus," *Mershon International Studies Review*, vol. 42, no. 1 (May 1998), pp. 29–61.

"President Bush Commends Israeli Prime Minister Sharon's Plan," April 14, 2004, available from www.whitehouse.gov/news/releases/2004/04/20040414-4.html#; Internet; accessed May 20, 2005.

"President Bush Meets with British Prime Minister Tony Blair," December 7, 2006, available from www.whitehouse.gov/news/releases/2006/12/20061207-1.html; Internet; accessed December 30, 2006.

"President Bush Meets with President Abbas of the Palestinian Authority," April 24, 2008, available from www.whitehouse.gov/news/releases/2008/04/20080424-10.html; Internet; accessed May 6, 2008.

"President Welcomes Palestinian President Abbas to the White House," October 20, 2005, available from www.whitehouse.gov/news/releases/2005/10/20051020.html; Internet; accessed December 23, 2006.

Project for the New American Century. "Statement of Principles," June 3, 1997, available from www.newamericancentury.org/statementofprinciples.htm; Internet; accessed January 11, 2007.

Prusher, Illene R. "Israel's Gaza Balancing Act," *Christian Science Monitor,* July 3, 2006.

Puder, Joseph. "The Arab Lobby Can't Buy Support," *The Bulletin,* September 17, 2007, available from www.thebulletin.us/site/news.cfm?newsid = 18823821&BRD = 2737&PAG = 461&dept_id = 576361&rfi = 6; Internet; accessed April 7, 2008.

Puschel, Karen L. *US-Israeli Strategic Cooperation in the Post-Cold war Era, An American Perspective* (San Francisco, CA: Westview Press, 1993).

"Pushing the Arab Cause in America," *Time,* June 23, 1975.

Quandt, William B. *Decade of Decisions: American Foreign Policy toward the Arab-Israeli Conflict, 1967–1976* (Berkeley, CA: University of California Press, 1977).

——. *Peace Process: American Diplomacy and the Arab-Israeli Conflict Since 1967* (Washington, DC: Brookings Institution Press, 2005).

Quandt, William B. (ed.). *The Middle East: Ten Years after Camp David* (Washington, DC: Brookings Institution Press, 1988).

Rahn, Wendy M., John H. Aldrich, and Eugene Borgida. "Individual and Contextual Variations in Political Candidate Appraisal," *American Political Science Review,* vol. 88, no. 1 (March 1994), pp. 193–99.

Randal, Jonathan. *Osama: The Making of a Terrorist* (London: I. B. Tauris, 2004).

Rasler, Karen, William R. Thompson, and Kathleen Chester. "Foreign Policy Makers, Personality Attributes, and Interviews: A Note on Reliability Problems," *International Studies Quarterly,* vol. 24, no. 1 (March 1980), pp. 47–66.

Ray, James Lee. *Democracy and International Politics: An Evaluation of the Democratic Peace Proposition* (Columbia, SC: University of South Carolina Press, 1995).

——. *The Future of American-Israeli Relations* (Lexington, KY: University Press of Kentucky, 1985).

Reagan, Ronald. "Letter to the Speaker of the House of Representatives and the President of the Senate on the Sale of AWACS Aircraft to Saudi Arabia," June 18, 1986, available from www.reagan.utexas.edu/archives/speeches/1986/61886e.htm; Internet; accessed January 11, 2007.

Regan, Tom. "They Hate Our Policies, Not Our Freedom: Pentagon Report Contains Major Criticisms of Administration" *Christian Science Monitor,* November 29, 2004.

Reich, Bernard. *Securing the Covenant: United States-Israel Relations after the Cold War* (Westport, CT: Greenwood Press, 1995).

Reinhart, Tanya. *Israel/Palestine: How to End the 1948 War* (St. Paul, MN: Seven Stories Press, 2002).

Rice, Condoleezza. "Dr. Condoleezza Rice Discusses the Roadmap for Peace in the Middle East," June 3, 2003, available from www.whitehouse.gov/news/releases/2003/06/20030603-6.html; Internet; accessed January 9, 2007.

Richburg, Keith B. "U.N. Court Rejects West Bank Barrier, Israel Says Security Fence Will Stay," *Washington Post,* July 10, 2004.

Richman, Alvin. "A Report: American Attitudes Toward Israeli-Palestinian Relations in the Wake of the Uprising," *Public Opinion Quarterly,* vol. 53, no. 3 (Autumn 1989), pp. 415–30.

Richman, Sheldon L. "The Economic Impact of the Israeli Loan Guarantees," *Journal of Palestine Studies,* vol. 21, no. 2 (Winter 1992), pp. 88–95.

Ripley, Brian. "Psychology, Foreign Policy, and International Relations Theory," *Political Psychology,* 14 (1993), pp. 403–16.

Ripley, Randall B. and James M. Lindsay (eds). *Congress Resurgent: Foreign and Defense Policy on Capitol Hill* (Ann Arbor, MI: University of Michigan Press, 1993).

Risse-Kappen, Thomas. "Public Opinion, Domestic Structure, and Foreign Policy in Liberal Democracies," *World Politics*, vol. 43, no. 4 (July 1991), pp. 479–512.

Rittberger, Volker. "On the Peace Capacity of Democracies: Reflections on the Political Theory of Peace," *Law and State*, 39 (1989), pp. 40–57.

Rokach, Livia. *Israel's Sacred Terrorism*, 3rd edn (Washington, DC: AAUG Press, 1986).

Rosati, Jerel A., Michael W. Ling, and John Creed. "A New Perspective on the Foreign Policy Views of American Opinion in the Cold War and Post-Cold War Eras," *Political Research Quarterly*, vol. 51, no. 2 (June 1998), pp. 461–79.

Rosenau, James N. (ed.). *Comparing Foreign Policies: Theories, Findings, and Methods* (New York: Sage-Halsted, 1974).

——. *Domestic Sources of Foreign Policy* (New York: Free Press, 1967).

——. *International Politics and Foreign Policy: A Reader in Research and Theory* (New York: Free Press, 1969).

Rosenthal, Andrew. "Bush Acts to Calm Israel Aid Uproar," *New York Times*, September 21, 1991.

Rothkopf, David. *Running the World: The Inside Story of the National Security Council and the Architects of American Power* (New York: Public Affairs, 2006).

Rouleau, Eric. "US-Israel Relations," *Journal of Palestine Studies*, vol. 6, no. 4 (Summer 1977), pp. 169–77.

Rozell, Mark J. *Media Power, Media Politics* (Lanham, MD: Rowman and Littlefield, 2003).

Rubenberg, Cheryl A. *Israel and the American National Interest: A Critical Examination* (Chicago, IL: University of Illinois Press, 1986).

——. *The Palestinians: In Search of a Just Peace* (Boulder, CO: Lynne Rienner, 2003).

Rubenberg, Cheryl A. (ed.). *Encyclopedia of the Israeli-Palestinian Conflict* (New York: Lynne Rienner, forthcoming, 2009).

Rudin, A. James. *Israel for Christians: Understanding Modern Israel* (Philadelphia, PA: Fortress Press, 1983).

Ryan, Sheila. "Israel's Invasion of Lebanon: Background to the Crisis," *Journal of Palestine Studies*, vol. 11, no. 4, Special Issue: The War in Lebanon (Summer 1982), pp. 23–37.

Ryder, Denny and Ali Omar. *Opening Pandora's Box* (Baltimore, MD: Publish America, 2004).

Sabato, Larry J. (ed.). *The Sixth Year Itch: The Rise and Fall of the George W. Bush Presidency* (New York: Pearson-Longman, 2008).

Safran, Nadav. *The United States and Israel* (Cambridge, MA: Harvard University Press, 1963).

Said, Abdul Aziz. *Ethnicity and U.S. Foreign Policy* (New York: Greenwood Publishing Group, 1981).

Said, Edward W. "A Troubling Accord," in Arab American Institute, *Nota Bene*, The Peace Accord – A Special Edition (October 1993), pp. 1–3.

——. *Orientalism* (New York: Vintage Books, 1979).

——. *Peace and its Discontents: Essays on Palestine in the Middle East Peace Process* (New York: Vintage Books, 1995).

——. "Reflections on Twenty Years of Palestinian History," *Journal of Palestine Studies*, vol. 20, no. 4 (Summer 1991), pp. 5–22.

——. *The End of the Peace Process: Oslo and After* (New York: Pantheon Press, 2000).

——. *The Politics of Dispossession: The Struggle for Palestinian Self-Determination, 1969–1994* (New York: Vintage Books, 1995).

——. "Truth and Reconciliation," *Al-Ahram Weekly On-Line*, January 14–20, 1999, available from http://weekly.ahram.org.eg/1999/412/op2.htm; Internet; accessed January 28, 2007.

Said, Edward W. and David Barsamian. *Culture and Resistance: Conversations with Edward W. Said* (Boston, MA: South End Press, 2003).

Saigh, Yezid and Avi Shlaim (eds). *The Cold War and the Middle East* (Oxford: Oxford University Press, 1997).

Sayigh, Yezid. *Armed Struggle and the Search for State: The Palestinian National Movement, 1949–1993* (Oxford: Oxford University Press, 1999).

Samhan, Helen Hatab. Executive director of Arab American Institute Foundation. Interview by the author, Washington, DC, March 16, 2006.

——. "Politics and Exclusion: The Arab American Experience," *Journal of Palestine Studies*, vol. 16, no. 2 (Winter 1987), pp. 11–28.

Satloff, Robert. "Shifting Sands," *New Republic*, June 1, 1998.

——. "U.S., Israel Still Need Each Other," *Newsday*, October 14, 1998.

Saudi Aramco. "Who We Are," available from www.saudiaramco.com/bvsm/JSP/content/channelDetail.jsp?BV_SessionID=@@@@@0380322060.1168761664@@@@&BV_EngineID=cccfaddjljmfjfgcefeceefdfnkdfhl.0&datetime=01%2F14%2F07+11%3A01%3A04&SA.channelID =-11681; accessed January 14, 2007.

Schilling, Warner R., Paul Y. Hammond, and Glenn H. Snyder. *Strategy, Politics, and Defense Budgets* (New York: Columbia University Press, 1962).

Schlesinger, Jr., Arthur M. *The Imperial Presidency* (New York: Houghton Mifflin Company, 2004).

Schoenbaum, David. *The United States and the State of Israel* (New York: Oxford University Press, 1993).

Schultz, George. "The United States and Israel: Partners for Peace and Freedom," *Journal of Palestine Studies*, vol. 14, no. 4 (Summer 1985), pp. 122–28.

Schwartz, Stephen. *Is It Good for the Jews? The Crisis of America's Israel Lobby* (New York: Doubleday, 2006).

Schwartz, Yossi. "Israel/Palestine: Two States or One Bi-National State," available from www.marxist.com/MiddleEast/israel_binational_state.html; Internet; accessed April 22, 2007.

Scott, James M. *After the End: Making U.S. Foreign Policy in the Post-Cold War World* (Durham, NC: Duke University Press, 1998).

Segev, Samuel. "Turning a Page in the Middle East," *American Foreign Policy Interests*, 23 (2001), pp. 71–86.

Seib, Gerald F. and Michel McQueen. "Poll Finds Americans Feel Hawkish Toward Iraq but Would Grant Some Concessions to Avoid War," *Wall Street Journal*, December 13, 1990.

Seliktar, Ofira. *Divided We Stand: American Jews, Israel, and the Peace Process* (Westport, CT: Praeger, 2002).

Shadid, Mohammed K. *The United States and the Palestinians* (New York: St. Martin's Press, 1981).

Shaheen, Jack. *Reel Bad Arabs: How Hollywood Vilifies a People* (Northampton, MA: Interlink Publishing Group, Inc. 2001).
——. *The TV Arab* (Bowling Green, OH: Bowling Green State University Popular Press, 1984).
Shain, Yossi. "Arab-Americans at a Crossroads," *Journal of Palestine Studies*, vol. 25, no. 3 (Spring 1996), pp. 46–59.
Shalom, Zaki. *The Superpowers, Israel and the Future of Jordan, 1960–1963: The Perils of the Pro-Nasser Policy* (Portland, OR: Sussex Academic Press, 1999).
Shannon, Vaughn P. *Balancing Act: US Foreign Policy and the Arab-Israeli Conflict* (Burlington, VT: Ashgate Publishing Company, 2003).
Shapiro, Robert Y. and Benjamin I. Page. "Foreign Policy and the Rational Public," *The Journal of Conflict Resolution*, vol. 32, no. 2 (June 1988), pp. 211–57.
Sharon, Ariel. "Landmark Address," *Near East Report*, vol. XLVIII, no. 1 (January 12, 2004), p. 2.
Sharp, Gene. "The Intifada and Nonviolent Struggle," *Journal of Palestine Studies*, vol. 19, no. 1 (Autumn 1989), pp. 3–13.
Shavit, Ari. "Survival of the Fittest," *Ha'aretz*, January 9, 2004.
Sheehan, Edward. "Step by Step in the Middle East," *Journal of Palestine Studies*, vol. 5, no. 3/4 (Spring 1976), pp. 3–53.
Sheffer, Grabriel (ed.). *U.S.-Israeli Relations at the Crossroads* (Portland, OR: Frank Cass, 1997).
Sheinwald, Sir Nigel. British ambassador to the United States. Conversation with the author at the Chicago Council on Foreign Relations, Chicago, IL, April 25, 2008.
Shipler, David K. "On Middle East Policy, A Major Influence," *New York Times*, July 6, 1987.
Shrewder, R. and R. Levine (eds). *Culture Theory: Essays on Mind, Self, and Emotion* (Cambridge: Cambridge University Press, 1984).
Shukrallah, Hani, Sana Kamal, Mona Zaide, Marlin Dick, and Cengiz Candar. "The Street Reacts to Operation Defensive Shield: Snapshots from the Middle East," *Journal of Palestine Studies*, vol. 31, no. 4 (Summer 2002), pp. 44–65.
Shull, Steven A. *Presidential Policy Making: An End of Century Assessment* (Armonk, NY: M. E. Sharpe, 1999).
Simarki, Lyn Teo. "The Rhetoric of Reassurance at AIPAC's 31st Annual Policy Conference," *Journal of Palestine Studies*, vol. 20, no. 1 (Autumn 1990), pp. 92–100.
Simes, Dimitri K. "Unrealists," *The National Interest*, May 26, 2006.
Simon, Reeva S. *The Middle East in Crime Fiction: Mysteries, Spy Novels, and Thrillers from 1916 to 1980* (New York: Lilian Barber Press, 1989).
Singer, Eric and Valerie Hudson (eds). *Political Psychology and Foreign Policy* (Boulder, CO: Westview Press, 1992).
Singer, J. David and Paul Diehl. *Measuring the Correlates of War* (Ann Arbor: University of Michigan Press, 1991).
Singer, J. David and Daniel Geller. *Nations at War: A Scientific Study of International Conflict* (Cambridge: Cambridge University Press, 1998).
Slater, Jerome. "Muting the Alarm over the Israeli-Palestinian Conflict," *International Security*, vol. 32, no. 2 (Fall 2007), pp. 84–120.
Small, Melvin. *Democracy and Diplomacy: The Impact of Domestic Politics on U.S. Foreign Policy, 1789–1994* (Baltimore, MD: Johns Hopkins University Press, 1996).
Smith, Charles D. *Palestine and the Arab-Israeli Conflict* (New York: St. Martin's Press, 1988).

Smith, Tony. *Foreign Attachments: The Power of Ethnic Groups in the Making of American Foreign Policy* (Cambridge, MA: Harvard University Press, 2000).

Snyder, Richard C., H. W. Bruck, and Burton Sapin, *Decision Making as an Approach to the Study of International Politics*. Foreign Policy Analysis Project series no. 3 (Princeton, NJ: Princeton University Press, 1954).

Sobel, Richard. *The Impact of Public Opinion on U.S. Foreign Policy Since Vietnam: Constraining the Colossus* (New York: Oxford University Press, 2001).

Solomon, Norman and Jeff Cohen. *Behind the Curtain of Mainstream News* (New York: Common Courage, 1997).

Southern Political Science Association Conference. "Panel on U.S. Foreign Policy and Conflict Management," New Orleans, LA, January 3–7, 2007.

Spanier, John. *American Foreign Policy Since World War II*, 12th edn (Washington, DC: CQ Press, 1991).

Spiegel, Steven L. *The Other Arab-Israeli Conflict: Making America's Middle East Policy, From Truman to Reagan* (Chicago, IL: University of Chicago Press, 1985).

Sprout, Harold and Margaret Sprout. *The Ecological Perspective on Human Affairs with Special Reference to International Relations* (Princeton, NJ: Princeton University Press, 1965).

Steger, Manfred B. *Globalization: A Very Short Introduction* (Oxford: Oxford University Press, 2003).

Steger, Manfred B. (ed.). *Rethinking Globalism* (New York: Rowman and Littlefield, 2004).

Stein, Dorothy. "Palestine: The Return of the One-State Solution," *Asian Affairs*, vol. XXXV, no. 3 (November 2004).

Stephens, Bret. "The Gaza Breakout," *Wall Street Journal*, January 29, 2008.

Stephens, Elizabeth. *US Policy Toward Israel: The Role of Political Culture in Defining the "Special Relationship"* (Brighton: Sussex Academic Press, 2006).

Steger, Manfred B. *The Rise of the Global Imaginary: Political Ideologies from the French Revolution to the Global War on Terror* (Oxford: Oxford University Press, 2008)

Stimson, James A. *Public Opinion in America: Moods, Cycles, and Swings* (Boulder, CO: Westview, 1991).

Stimson, James A., Michael B. Mackuen, and Robert S. Erikson. "Dynamic Representation," *American Political Science Review*, vol. 89, no. 3 (September 1995), pp. 543–65.

Stockwell, John. *The Praetorian Guard: The U.S. Role in the New World Order* (Cambridge, MA: South End Press, 1991).

Stolberg, Sheryl Gay. "Bush Meets Abbas, but Palestinians Criticize Plans for Trip," *New York Times*, April 25, 2008.

Stork, Joe. "Israel as a Strategic Asset," *MERIP Reports*, no. 105, Reagan Targets the Middle East (May 1982), pp. 3–13, 32.

Stork, Joe and Rashid Khalidi. "Washington's Game Plan in the Middle East," *Middle East Report*, no. 164/165, Intifada Year Three (May-August 1990), pp. 9–11.

Suleiman, Michael. "Development of Public Opinion on the Palestine Question," *Journal of Palestine Studies*, vol. 13, no. 3 (Spring 1984), pp. 87–116.

Suleiman, Michael (ed.). *U.S. Policy on Palestine from Wilson to Clinton* (Normal, IL: Association of Arab-American University Graduates, 1995).

Sweilam, Ashraf. "Police Reinforce Gaza-Egypt Border After Palestinian Militants Blast Hole in Wall," from *Associated Press*, June 29, 2006.

Swisher, Clayton E. *The Truth about Camp David: The Untold Story about the Collapse of the Middle East Peace Process* (New York: Nation Books, 2004).

Sylvan, Donald A. and Stuart J. Thorson. "Ontologies, Problem Representation, and the Cuban Missile Crisis," *Journal of Conflict Resolution*, 36 (1992), pp. 709–32.

"Syracuse Coalition Supports Palestinian State," *The Post-Standard*, December 21, 1988.

T'Hart, Paul, Eric K. Stern, and Bengt Sundelius (eds). *Beyond Groupthink: Political Group Dynamics and Foreign Policy-making* (Ann Arbor, MI: University of Michigan Press, 1997).

Talhami, Ghada Hashem. *Palestinian Refugees: Pawns to Political Actors* (New York: Nova Science Publishers, 2003).

——. *Syria and the Palestinians: The Clash of Nationalisms* (Miami, FL: University of Florida Press, 2001).

Telhami, Shibley. *The Stakes: America in the Middle East, Consequences of Power and the Choice for Peace* (Boulder, CO: Westview Press, 2004).

Tenet, George. *At the Center of the Storm: My Years at the CIA* (New York: HarperCollins, 2007).

——. "The Tenet Plan: Israeli-Palestinian Ceasefire and Security Plan," June 13, 2001; available from www.yale.edu/lawweb/avalon/mideast/mid023.htm; Internet; accessed July 6, 2006.

Terry, Janice J. *Mistaken Identity: Anti-Arab Stereotypes in Popular Literature* (Washington, DC: Arab-American Council, 1985).

——. *U.S. Foreign Policy in the Middle East: The Role of Lobbies and Special Interest Groups* (Ann Arbor, MI: Pluto Press, 2005).

Tetlock, Philip E. "Identifying Victims of Groupthink from Public Statements of Decision Makers," *Journal of Personality and Social Psychology*, 37 (1979), pp. 1314–24.

"The Declaration of the Establishment of the State of Israel." May 14, 1948, available from www.mfa.gov.il/MFA/Peace%20Process/Guide%20to%20the%20Peace%20Process/Declaration%20of%20Establishment%20of%20State%20of%20Israel; Internet; accessed June 11, 2007.

"The Madrid Peace Conference," *Journal of Palestine Studies*, vol. 21, no. 2 (Winter 1992), pp. 117–49.

"The New U.S. Administration," *Journal of Palestine Studies*, vol. 18, no. 2 (Winter 1989), pp. 168–71.

"The Palestine Problem in Public Debate," *Journal of Palestine Studies*, vol. 13, no. 4 (Summer 1984), pp. 187–98.

"The Talk of the Town," *New Yorker*, June 17, 1996.

Tilley, Virginia. *The One-State Solution: A Breakthrough for Peace in the Israeli-Palestinian Deadlock* (Ann Arbor, MI: University of Michigan Press, 2005).

Tillman, Seth P. "United States Middle East Policy: Theory and Practice," *American-Arab Affairs*, no. 4 (Spring 1983), pp. 9–10.

Timco, Peter. Director of the Office of the President, Arab American Institute. Telephone interview by the author, April 25, 2008.

Tivnan, Edward. *Jewish Political Power and American Foreign Policy* (New York: Simon and Shuster, 1987).

Triandis, Harry C. *Culture and Social Behavior* (New York: McGraw-Hill, 1994).

Trice, Robert H. "Foreign Policy Interest Groups, Mass Public Opinion and the Arab-Israeli Dispute," *Western Political Quarterly*, vol. 31, no. 2 (June 1978), pp. 238–52.

Trofimov, Yaroslav. *Faith At War: A Journey on the Frontlines of Islam, from Baghdad to Timbuktu* (New York: Henry Holt and Company, 2005).

Turki, Fawaz. "The Passions of Exile: The Palestine Congress of North America," *Journal of Palestine Studies*, vol. 9, no. 4 (Summer 1980), pp. 17–43.

United Nations Security Council Resolutions, available from www.un.org/documents/scres.htm; Internet; accessed August 21, 2005.

United States Internal Revenue Service. Section 501(c)(3) Organizations, available from www.irs.gov/publications/p557/ch03.html#d0e7391; Internet; accessed January 14, 2007.

United States Senate. "Israel in the US Senate," *Journal of Palestine Studies*, vol. 4, no. 4 (Summer 1975), pp. 167–69.

Urbina, Ian. "Rogues' Gallery: Who Advises Bush and Gore on the Middle East?" *Middle East Report*, no. 216 (Autumn 2000), pp. 9–12.

Ursano, Robert J. and Ann E. Norwood (eds). *Emotional Aftermath of the Persian Gulf War: Veterans, Families, Communities, and Nations* (Washington, DC: American Psychiatric Press, 1996).

Verter, Yossi. "Poll: Most Israelis Back Direct Talks with Hamas on Shalit," *Ha'aretz*, February 27, 2008.

Wagner, Don. "For Zion's Sake," *Middle East Report*, no. 223 (Summer 2002), pp. 52–57.

Walt, Stephen M. "Beyond bin Laden: Reshaping U.S. Foreign Policy," *International Security*, vol. 26, no. 3 (Winter 2001/02), pp. 56–78.

Walker, Stephen G. "The Interface Between Beliefs and Behavior: Henry A. Kissinger's Operational Code and the Vietnam War," *Journal of Conflict Resolution*, 21 (1977), pp. 129–68.

——. "The Motivational Foundations of Political Belief Systems: A Re-Analysis of the Operational Code Construct," *International Studies Quarterly*, vol. 27, no. 2 (June 1983), pp. 179–202.

Wettstein, Howard (ed.). *Diasporas and Exiles: Varieties of Jewish Identity* (Berkeley, CA: University of California Press, 2002).

Wilbur, Rich (ed.). *The Politics of Minority Coalitions: Race Ethnicity and Shared Uncertainties* (New York: Praeger 1996).

Wilcox, Clyde. *Onward Christian Soldiers?: The Religious Right in American Politics* (Boulder, CO: Westview Press, 2000).

Wingfield, Marvin. Director of Education and Outreach for American-Arab Anti-Discrimination Committee. Telephone interview by the author, December 19, 2006.

Wisse, Ruth R. "Harvard Attack on 'Israel Lobby' is Actually a Targeting of American Public," *Jewish World Review,* March 23, 2006.

Wolfsfeld, Gadi. *Media and Political Conflict: News from the Middle East* (Cambridge: Cambridge University Press, 1997).

Wood, B. Dan and Jeffrey S. Peake. "The Dynamics of Foreign Policy Agenda Setting," *American Political Sciences Review*, vol. 92, no. 1 (March 1998), pp. 173–84.

Woodward, Bob. *State of Denial: Bush at War, Part III* (New York: Simon and Schuster, 2006).

Wright, John R. *Interest Groups and Congress, Lobbying, Contributions, and Influence* (Needham, MA: Allyn and Bacon, 1996).

Wright, Robin. "Iranian Unit to Be Labeled 'Terrorist,' U.S. Moving Against Revolutionary Guard," *Washington Post*, August 15, 2007.

Xinhua Newswire. "US Rejects Iraq's 'Peace Initiative' on Gulf Crisis," available from *Xinhua General Overseas News Service*, August 12, 1990.

Yalla Vote. "About Yalla Vote," available from www.yallavote.org/; Internet; accessed April 30, 2008.

Yaqub, Salim. *Containing Arab Nationalism: The Eisenhower Doctrine and the Middle East* (Chapel Hill, NC: University of North Carolina Press, 2004).

Young, Jason, Eugene Borgida, John Sullivan, and John Aldrich. "Personal Agendas and the Relationship Between Self-Interest and Voting Behavior," *Social Psychology Quarterly*, vol. 50, no. 1 (March 1987), pp. 64–71.

Yusof, Zainal Aznam. "It All Comes Down to the Palestinian Problem," *New Straits Times Press* (Malaysia), July 29, 2006.

Zakaria, Fareed. "Realism and Domestic Politics," *International Security*, 17 (1992), pp. 177–98.

——. "The Politics of Rage: Why do They Hate Us?" *Newsweek*, October 15, 2001.

Zimmerman, Bennett, Roberta Seid, Michael L. Wise, and Yoram Ettinger. "The Fourth Way: An Integrated Strategy to Strengthen Israel's Unilateral Political and Security Options – A New Demographic, Electoral, and Political Paradigm for Israel," produced by American-Israel Demographic Research Group, January 21, 2007, available from www.pademographics.com/4th%20Way%20Israel%20Summary% 20Januar%2021%202007.doc; Internet; accessed January 30, 2007.

Zogby, James R. "Israeli Impediments Cripple Commerce," *Washington Times*, March 31, 1996.

——. "Likud Uses City as Wedge Issue," *Washington Times*, February 21, 1996.

——. "New Thinking for Israeli-Palestinian Peace," AAI Publication (1991).

——. President and co-founder of Arab American Institute, co-founder of Palestine Human Rights Campaign, co-founder and former executive director of American-Arab Anti-Discrimination Committee. Telephone interview by the author, April 26, 2008.

——. "The Lingering Image of Arafat," *Washington Post*, October 21, 1995.

——. "The Stakes Have Never Been Higher: The Need to Debate U.S. Mideast Policy in the 2008 Election," *Washington Watch*, March 3, 2008.

——. "Viewpoint: John Mearsheimer and Stephen Walt," *Dubai Television*, December 20, 2007.

Zogby, Jim and Joe Stork. "Jim Zogby: 'They Control the Hill, but We've Got a Lot of Positions Around the Hill,'" *MERIP Middle East Report*, no. 146, Twenty Years After (May-June 1987), pp. 24–27.

Zogby Poll, Zogby International, 7/6/2003–7/9/2003.

Zunes, Stephen. "The Israel Lobby: How Powerful is it Really?" *Global Politician*, May 24, 2006, available from http://globalpolitician.com/articledes.asp?ID = 1793&cid = 2&sid = 1; Internet; accessed June 14, 2006.

Index

9/11 *see* September 11 terrorist attacks
Abbas, Mahmoud (Abu Mazin) 78
Abdel Nasser, Gamal 30; on lobbying
    210*n*204
Abou-Chedid Rebecca: on Cold War
    end 99; on Gulf War (1991) 97; on
    pro-Arab lobby 118; on US policy
    fairness 106; on terrorism 208*n*161
Abramoff, Jack 213*n*27
Abrams, Elliot 178*n*150
Abunimah, Ali: on one-state solution
    212*n*15; "The Palestinian Right of
    Return," 206*n*121
academia 203*n*27; and pro-Israel lobby
    9, 12, 55, 63, 70; and consideration of
    pro-Arab lobby 116
Adelman, Kenneth 178*n*150
Afghanistan: and Taliban removal
    49–50, 147; war on terrorism in 13,
    51, 75–76
airspace 124, 126
al-Aqsa Intifada 21, 54, 72, 108, 145,
    195*n*86; American public opinion on 45;
    and first Intifada (1987–93) 45–46, 70;
    and Sharon's march on the Dome of
    the Rock 45
al-Maliki, Nouri 215*n*52
al-Masri Hani 136
al-Qa'eda 47, 72, 108–9, 114, 148,
    196*n*104
al-Sadat, Anwar 53, 90, 202*n*44
Ambrosio, Thomas 73
American Civil Liberties Union
    (ACLU) 94, 206*n*127
American Friends Service Committee
    (AFSC) 156
American Israel Public Affairs
    Committee (AIPAC) 23, 28, 42, 57,
    59–74, 76–84, 111–18, 124–25, 129,

135, 140–44, 156, 174*n*102, 190*n*14;
    challenges to hegemony of 86, 89, 94,
    191*n*20, 203*n*67, 210*n*196, *see also*
    pro-Arab lobby *and* Jewish American
    groups; and Christian alliance
    193*n*67; domestic lobby designation
    of 24, 59; framing of terrorism by
    72–73, 121; influence of 5, 33, 56–57,
    60, 62–63, 68, 110, 188*n*167, 189*nn*4–5,
    9, 191*n*21, 194*n*73, 208*n*165, 211*n*12;
    and international developments 44,
    66, 204*n*87; and Israel 195*n*93,
    196*n*116, 212*n*14; the leading
    pro-Israel group 14, 59, 190*n*13;
    opposition to Palestinian rights/state
    by 4, 15, 64, 77–78, 80–81, 122,
    197*nn*122, 127; and strategic alliance
    56, *see also* Memorandum of
    Understanding (1981); support of
    regime change by 76; *see also* pro-Israel
    lobby
American Jewish Committee (AJC)
    156; *see also* pro-Israel lobby
American Jews *see* Jewish Americans
American League of Muslims (ALM):
    political contributions by 163; *see*
    also pro-Arab lobby
American Muslim Alliance (AMA):
    political contributions by 163; *see*
    also pro-Arab lobby
American Muslim Council (AMC) 156;
    see also pro-Arab lobby
American Muslim Institute (AMI):
    political contributions by 163; *see*
    also pro-Arab lobby
American policymakers 22–24, 27, 42–44,
    48, 81, 86–87, 99, 103, 106–7, 109,
    113–17, 119, 121, 140–46, 148; and
    Cold War 20, 54, 100, 106, 176*n*131,

and Christian Zionism 46; expansion of 44, 159; as obstruction to Palestinian state 3, 54, 128, 133, 139–40; and pro-Arab lobby14, 211–12*n*13; and pro-Israel lobby 81, 197*n*122; US policy on 36–37, 47, 75, 77, 82, 122–24, 186*n*131, 187*n*140; *see also* Israeli occupation
Shadid, Mohammed 16, 29, 61
Shain, Yossi 88, 97
Shalit, Galid 126, 214*n*43
Shannon, Vaughn 5
Sharon, Ariel 25, 73, 125, 176*n*127; and AIPAC 79; Dome of the Rock march by 45; and Gaza disengagement 81; and politicide 215*n*96; and settlements 47, 122, 140, 167*n*21, 186*nn*126, 131, 187*n*140, *see also* Israeli settlements
Shavit, Ari 134
Sheinwald, Sir Nigel 146
Shuraydi, Muhammad 70
Simpson, O. J. 43
Six-Day War *see* June 1967 war
Small, Melvin 5
Sobel, Richard 15
South Africa 135, 137
Soviet Union 184*n*84; American-Israeli alliance against 55, 58, 90, 99, 106, 120, 165*n*4, *see also* Memorandum of Understanding (1981); and Arab states 30, 98–99; collapse of 6, 10, 15, 28, 34, 90, 98, 117, 121, 144, 176*n*131, *see also* Russian Federation; US rivalry with 3, 19, 182*n*43, *see also* Cold War
special relationship 23; and discourse on Israel 9; and pro-Israel advocacy 55; and US government 56; *see also* Memorandum of Understanding (1981) *and* strategic alliance
State Department 62, 67, 127, 151
Steger, Manfred 195*n*89
strategic alliance 21, 27, 90, 93; against communism 16, 29, 34, 42, 55–56, 106, 116, 144, 171*n*64, *see also* Cold War; and Palestinians 1, 34, 60, 87–88, 90, 100, 104, 120, 144; and pro-Israel lobby 9, 12, 14–15, 53, 58–60, 64, 71, 89; and US policy 2–3, 10, 16, 30, 33–34, 59; *see also* Memorandum of Understanding (1981) *and* special relationship
Strategic Peace Initiative Package (SPIP) 98; *see also* Madrid (1991)

Supreme Court, US 46
Syria 12, 156; AIPAC on 80; Americans originating from 164; and Madrid (1991) 65

Talhami, Ghada 183*n*52, 196*n*114, 206*n*121
Telhami, Shibley: demand side of terrorism 113
Tenet, George 187*n*151; peace plan (2001) 72
terrorism 3, 5, 10, 17, 19, 50, 54–55, 58, 63, 87, 114, 132, 138, 158; democracy as a weapon against 109–10, 148; and Iran 198*n*141; and Israel 171*n*64, 185*n*99, 195*n*99, 196*n*102; and Lebanon war (2006) 126–27, 198*n*142; and Palestinians 17, 31, 43, 48, 66, 71–79, 90, 102, 105, 109, 113–16, 121, 125, 186*n*129, 195*n*89, 218*n*110; and pro-Arab lobby 25, 71, 88, 97–98, 105, 108–15, 146, 156, 208*n*161; and pro-Israel lobby 11–12, 14, 16, 43–44, 72–73, 78–81, 105, 114, 121, 144, 146, 211*n*7, 212*n*14; and public opinion 48–49; roots of 148; war against 7, 11–12, 14, 19, 21–22, 25, 47, 49, 70, 72, 75–76, 81–82, 109, 117, 120–21, 147–48, 187*n*151, 195*n*88, *see also* global war on terrorism (GWOT)
think tanks: and information dissemination 69–70; and Israel lobbying 194*nn*77, 79; policy influence by 67, 118
Tilley, Virginia 216*n*72; on Arab Israelis 167*n*17; on Israeli settlements 167*n*21, 186*n*131; on Palestinians 124, 139, 197*n*130, 213*n*26; on security fence 80; on resolving the Israeli-Palestinians conflict 128, 212*n*19, *see also* one-state solution
Tillman, Seth 63, 192*n*48
Timco, Peter: on Arab American political sophistication 118
Trice, Robert: on pro-Arab lobby 190*n*10; on pro-Israel lobby 180*n*18; on public opinion 27, 178*n*1
Truman Institute for the Advancement of Peace: polls of Israelis and Palestinians 122, 188*n*170, 212*n*16, 218*n*116